"As a magisterial scholar of Jewish law and philo: alleled ability to write in a balanced and clear r produced a comprehensive book on Conservati write. The documents and explanations he offers the distinctive legal-historical-religious character ᴏꜰ ᴛʜᴇ ᴄᴏɴꜱᴇʀᴠᴀᴛɪᴠᴇ ᴍᴏᴠᴇᴍᴇɴᴛ to shine forth. All who seek a comprehensive and detailed knowledge of the movement and its evolution and postures will find themselves richly rewarded by this work. *Modern Conservative Judaism* is required reading for scholars and laypersons alike, and all students of American Judaism and American religion will delight in its pages!"
—RABBI DAVID ELLENSON, director of the Schusterman Center for Israel Studies at Brandeis University and chancellor emeritus and former president of Hebrew Union College—Jewish Institute of Religion

"I cannot think of another work that provides such a detailed survey of historical and internal documents relating to the history of Conservative Judaism, let alone with this level of firsthand insight into the interior thought processes of the movement's most important authors and thinkers. The author's appreciation of the importance of the documents cited and his talent at abridging them thoughtfully and well will make them accessible even to readers to whom they are entirely new. The worth of *Modern Conservative Judaism* will be obvious to any student of modern Jewish history."
—RABBI MARTIN S. COHEN, senior editor of *The Observant Life: The Wisdom of Conservative Judaism for Contemporary Jews*

"Conservative Judaism continues to remain a mystery even to many of its adherents, in part because it is a complex movement, with sophisticated underlying principles. *Modern Conservative Judaism* is therefore a very significant contribution to helping make the Conservative Movement widely understood. With a multitude of original materials, encompassing earlier debates within the movement through current 'hot topics,' and Rabbi Dorff's illuminating introductions, members of Conservative congregations will find the book enlightening—helping them to more fully appreciate the ideas, approach, and practices of their Jewish home."
—RABBI WAYNE FRANKLIN, senior rabbi of Temple Emanu-El, Providence, Rhode Island

MODERN CONSERVATIVE JUDAISM

If there is a person on Planet Earth capable of positing a cogent set of words about Conservative Judaism, past, present, or future, it is Rabbi Elliot Dorff, PhD, Rector and Sol and Anne Dorff Distinguished Service Professor of Philosophy at the American Jewish University.

During the thirty-some years I have been within Elliot's sphere of influence, I have known him to have a smiling, perpetually thoughtful, inquisitive, and sweet countenance.

He fits the phrase: "Some men are too gentle to run with wolves."

Elliot, you walk, run, stroll, live, and breathe Torah.

Your friend,
Bruce Whizin

JPS ANTHOLOGIES
OF JEWISH THOUGHT

University of Nebraska Press | Lincoln

Modern Conservative Judaism

Evolving Thought and Practice

Elliot N. Dorff

Foreword by Julie Schonfeld

A co-publication of the Jewish Publication Society and the Rabbinical Assembly

Acknowledgments for the use of copyrighted
material appear on pages 389–90, which constitute
an extension of the copyright page.

Library of Congress Cataloging-in-Publication Data
Names: Dorff, Elliot N., author.
Title: Modern Conservative Judaism: evolving thought and
practice / Elliot N. Dorff; foreword by Julie Schonfeld.
Description: Lincoln: University of Nebraska Press,
[2018] | Series: JPS Anthologies of Jewish Thought |
Includes bibliographical references and index.
Identifiers: LCCN 2017026972 (print)
LCCN 2017028009 (ebook)
ISBN 9780827613874 (epub)
ISBN 9780827613881 (mobi)
ISBN 9780827613898 (pdf)
ISBN 9780827613102 (pbk.: alk. paper)
Subjects: LCSH: Conservative Judaism—History—20th century.
Classification: LCC BM197.5 (ebook)
LCC BM197.5 .M63 2018 (print)
DDC 296.8/342—dc23
LC record available at https://lccn.loc.gov/2017026972

Set in Merope by Mikala R Kolander.
Designed by N. Putens.

With deep appreciation for the people and institutions of the Conservative movement. They gifted me with a form of Judaism that is totally honest and intellectually challenging while also being vibrant, joyful, caring, morally sensitizing, and profoundly meaningful.

Elliot N. Dorff

Contents

Foreword

Rabbi Julie Schonfeld

Our revered colleague, Rabbi Elliot N. Dorff, stands on the shoulders of generations of rabbis and scholars who have shaped the Conservative movement, first as it emerged in North America in the late nineteenth and twentieth centuries and now as it continues to grow all over the world (where it is known as Masorti, meaning Traditional Judaism).

Conservative Judaism is sometimes mischaracterized as being a middle ground between Reform and Orthodoxy. Not so here. From this book's first paragraph to its last, Rabbi Dorff clearly articulates Conservative Judaism's essential, vital, and unique character—a resilient, authentic understanding of Judaism that balances response to the rapid pace of change in contemporary life with the eternal values of Judaism. The book's subtitle—"evolving thought and practice"—also expresses this well.

As Rabbi Dorff explains, the Committee on Jewish Law and Standards (CJLS) of the Rabbinical Assembly, the seventeen-hundred-member international organization of Conservative rabbis, addresses questions of law that have evolved over millennia and are rooted in a multiplicity of texts. Rabbi Dorff turns to the CJLS responses, or *teshuvot*, as primary sources in his analyses of the evolving nature of Conservative Judaism. Some of the questions the committee has addressed—such as whether women may serve as rabbis and whether same-sex couples may wed under Jewish law—have shaped a generation (see chapters 6 and 11, respectively). Other queries, while seemingly small—such as whether quinoa is kosher for Passover—are nonetheless vehicles for testing and reinforcing the mechanisms by which change is made in the Conservative movement.

Rabbi Dorff's publications include more than two hundred articles on Jewish thought, law, and ethics, together with twelve books he wrote and another fourteen he edited or coedited. We might suggest that Rabbi Dorff's extensive teaching, speaking, and writing constitute a lifetime of preparation for this new book. Here he draws on history and philosophy, explains the Conservative movement's contributions in critical areas such as theology and prayer, and details how the CJLS works to illuminate the Conservative/Masorti movement's unique, evolutionary perspective. He also zeroes in on Zionism and the Masorti movement in Israel, where the approach of "evolving thought and practice" is finding increasing resonance among citizens of the Jewish state.

The journey that began in the early nineteenth century as emancipated Jews began to take their place in modern society while maintaining a deep devotion to Jewish tradition and values continues today. We are indebted to scores of colleagues, including Rabbi Dorff, for their many decades of work on the Committee on Jewish Law and Standards. And we are especially indebted to Rabbi Dorff for drawing together all the strands that define the Conservative movement—theological, legal, philosophical, historical—into a tapestry that represents this uniquely American movement, which has spread far beyond these borders. The breadth and depth of Rabbi Dorff's work will resonate with his colleagues and provide an extraordinary source for teaching and preaching, enlighten Conservative Jews about the essential nature and significance of their movement, and provide scholars with an abundance of primary material for their future research and writing. The transmission of Jewish tradition begins in the Torah when Moses chooses Joshua as his successor, and from this ancient origin it passes through hundreds of generations, coming to rest on those whose life's work is the preservation and perfection of this tradition. And in our generation Rabbi Elliot Dorff adds a link to this chain of tradition forged by all those who have gone before.

May we continue to imbibe their wisdom in the spirit of Yose ben Yoezer (Pirke Avot 1:4): "May your house be a meeting house for Sages. . . . Drink their words thirstily."

Preface

What This Book Is

The heart of this book is an introspective, thought-provoking discussion of Conservative Judaism's emerging beliefs and practices over the last fifty years.

Sometimes the Conservative thought and practice of fifty years ago look very different from those of today, while in other arenas there has been more constancy than change. Sometimes Conservative ideas and observances have found unity and standardization throughout the movement; at other times, divergent perspectives are accepted and practiced in various communities. Occasionally, Conservative Judaism in North America has differed from Masorti/Traditional Judaism, as it is known outside of the United States and Canada. Always, however, Conservative beliefs and practice are rooted in and grow from Jewish tradition, law, and moral values.

This book is an insider's guide to why and how the movement's thought and practices have evolved — or stayed the same — over the last half century. Having played a leadership role in many of the key historical events and texts, I try to offer curious readers and students of history an understanding of the creation of the modern movement's most important laws, policies, and documents — which, for the first time, have been excerpted and contextualized all in one place. Sometimes the thought processes and conclusions on matters of belief or practice have been largely unified; at other times they have been more diverse — and, occasionally, contentious. Some issues, particularly those in which the movement is unified, have been addressed to the current movement's satisfaction. Other, more controversial matters remain in flux, open to interpretation and deliberation in this and perhaps succeeding generations.

The Structure of This Book

Unlike Christianity and Islam, Judaism has never had a creed, an official set of beliefs that an adherent must affirm to be a member. Yet Judaism definitely has beliefs, and a medieval Jewish saying nicely summarizes them: "Israel, Torah, and God are one." This book follows that triad, although in reverse order.

Part 1 of this book is thus on God. Chapter 1 examines Conservative movement theologies: an official Conservative movement perspective through the lens of *Emet Ve-Emunah*, followed by the viewpoints of various Conservative thinkers that illustrate the diversity of theological thought within the movement. Chapter 2 explores distinct approaches to God through prayer.

Part 2 addresses Torah in both its meanings of study and of instruction for action through both law and moral guidance. Chapter 3 describes the modes of study through which Conservative Judaism understands Jewish tradition, how Jews historically interpreted and applied that tradition, and modern methods for doing so. Chapter 4 discusses a variety of legal theories articulated by Conservative movement thinkers. Chapter 5 describes how the Conservative movement makes decisions about Jewish practice. Subsequent chapters delve into legal decisions and moral guidance: on women (chapter 6), bioethics (chapter 7), business ethics (chapter 8), ritual observance (chapter 9), social issues (chapter 10), and sex and family life (chapter 11).

In part 3 of the triad—Israel—chapter 12 discusses the Conservative movement's commitments to the People Israel, our fellow Jews. Chapter 13, on Zionism, explores why and how the movement as a whole has always been committed to Zionism and why Conservative leaders today remain personally committed to Israel even when they may disagree with official Israeli policy. Chapter 14 describes how the Conservative movement has responded to challenges specific to the State of Israel, such as the status of Jewish marital and ritual laws in the Jewish state.

There is more. The epilogue describes an ideal Conservative Jew. The list of authors whose work has been excerpted in this volume details their manifold accomplishments and contributions to Jewish life generally and to the Conservative movement in particular. The bibliography includes and augments the suggestions for further reading that appear at the end of each chapter. And the appendix describes all the national Conservative movement organizations and affiliates.

Two notes about style. First, many of the people whose writings are excerpted in this book are rabbis and have doctoral degrees besides. Because this book is about a religious movement, however, I have chosen to identify those who are rabbis as rabbis, leaving it to the descriptions at the end of this book to list their other graduate degrees, if any, as well as their other achievements. In general, following academic style, I have identified them as Rabbi X the first time they are mentioned in a given chapter but only by their last name thereafter.

Second, except when it is really awkward, throughout this volume, whenever there has been occasion for me to reference a legal theory, responsum, book, or other creative work of my own, I have chosen to refer to myself in the third person. In this way, I maintain a consistent style of how I refer to people. I also do my best to take an arm's-length posture vis-à-vis my own writings so that I do not privilege my own views over those of anyone else in the process of analyzing and evaluating the strengths and weaknesses of each document discussed in this volume.

How to Use This Book

Modern Conservative Judaism: Evolving Thought and Practice is designed to be accessible to all readers: knowledgeable Jews as well as both Jews and people of other faiths with little understanding of Jewish law or practice. Rabbis and educators in the Conservative movement are encouraged to use the book for adult and teen education classes. Rabbis and educators in other movements may also find the book useful for young adult and adult education, particularly in a course that compares how and why their movement differs from Conservative Judaism's stances.

The book's structure also lends itself to college courses on contemporary American Judaism or on world religions: it provides relevant excerpts from the primary sources that students on a university level need to study, as well as explanatory material to put those sources in context. Hillel educators may want to use this book to introduce Conservative Judaism to college and graduate students in a more informal way.

For those readers who grew up in the Conservative movement, this book may serve as an illuminating backstory you may have never known, explaining not only what the movement believes and practices but how and why it arrived at these conclusions. For those who grew up in other expressions of Judaism, I hope the book will deepen your understanding of Conservative Judaism beyond the one-dimensional "Orthodox Judaism watered down" or "Reform Judaism beefed up" and impel you to engage with its teachings on its own terms.

Finally, *Modern Conservative Judaism: Evolving Thought and Practice* is also meant to be savored, slowly and thoughtfully, by all those adults interested in the Conservative movement and/or in the continuing evolution of the Jewish religion today.

Acknowledgments

Rabbi Barry Schwartz, director of the Jewish Publication Society (JPS), asked me to write this book as part of the JPS Anthologies of Jewish Thought series on the various forms of modern Jewish identity. In 1977 the United Synagogue of Conservative Judaism had published my book *Conservative Judaism: Our Ancestors to Our Descendants,* and in 1996 a substantially revised, updated version was released, so, frankly, I had never considered writing another book about the movement. Rabbi Schwartz, however, convinced me that the kind of book he wanted me to write was different in audience and tone from my previous book and that, in any case, much had happened in the intervening twenty years. He not only initiated this project; he also shepherded me along the way, so that it includes topics that I had not thought to cover and excludes others he rightfully saw as not relevant. Thank you, Barry, for prodding me to undertake this project and for working with me to see the vision you had for it.

Joy Weinberg, JPS managing editor, did a yeoman's job in helping me cut down an original manuscript of some 216,000 words to the more reasonable 150,000 or so. Her skill at seeing what was needed and what was not, in articulating some points more sharply than I had first formulated them, and in keeping me focused on the audience for this book truly shaped whatever is good in it. Thank you also, Joy, for your enthusiasm for this project and for your kindness in keeping me in line.

In the process of writing this book, it became evident early on that many of the materials that I needed to use to describe developments in the Conservative movement had been produced by the Rabbinical Assembly (RA). At that point I suggested to Rabbi Schwartz that we ask the Rabbinical Assembly to copublish this book. Rabbi Julie Schonfeld, CEO of the RA; Rabbis William Gershon and Philip Scheim, successive presidents of the RA during the time this book was being created; and members of the RA Executive Council during this period were immensely helpful in approving a copublishing agreement and very generous in allowing JPS and me to use the many RA materials contained in this book. More broadly, much of my own thinking about Judaism in general and ethics in particular has been shaped by my colleagues on the RA's Committee on Jewish Law and Standards (CJLS), to which I was first appointed in December 1984 and which I now have the privilege to chair. Thank you to my friends and colleagues on the CJLS during all those years and in the RA generally for enabling this book to come to light.

The University of Nebraska Press (UNP), JPS's copublisher of this volume, has been the third partner in making it a reality. Many thanks to the good people at UNP for overseeing its beautiful production. These especially include Joeth Zucco, senior project editor, and Mary M. Hill, copyeditor of my book.

I have been blessed since 1971 to be on the faculty of what was originally called the University of Judaism and is now the American Jewish University. Throughout all these years, rabbinical students, in particular, have prodded me to clarify my thinking and to think new thoughts. I am deeply appreciative of all my students over the years and of the university's administration, board, faculty, staff, and supporters for creating a place where I can have these interactions.

Finally, I would like to thank my wife of fifty-plus years, Marlynn, for tolerating my spending yet more time on another book. That this book was about Conservative Judaism, to which she has devoted her life as much as I have mine, made that sacrifice somewhat easier for her to bear, or so she tells me, but it was a sacrifice nonetheless. As such, this is yet another expression of the love she has for me and I have for her.

MODERN CONSERVATIVE JUDAISM

Introduction

The Roots of Conservative Judaism

Before we enter into the Conservative movement's evolution over the last half century (chapter 1), the question arises: How did the movement first emerge?

It began (as you will see) with the thought of Zacharias Frankel in 1840s Germany, evolved in the work and thought of its U.S. founders in the late nineteenth and early twentieth centuries, and has continued developing ever since. For a more thorough treatment of the movement's early years, see *Tradition and Change*, edited by Mordecai Waxman (Rabbinical Assembly, 1958), as well as other books in this introduction's list of suggestions for further reading.

Conservative Judaism's European Beginnings

Since at least the time of the Romans, a corporate structure governed European countries in which subgroups of the population were assigned legal rights and duties as a group. In this mode of organization, at best Jews were treated as second-class citizens, with limited rights and often higher taxes, and at worst they were persecuted or expelled.

By the seventeenth and eighteenth centuries, however, thinkers such as John Locke, Benedict Spinoza, Jean-Jacques Rousseau, and Claude Montesquieu had laid a philosophical framework that saw each person as possessing "inalienable rights," as Locke and Thomas Jefferson phrased it. Each individual, regardless of religion or any other factor, was to be treated as the equal of any other person. At the time, the reality in these countries did not match the theory, but this view ultimately produced the founding documents of the American and French revolutions in the latter half of the eighteenth century and similar political changes in Germany.

As a result, by 1800 Jews in parts of Western Europe (Germany, France, Holland, and, to a certain extent, England) had generally been allowed to study at universities, enter the professions and government, and develop freely as Jews. The approximately forty years from 1760 to 1800 later became known as the Emancipation—the period in which Jews in central and western European countries were freed from multiple restrictions and became full citizens of their nations.

The Emancipation was not an unmixed blessing, however. As Jews took advantage of their new freedoms and opportunities, they increasingly considered themselves not only Jews but also citizens of Germany, France, or England. This created a new problem for them: How were they to identify both as Jews and as citizens of the modern, secular, Western world? After all, as Jews they were supposed to observe the dietary laws and the Sabbath, for example, but how could they do that if being successful in business required eating at all sorts of restaurants with both Jewish and non-Jewish customers and keeping their businesses open on Saturday? And how could they become lawyers or doctors and still remain Jewish if they had to attend classes in law school or medical school on Saturday and other Jewish holy days and subsequently work on those days? Aside from these specific problems, Jews found that non-Jews were willing to do business with them and treat them as equals only if Jews forgot about their Jewishness (or at least hid it) and acted like any other German, French, or English citizen.

The first generation of Jews living under these new rules sought to balance their Jewish and national identities often by compartmentalizing the various parts of their lives; as Moses Mendelssohn wrote in the late 1700s, "Be a German in the streets and a Jew at home." Subsequent generations of Jews, however, did not struggle with their dual identity. They considered it impossible to be both Jews and full citizens of the modern world. Because they valued their new freedoms, they abandoned their Jewish identity, sometimes through outright conversion to Christianity, sometimes through intermarriage, and sometimes through simply denying that they were Jews.

Modern Orthodoxy, the Reform movement, and the early Conservative movement all emerged as reactions to this new phenomenon of the 1820s through the 1850s. Each of the three movements said to Jews that it was both possible and desirable to affirm its particular interpretation of Jewish faith and practice while also taking full advantage of the freedoms newly granted to Jews.

The individual most responsible for shaping the convictions of the early Conservative movement was Rabbi Zacharias Frankel, head of the Jewish Theological Seminary of Breslau, Germany. Together with a number of other European scholars, he developed the "positive-historical" approach to Judaism, "historical" in several of the following senses.

Method

When Jews examined Jewish texts, Frankel asserted, they were obligated to use the generally accepted techniques of literary analysis utilized in analyzing other documents created by any other group of people. So, for example, in any Jewish writing, Jews needed to distinguish between the meaning the author intended (the *peshat*) and the meaning(s) given the text by the later tradition (the *derash* or midrash). Given that the *derash* came later, it might have a very different meaning from the one contained in the original text—even if later authorities justified their philosophies and legal decisions by quoting earlier sources in the Bible and Talmud. Distinguishing the laws and ideas appearing in the Bible from those that developed later, in fact, constituted an important way for Jews to learn about Jewish history.

Understanding the text's original meaning involved understanding the events and ideas underlying it. Jews were instructed to learn the relevant languages, ideas, and practices of surrounding nations, much of which likely influenced their ancestors' thoughts, speech, and practices.

In short, discerning the original meaning of the text depended crucially upon comprehending both its historical and its literary contexts.

Identifying the text's original meaning did not mean, however, that later interpretations were wrong and the original meaning was correct. Sometimes text interpretations or embellishments could even be more historically or legally important than the text itself! At its essence, the historical method ensured that the various levels of meaning over time could be distinguished.

In contrast, Orthodox Judaism taught (and continues to teach) Jews to consult classical Jewish commentators (e.g., Rashi) to understand a biblical text's divinely intended meaning. From the Orthodox perspective, God revealed the written text of the Torah and the interpretations God intended at Sinai, and then those interpretations were passed down from generation to generation until they were ultimately written down in the Mishnah, Talmud, collections of Midrash, and medieval Jewish commentaries. Any perceived contradictions between the original text and the traditional interpretations of them were of no consequence: the *peshat* was to be seen exclusively through the *derash*, because God's intent was manifest in the *derash*.

Intellectual Result

Studying Judaism using historical techniques also revealed that Judaism was not the same during all the years of its existence. Instead, the various peoples among whom Jews lived, as well as the Jews' changing political, social, and economic conditions, influenced Jewish thought and practice through time. Sometimes, change happened deliberately and quickly; other times, change developed almost unconsciously and slowly. Always, Jewish ideas, values, and practices continued to change organically in response to new conditions.

That said, modern forms of Judaism still had much in common with the Judaism of Moses. Moreover, Jews could trace the very process by which Judaism changed in form and sometimes in content from Moses to their own day.

Rabbi Alexander Kohut, who helped found the Jewish Theological Seminary of America in 1886 and who was a spokesman for the new movement on ideological matters, stated the intellectual result of the historical method this way: "Judaism is a consistent whole. The Mosaic, prophetic, talmudic-rabbinic Judaism is an organic totality. . . . The Judaism of history is a unity, an organic development. May Moses be its head, the prophets its heart, the Rabbis its links: one without the other is a halfness, a wanton mutilation."[1]

To Conservative leaders, each period in Jewish history contributed its part to the ongoing tradition. Some periods might be more productive than others, and modern Jews might like some developments more than others, but an objective study of Jewish tradition had to consider them all.

Practical Result

Moreover, Judaism *should* change from one time and place to another. The world did not stand still, all living entities had to adapt in order to survive, and Judaism was no exception. As such, Judaism changed in the past by including new ideas and practices and modifying or dropping old ones, but it must continue to change in all these ways in the present and the future in order to continue to be a part of history, an ongoing concern of a living people.

Once again Kohut expressed the point clearly and strongly:

The chain of tradition continued unbroken from Moses through Joshua, the Elders, the Prophets and the Men of the Great Synagogue, down to the latest times. On this tradition rests our faith, which Moses first received from God on Sinai. On this foundation rests Mosaic-rabbinical Judaism today; and on this foundation we take our stand. . . .

But you may ask: Shall the fence around the garden, shall reverence be extended around everything that the past hedged in . . . ? "Remember the days of old," said Moses, *and have regard to the changes of each generation* (Deuteronomy 32:7). The teaching of the ancients we must make our starting-point, but we must not lose sight of what is needed in every generation. . . .

And as these elders did, so can—yes, so must we, the later Epigoni [successors]—do in the exigencies of our own day. If the power to make changes was granted to the Elders, is not the power given equally to us? "But they were giants," we are told, "and we, compared with them, are mere pygmies." Perhaps so; let us not forget, however, that a pygmy on a giant's shoulder can see further than the giant himself.

Let us now revert to the question raised at the outset: Is Judaism definitely closed for all time, or is it capable of and in need of continuous development? I answer both Yes and No. I answer Yes, *because Religion has been given to man*; and as it is the duty of man to grow in perfection as long as he lives, he must modify the forms which yield him religious satisfaction, in accordance with the spirit of the times. I answer No, insofar as it concerns the word of God, which cannot be imperfect. . . . You Israelite, imperfect as you are, strive to perfect yourself in the image of your perfect God. Hold in honor His unchangeable law, and let it be your earnest task to put new life into the outward form of our religion.[2]

Similarly, Kohut left no doubt that in matters of belief too we might well differ from our ancestors:

Ought we to maintain two kinds of logic, one for theology and the other for science? I believe decidedly, no! The indubitable results of science can and must agree with the truths of religion, for a religion which cannot bear the light of science or must first soften it through all kinds of lenses is to be classed with the dead. Such a religion could vegetate among the lower classes, lead a sad existence, become sometimes dangerous by fanaticism, but could not exercise a decisive influence upon the development of mankind.

Fortunately the Mosaic religion does not belong to religions that fear the light. . . . There never existed a time or party or sect which required, recommended, or even asserted as admissible, to neglect the use of reasoning.[3]

The "Positive" Part of "Positive-Historical Judaism"

What did the Conservative movement founders wish to convey by appending the word "positive" to "historical Judaism"?

In this context, "positive" could have had one or two meanings. First, it may have meant "concerned only with observable, empirical data." In this sense, "positive-historical Judaism" would describe a study method that analyzes Jewish history, ideas, and practices as objectively and dispassionately as possible. Certainly, this meaning was intended.

"Positive," though, can also denote enthusiasm, as when we say a person has a positive attitude toward something. This interpretation is almost the opposite of the other: the first denotes dispassionate objectivity, and the second passionate involvement.

Whether the original members of the "positive-historical school" intended the latter meaning as well is questionable, but it aptly describes their deep interest in promoting a positive attitude toward Judaism, which Jews would honor, hold dear, and seek to preserve. In effect, Jews were asked to be as honest and objective as possible when studying Jewish history and simultaneously to be as passionate and involved as possible when participating in its present and future.

Ultimately, the founders named their movement "the Conservative movement" because they sought to *conserve* as much of the Jewish tradition as possible rather than reform it, as Reform leaders sought to do. At that same time, in contrast to Orthodoxy, Conservative leaders recognized that to be authentic to Judaism historically, Jews had to be prepared to change it in a variety of ways, as their ancestors had done for generations.

At first, Frankel and other Jewish leaders were largely aligned with Reform thinkers, as both groups had adopted the positive-historical study method. In matters of practice, however, the Reform rabbis in Germany differed among themselves. That became intolerable for the more traditional rabbis among them when the majority of the Reform rabbis, meeting in 1845, decided to drop Hebrew from the liturgy either entirely or predominantly in favor of praying in German, the vernacular. Upset by the plan, Frankel and his more traditional colleagues left the Reform movement. (Their ideology would not be named "Conservative" until decades later in nineteenth-century America.)

In some ways the splitting of the ways was ironic, because according to Jewish law one may fulfill one's obligations to pray in any language.[4] The refusal of Frankel and his followers to substitute the vernacular for Hebrew in the liturgy, however, indicated their early conviction that Jewish identity is a matter not solely of religion and morals, as the Reformers saw it, but also of community. This communal emphasis was to become ever more important as Conservative Judaism took root in America.

Taking Root in America

In America, hundreds of thousands of Russian and eastern European Jews arrived between 1881, when Czar Alexander II unleashed devastating pogroms on Russian Jews, and 1924, when a change in U.S. laws limited immigration.

At first, Conservative Judaism did not catch on in the States. Most Jews of that generation were working long and hard hours just to earn a living and learn English. In religious matters they were quite content to transfer to these shores whatever Jewish identity they had in Europe, from secular to Orthodox.

Two groups of Jews who had already settled in America before this wave of immigration, however, were interested in promoting the traditional and modern synthesis that Conservative Judaism represented. One group was Sephardic Jews—that is, Jews whose ancestors came from Spain and other nations of the Mediterranean basin and the Middle East. Descendants of the very first Jews to have arrived in America in 1654, they sought a form of Judaism that would be both traditional and tolerant of variations in practice and thought. They were too traditional to be part of the emerging American Reform movement, which, according to its 1885 Pittsburgh Platform, maintained that the ritual laws of Judaism were not binding. On the other hand, they were open to studying and practicing Judaism in a variety of ways. So it was no accident that leaders of the

Sephardic synagogue in Philadelphia were instrumental in creating the Conservative movement's first seminary, the Jewish Theological Seminary of America, in 1886 and that JTS's first two presidents, Sabato Morais and Henry Pereira Mendes, were Sephardic Jews.

Ironically, Reform lay leaders such as Jacob Schiff constituted the other group involved in creating the seminary and thus the seeds of the Conservative movement in America. These were the children of German Jews who had come to America in the third quarter of the nineteenth century, and some of them had become quite wealthy. Several were frankly embarrassed by what they saw as uneducated and unsophisticated eastern European Jews, who were flooding into America. Understanding that these new Jews would not embrace the Reform Judaism that they did, they sought to create a different kind of Judaism for the new arrivals, one that would be sufficiently traditional to attract them but also sufficiently modern to help them adjust to America. Because of their influence, English rather than Yiddish or Hebrew became the language of instruction at the Jewish Theological Seminary of America. After all, the rabbis educated at the seminary would be the very people who taught eastern European Jews that they could be modern as well as traditional.

This latter group also ultimately prevailed in appointing Rabbi Solomon Schechter as the seminary's third president. A professor of Semitics at Oxford University in England, Schechter embodied the very synthesis of tradition and modern respectability sought by the Reform leaders.

In 1913 Schechter created the United Synagogue of America, thus transforming Conservative Judaism in America from a rabbinical school with a particular way of studying Jewish texts to a full movement, with synagogues, schools, and later camps, a youth group (United Synagogue Youth), and adult groups for men and women.

Rabbi Solomon Schechter's Concept of "Catholic Israel"

Schechter also transformed the Conservative methodology for accepting changes in Jewish thought and practice. He asked: How can the Conservative movement embrace the method and implications of positive-historical

Judaism, thus recognizing changes in Jewish law, and, at the same time, conserve Judaism? The answer, he asserted, lay in making the decision of when, what, and how to change a law a matter for *communal* decision. Although there was no guarantee that the judgments of a given community or its representatives would be any wiser than those of a single individual, employing communal practice to shape contemporary Jewish law would at least enable Conservative Judaism to draw upon the collective wisdom and customs of the people—the very method that had preserved Judaism until now.

Two different approaches to communal decision making soon emerged.

Kohut declared that legal decisions should be made by the rabbis of each generation. This was how most Jewish legal matters had been decided from biblical times on, for Judaism had always entrusted the law to those who knew most about it. The Jewish community had never chosen its legal interpreters by popular vote or by a person's wealth or power. From the prophet Ezra's time on, a person who wanted to gain authority in Jewish law first had to learn enough to earn the authorization to act as a teacher or judge. And from the first century CE on, those who gained that authorization were called "rabbis," meaning both masters of the tradition and teachers of it. They had made Jewish legal decisions from then until the present day, and, Kohut argued, this practice should continue.

Another factor, however, had also influenced Jewish law over time: the custom of the people. When, occasionally, the rabbis' decisions and the people's practices were at odds, the rabbis sometimes attempted to change the people's customs to fit the law, and at other times the rabbis adjusted the law to fit the customs. In fact, in some instances the customs became so strong that the rabbis claimed that "custom uproots a legal decision."[5] In any case, Jewish law had always been the product of an interaction between the rabbis and the rest of the Jewish people.

In recognition of this, Schechter avowed that Jewish law should be determined by "catholic Israel," here the word "catholic" meaning "the whole of," in other words, "the whole of Israel" or "the whole of the Jewish community." In so translating the Hebrew term *klal Yisra'el*, Schechter contended that decisions in Jewish law should be determined by the practices of the whole Jewish community.

So, for example, in Conservative synagogues, even in Schechter's time, men and women sat together for prayer, and boys and girls learned the same curriculum together in the same classes—both deviations from Orthodox practice. On the other hand, Conservative congregations continued to pray in Hebrew—the Jewish practice over millennia—even as prayers in English (the native tongue of most worshippers) figured predominantly in American Reform services.

At the time, most Jews who joined Conservative synagogues were observant, and so basing decisions in Jewish law upon Jewish communal practices made legal sense. Today, though, when a great many Conservative Jews do not follow Jewish law, the Conservative movement has largely accepted Rabbi Robert Gordis's reinterpretation of Schechter's teaching: to consider only the practices *of Jews who try to observe Jewish law* in making decisions—an approach that is both modern and historically authentic.[6]

In those days, however, the ideas and practices inherent in positive-historical Judaism and catholic Israel were more than enough to launch the new movement in America and give it its distinctive character.

Taking Off in America

The second generation, the children of American immigrants from eastern Europe, took to Conservative Judaism. By the mid-twentieth century, they would make it the most popular form of Judaism in America.

By the 1930s, 1940s, and 1950s, thanks to their parents' prodding and their own hard work, many native-born Jewish Americans had graduated from college and professional school and/or established businesses, increasingly making it into the middle class. They also wanted to blend into American society socially. Conservative Judaism, which took Judaism seriously and also advocated integration into the larger society, served their social needs precisely. Because belonging to a church was then customary among Christian Americans, Jews striving to be recognized as Americans in the fullest sense realized they needed to belong to a Jewish equivalent. Consequently, many Jews who knew little about Judaism and had dropped most of its practices nevertheless affiliated with synagogues.

Conservative appearance and practice changed as a result. American Jews wanted synagogues that were similar in form to Protestant churches so that it would be clear to both Jew and Christian alike that this was a Jewish form of an unquestionably American institution. Both Conservative and Reform synagogues were therefore built using a church floor plan, in which congregational leaders faced the audience from an elevated platform, rather than the traditional Jewish arrangement, in which the cantor stood on a platform and faced the ark with his back to the congregation. Rabbis and cantors donned robes, like Protestant ministers. Decorum became a major value, as it was in church. Since "full" Americans attended American public schools, the more extensive religious education offered in Orthodox Jewish day schools was considered un-American; instead, congregations established religious schools that held classes in the late afternoon hours and on the weekends, like their Christian counterparts, thereby changing Jewish education from full- to part-time. Moreover, most Reform and many Conservative congregations instituted a confirmation program—another borrowing from Protestant churches—for those teenagers who wanted to attend Jewish schools only on Sunday mornings.

From approximately 1945 to 1980, Conservative Judaism was the largest Jewish religious movement in America. Its dominance, its role as the middle movement, and its commitment to pluralism enabled Jews of all persuasions to work together on communal institutions such as federations, boards of rabbis, and organizations created to free Soviet Jewry and support Israel. Conservative Jewish leaders in mid-twentieth-century America were pleased that Jews were joining Conservative synagogues but not at all happy about their Jewish ignorance and increasing nonobservance. To intensify Jewish education and religious commitment, Conservative religious and lay leaders founded a variety of educational and religious organizations for children, teenagers, and adults. These national efforts were matched on the congregational level by a continually expanding roster of adult education classes and an attempt to set minimum standards of Jewish education for bar or bat mitzvah.

Rabbi Mordecai Kaplan's Concept of "Judaism as a Civilization"

Along with these new sociological and institutional developments arose a new, influential articulation of Conservative Jewish ideology by Rabbi Mordecai M. Kaplan. Raised as an Orthodox Jew, Kaplan was ordained a rabbi by the Jewish Theological Seminary of America and embraced its teachings of positive-historical Judaism and catholic Israel and then extended their implications.

In his groundbreaking book, *Judaism as a Civilization* (1934), Kaplan asserted that Judaism was much more than a religion of beliefs and rituals. Judaism was, rather, a full civilization with an attachment to a particular land (Israel) and language (Hebrew), as well as to art, music, dance, literature, and philosophy. This illuminated why even Jews who were not religiously observant strongly identified as Jews; for them, facets of Jewish civilization embodied their Jewishness.

At the same time, Kaplan emphasized that Judaism was an evolving religious civilization with religion at its core. That explained why Israel was the Jewish homeland, even though most of the world's Jews had not lived there for most of Jewish history; why Hebrew, the language of the Bible, Mishnah, and prayer book, was the Jewish language, even though most Jews did not speak it; and why Jewish foods could be from multiple cuisines, but only if they were kosher. Jews who neglected the religious core of the Jewish civilization were missing Judaism's central meanings.

Kaplan's ideology had immediate practical implications. Jews, he said, needed to commit to learning Hebrew as a living language—the language of the then-fledgling Jewish community in Palestine that would ultimately become the State of Israel—beyond the Hebrew language of religious texts. This meant, for example, that congregational afternoon schools were called "Hebrew schools" because Hebrew was a major part of the curriculum and, even more pervasively, that conversational Hebrew was taught at the movement's Ramah summer camps.

The synagogue, Kaplan said, should be not only a place of worship, study, and assembly, as its three Hebrew names (*beit tefillah*, *beit midrash*, and *beit kenesset*) suggested, but also "a synagogue center," home to Jewish art, dance, music, literature, philosophy, and even athletics ("a shul with a pool," as some described it). This vision greatly influenced how American synagogues—especially, but not exclusively, in the Conservative movement—developed in the middle of the twentieth century. Many called themselves the "So-and-So Synagogue Center," whether they had athletic facilities or not.

Recognizing that children could best learn about Judaism as a full way of life, Kaplan was also instrumental in creating Jewish summer camps, which integrated religious and civilizational elements 24/7. This introduced what is now three or four generations of children and staff to an all-encompassing form of Judaism that was both serious and broad in its content and also participatory and joyful in its mode. Campers came back to their congregations wanting the same kind of Judaism. This led in the 1960s to the creation of alternate services in many synagogues (the "synaplex"), some led entirely by congregants, and many experimenting with contemporary music. It also ushered in new forms of Jewish theology, moral thought, music, and art and spawned a major focus on social action projects under the rubric of *tikkun olam* (repairing the world) that continues to this day.

In 1968, frustrated at the slow pace of egalitarianism in the Conservative movement, Kaplan broke with the movement by establishing the Reconstructionist Rabbinical College, and some congregations that had identified as Reconstructionist since the 1940s dropped their concurrent membership in the Conservative movement. In 1922 his daughter became the first woman to have a bat mitzvah ceremony. It would take many decades for the full egalitarianism Kaplan had espoused to become a predominant reality in the Conservative movement (see chapter 6 for details), but by the 1950s most Conservative synagogues had bat mitzvah ceremonies.

Meanwhile, ultra-Orthodox Jews and even many Modern Orthodox Jews dismissed all Conservative developments in Jewish law or thought as heretical. Some Modern Orthodox synagogues, however, went on to follow the Conservative movement's lead in creating their own form of bat mitzvah ceremony and in being staunchly Zionist. The Reform movement followed the Conservative movement's lead in creating summer camps, including more Hebrew in its prayer books, joining the Zionist movement, and cultivating Jewish productivity in thought, music, and art.

Articulating Conservative Judaism's Faith and Practice

It was never a primary movement objective to spell out the tenets of Conservative Judaism's faith and practice, even though this had been attempted in the past.[7] In fact, Conservative rabbis and lay leaders reveled in the diversity of opinion and practice within the movement. They did not want to squelch its creativity and liveliness, and, furthermore, they believed it would be Jewishly inauthentic to adopt a rigid definition of what a Conservative Jew must believe or do. Furthermore, Conservative leaders did not want to upset their standing as the largest movement in American Judaism by defining some people as outside its bounds.

Yet, the growth of the other major movements, independent prayer groups (minyanim), and social groups (ḥavurot) changed the midcentury pattern of most American Jews affiliating with the Conservative movement simply to be churched in both Jewish and modern ways. Third- and fourth-generation descendants of their Eastern European forebears no longer felt the need to join a synagogue—but if they were going to affiliate, they needed good reasons to choose a Conservative congregation. Furthermore, Conservative rabbis and lay leaders were increasingly asking for specification regarding points of substantial agreement in Conservative Jewish belief and practice, as well as descriptions of various options where consensus did not exist.[8] In recent times, Jewish millennials, like those of other faiths, were increasingly averse to joining any institution, preferring to cultivate their own individuality on their own (*The Jew Within*, as Steven M. Cohen and Arnold Eisen titled their 2000 book). They were also postponing marriage and children until their thirties or even forties, thus reinforcing their sense that they need not join a synagogue to educate their children and be part of a community of others in the same situation. As a result, as the Pew study of American Jews demonstrated in 2013, a full 32 percent of millennials (born after 1980), both Jews and those of other faiths, were not affiliating with any of the religious movements. Ultra-Orthodox Jewry and fundamentalists of other faiths as well were gaining in numbers somewhat, but all modern expressions of religion were losing members. Furthermore, because Orthodox Jews were having larger families than Conservative Jews were, Conservative Jewry was comparatively aging.

Conservative leaders felt the beginnings of these changes as early as the mid-1980s. Although individual Conservative rabbis from the 1940s through the 1980s had written books about the movement's convictions, history, and sociology, Conservative leaders felt the need for an official movement statement that articulated the philosophy of Conservative Judaism and thus would hopefully draw young Jews to our ranks.[9]

The principal effort to do this was the publication in 1988 of *Emet Ve-Emunah: Statement of Principles of Conservative Judaism*, created by the Commission on the Philosophy of Conservative Judaism. Representatives from all five of the movement's major arms at the time — the Jewish Theological Seminary of America, the Rabbinical Assembly, the United Synagogue of Conservative Judaism (then the United Synagogue of America), the Women's League of Conservative Judaism, and the Federation of Jewish Men's Clubs — served together on this commission under the chairmanship of Rabbi Robert Gordis.

The commission met every month for three years. At the outset, members submitted papers describing their individual theologies, and the members of the commission discussed these theologies' similarities and differences. Subsequently, a group of commission rabbis wrote a draft of the Conservative statement and principles. The larger commission discussed the first and many subsequent drafts of each section. The commission's editorial committee (consisting of Gordis, Rebecca Jacobs, Rabbi David Lieber, Rabbi Gilbert Rosenthal, and me) eventually styled various pieces to speak in a coherent voice.

The commission selected the title *Emet Ve-Emunah* (Truth and faith), the very words that immediately follow the *Shema* in the *Ma'ariv* (evening) daily service, as a way to link the name of the document to the tradition and describe its contents simultaneously.

The final document (accessible by Googling "Emet Ve'Emunah" and following the second link, "Masorti Olami") remains the only official statement of Conservative beliefs to date. The fact that nearly thirty years have passed without pressure to revisit the document suggests that its ideology continues to stand the test of time. (This stands in marked contrast to the four Reform movement platforms adopted by leading rabbis in 1885, 1937, 1976, and 1999.)

That said, the movement's Committee on Jewish Law and Standards went on to issue a great many rulings governing Conservative practice in old and new aspects of life, and some movement arms have produced other guidelines (all covered in later chapters). In addition, rabbis and others affiliated with the Conservative movement have written books and essays on their own Jewish theology, their theories of Jewish law, and other aspects of Conservative Jewish life (some of which are excerpted in this book).

Definitions and Demographic Declines

By the 1980s the Conservative movement had long ceased being a "catch-all" movement for a majority of Jews, as it largely had been in the middle of the twentieth century. The process of defining what it was necessarily involved setting limits, and excluding certain practices and beliefs led to defections on both the left and right.

The Jews who identified with the Conservative movement's Reconstructionist wing had established their own rabbinical seminary in 1968 in large part to grant women equal roles and responsibilities, which were slower in coming within the Conservative movement. Almost twenty years later, once the movement's Jewish Theological Seminary had ordained its first woman in 1985, some Conservative Jews on the far right of the movement left it and ultimately established their own seminary.

Ideologically, the painful loss of the far left and right ends of the movement depleted its rich reservoir of belief and practice. At the same time, however, these developments helped to define Conservative stances more clearly and strengthen the commitment of Jews who identified with them.

Reading This Book

A hallmark of the Conservative movement has been to recognize the pluralism that has characterized Judaism historically and to assert that pluralistic ways of living and thinking about Judaism should characterize Judaism today. Conservative thinkers and leaders will affirm with some justification that the synthesis of tradition with modernity that Conservative Judaism represents is historically the most authentic form of Judaism and the healthiest form of Judaism for the future. I believe readers of this book will learn why both of these claims are true.

Suggestions for Further Reading

Michael R. Cohen. *The Birth of Conservative Judaism: Solomon Schechter's Disciples and the Creation of an American Religious Movement.* New York: Columbia University Press, 2012.

Moshe Davis. *The Emergence of Conservative Judaism.* Philadelphia: Jewish Publication Society, 1965.

Daniel J. Elazar and Rela Mintz Geffen. *The Conservative Movement in Judaism: Dilemmas and Opportunities.* Albany: State University of New York Press, 2000.

Robert E. Fierstien, ed. *A Century of Commitment: One Hundred Years of the Rabbinical Assembly.* New York: Rabbinical Assembly, 2000.

Neil Gillman. *Conservative Judaism: The New Century.* New York: Behrman House, 1993.

Pamela S. Nadell. *Conservative Judaism in America: A Biographical Dictionary and Sourcebook.* New York: Greenwood Press, 1988.

Marshall Sklare. *Conservative Judaism: An American Religious Movement.* Glencoe IL: Free Press, 1955.

Mordecai Waxman, ed. *Tradition and Change: The Development of Conservative Judaism.* New York: Burning Bush Press [of the Rabbinical Assembly of America], 1958.

PART ONE

God

CHAPTER ONE

Emunah

Theology

The word "theology," although etymologically "the study of God," also includes a religion's understanding of human beings, nature, and the relationships among all three. Although Conservative leaders have openly articulated their approaches to Jewish law, study, and practice, by and large they have been reticent to address matters of theology in an official way.

There are several reasons for this. The leaders wished to open the tent of Conservative Judaism as wide as possible, given the considerable spectrum of God beliefs among Jews. They further wished to uphold a central tenet of Conservative Judaism — be historically authentic — knowing that Jews from biblical times and throughout the ages have also articulated a wide variety of theologies. Also underlying their thinking was the understanding that Jews have always identified themselves as Jews through their adherence to law and ethnicity, not theology.

This last factor is not true of Christianity and Islam. Both are creedal religions, defining themselves by official theological beliefs and welcoming to the religion only those who affirm those beliefs. One cannot be a Christian without believing, in some manner, that Jesus is Christ, and one cannot be a Muslim without believing Muhammad is the primary prophet of God.

Judaism, in contrast, defines a Jew through matrilineal descent or conversion. A Jew can therefore be an agnostic or atheist or believe all kinds of other things about God (except perhaps that God is more than one or incarnated in a particular person) and still be a Jew, because for the vast majority of Jews, Jewish identity is defined not by ideology but by biology.

Jewish identity is thus akin to American identity. A person born in the United States is an American citizen, even if he or she does not speak English and has never heard of George Washington. Conversely, a person born in France who serves as professor of American studies at the Sorbonne may know more about the United States than 95 percent of American citizens and yet not have American citizenship.

This said, Judaism does uphold certain theological and related beliefs. In the medieval period, under pressure from Christians and Muslims, a number of Jewish thinkers sought to articulate these beliefs. Moses Maimonides, for example, pronounced Thirteen Principles of the Faith. But as soon as he did, other thinkers took issue with his list; Joseph Albo, for example, trimmed the tenets down to three.

Beyond the numbers, Maimonides's principles were open to interpretation. Rabbi Louis Jacobs's *Principles of the Jewish Faith* (1964) cataloged the wide variety of Rabbinic and other interpretations that emerged over the centuries, listing, for example, thirty different understandings just of Maimonides's single tenet that God is one![1]

Emet Ve-Emunah on Theology

In 1988, responding to movement-wide calls for a document articulating the beliefs of Conservative Judaism, its leaders issued the first and still only official statement of essential Conservative convictions: *Emet Ve-Emunah: Statement of Principles of Conservative Judaism*. (For more on this process, see the introduction to this volume.) Committed to showing diversity within the movement, *Emet Ve-Emunah* presented a variety of viewpoints concerning four theological topics: God, revelation, evil, and eschatology (how we envision the future and what that means for us at present). To keep this book reasonable in size, this chapter includes excerpts from *Emet Ve-Emunah* solely on the first three topics and explores only the topic of God in some depth, omitting the range of Rabbinic perspectives on revelation, evil, and eschatology. To learn more about all four topics, see this chapter's suggestions for further reading.

The following passages from *Emet Ve-Emunah* discuss God, revelation, and the problem of evil. Note that when this document was written in 1988, sensitivity to gender-neutral language, especially with regard to God language, was in its infancy. Today, the text affirming "the kingship and fatherhood of God" would undoubtedly have been written differently while still avowing God's sovereignty and parental care for us. This is not only a matter of political correctness; it is also theologically important. As Maimonides asserted, God, when properly understood, does not have a physical body of any sort, male or female. Nonetheless, since human beings generally can relate to God more easily when picturing God as embodying a humanlike form, contemporary translators, thinkers, and liturgists tend to either use gender-neutral language for God or alternate between male and female images.

God

We believe in God. Indeed, Judaism cannot be detached from belief in, or beliefs about God. Residing always at the very heart of our self-understanding as a people, and of all Jewish literature and culture, God permeates our language, our law, our conscience, and our lore. From the opening words of Genesis, our Torah and tradition assert that God is One, that He is the Creator, and that His Providence extends through human history. Consciousness of God also pervades Jewish creativity and achievements: the sublime moral teachings of the prophets, the compassionate law of the Rabbis, the spiritual longings of our liturgists, and the logical analyses of our philosophers all reflect a sense of awe, a desire to experience God in our lives and to do His will. God is the principal figure in the story of the Jews and Judaism.

Although one cannot penetrate Jewish experience and consciousness without thinking of and speaking of Him, God is also a source of great perplexities and confusions. Doubts and uncertainties about God are inevitable; indeed, they arose even in the hearts and minds of biblical heroes such as Abraham, Moses and Job, the biblical prophets and Wisdom teachers, among the greatest masters of rabbinic *midrash,* and in the writings of renowned Jewish thinkers and poets to the present day. One can live fully and authentically as a Jew without having a single satisfactory answer to such doubts; one cannot, however, live a thoughtful Jewish life without having asked the questions.

Does God exist? If so, what sort of being is God? Does God have a plan for the universe? Does God care about me? Does He hear prayer? Does God allow the suffering of the innocent? Every one of these questions, and many others, have been the subject of discussion and debate among theologians and laypersons alike for centuries. The biblical book of Job agonizes over each of these, concluding that God and His ways cannot be comprehended fully by human beings. The Jewish tradition continually has taught that we must live with faith even when we have no conclusive demonstrations.

Conservative Judaism affirms the critical importance of belief in God, but does not specify all the particulars of that belief. Certainly, belief in a trinitarian God, or in a capricious, amoral God can never be consistent with Jewish tradition and history. Valid differences in perspective, however, do exist.

For many of us, belief in God means faith that a supreme, supernatural being exists and has the power to command and control the world through His will. Since God is not like objects that we can readily perceive, this view relies on indirect evidence. Grounds for belief in God are many. They include: the testimony of Scripture, the fact that there is something rather than nothing, the vastness and orderliness of the universe, the sense of command that we feel in the face of moral imperatives, the experience of miraculous historical events, and the existence of phenomena that seem to go beyond physical matter, such as human consciousness and creativity. All of these perceptions are encounters that point beyond us. They reinforce one another to produce an experience of, and thus a belief in, a God who, though unperceivable, exists in the usual sense of the word. This is the conception of God that emerges from a straightforward reading of the Bible.

Some view the reality of God differently. For them, the existence of God is not a "fact" that can be checked against the evidence. Rather, God's presence is the starting point for our entire view of the world and our place in it. Where is such a God to be found and experienced? He is not a being to whom we can point. He is, instead, present when we look for meaning in the world, when we work for morality, for justice, and for future redemption. A description of God's nature is not the last line of a logical demonstration; it emerges out of our shared traditions and stories as a community. God is, in this view as well, a presence and a power that transcends us, but His nature is not completely independent of our beliefs and experiences. This is a conception of God that is closer to the God of many Jewish philosophers and mystics.

The two views broadly characterized here have deep roots in the Bible and in the rest of Jewish tradition. They are both well represented in Conservative Jewish thought and coexist to this day in our movement. They, in fact, have much in common. In particular, they both insist that the language and concepts traditionally used to speak of God are valid and critical parts of our way of life. Although proponents of both views use metaphors to speak of God, we all affirm the power of traditional terms (such as the kingship and fatherhood of God) to influence our lives in very positive ways. Our liturgy and our study of classical texts reflect that acknowledgement of the power of God in our lives.

That there are many questions about God that are not fully answered does not mean that our beliefs on these issues do not matter. On the contrary, they can change the world, for what an individual believes about God will both shape and reflect his or her deepest commitments about life. A belief in the unity of God, for example, creates and reinforces a belief in the unity of humanity and a commitment to standards of justice and ethics. Similarly, a people that believes in a God who "adopts orphans and defends widows" and commands us to do likewise will construct a society vastly different from that of a community that glorifies only the autonomy of human beings. God's elusive nature has always given us many options in deciding how we shall conceive of Him and how that will affect our lives. The human condition being what it is, some choices in these matters must inevitably be made. In our own fragile world, the tenacious belief in God that has characterized our history since Abraham and Sarah stands as instruction and inspiration, and continues to call us to pattern our lives after the God in whom we believe.

Revelation

Conservative Judaism affirms its belief in revelation, the uncovering of an external source of truth emanating from God. This affirmation emphasizes that although truths are transmitted by humans, they are not a human invention. That is why we call the Torah *torat emet* [a Torah of truth]. The Torah's truth is both theoretical and practical, that is, it teaches us about God and about our role in His world. As such, we reject relativism, which denies any objective source of authoritative truth. We also reject fundamentalism and literalism, which do not admit a human component in revelation, thus excluding an independent role for human experience and reason in the process.

The nature of revelation and its meaning for the Jewish people have been understood in various ways within the Conservative community. We believe that the classical sources of Judaism provide ample precedents for these views of revelation.

The single greatest event in the history of God's revelation took place at Sinai, but was not limited to it. God's communication continued in the teaching of the Prophets and the biblical Sages, and in the activity of the Rabbis of the Mishnah and the Talmud, embodied in Halakhah and the Aggadah (law and lore). The process of revelation did not end there; it remains alive in the Codes and Responsa to the present day.

Some of us conceive of revelation as the personal encounter between God and human beings. Among them there are those who believe that this personal encounter has propositional content, that God communicated with us in actual words. For them, revelation's content is immediately normative, as defined by rabbinic interpretation. The commandments of the Torah themselves issue directly from God.

Others, however, believe that revelation consists of an ineffable human encounter with God. The experience of revelation inspires the verbal formulation by human beings of norms and ideas, thus continuing the historical influence of this revelational encounter.

Others among us conceive of revelation as the continuing discovery, through nature and history, of truths about God and the world. These truths, although always culturally conditioned, are nevertheless seen as

God's ultimate purpose for creation. Proponents of this view tend to see revelation as an ongoing process rather than as a specific event.

The Problem of Evil

The existence of evil has always provided the most serious impediment to faith. Given the enormity of the horror represented in Auschwitz and the threat of nuclear destruction symbolized by Hiroshima, this dilemma has taken on a new, terrifying reality in our generation. The question of how a just and powerful God could allow the annihilation of so many innocent lives haunts the religious conscience and staggers the imagination.

Despite centuries of debate, we must realize that no theology can ever justify the mass slaughter of the blameless, the death of a single child, or the seeming randomness with which natural disaster strikes. The Torah itself reflects the tension between the inscrutability of God's will and God's own assertions that He is the Author and Prime Exemplar of morality.

Ultimately, we cannot judge God because we cannot discern His workings from beginning to end. A discrepancy will always exist between our finite characterizations of God and His own infinite nature.

Although we cannot always reconcile God's acts with our concept of a just God, we can seek to further our understanding of His ways. By creating human beings with free will, God, of necessity, limited His own future range of action. Without the real possibility of people making the wrong choice when confronted by good and evil, the entire concept of choice is meaningless. Endowing humankind with free will can be seen as an act of divine love that allows for our own integrity and growth, even if our decisions can also bring about great sorrow.

We must recognize that much of the world's suffering directly results from our misuse of the free will granted to us. Poverty and war are often the product of human sloth and immorality. Our own passivity or injudicious behavior can exacerbate the ravages of hunger or disease. Given the organic relationship that binds all humankind together, the cruelty or stupidity of some can have wide-ranging, hurtful effects on others, especially when such acts go unchallenged. We can honestly assert that our actions do have consequences. Even if ultimately vindication or recompense is delayed, it is true that in general, right-doing does lead to well-being while wrong-doing results in disaster.

At times, however, we are confounded and even angered when we cannot discern the purpose of suffering or the warrants of evil's targets. We deny as false and blasphemous the assertion that the Holocaust was the result of its victims' transgressions or of the sins of Jewry as a whole. But even when the causes of human evil are traceable, the justification of natural disaster or genetic disease remains a mystery to us. When words fail us, when our understanding cannot grasp the connection between suffering and our deeds, we can still respond with our acts. Tragedy and personal suffering can spur us on to new levels of compassion, creativity, healing and liberation of the human spirit.

When caught in the throes of pain, the sufferer can find little comfort in theodicy. Thus, attempts to vindicate God by posting tragedy as a necessary condition of life, or by asserting that evil is either the mere absence of good or the work of an autonomous demonic realm, may have some philosophic value, but they cannot alleviate the immediacy and intensity of sorrow. During moments of travail, we can find solace in God who identifies compassionately with us in our struggles. When the world seems chaotic following bereavement, the traditional blessing *barukh dayan ha-emet* ("blessed is the righteous Judge") and the *kaddish* can provide a sense of stability and order. They serve as signposts on the road from mourning to consolation while affirming our belief that all is not chance, that there is a divine plan even when we cannot clearly discern its contours. The image of *olam ha-ba* (a hereafter) can offer hope that we will not be abandoned to the grave, that we will not suffer oblivion. Stripped of all illusions of self-sufficiency by the reality of death, we can gain a deeper consciousness of God who caringly grants us the fortitude to endure, and the ability to find meaning even in our loss.

We maintain our faith in God whose will it is that good triumph over evil, even if that triumph is experienced only fitfully in historical time. Humanity can delay God's plan of a world freely united in love and righteousness with Him, but it cannot prevent its ultimate fulfillment. Even if the "Kingdom of God" remains a vision of a distant future, we can attain kinship with the divine by restraining our hurtful, self-aggrandizing impulses and by dealing justly and compassionately with one another.

Modern Conservative Theologies

Modern Conservative/Masorti Jews have voiced a variety of perspectives on God. Many of these theories can be categorized as forms of various schools of thought—for example, of rationalism, religious naturalism, process theology, mysticism, or feminist theology—but theologians within each school of thought may articulate different theological understandings. Furthermore, many of these thinkers have not characterized their beliefs as belonging to a particular theological school of thought. I have nonetheless described the forthcoming theologies in these terms to help readers discern the variations in theological perspectives.

A book of this size cannot possibly include theological writings in all schools of thought from all the important contemporary Conservative thinkers. Here is a sampling of views, organized by theological theory, with no claim to completeness.

Rationalism

Rationalism (from the Latin *ratio*, "reason") stresses the power of reason to give us knowledge about ourselves and our world. It is often contrasted with empiricism, which instead stresses the role of sense experience in imparting such knowledge. Of course, both reason and sense experience are involved in teaching us what we know, as do our interactions with people and our learning more generally through the process of living life.

What distinguishes rationalism from other theories is the attempt to use reason as much as possible to learn about ourselves, our environment, and God. This school of thought goes back to Plato and includes Descartes and Kant among its more modern expositors.

Two Conservative theological perspectives within the rationalist school of thought follow.

In the first excerpt, Rabbi Elliot Dorff examines how we use reason generally to learn truths about our lives and then applies that analysis to how we can come to know about a personal God very much akin to that of Judaism's classical biblical and rabbinic writings and embedded in its prayer book in ways that resemble how we come to know other people. The second excerpt from Dorff's writings describes the core of the experience of being in relationship with that personal God as articulated in the covenant between God and the Jewish people.

In the third excerpt, Rabbi Neil Gillman explores what we can learn from anthropology about using myths to describe our fundamental beliefs. While in common parlance "myth" means falsehood, as in "It is a myth that girls cannot learn physics," Gillman's use of the term has the opposite meaning common in anthropology, namely, myths are truths that express our ultimate convictions about life that we cannot describe in straightforward language because they are too fundamental and abstract but that we can capture at least in part through stories. When such myths are real for us, he explains, we can use them to understand ourselves and our world and to decide how to live in that world.

For Jews, these kinds of myths have Jewish legal consequences, for, as Gillman asserts, there can be no Judaism without Jewish law. The practice of Jewish law, then, is, for Gillman, how we live out in practice what we believe as articulated in those myths most meaningful to us.

Epistemological Moorings

Elliot N. Dorff

I begin with one fundamental belief concerning the human ability to know. I am deeply convinced of both the value and the limitations of human knowledge. I honor and pursue knowledge, pushing reason as far as it will take me in understanding my experience; in that sense I am a rationalist. At the same time, I assume from the beginning that ultimately there will be features of my experience that will not fit into a neat, intellectual system, sometimes because of my own individual failings to understand, and sometimes because no human being does or can understand them. I therefore do what I think the Rabbis, in contrast to the Greeks, did—that is, I entertain and pursue any explanation that sheds light on an issue; I expect that conflicting analyses may each be true and helpful to some degree, conflicting though they be; and I prefer to live with inconsistency rather than distort or ignore features of my experience that do not fit into a given theory, however helpful that theory may be in explaining other facets of my experience. Keeping the limitations of human knowledge in mind does not make me abandon the effort to know, but it does afford me a healthy sense of epistemological humility and humor; I must let go of the human quest for certainty and adopt instead a mellow, almost playful, posture vis-à-vis earnest human attempts to understand everything.

In practice, what that means with reference to God is that I am a "constructivist": that is, I think that we human beings have no unmediated knowledge of God but that we rather have to construct our conceptions of God on the basis of the experiences we have. Like most other conceptions (except perhaps more so), our understanding of God will therefore be built not only upon those experiences that we all share but also upon those that are unique to each one of us. . . .

If that is my fundamental methodological belief in these matters, my root experience is that "God" is a term that means one thing to me in moments of thought and another in moments of prayer and action. When *thinking* about God, "God" signifies, among other things, the superhuman (and maybe supernatural) powers of the universe; the moral thrust in human beings; the sense of the beauty in life; and the ultimate context of experience. While these phenomena do not offer proof of God, they persuade me that theological language is appropriate in describing experience and ultimately more adequate than a totally secular conceptual framework.

The depictions of God produced by reason, however, are very abstract. That, I have come to recognize, is more a result of the character of reason than it is a reflection of God. Reason by its very nature seeks to generalize over specific phenomena and draw analogies among them. In contrast, when I experience God in prayer or action, the God I encounter is a unique personality who interacts with the world, most especially in loving us by commanding everyone to obey the laws of morality and the People Israel to observe the *Mitzvot*. It is the one, unique God who cannot be reached by generalization. . . .

This has led me in recent years to examine personal interactions with God—not "kooky" or even mystic experiences (I am too much of a rationalist for that), but evidence of a personal God in everyday experience. We learn most about other people and we foster relationships with them not by creating proofs for their existence but rather through doing things together and through talking with them. Observation and cogitation have limited value in such contexts. Because the classical Jewish tradition has portrayed God as personal, human experience would suggest that we come to know God just as we learn about people—namely, through mutual action and verbal communication. Moreover, the Jewish tradition would suggest this, for historically Jews have experienced God not so much in thinking about God but rather in the process of carrying out God's commandments, in God's actions in history, in revelation, and in prayer. [The following sections of this essay and separate chapters of my book *Knowing God* discuss how we come to know God in these four ways.]

"In Search of God," 112–14

The Soul of the Covenant with God

Elliot N. Dorff

[The central] Jewish story that defines the consciousness of Jews as Jews is the Exodus from Egypt followed by the Revelation at Mount Sinai (Horeb) and the trek to the Promised Land. In the story, the model for understanding Jewish law is the covenant between God and the People Israel. Although the Torah records that God previously entered into covenants with Noah and Abraham and had renewed the latter with Isaac and Jacob,[2] it is at Mount Sinai that the covenant is specifically with the whole People Israel, and it is only there that both the basic assumptions about the relationship between God and Israel and its underlying values are articulated. Israel's covenantal relationship with God thus expresses the soul of Jewish law.

"Covenant" is not a word or concept that is imposed on Jewish law from external sources: It comes from the very roots of the Jewish tradition. It is one of the primary ways in which the tradition expressed and understood itself.

[But] what understanding of covenant [do] we mean to apply to Jewish law? For even in the Bible the word "covenant" (*brit*) is used for a wide variety of relationships. . . .

From the time of Abraham . . . Jewish tradition has understood God to be not only powerful but good. Therefore the relationship with this Sovereign, powerful though He be, is not based on might makes right. On the contrary, as Moses tells the people, the point of the covenant is to help us flourish: "The Lord commanded us to observe all these laws, to revere the Lord our God, for our lasting good and for our survival. . . . It will be therefore to our merit before the Lord our God to observe faithfully this whole Instruction, as He has commanded us" (Deut. 6:24–25). God informs us that there will be negative consequences if we fail to abide by the Covenant (Lev. 26; Deut. 28, 29), but the Torah gives us the clear message that God did not enter into this covenant primarily to demonstrate and exert His authority. He rather created this covenant with the People Israel *for their good*—specifically, so that they can be "a kingdom of priests and a holy nation" (Exod. 19:6).

In more contemporary terminology, the soul of the covenant with God is *tikkun olam*, "fixing the world," where the morals of the Jewish tradition apply directly to this task, and its rituals bring together and identify the community, remind it of its mission and moral obligations (Num. 15:37–41), and make life an art.[3]

The covenant between God and Israel establishes the basis for the love that Jews should have for each other. The verse "Love your neighbor as yourself" ends with "I am the Lord" (Lev. 19:18), indicating that this social bond is to be rooted in the recognition that God created and reigns over us all. Rabbi Akiva identifies this verse as "a fundamental principle of the Torah,"[4] and Hillel maintains that all of the rest of the Torah is simply commentary to this central value: "Hillel said: 'What is hateful to you, do not do to your neighbor. That is the whole Torah; the rest is commentary. Go and learn it.'"[5] . . . The Rabbis understood this verse to require not merely that we have a positive attitude toward our neighbor but also that we fulfill specific obligations toward all other Jews. This leads to the rabbinic assertions that "all Israelites are responsible for one another"[6] and that one may not separate oneself from the community.[7]

Israel's covenant with God also establishes the standard that Jews as a community should relate to non-Jews with love. . . . Jewish tradition is remarkably concerned for non-Jews as well . . . "remarkably" because . . . the Torah and the Rabbis articulated these obligations during periods when non-Jews were more likely to be persecuting Jews than aiding them. In sharp contrast, no fewer than 36 times, by the Talmud's count—and some say 46—the Torah warns Jews not to wrong a stranger.[8] One must even "love the stranger, for you were strangers in the land of Egypt" (Deut. 10:19), again made even more explicit here: "When a stranger resides among you, with you in your land, you shall not wrong him. The stranger who resides with you shall be to you as one of your citizens; you shall love him as yourself, for you were strangers in the land of Egypt; I the Lord am your God" (Lev. 19:33–34).

For the Love of God and People, 88–95

The Complex Torah Myth

Neil Gillman

I believe, first, that the function of religion is to discern and describe the sense of an ultimate order that pervades the universe and human experience. With that sense of an ordered world intact, we human beings also have a place, we belong, we feel ultimately "at home"; without it, we are in exile, "homeless" and our lives are without meaning. The whole purpose of religion, its liturgies, rituals, and institutions, is to highlight, preserve, and concretize this sense of cosmos, and to recapture it in the face of the chaos that hovers perpetually around the fringes of our lives as we live them within history. . . .

I [also] believe that all human characterizations of God are metaphors borrowed from familiar human experience. Precisely because God transcends all human conceptualization, we can only think of God through metaphors. Our ancestors discovered God in their experience of nature and history. Those experiences, as understood, interpreted, and then recorded in Torah and the rest of our classical literature, serve as the spectacles through which we recapture the experience of God for ourselves. They teach us what to look for, how to see, and how to interpret what we see. We discover God, but we invent the metaphors that capture the variegated qualities of our experiences of God. They bring God into our lives and then in turn, help us discover God anew.

Our tradition provides us with a rich kaleidoscopic system of metaphors for God. We appropriate some of these, reject others, and add some of our own that reflect our personal experience of God. . . . Knitted together, these metaphors form the complex Torah myth. This myth provides the structure of meaning that explains why things, including all of nature and history together with the realities of the human experience in all its complexity, are the way they are for us as Jews. . . .

[And] I believe that the covenant is the linchpin of the Jewish myth, the primary metaphor for Jewish self-understanding. But the covenant is itself the implication of a far more subtle characterization of God, what [Abraham Joshua] Heschel tried to capture in his use of the term "God's pathos." God entered into a covenant with the Jewish people because ultimately God cares desperately about creation, about people, and about our social structures. A caring God enters into relationships with communities. The fact that our ancestors used this metaphor for their relationship with God is further testimony of their concern with structure, for it is precisely their sense of convenantedness that led to their further understanding of law as the primary form of Jewish religious expression. . . .

Doing Jewish Theology, 3–4

Religious Naturalism

Dating back to Aristotle, the doctrine known as empiricism holds that sense experience is and should be the primary road to knowledge. In science, empiricism has produced the scientific method of testing results. In analyzing religion, empiricism has taken several forms, one of which is called "religious naturalism": religion is seen as a response to nature, and God is interpreted as particular aspects of nature or of our human lives within it.

For religious naturalists, God is superhuman but not supernatural. In other words, while God is beyond what any human being can understand or do, God is not beyond nature but is rather an essential part of it.

Among Conservative thinkers, Rabbi Mordecai M. Kaplan (1881–1983) was an early advocate of religious naturalism. He understood God as the power in nature to actualize potential for good—the power, for example, that transforms the acorn into the oak tree, or spurs a creative idea, or sparks love. Both Rabbis Harold Kushner and Harold Schulweis, two more contemporary advocates of religious naturalism whose writings are excerpted here, studied with Kaplan and were very influenced by his thought. Both, however, are prompted to use God language by different aspects of human experience.

For Kushner, whose son died at age fourteen of a tragic disease that rapidly aged him, God is not omnipotent (all-powerful), for how could a good God allow that to happen? God is good, though, and so God is not in the disease that Kushner's son suffered but in the supportive human reactions to it: in the caring concern of loved ones who comforted his family and in researchers' ongoing efforts to prevent or cure the disease. In so conceiving of God, Kushner sacrifices God's perceived power in order to preserve God's goodness. Kushner, like most religious naturalists, also sees God in the awesomeness of creation. While a scientific approach to nature would seek to analyze it, this religious approach expresses appreciation for nature's wonders.

Schulweis similarly defines God as the goodness we can find in people's reactions to tragedies, but he expands this understanding to include (among other things) the goodness expressed in the world as people cooperate, form community, and enrich society. In the following excerpt, however, he addresses different issues: How can we speak of God in a world of concrete objects and forces? If God is a part of nature, does that mean everything in nature?

Years ago, I, Elliot Dorff, was sitting with my three-year-old son on his bed reading him a bedtime story when he asked me, "Is God everywhere?" When I hesitatingly answered, "Yes," he inquired, "Does that mean that we are sitting on God?" and he burst out laughing. Schulweis, faced with a similar query from his daughter, explores what it means to identify

36

God with more abstract features of nature than the objects and forces in it—in his case, love.

When Bad Things Happen to Good People

Harold Kushner

Innocent people do suffer misfortunes in this life. Things happen to them far worse than they deserve—they lose their jobs, they get sick, their children suffer or make them suffer. But when it happens, it does not represent God punishing them for something they did wrong. The misfortunes do not come from God at all.

There may be a sense of loss at coming to this conclusion. In a way, it was comforting to believe in an all-wise, all-powerful God who guaranteed fair treatment and happy endings, who reassured us that everything happened for a reason, even as life was easier for us when we could believe that our parents were wise enough to know what to do and strong enough to make everything turn out right. But it was comforting the way the religion of Job's friends was comforting: it worked only as long as we did not take the problems of innocent victims seriously. When we have met Job, when we have *been* Job, we cannot believe in that sort of God any longer without giving up our own right to feel angry, to feel that we have been treated badly by life.

From that perspective, there ought to be a sense of relief in coming to the conclusion that God is not doing this to us. If God is a God of justice and not of power, then He can still be on our side when bad things happen to us. He can know that we are good and honest people who deserve better. Our misfortunes are none of His doing, and so we can turn to Him for help. Our question will not be Job's question, "God, why are You doing this to me?" but rather "God, see what is happening to me. Can You help me?" We will turn to God, not to be judged or forgiven, not to be rewarded or punished, but to be strengthened and comforted.

If we have grown up, as Job and his friends did, believing in an all-wise, all-powerful, all-knowing God, it will be hard for us, as it was hard for them, to change our way of thinking about Him (as it was hard for us, when we were children, to realize that our parents were not all-powerful, that a broken toy had to be thrown out because they *could not* fix it, not because they did not want to). But if we can bring ourselves to acknowledge that there are some things God does not control, many good things become possible.

We will be able to turn to God for things He can do to help us, instead of holding on to unrealistic expectations of Him which will never come about. The Bible, after all, repeatedly speaks of God as the special protector of the poor, the widow, and the orphan, without raising the question of how it happened that they became poor, widowed, or orphaned in the first place.

We can maintain our own self-respect and sense of goodness without having to feel that God has judged us and condemned us. We can be angry at what has happened to us, without feeling that we are angry at God. More than that, we can recognize our anger at life's unfairness, our instinctive compassion at seeing people suffer, as coming from God who teaches us to be angry at injustice and to feel compassion for the afflicted. Instead of feeling that we are opposed to God, we can feel that our indignation is God's anger at unfairness working through us, that when we cry out, we are still on God's side, and He is still on ours.

When Bad Things Happen to Good People, 44–45

Touch My Love

Harold Schulweis

In our home, the children were put to bed at night with some conversation and prayer. One evening my daughter, then six or seven, asked the perennial question, "Where is God?" following the prayer proclaiming God, the Lord, as One. In her book, *Today's Children and Yesterday's Heritage*, Sophia Fahs, a thoughtful religious educator, suggested a game to answer the "where" question. I decided to adapt her game with my daughter. I asked her to touch my arms. She did. I asked her to touch my chest. She did. I asked her to touch my nose. She did. I then asked her to touch my love. She stopped for a moment and reached out to touch my chest and my arms. I pointed out that she had already done so. "Now touch my love." She could not. She smiled. The exercise was an introduction to a deeper understanding of faith. . . .

For some, the religious exercise may appear oblique. But such patient introduction to religious belief is important to maintain a respect for religious wisdom. There is too great a temptation to rush to the word *God*. God should come at the conclusion of the argument. The Book of Genesis does not begin with the name of God. God's name comes after "in the beginning." . . .

Theologians consider ineffability, the inability to express certain experiences in words, as a sign of mystical experience. But the mystery experience in "touch my love" does not come from another world different from the one in which we live and breathe. . . . The power, mystery, and significance of transcendence, something beyond the limits of the five senses, are grounded in earthly love. . . .

Godliness, like love, is located not "in me" or "in you" but "between us." . . .

In Judaism, the importance of "betweenness" is expressed in the high value the tradition places on community. Acts of holiness, such as the recitation of the mourner's kaddish and the public reading of the Torah, require a minyan. . . . The noblest form of communion with God is through community. . . .

There are other lessons in that religious exercise. "Touch my love" teaches that love cannot be manipulated. I cannot make my daughter love me, nor can she make me love her. Tables and chairs can be "made." Love is a relationship that cannot be manufactured or ordered. The biblical imperative does not command that we love our parents, but that they be respected. God cannot force people to love Him. Therein lies part of the uniqueness and mystery of the love of God. . . .

For Those Who Can't Believe, 22–25

Process Thought

Process thought, dating back to Aristotle and developed by the early twentieth-century thinker Alfred North Whitehead, is another form of religious empiricism. Unlike religious naturalism, though, its theology does not emphasize the wondrous features of nature (including human life) that stir us to speak in God language; instead, it emphasizes the dynamic forces within nature and human life that continually transform our world—some of which, such as earthquakes and illness, unleash harm upon it. When

God is understood as an ever-changing natural force, bad outcomes are not a conscious God's moral responsibility but simply the amoral forces of nature at work.

Although viewing God as a force might logically seem to require seeing God as amoral (i.e., with no moral qualities, positive or negative, and thus no moral import for humans), process theologians nonetheless tend to see God as ultimately good. Perhaps this is because they tend to focus on the positive aspects of natural forces. Or perhaps, driven by the desire to derive morally positive lessons for society, they relieve God of the moral burden of having caused unjust harm to human beings.

In the brief excerpt that follows, God, in Rabbi Tamar Elad-Appelbaum's view, is constantly changing, ever creating and destroying, but in uniformly constructive ways: making order out of chaos in human society, language, ethics, and the world itself. Moreover, God promises to do this in the present and future as well. By linking ourselves with God, we become God's partners in this process.

In the subsequent excerpt, Rabbi Bradley Shavit Artson describes all beings as recurrent patterns of energy (rather than substances) and God as the one who makes relationships among these energy patterns possible. Here, God is not morally neutral. According to Artson, God lures us, by persuasion, to the good—to maximize our "experience, justice, compassion, and love" individually and collectively. When we act upon our intuitive understandings of morality, God extends the prize of a better life. When we make bad choices and endure the consequences, God suffers with us.

Radical Divinity

Tamar Elad-Appelbaum

Divinity is the radical force that moves the entire cosmos, from one end of the world to the other, and the goal of the Jewish story is to serve witness to this. Thus, in the creation story, God took the world of chaos, broke down both its concepts and its reality, and rebuilt them in the form of heaven and earth, luminaries, plants, and living beings, finally establishing humankind in God's image and likeness. The story of the beginning of the world is a story of deconstruction, of chaos, and of new creation by means of the Divine. The same follows from the story of Noah and the Flood—breaking down and rebuilding, and reassembly of humankind; the tower of Babel—breaking down and reconstructing language and attitude toward life; Abraham—breaking down and reconstructing ethics; Egypt—destroying slavery and subjugation and building within the people a new reality of freedom.

Numerous biblical stories are characterized by the tension between creation and destruction in God's world, by the quest for that same intensely sought "and it was good." . . . This includes not only stories of the past, but also the vision for the future. Prophetic visions denounce the rot of unethical behavior and sketch upon the religious horizon the possibility of a new reality better suited to the dwelling place of the God of justice and mercy, as is implied in the words of the prophet Isaiah: "For behold! I am creating a new heaven and a new earth; the former things shall not be remembered, they shall never come to mind" (Isaiah 65:17). The Tanakh [Hebrew Bible] is filled with stories of the radical God, who breaks down reality and creates a new one from its ashes, smashes humankind's dreams of an idyll and creates another in its place. But the miraculous nature of divine radicalism lies in the fact that every act of breaking down is simultaneously a new putting together. The Divine never breaks things down merely to leave reality in ruins; rather, God takes things apart in order to create a new and better order: "He did not create it a waste, but formed it for habitation" (Isaiah 45:18). . . .

When God brings forth knowledge within humankind—that is to say, the power of cognition and of creativity—humankind is destined to inherit and nullify anew its god, its world, and its own consciousness. Thus, humankind and God are transformed into partners in the secret order of the world and in its constant change.

"The Radical Divinity," 162–63

God, Energy, and Humanity
Bradley Shavit Artson

The world and God are expressions of continuous, dynamic relational change. We label that process as creativity. The mutual commitment to that process is faithfulness (*emunah*), which rises above any faith (doctrine or creed).

We and the world are not solid substances, but rather recurrent patterns of energy, occasions that change with each new instantiation but also maintain continuity from moment to moment.

We are interconnected, each to each and each to all. Therefore all creation—not just humanity or a subset of humanity—has value and dignity.

Every occasion has an interiority (first person mode, subjective) appropriate to its nature as well as an outer (third person, objective) way of related interaction and becoming. That is, we are all selves-in-relation.

We and every occasion relate to each and all creation instantaneously and intuitively. We respond to the decisions of each other and of the totality, as we ourselves are re-created in each instant.

God is the One who makes this relating possible, who creates the openness of a future of real novelty and the variety of its possibilities, and who relates to each of us in our particular individuality.

God is the One who invites us—and empowers us—in our particularity (hence, God knows us and relates to us as individuals) to select the optimal choice for our own flourishing (optimal in terms of maximizing experience, justice, compassion, and love) and for our mutual flourishing. To exist is to be self-determining, interconnected, and creative to some degree.

We and everything in the cosmos become co-creators with God in fashioning the present (which has primacy) out of the possibilities offered by the future and the constraints imposed by the past. God's primary mode of power is persuasive, not coercive. That goes for us, too.

Once the present becomes actual, it is known eternally by God and cherished forever. . . .

It remains our privilege to discern the Divine's optimal possibilities and to make choices that advance or get in the way of that best option. What is God's role in how we make those choices? How does God extend that relationship into conversation and content?

The dominant Western way of thinking about God's involvement in our choices posits a bully in the sky who compels behavior or results from unwilling, passive agents or who restrains behavior and precludes outcomes that sinning creatures would otherwise pursue. A key shift for process theology is that God does not exercise such coercive power. Rather, God exercises persuasive power. Process thinking asserts that God works through persuasion and invitation, through persistently inviting us to make the best possible choices, then leaves us free to make the wrong choice. The instant we have made our choice, God persistently urges us toward making the best possible subsequent choice.

In exercising this persuasion, God does not break the rules to force a desired outcome, but instead works with and through us, with and through natural propensities. Here is timely assurance from Midrash Tanhuma:

> All might, praise, greatness, and power belong to the Sovereign of sovereigns. Yet God loves law. It is the custom of the world that a powerful tyrant does not desire to do things lawfully. Rather, he bypasses law and order by coercing, stealing, transgressing the will of the Creator, favoring his friends and relatives while treating his antagonists unjustly. But the Blessed Holy One, the Majesty of majesties, loves law, and does nothing unless it is with law. This is the meaning of "Mighty is the Majesty who loves law."[9]

The ancient Rabbis decontextualize this verse and construe it to teach that when one talks about God's might, one celebrates God's willingness to live within natural propensities, or law. Process theologians agree. . . . The way God works on us, in us, and through us is called the "lure." . . . That is to say, at this very moment—and at every moment—God meets each of us and all of creation, offering us the best possible next step. We have the opportunity and the freedom to decide whether to take that best possible next step or not. . . . That next step—the initial aim—becomes for us our subjective aim, what we choose to do.

We know what the initial aim is . . . intuitively because we prehend it, Whitehead's term for immediate, internal intuition. We do not have to be told; we are each connected to all and to the creative-responsible love that God offers. So we intuit the lure from the inside. Sometimes we choose not to make the right choice. . . . We offer a wide array of excuses for our subjective aim perverting God's initial aim, which leaves God in covenant, hence vulnerable.

When Israel performs the will of the Holy One, they add strength to the heavenly power. When, however, Israel does not perform the will of the Holy One, they weaken (if it is possible to say so) the great power of the One who is above.[10]

God of Becoming and Relationship, xv–xvi, 17–19

Mysticism

While rationalists focus on reason to help us understand the world and live in it, and empiricists use sense experience to accomplish the same tasks, mystics think that the world we experience through those two faculties is ultimately an illusion. Indeed, it is a trap, for our reason and experience lure us into thinking that the world of objects and forces is real when it is not. It is here today and gone tomorrow, just as we are ourselves. Furthermore, the material world prompts us to do all kinds of things that, on reflection, we know we should not do but pursue anyway because we are so devoted to obtaining its pleasures. The material world thus becomes our idol of daily worship.

Instead, the mystic turns inward to find the real, eternal world. Mystics throughout the world do this in varying ways, depending upon the form of mysticism. Some use exercises or dances, some meditate, some flagellate or torture themselves.

There are two general types of classical Jewish mysticism. The earlier form, prevalent from the thirteenth through the sixteenth century, was primarily Sephardic, intellectual, halakhic, and literary (it produced books). Mystics studied the Torah for its secret meanings (*sod*) beyond its *peshat* (contextual meaning), its *midrash* (interpreted or applied meaning), and its *remez* (hinted meanings). Interpreting Jewish practices in new ways enabled them to see rituals as methods of becoming one with God—and, for some, even repairing God along with the world.

The second type of classical mysticism, Hasidism, was prevalent in the eighteenth to the twentieth century in Eastern Europe. It was Ashkenazic, anti-intellectual (one comes to God through ecstasy generated by dancing and singing rather than by thinking and writing), and nonliterary (primarily producing stories and songs). It was also quasi-halakhic. Many Hasidic stories praise going beyond the bounds of *halakhah* to reach God by, for example, whistling instead of reciting the traditional liturgy, or chopping down a tree and lighting a fire for a widow on Friday night after the Sabbath laws would forbid such actions.

Modern mystic Rabbi Arthur Green shares with the classical mystics the sense that ultimate reality is different from what we experience in our day-to-day lives. As he says in the following excerpt, "[When] that *mask of ordinariness* falls away, our consciousness is left with a moment of nakedness. . . . The astonishment of such moments . . . is the starting point of my religious life."

Yet his thoroughly modern way of religious seeking differs substantially from the Jewish mystics of yore. Whereas their mysticism led them to retreat into an alternative universe, his leads him to take an active role in the world.

The Mask of Ordinariness Falls Away

Arthur Green

I have understood since childhood that I am a deeply religious person, one easily moved by the power of sacred language, rites, and symbols. Through them I am sometimes able to enter into states of inner openness to a nameless and transcendent presence, that which I choose to call "God." . . .

At the same time, I have long known that I am not a "believer" in the conventional Jewish or Western sense. I simply do not encounter God as "He" is usually described in the Western religious context, a Supreme Being or Creator who exists outside or beyond the universe, who created this world as an act of personal will, and who guides and protects it. Indeed, I do not know that such an "outside" or "beyond" exists. . . .

What can it mean to "be religious," in a Jewish (and not Buddhist) context, if one does not "believe in God," at least as defined in the above parameters? It means that I still consider the sacred to be the most important and meaningful dimension of human life. "The sacred" refers to an inward, mysterious sense of awesome presence, a reality deeper than the kind we ordinarily experience. Life bears within it the possibility of inner transcendence; the moments when we glimpse it are so rare and powerful that they call upon us to transform the rest of our lives in their wake. These moments can come without warning, though they may be evoked by great beauty, by joy, by terror, or by anything else that causes us to stop and interrupt our ordinary, all-encompassing, and yet essentially superficial perception of reality. When that *mask of ordinariness* falls away, our consciousness is left with a moment of nakedness, a confrontation with a reality that we do not know how to put into language. The astonishment of such moments, that which my most revered teacher termed "radical amazement," is the starting point of my religious life. I believe, in other words, in the possibility and irreducible reality of religious experience. Such experience stands behind theology; it is the most basic datum with which the would-be theologian has to work. The awareness that derives from that range of human experiences, distilled by reflection, is the basis of religious thought. . . .

What is the nature of this experience? It is as varied as the countless individual human beings in the world, and potentially as multifarious as the moments in each of the human lives. In the midst of life, our ordinariness is interrupted. This may take place as we touch one of the edges of life, in a great confrontation with the new life of a child, or of an approaching death. We may see it in wonders of nature, sunrises and sunsets, mountains and oceans. It may happen to us in the course of loving and deeply entering into union with another, or in profound aloneness.

Sometimes, however, such a moment of holy and awesome presence comes upon us without any apparent provocation at all. It may come as a deep inner stillness, quieting all the background noise that usually fills our inner chambers, or it may be quite the opposite, a loud rush and excitement that fills us to over-flowing. It may seem to come from within or without, or perhaps both at once. The realization of such moments fills us with a sense of magnificence, of smallness, and of belonging, all at once. Our hearts well up with love for the world around us and awe at its grandeur. The experience is usually one that renders us speechless. But then we feel lucky and blessed if we have enough ties to a tradition that gives us language, that enables us to say, "The whole earth is filled with God's glory!" . . .

I believe with complete faith that every human being is capable of such experience, and that these moments place us in contact with the elusive inner essence of being that I call "God." It is out of such moments that religion is born, our human response to the dizzying depths of an encounter we cannot—and yet so need to—name. . . . Through the profound echo chamber of countless generations, tradition offers a way to respond, to channel the love and awe that rise up within us at such times, and to give a name to the holy mystery by which our lives are bounded.

Radical Judaism, 1–5

Feminist Theology

Since the feminist movement began with Betty Friedan's 1963 book, *The Feminine Mystique*, at least two types of feminism have developed. Liberal feminism maintains that aside from physiology, men and women are essentially the same and therefore should be treated as equals in all matters. In contrast, radical feminism asserts that the two genders are different and equal. Adherents of this latter theory point to differences in how boys and girls play on the playground (Carol Gilligan's *In a Different Voice*, 1982); what men and women variously mean when they both say the same things (Deborah Tannen's *You Just Don't Understand! Women and Men in Conversation*, 1991); how men and women interact with each other (John Gray's *Men Are from Mars, Women Are from Venus*, 1992); and even how MRI brain scans indicate that different brain areas are used when men and women respond to the same questions.

In the following excerpt, Rabbi Amy Eilberg seeks God through personal experience. This is a classic feminist approach: the religious (or the political) becomes personal. At the same time, she believes in mediating one's personal relationship with God through the Jewish people's relationship with God, past and present, and through living in accordance with God's commandments as an expression of that relationship.

Finding God

Amy Eilberg

Raised in a nominally Conservative Jewish family, I absorbed a form of Jewish spirituality based on social action, ethics, and justice for the oppressed and the underprivileged. This kind of spirituality-in-motion bred in me a commitment to *tikkun olam*, to seeing myself as a partner in the work of healing the world. . . .

Later, as a teenager, I discovered the world of traditional Jewish ritual, a life of Torah and *mitzvot* (commandments; sacred obligations). I began to connect deeply with Jewish ritual, experiencing the quiet sustaining moment of *Shabbat* (Sabbath) candle lighting, the exuberant joy of *Shabbat* meals shared with family and friends, the deep connectedness of wishing friends in synagogue "*Shabbat Shalom*" (good Sabbath; literally, a Sabbath of peace). . . .

But when, as an adult, I experienced private pain and struggle, the spirituality I had known failed me. I needed something that would be available to me between rallies, between legislative campaigns. For all the richness of Jewish ritual, I still lacked a way to relate to God between Jewish holidays, between Sunday and Friday, when there was no major life passage at hand, when it wasn't time to *daven Minḥah* (pray the daily afternoon service), nor *Ma'ariv* (daily evening service). I needed a spiritual discipline that could speak to the private places of pain and joy within me. I needed a God who could envelop me when I suffered shame or grief or loneliness, a God who could celebrate with me when life was full of beauty and blessing.

I spent about ten years of my life at The Jewish Theological Seminary. Despite the name of the institution, I was never asked who or what God was in my life, never supported in the difficult and wonderful process of working out a personal theology that could be a resource to me.

Then I landed at a place called Methodist Hospital, and, in a moment of pain, a Christian pastor-friend asked me, "Where is God for you?" The question gave rise to many other fruitful questions. . . . Why have we as Jews moved so far away from heartfelt experiences of God / the Creator / the Source of Being / A Higher Power? How do we go about retrieving this essential part of who we are? . . . What soothes our pain when we hurt, gives us hope when life is cruel, fills in the gaps when we feel wounded and empty? How do we connect our own spiritual lives with our people's collective journey? . . . Teachers began to show up in many unlikely places.

Years before . . . I had been deeply engaged in exploring the meaning of the fact that Jewish liturgy predominantly imagines God in male terms, as father, king, warrior, judge, and lawgiver. Now, in feminist spiritual communities, I began to experience the different texture of women's spirituality, the sense of feminist religious community as a source of nurturance rather than judgment, of comfort more than command, as midwife to growth, connection, and spiritual immediacy. I wondered how we might expand our images of God to embrace women's experience as well as men's. More and more often, I asked myself, "What kind of God do you believe in?" Answers began to appear everywhere—everywhere, that is, that I brought my full attention, every time I could become conscious of the gifts of life.

Then, I gave birth to my daughter. Exhausted for some days afterwards, I let ten days go by without davening (praying), despite my years-long practice of praying every morning. On the second *Shabbat* of Penina's life, I was again physically and emotionally able to open the *siddur* (prayer book). For an exquisitely clear moment, I realized that, before giving birth, I had a very specific image of God in my head. It was a male God, a punitive God, a judge, who would be critical of my allowing days to pass without praying to Him, even as I healed from surgery and cared for a newborn baby. This was the old-man-with-the-long-white-beard-God of my childhood, reinforced, I must admit, by my internalized image of some of my teachers at the Seminary. This, I now painfully realized, was the God to whom I had always prayed.

In my prayer that extraordinary evening, I encountered a new (read: ancient) image of God—feminine, loving, embracing, joyful. Far from wanting to judge me for the lapse in performing my normal religious obligations, this Mother God rejoiced in just how sacred these last days had been. I had not prayed from the *siddur*, but I had been filled with silent prayers as I anticipated Penina's birth. I was overwhelmed with gratitude when she emerged healthy. I was struck by the utter holiness of the tasks of caring for her, nursing her, rocking her, marveling at her.

The God I encountered for the first time that night understood all this very well. The Mother God rejoiced in my birth as a mother.

This experience helped me shift the site of my theological journeying from my head down toward my heart. . . . God was becoming for me an answer to a different set of questions: What is it that makes life worth living? . . . How do I cultivate a sense that life is good, that I am cared for, that I am not alone, even in difficult times? What can I do to nourish sanctity in my life?

I began to experience God in unpredictable times and places. Gradually, I found myself no longer needing to wait only for the grand peak moments of life—the birth of a child or visit to Grand Canyon—or the great Jewish peak moments like *Kol Nidrei* (*Yom Kippur* eve service) or the arrival of the planeload of Soviet Jews in Israel. I would find myself stopping in the midst of everyday activities and noticing, with wonder and satisfaction, that I felt myself standing on holy ground. There was sanctity, there was an awareness of a Higher Power, there was a sense of divine revelation for me when: One bereaved family turned to comfort another in the waiting room of an intensive care unit, after the death of their own loved one; a woman dying of anorexia told me of her hope that she might learn to experience the small miracles in life—like the presence of someone who cared on a day when she felt very low; a woman struggling with profound depression spontaneously opened her well-worn Bible to Psalm 126 and joyfully read to me, "Those who sow in tears will reap in joy"; a friend spoke to me from a place of deep genuineness and caring, and, listening, it suddenly clicked for me—this is the voice of God.

I have been finding God at absolutely ordinary moments: When a stranger admires the natural streak of white in my hair, when the clouds hang in a particularly beautiful way over the hills where I live, when my daughter reaches for my hand, when a friend calls to say "I was thinking about you." . . .

I am beginning really to know that I can find God within me as well; for me, the teaching of the first chapter of Genesis—that we are all created in the image of God—means that God is present within me. When I am really present to myself, when I say "no" to the noise and distractions that keep me from my innermost sense of what is true, when I slow and quiet down and listen to the still, small voice within, the voice of God can speak to me and through me. . . .

I have learned that God is in every breath I breathe. This is precisely the biblical teaching: That humanity was created as the union of dust of the earth and the breath of God. If I am quiet enough, attuned enough, ready enough, I can find the presence of God moving through me with each breath.

This is implied, too, in the teaching of the last verse of the Book of Psalms: *"Kol haneshamah tehallel yah"* (with every breath I praise God). Every moment can be an opportunity for gratitude, for awareness of everyday blessings, for a sense of the miraculous. My very breath, my every breath, can be a vehicle for awareness of God in my life at any moment. . . .

Some days it is the *Modim* (thankfulness) prayer of the *Amidah* (series of blessings that is the centerpiece of every prayer service) that most powerfully claims my attention. *Modim anahnu lakh* . . . "Thank you, God, for our lives that are placed in Your hands, for our souls that are entrusted in Your care, for the miracles that are with us every day, the wonders and the goodness that are in each moment, morning, noon, and night. God of goodness, Your mercy is unbounded. God of Compassion, Your lovingkindness is everlasting. We turn always to You." This is a powerful lesson in gratitude and surrender.

At other times, when I am fearful or agitated, out of balance or confused, I am helped to place my life in God's hands with the powerful words of the *Adon Olam* prayer: "In Your hand I place my soul, when I wake and when I sleep. My spirit and my body are in Your care. God is with me, I have no fear."

The question "Where is God for you?" is no longer so hard to pose or to answer. The language of this search may have grown foreign to us as Jews, but, thank God, we are beginning to reclaim it. The territory is not far from us. It is extremely close — embedded in our own lives and in our sacred texts. As with Moses, so with us, holy ground is right under our feet. We need only open our eyes and see.

"'Where Is God for You?': A Jewish Feminist Faith," 105–10

Suggestions for Further Reading

1. The books by Elliot Dorff, Neil Gillman, Harold Kushner, Harold Schulweis, Bradley Shavit Artson, and Arthur Green, from which selected excerpts appear in this chapter, are listed in this book's bibliography. Chapter 1's other selections were excerpted from articles in anthologies that include a broader range of Jewish perspectives than Conservative/Masorti thought. These anthologies are also good sources of further reading on this topic and appear in the bibliography as well.

2. The essays in the Conservative movement's Torah commentary, *Etz Hayim* (ed. David L. Lieber, as listed in the bibliography), relevant to theology—specifically, "The God of Israel" (beginning on p. 1390), "Revelation: Biblical and Rabbinic Perspectives" (p. 1394), "Medieval and Modern Theories of Revelation" (p. 1399), "The Nature of Revelation and Mosaic Origins" (p. 1405), "Prophecy and Prophets" (p. 1407), "The Covenant and the Election of Israel" (p. 1416), "Reward and Punishment" (p. 1430), and "Eschatology" (p. 1434).

3. See Abraham Joshua Heschel, *Heavenly Torah as Refracted through the Generations*, translated and edited by Gordon Tucker and Leonard Levin (New York: Continuum, 2005).

4. For a thorough discussion of Conservative Jewish approaches to revelation, consult Elliot N. Dorff, *Conservative Judaism: Our Ancestors to Our Descendants* (New York: United Synagogue of Conservative Judaism, 1977; 2nd, rev. ed., 1996), chap. 3, sec. D.

5. Those interested in the problem of evil may want to consult, among others, the following books by Conservative rabbis in order of publication: Richard Rubenstein, *After Auschwitz: Radical Theology and Contemporary Judaism*; Harold Kushner, *When Bad Things Happen to Good People* (short excerpt appears above); Harold Schulweis, *Evil and the Morality of God*; Elliot Dorff, *Knowing God: Jewish Journeys to the Unknowable*, chap. 5; David Blumenthal, *Facing the Abusing God: A Theology of Protest*; and Bradley Shavit Artson, *God of Becoming and Relationship: The Dynamic Nature of Process Theology*, chap. 5.

6. Those interested in eschatology might consult the following books by Conservative rabbis: Neil Gillman, *The Death of Death: Resurrection and Immortality in Jewish Thought*; and Elie Kaplan Spitz, *Does the Soul Survive? A Jewish Journey to Belief in Afterlife, Past Lives, and Living with Purpose*.

CHAPTER TWO

Tefillah

Prayer

Prayer is common to all the world's religions, and yet it is extremely complex. Each religion, and each denomination within that religion, may have varied, intricate ways of understanding the purpose of prayer and the prayer experience.

With this complexity in mind, in this chapter we explore teachings about prayer from *Emet Ve-Emunah* (the only official statement of Conservative belief); three different theories of the nature and goals of prayer as advanced by Conservative rabbis; an excerpt from the introduction of a recent Conservative prayer book, *Mahzor Lev Shalem*; and a description of new prayer forms taking hold in Conservative Judaism today.

Emet Ve-Emunah on Prayer

An essential Conservative message about prayer is its encouragement both within and outside the synagogue. This reflects Jewish tradition. According to the Talmud (*b. Menaḥot* 43b), a Jew should utter at least one hundred blessings each day, and saying the fixed prayers amounts to only sixty-five of them. That leaves at minimum thirty-five ways a day in which we are spontaneously supposed to praise God for the happenings in our lives—what Professor Max Kadushin of the Jewish Theological Seminary called "normal mysticism," that is, finding God in the normal course of the day.[1]

Emet Ve-Emunah speaks of the tension between *keva*, the fixed times and words of prayer, and *kavannah*, intention and meaning in prayer—a discussion dating back to the Rabbis of the Talmud as well as medieval Jewish thinkers. Ultimately, the conclusion is, both are important. An individual is not likely to achieve both completely in any given prayer experience, but still, one should seek to have both in one's prayers as much as possible. This means that Conservative Jews should pray *Shaḥarit* (the morning service), *Minḥah* (the afternoon service), and *Ma'ariv* (the evening service) daily, preferably in the context of a minyan, a quorum of ten Jews thirteen years of age or older. And they should participate in services on Sabbaths, festivals, and High Holy Days, all the while seeking to infuse attention and emotion into their prayers.

Emet Ve-Emunah also observes that the English word "prayer" is misleading, as it denotes prayer as petition, asking or begging, as in, "Do this, I pray." In fact, Jewish liturgy contains many kinds of prayers. Traditional Jewish prayers do include petitions, but the vast majority of the *Siddur* (the traditional, ordered liturgy) consists of praising God and giving thanks (with some attention given to confession).

The Hebrew word for prayer, *tefillah*, comes from the reflexive root *hitpallel*, which some understand to mean to "judge oneself." More likely, though, it means to try to see ourselves through God's eyes, to try to recognize how God would evaluate each of us—that is, to set ourselves up for judgment by God. This approach brings us out of ourselves and directs our attention instead onto human dependence on God and the world God created—hence, the many praises of God in the liturgy.

Emet Ve-Emunah also urges us to pray in the traditional Hebrew and to use the traditional musical modes for prayer at different times of the week and year. Both practices are understood to enhance our ties with our ancestors' prayers and those of Jews around the world and to give our own prayers more meaning. Praying in Hebrew also avoids misconceptions produced by translations (as in the meaning of the word "prayer"). To help less knowledgeable Jews read the prayers in Hebrew, the Conservative movement's Federation of Jewish Men's Clubs has produced two books, *Shalom Aleichem (the Friday Night Service)* and *Eyn Keylohenu (the Saturday Morning Service)*. Accompanying teachers' guides for each volume enable laypeople who can read the Hebrew prayers to help other Jews do so.

In addition, *Emet Ve-Emunah* delves into the music of prayer. Specific Jewish music is designed for prayer, and there are other musical modes for reading the Torah, the weekly section from the Prophets (the haftarah), and the five other scrolls read in synagogues throughout the year (Song of Songs, Ruth, Lamentations, Kohelet, and Esther). The same words are to be sung differently when they appear variously in weekday, Friday night, Saturday morning, Saturday afternoon, festival, and High Holy Day services; in each setting they thereby take on completely different meanings and emotional tones. (Try this yourself by singing any sentence you wish to a bouncy melody, then to a romantic melody, and finally to a mournful melody.) During the course of one year, the *Kaddish* is traditionally sung to nineteen different melodies! This is quite a testament to how deeply Jewish tradition uses music to define and augment the moods and meanings of prayer.

Tefillah (Prayer)

We translate *tefillah* as "prayer," but the English word denotes petition, and the Jewish experience of *tefillah*, although it includes petition, is much richer than that. It includes acknowledgment of God's role in our lives, praise of God, confession, return to God (*teshuvah*), thanksgiving, the enunciation of ideals for both the Jewish people and the world, and study of our sacred literature from the Bible to this day. As the Hebrew root of *tefillah* suggests, its emphasis is not on petition but rather on self-examination as a prelude to self-improvement.

One who sees the world as pervaded by God responds to that with *tefillah* on many occasions throughout each day. The synagogue and special seasons or events can be catalysts for prayer, but only in the soul of one who is ready to seek God.

Keva and Kavanah

The Jewish tradition establishes a structure, called *keva*, for the times, content, and order of prayer. Thus, Jewish law requires that we pray at fixed times to assure our continual awareness of God and of Jewish tradition. Moreover, *keva* enables us to pray as a community; only by coordinating the times and content of prayer can we pray together. Setting a fixed tine for prayer adds meaning to life by marking its special moments and endowing it with a rhythmic pattern.

Nevertheless, the ideal goes beyond *keva* and calls upon us to pray with *kavanah*, intending and feeling our prayers. In their attempts to make prayer live for contemporary people, Conservative congregations will differ in their services, and, for that matter, a given congregation may vary the form of its worship from time to time or offer alternative services. All of these variations are part of the Jewish tradition of liturgical creativity. The *Siddur*, the traditional prayer book, evolved over time through both addition and deletion. This creative process enabled the Jew to mix the traditional with the modern and thus to pray with more *kavanah*. The prayer books and other liturgical publications of the Conservative community embody this balance between old and new, *keva* and *kavanah*.

Although there are minimum, fixed times for prayer each day, a Jew is encouraged to pray at any time he or she is moved to pray, either within or outside the usual rubric of prayer. When one is unable to perform the prescribed ritual as part of a community (minyan), one should recite the prayers in private. Even communal forms of prayer begin with the individual soul of every Jew.

The Spiritual Meanings of Prayer

The many types of prayer—petition, confession, thanksgiving, praise of God, emotional expression, affirmation of ideals, and study of Torah— make it possible for every Jew to gain spiritual meaning from prayer to differing extents and in any of the following ways:

Perspective, appreciation, and meaning. The many praises of God in the liturgy may seem redundant, but focusing our attention on God and His qualities enables us to transcend ourselves, to see the world from God's perspective, as it were, so that our concern may extend to people beyond ourselves and we may appreciate values that transcend our own needs and wants. Above all, the goal of prayer is to involve us with a sense of the holiness of God, which fills the universe.

Communal and historical roots. Our inescapable egocentrism presents yet another problem: we are separate and lonely. To be psychologically healthy, we must form our own individual personalities, but we must also create ties to others. Jewish liturgy helps us transcend our loneliness by indicating a preference for worshipping with a community (minyan), by the constant use of the first-person plural in the prayer book, and by the repeated references to the Jewish people of the past, present, and future. All these factors together help produce a powerful sense of community and rootedness.

Knowledge of the tradition. Sometimes prayer is effective because it teaches us about our heritage. Judaism regards study as one of the highest forms of worship. This is apparent in the communal reading of the Torah, together with its exposition and discussion. Learning Torah, one reenacts the hearing and acceptance of the Torah at Mount Sinai. The *Siddur* itself is a book of theology for the Jewish people as a whole, and Jewish prayer, then, is nothing less than a continual renewal of one's attachment to the heart and mind of Judaism.

Aesthetic and emotional impact. We Jews strive to make our experience of prayer beautiful (*hiddur mitzvah*). In addition to the sheer beauty of the synagogue and service, worship can enable us to express our feelings and hopes. Prayer is a potent way to express our present emotions and feel new ones.

Moral effects. The set times for prayer remind us of our moral commitments, with the result that we are more likely to make them a part of our lives. Prayer can stimulate us to act as we should. It can help us to become holy like God: "You shall be holy for I, the Lord your God, am holy" (Leviticus 19:2).

Fulfilling a mitzvah: prayer as a discipline. There are times when one is not in the mood to pray. Jewish law obligates us to pray nevertheless. This requires discipline and a sense of obligation, but it may ultimately lead us to pray with attention and feeling.

The efficacy of prayer: God as the hearer of our prayers. For the worshipper, prayer can be a vibrant link to God and the Jewish people. People understand this link differently. Some believe that even communal prayer remains a personal expression of the individual worshipper, albeit one heightened in its meaning by an awareness of oneself, one's people, and God. Others believe that prayer is a form of direct communication with God. That view is probably more personal and comforting, but it raises the difficult issues of the efficacy of prayer. Can God, and does God, answer our prayers? How do we know? Sometimes our prayers are answered because we become transformed in the process, and thus our goal is achieved. This is true of collective as well as individual prayer. Thus, centuries of Jewish prayer for the restoration of Zion, which kept alive the hope of return in the hearts of our people, found its fulfillment in the rebirth of the State of Israel. But however we understand the phenomenon of prayer, much of its significance lies in its ability to give voice to our yearnings and aspirations, to refine our natures, and to create a strong link to God.

The Language and Music of Prayer

According to Jewish law, one's obligation to pray can be fulfilled in any language. Nevertheless, Conservative Jews, like Jews throughout the centuries, pray largely in Hebrew. Religion employs intellectually abstract and emotionally powerful terms to convey its message. Such terms, when translated, tend to change both in denotation and connotation. Hence we pray in Hebrew to preserve all the original nuances of meaning. Hebrew has always been the primary language of Jewish worship, *leshon ha-kodesh* (the holy tongue). As a result, through Hebrew prayer we link ourselves to Jews praying in all times and places. One who learns the *Siddur* and its music develops an emotional attachment to the very sound and rhythms of the words and music.

For all of these reasons, the Conservative movement urges contemporary Jews to master the art of traditional Jewish prayer, including the Hebrew words and the prayer's music. A variety of educational programs within the movement seek to help people learn the necessary skills so that they can participate in the largely Hebrew prayers of Conservative synagogues. At the same time, as Jews have done throughout time, we in the Conservative movement enhance Jewish liturgy and the experience of worship through new prayers in both Hebrew and the vernacular and through the use of new melodies. We thus avail ourselves of the legitimacy, immediacy, and creativity of prayer in our native tongue, and we "sing a new song" while preserving the many values of singing the Hebrew prayers and melodies hallowed by our tradition.

A Life Imbued and Inspired by Prayer

The Conservative movement also teaches that there are prayers and special blessings (*berakhot*) that are to be said in a variety of circumstances, both within the synagogue and without, and it encourages Jews to recite them at the appropriate times. Thus we become sensitive to each occasion and learn how to respond to it. By offering thanks to God, we remind ourselves that neither food nor drink nor any phenomenon of nature, nor indeed the gift of life itself, is to be taken for granted.

The prayers that mark the milestones of the life cycle and the Sabbaths and festivals endow these occasions with high significance. In this way, prayer expands our awareness of God beyond limited times and places and imparts a sacred dimension to our lives as a whole.

Introducing Conservative/Masorti Theories of Prayer

What constitutes success in prayer? Are our prayers for God or for us? How are they—or should they be—related to our emotions, relationships, and actions? These are precisely the kinds of hard questions that people who write theories of prayer seek to address.

Although many Conservative/Masorti authors and others have written theologies (views of God, human beings, and their interactions), new prayers, and full liturgies, very few have written theories of prayer that seek to respond to these questions. That may be because prayer is the most complex of all religious phenomena, involving multiple elements and levels of meaning. Jewish prayer in particular demands a whole set of skills— knowledge of Hebrew, the prayer book, prayer traditions, musical modes, choreography (when to stand, sit, bow, kiss the Torah), and accoutrements (how and when to put on a tallit and tefillin)—plus the ability to integrate all this with intention and emotion. Moreover, whereas we can generally understand the elements of a wonderful Shabbat experience without too much probing, when it comes to prayer, we first have to determine:

* Who is praying (the individual, the community, or both)?
* To whom (a God who listens, or some other God concept)?
* For what (praise, thanksgiving, petition, other)?
* What constitutes success in prayer? If, as *Emet Ve-Emunah* says, prayer has multiple goals, at a given time we may succeed admirably in one but fail miserably in all the others. Is that enough to count as a good prayer experience?

Conservative/Masorti thinkers Rabbis Mordecai Kaplan, Bradley Shavit Artson, and Elliot N. Dorff, however, all took up the challenge to articulate their own theory of prayer. When you read their theories (excerpts will follow), consider these questions:

1. What are the goals of prayer as the author articulates them?
2. Why are these goals important to strive for?
3. Why should a person use prayer to achieve these goals (rather than something else, such as literature, drama, or music)?
4. How can a worshipper know if he or she has achieved these goals?
5. How does the God concept underlying each author's theory of prayer affect how the author understands what prayer can and should do?
6. Why should Jews use traditional liturgy rather than just say what they want to say when they want to say it?

Rabbi Mordecai Kaplan

Rabbi Mordecai Kaplan (1881–1983), the founder of what was originally the Reconstructionist wing of Conservative Judaism and later a separate movement and a leading Conservative Jewish thinker during much of his life, believed that God is "the force that makes for salvation"—that is, the power in nature that actualizes potential for good. God is not a personal deity; rather, God is the power in nature that produces both personal and collective goodness, for example, turning the acorn into the oak tree, giving us a good idea, or inducing us to fall in love.

Not believing in a personal deity should not preclude worshippers from using personal pronouns when referring to God and/or remarking on God's human-like attributes. To Kaplan, this was comparable to citizens approaching their government through administrative officials who represent that government's process.

With this theology as the foundation, Kaplan believed that the primary goal of prayer is to reconnect the person praying with the powers in nature that motivate and thus actualize the potential for goodness. A second purpose is to reconnect the person praying with the Jewish community and its heritage.

Kaplan suggested multiple ways to achieve these prayer goals. He created new prayers and encouraged Jews to develop others for a variety of life events not fully addressed by the traditional liturgy. In addition, he inspired Jews with artistic talents to produce new musical, poetic, and dramatic liturgical renditions that would engage worshippers more fully in prayer—and thereby intensify its significance in their lives. As the first Conservative leader to espouse egalitarianism, he also encouraged both women and men to create new prayers and lead public worship.

Here is his theory of prayer as it pertains to public worship and having a personal experience with God.

On Public Worship

Public worship is far from incompatible with the modern outlook on life. It has far more exalted uses than that of setting in motion forces that might fulfill one's private desires. . . .

[It] meets two essential needs of human nature: the need for selecting and retaining those aspects of reality that make life significant, and the need for identifying oneself with a community which aspires to make life significant. Public worship meets this twofold need because it affirms the meaning of life and the primacy of its moral and spiritual values, and because it gives reality, purpose, and self-consciousness to the collective spirit of a people. The usual objection to the traditional liturgy is that it abounds in endless praises of the Deity. But even that objection can easily be overruled. Only a philistine literalism can miss the poetic beauty and majesty of the traditional type of hymnologies. Primitive man, no doubt, resorted to praising his deity as a means of eliciting favors from him. But in the higher civilizations, when the pious sang praises to God, they gave utterance to the ineffable delight they derived from communion with him. The modern equivalent of that experience is a glimpse into life's unity, creativity, and worthwhileness. To articulate that experience in the midst of a worshipping throng is a spiritual necessity of the normal man. He needs it as a means of affirming the meaning of life and of renewing his spirit.

There are some principles which must be reckoned with in reinstating worship as part of Jewish folk religion. It should intensify one's Jewish consciousness. . . . It should interpret the divine aspect of life as manifest in social idealism. It should emphasize the high worth and potentialities of the individual soul. It should voice the aspiration of Israel to serve the cause of humanity.

To achieve these purposes, Jewish worship will have to conform to the following conditions:

In the first place, the language and the atmosphere of the worship should be entirely Hebraic. . . . If the synagogue were to substitute the vernacular for the Hebrew, the Jews of one country could not unite in worship with the Jews of another.

Secondly, worship must be highly aesthetic. Since it is effective mainly through the aesthetic appeal, the synagogue should enlist the creative ability of Jews. The talents of the Jewish architect, musician, poet, or dramatist should be encouraged to create forms embodying the ideas expressed in Jewish worship. . . .

Thirdly, the content of Jewish worship should deal not only with the past, but also with the present interests of the Jews, collectively and individually. The renascence of the Jewish spirit and the reclamation of the ancient homeland [in Israel] should have a foremost place in the ritual. Likewise, the yearning for peace, for justice, and for freedom should be given more specific expression than that implied in the various prayers for the establishment of the kingdom of God.

Judaism as a Civilization, 346–48

Personal Experience with God Explained

As the power that makes for world order and personal salvation, God is not a person but a Process. Nevertheless, our experience of that Process is entirely personal. That should not be surprising. Choosing, learning, loving are all processes, yet they are all personal; they can only be understood as aspects of the personal life. There is no denying that, in genuine prayer, there is a personal experience of God, but that does not mean that God is a person. Critics of the conception of God as Process object to it on the ground that it reduces prayer to a form of talking to oneself. In a sense that is true, but we must understand in *what* sense it is true.

All thinking—and prayer is a form of thought—is essentially a dialogue between our purely individual egocentric self and our self as representing a process that goes on beyond us. When we pose a problem, for example, we expect an answer or solution. But clearly that solution does not come from the person who asked the question, since there would be no question if he had the answer. In seeking a solution through thought, we expect that the answer comes to us from that side of our human nature which is open to, and represents, the divine Process. In a moral problem, we seek our answer not from the self that is identified with our appetites, passions and ambitions, but from the higher self, which represents the good of society and, in the last analysis, the goal of the Cosmic Process that governs the evolution of mankind.

Just as, when we want to approach the government of our country, we can do so only through some person—legislator, judge, or administrative official—who *represents* the process of government, so when we wish to establish contact with the Process that makes for human salvation, we can do so only by an appeal to the higher self that represents the working of that Process in us. From that higher self, which is identical with our conscience, the moral censor of our acts, and which represents God as operative in our life, we seek the answer to prayer. That answer comes in the greater power to transcend our self-centered drives, control our aggressive impulses, banish our fears, and achieve a creative and happy adjustment to the conditions of our personal life. . . .

Questions Jews Ask: Reconstructionist Answers, 105–6

Rabbi Bradley Shavit Artson

A contemporary process theologian, Rabbi Bradley Shavit Artson explores what it means to pray to a God one understands to be a process embedded in nature and therefore in all human beings. (For more on his theology, see chapter 1.) God, he says, is not an all-knowing, unchanging, supernatural being whom we might petition for an intervention that violates natural laws; rather, God is the process in nature that is "tirelessly luring creation toward its optimal expression—greater love, greater justice, greater engagement."

In the excerpts that follow, he also explains why a fixed liturgy and spontaneous prayer are both important and complementary.

Prayer Elevates Our Sense of the Possible

What are we doing when we pray? At the simplest level, with spontaneous prayer or wordless prayer, we re-center ourselves with God at the core. When I was a child, I used to run my magnet through the soil in an abandoned field near my home. The magnet would attract the iron filings in the earth, and those filings would align themselves with the magnet as it passed by. With God as our magnet, prayer allows us to orient ourselves around optimal love, justice, experience, and compassion. We elevate our own sense of what is possible, the significance of our choices, and our capacity to make a difference. Since God works with the world as it is, that new/renewed energy and determination is now available for God's wondrous work.

We don't turn to God as magician and rule breaker. God works with, in, and through creation as it is. But God is persistently, tirelessly luring creation toward its optimal expression—greater love, greater justice, greater engagement. Rather than breaking the rules, our praying opens us to renewed expression of that lure, and fresh zeal for its advance.

Scripted and Spontaneous Prayer: A Symbiotic Relationship

For many people, the only prayer they encounter is a communal activity that consists of liturgical reading from a book. Please rise. Please be seated. Please rise. Please be seated. Often the book is very old. For example, the *Siddur*, Jewish prayer book, contains prayers that range in age from thousands to hundreds of years old. How does reading someone else's words open us to a more attentive responsiveness to God's lure? Wouldn't we commune better if we prayed spontaneously and from the heart? . . . There is much to be said for the spontaneous outpouring of the heart. It is noteworthy that in Jewish tradition two of the earliest biblical examples of prayer are exactly that: . . . Hagar . . . and Hannah. . . .

But . . . the choice isn't limited to the dichotomy of one or the other, either spontaneous outpouring or scripted liturgy. Indeed, the weight of Jewish precedent affirms the symbiotic relationship between the two. We will be best prepared for the unscripted exclamation if we devote the discipline to regular scheduled prayer. The resonance of that scripted communal recitation will be that much richer because of the trails blazed by unscripted moments of crying out, in anguish, need, or gratitude.

Liturgical prayer, then, is like reading a script. A great actor will allow the script to provide the content and context for their own personality as a character. The actor becomes the character portrayed in the script, feels the character's feelings, motivations, anxieties, and aspirations that shape the character's personality. So too, the person at prayer becomes the righteous questing soul portrayed in the prayer book. We make ourselves into vessels to be sculpted by the values, aspirations, and memories provided by the *Siddur*. In emptying ourselves to be so filled, we express ourselves not as discontinuous and solitary moderns, but as instantiations of *klal Yisrael*, children of Israel, at one with our Maker. For the duration of our praying, those words become our words, those sentiments become our yearning. We expand beyond the confines of our own limited lives, the constrictions of our own age and place, and enter into a flowing stream of ancient and timely tradition. Such praying can make us more than we are alone. We grow to include our people around the world and across the ages. Through that expansive sense of *Yisrael*, we take on concern for all humanity and serve as stewards for all creation.

Praying for Someone's Recovery When God Is Not a Magician

When we pray for someone else, a form of intercessory prayer, a prayer for healing or for the diminution of pain, what are we doing? Particularly since we've abandoned the notion of God as magician and prayer as insurance policy, what does it mean for us to pray for someone's recovery? . . .

Knowing that illness and death are part and parcel of the human condition, we feel the need to do something, to speak hope and determination in the face of our own and each other's suffering, to strengthen our connections and to affirm our shared becoming. God works in, with, and through us. As we lift up another in our prayer, we focus our attention and energy on them, offering God and the world this new level of focus as a tool for renewed connection and integration. . . .

Perhaps such prayer can nudge the trajectory of a disease; the scientific studies of such matters are ambivalent in their findings.

Prayer can [also] speak to the depths of the sick, the struggling, the sad, affirming that they are not alone, not abandoned, and making it possible for us to meet them in God and mobilize untapped resources on their behalf, their own, ours, and God's.

God of Becoming and Relationship, 125–29

Rabbi Elliot N. Dorff

What can prayer mean if you conceive of God as both inherent in nature and supernatural (separate from the universe)? Does petitionary prayer, asking for God's intervention, serve any other purpose beyond trying to actualize, through supernatural intercession, an outcome that might violate natural laws?

For Rabbi Elliot N. Dorff, a theological rationalist (and this book's author) who articulates a more traditional theology, God is both personal and powerful, although not all-powerful. God is also both within and separate from the universe. (For more on his theology, see chapter 1.)

Dorff theorizes that prayer has many possible goals, in part because humans can encounter God in many ways in life. We should not expect to achieve any single goal each time we pray, any more than a batter in professional baseball expects to get a base hit each time at bat. Instead, we should recognize that in baseball, getting a base hit in one out of three attempts is an unusually high average of 333, and so we should not expect even partial success in prayer any more often. Furthermore, just as batters can hit home runs over different fences — left field, center field, right field — in addition to inside-the-park home runs in professional baseball, we too can score different kinds of home runs in prayer.

How Prayer Is Like Baseball

Many Jews assume that prayer is one type of experience, and one either has it or does not. That, however, is false: prayer is a multifaceted experience that exists in a variety of forms and on many different levels. Some types and levels of prayer are more fulfilling than others, but all have value. Consequently, a Jew who is not fully competent in the skills described above can have important, meaningful experiences of prayer while acquiring the skills to deepen and broaden them. Such people should take comfort in the fact that even those who have considerable experience and skill in worship succeed in their prayers on the various occasions in which they pray to differing extents and in many different ways.

In this respect, prayer is very much like baseball. Both require skills. Some people are naturally talented, and for them the acquisition of the necessary skills is deceptively easy. It would be a mistake, though, to conclude from watching such people function that everyone should have the same ability. That would only produce embarrassment and frustration when one tried it oneself. It would also be a mistake to deduce that natural talent in and of itself is enough; even the most gifted must practice. It would be an even more serious error to think that only people to whom prayer or baseball comes easily can accomplish these tasks. Quite the contrary is true; for the vast majority of us, praying well demands the time and effort of extended preparation — just as deft baseball playing does — but, with that, both can be effectively done by almost everyone.

Prayer is also like baseball in that even professionals attain their goals to differing degrees each time they engage in the practice. Sometimes even people who have prayed daily for years strike out in prayer. They cannot concentrate at all on what they are doing and perhaps even resent the time they devoted to prayer that day.

At other times, prayer is the rough equivalent of a walk in baseball. On such occasions, the person praying is not moved by any of the prayers but, nevertheless, is glad to have spent the time in prayer. It was, at least, a brief time spent away from the hectic schedule of the day. Even if one's mind wandered throughout the time one was saying the words of the liturgy, the exercise still carved out some time for meditation. Moreover, one might appreciate that, in more attentive moments, these prayers articulate some of the most significant aspects of one's life. Today's experience of prayer was thus worthwhile even if it was only a walk through the prayer book.

Sometimes one gets the equivalent of a base hit. A particular prayer, or sentence, or even phrase happens to hit home. That may be because it speaks to the particular problems one has at the moment, or because it stimulates one's thought, or because it reminds one of an important value, or because it adds a bit of beauty to the day, or because it gives one a sense of the meaning of being a human being and a Jew. In other words, just as one can get a base hit in baseball by hitting the ball to a variety of areas within the ballpark, so too one can score a base hit in prayer through a variety of different experiences. What makes them all a base hit is that one of the prayers has enabled the person praying to reach one of the goals of prayer.

At other times one achieves the equivalent of a double or triple in baseball. Several of the prayers hit their mark, perhaps in very different ways, and one is left with an awareness of how important it was to pray. One's day, one's week, and perhaps even one's life have been enriched.

And then, once in a while, one hits a home run. It would not be realistic or fair to expect a home run each time one is at bat in prayer any more than it would be in baseball. Those who pray very little often make that mistake. A home run in prayer, like one in baseball, requires much practice, many trials and errors, and, ultimately, consummate skill. Even that is not enough. One needs some luck, too. The conditions have to be just right, and one's body, mind, and emotions have to be perfectly attuned to one another and to the task at hand. This does not happen very often.

Moreover, one should not pray only in hopes of having such an experience—any more than one plays baseball only for the times one hits a home run. In fact, some of us will play baseball all our lives and never hit a home run. Indeed, if our praying or baseball playing were to succeed on every level each time we tried, we would be very different individuals and societies from what we know, and prayer—and baseball— would have to be restructured to speak to our needs. The fact that prayer (or anything else) cannot remake us into ideal human beings does not negate its value, however, for prayer *can* remind us what to strive for and motivate us to try. Although it cannot move us in all its dimensions every time, it *can* affect us on some level on many occasions. It thus can be a valuable practice even if it is not always or totally successful.

Gaining Spiritual Meaning from Prayer

What . . . constitutes "success" in prayer? Even if we do not expect to hit a home run immediately, for what should we aim? We know where the outfield fence is in baseball, but what kind of experience is a home run in prayer?

When one looks at the traditional prayer book, one finds prayers of petition, thanksgiving, confession, praise of God, and emotional expression, as well as provision for periods of study. There are, in other words, many ways to hit a home run, often independent of one another, just as there are many directions in which a home run in baseball can be hit and many places in which the ball can cross the outfield fence.

These varied forms of worship together develop the spiritual side of our being. Indeed, in contrast to the frenzy of the cults and the solitary meditation of some Oriental religions, Jewish communal prayer and study are the major repositories of Jewish spirituality.

Some modes of Jewish prayer place the individual praying at the center of consciousness, while others are more God-centered. This explains why people who have not developed a clear conception of God can nevertheless gain meaning from many aspects of Jewish worship. . . . They can focus on the more person—centered aspect of Jewish prayer at first and then gradually move toward the more God—centered elements. . . . This, in fact, is a prime way in which prayer informs us about God: we begin thinking about ourselves and find ourselves drawn by prayer into thinking about God. . . . We do need to be willing to set aside our intellectual conundrums for a while and jump into the dialogue with God, but this is no different from many other aspects of life in which we must engage in the experience before we have a clear conception of what we are doing. Indeed, we cannot expect to do accurate and adequate theology without such experiences upon which to build our thinking—just as we cannot hope to do accurate or adequate science without concrete experimentation first. The experience is, in other words, a prerequisite for the thought.

The common denominator of all forms of Jewish prayer, however, is that one goes beyond oneself or recedes within oneself and turns to the Holy One to at least some degree. One acknowledges one's dependence upon God and seeks to renew and strengthen one's relationships with the Eternal. As such, all forms of prayer constitute worship. Moreover, they all are necessary, for a broad relationship with God requires varying degrees of emphasis on the self. Sometimes, we *need* to express our own particular wishes or feelings; on other occasions, we *need* just as urgently to bury ourselves in God. Nothing is too personal, and nothing too sublime for prayer.

The multiplicity and variety of the elements of our spiritual being addressed and cultivated by prayer make it the crucial and enriching experience it is. On any given occasion, in fact, a Jew can gain spiritual meaning from prayer in any or all of the following ways.

1. Expression of Our Desires . . .
2. Perspective, Appreciation, and Meaning . . .
3. Communal and Historical Roots . . .
4. Knowledge of the Tradition . . .
5. Aesthetic and Emotional Effectiveness . . .
6. Moral Effects . . .
7. Fulfilling a Mitzvah and Coming into Contact with God

Knowing God, 154–58

Prayer through the Lens of Prayer Books

To articulate its understanding of Judaism in liturgical form, the Conservative movement produced a number of prayer books for the High

Holy Days, Sabbaths and festivals, and weekdays. The first prayer book to reflect a substantially new approach to Jewish liturgy, issued in 1946, was the *Sabbath and Festival Prayer Book*, edited by Rabbi Morris Silverman and published jointly by the Rabbinical Assembly of America and the United Synagogue of America.

In its introduction, Rabbi Robert Gordis, chair of the Joint Prayer Book Commission, explained three basic principles guiding the editor and commission members: continuity with Jewish tradition, relevance to the needs and ideals of their generation, and intellectual integrity. Prayers articulating the Chosen People concept were included (in contrast to Reconstructionist liturgy, where they were not), because that concept had played a critical role in traditional Judaism, and Conservative leaders deemed it unobjectionable when correctly understood.

In other instances, commission leaders departed from tradition, acknowledging that "the modern attitude varies from the traditional understanding of a concept."[2] For example, the editors changed the portion of the early morning blessings in which a free Jewish man expressed gratitude for his being obligated and able to fulfill all commandments, whereas non-Jews, slaves, and women were not so obligated because their places and roles in ancient society made it unrealistic to expect them to do so. Because the traditional liturgy's negative formulas ("Blessed are You, Adonai, who has *not* made me a Gentile, . . . a slave, . . . a woman") were easily read as denigrating non-Jews and women, the editors rephrased the blessings in positive forms: "who has made me in His image," "who has made me free," and "who has made me an Israelite"

Another instance of liturgical revision concerned animal sacrifice at the ancient Temple. Rather than retain the traditional liturgy, which spoke of looking forward to restoring this ancient practice, Conservative leaders reconfigured the prayers in the past tense; current worshippers should pray and hope to experience the fervor that had energized our ancestors when they worshipped this way but not expect or desire a return to this mode of worship. Similarly, the commission deleted the phrase "*ishei yisrael*," meaning the "fire offerings of Israel," from the *Amidah*, so that contemporary worshippers would ask God to be pleased with their prayers and not their animal sacrifices—which, after all, they were no longer offering and which Conservative leaders did not hope or expect to reinstate.

But the Prayer Book Commission and editor did retain *Musaf*, the additional service on the Sabbath and festivals that focuses most on the ancient animal sacrifices. Excluding *Musaf* would have meant destroying the entire structure of the traditional liturgy. It would have also meant forsaking valuable ideas and aspirations from the prayer book, among them the hope for the restoration of Palestine (now Israel) as the homeland of the Jewish people and the recognition that sacrifice is essential for fulfillment of all human ideals. Conservative leaders in 1946 also cherished the hope that Palestine would again become significant not only for Jews but also for the spiritual life of humankind. In addition, it was characteristic of Judaism to recall the sacrificial system as a legitimate stage in the evolution of Judaism and religion in general.[3]

Both *Siddur L'yimot Ha-Hol* (Weekday prayer book, 1961, primarily edited by Rabbi Gershon Hadas) and *Mahzor for Rosh Hashanah and Yom Kippur: A Prayer Book for the Days of Awe* (1972, edited by Rabbi Jules Harlow) incorporated these changes in the weekday and High Holy Day liturgies. They also ceased use of Elizabethan English, referring now to God as "You" rather than "Thou" and using "has" rather than "hath." In addition, the 1972 *Mahzor* included a number of new English readings in place of some of the medieval poems that had become part of traditional liturgy.

Next to arrive was *Siddur Sim Shalom* (1985, edited by Rabbi Jules Harlow), the Conservative movement's first comprehensive one-volume prayer book. Encompassing the liturgy for weekdays, Sabbaths, and festivals, it was designed both for the home and the synagogue. Rabbi Harlow and his colleagues were consciously asserting an essential tenet of Conservative ideology: Judaism in general and Jewish prayers in particular are not confined to the synagogue or to Sabbaths and festivals. Rather,

Jewish prayers are intended to infuse the entirety of our lives not only during study and worship but also at home, work, and play. *Siddur Sim Shalom* thus included home rituals, such as lighting candles on Sabbaths, festivals, and Hanukkah; various forms of *Kiddush* for Sabbaths, festivals, and Rosh Hashanah; blessings over meals and snacks; blessings for special occasions, such as seeing a rainbow or the sea or encountering a person of political power or with immense secular or Jewish knowledge; and prayers traditionally recited at night before going to sleep.

This comprehensive prayer book was also thick and heavy. Therefore, in succeeding years the Rabbinical Assembly produced two separate volumes, one for weekdays and another for Sabbaths and festivals, based on the original *Siddur Sim Shalom*.

Then in 1998 the Masorti movement in Israel and its Rabbinical Assembly region jointly produced a prayer book designed for Israelis. Published entirely in Hebrew, *Siddur Va-Ani Tefillati* (edited by Rabbi Simḥah Roth and overseen by Rabbi Michael Graetz, the *Siddur* committee chair) included some changes introduced into previous Conservative prayer books and new readings appropriate for the Israeli Masorti community.

Today, the Conservative movement's prayer books include two twenty-first-century volumes: *Maḥzor Lev Shalem* (literally, High Holy Day liturgy of the full heart), published in 2010, and *Siddur Lev Shalem* (Prayer book of the full heart) for Sabbaths, festivals, and weekdays, published in 2016 (both edited by Rabbi Edward Feld).

In addition, individual Conservative/Masorti rabbis have produced a variety of prayer books, some for their own synagogues, as well as booklets of supplementary readings for various occasions.[4]

Maḥzor Lev Shalem Offers a New Window into Conservative Prayer

Maḥzor Lev Shalem's introduction (excerpted here) well illustrates the depth and breadth of thinking about prayer, theology, history, language, tradition, and innovation that underlie each successive Conservative movement prayer book.

Overview

The prayerbook represents the theology of the Jewish people throughout the generations. Not only is it an expression of popular religious feeling, but it is also a textbook of, and gateway into, the world of Jewish thought and imagination of the past two thousand years.

The prayerbook is a work of collective genius. On the one hand, learned and artful poets turned biblical verses and commentary into prayer; they even made legal texts into liturgical poems. On the other hand, the basic liturgy is simple and direct, reflecting its origin in common communal experience. On several occasions, the will of the people overrode the decision of rabbis in determining the text and customary practice of prayer.

Our hope is that this High Holy Day mahzor will allow each congregant to engage the world of Jewish prayer in a vital way. In Jewish tradition, study and prayer have always been intimately linked. With this in mind, this mahzor consists of four main elements linking study and prayer — the liturgical Hebrew text, translation, commentary, and meditational readings — each carefully prepared with attention to the contemporary worshiper.

The Liturgy

All Jewish prayerbooks are anthologies of liturgical materials produced by generations of Jews living in many lands. Traditional *mahzorim* [prayer books for the High Holy Days] include biblical texts and prayers so old and so embedded in the liturgy that dating can only be approximated, sometimes only within hundreds of years. Moreover, because Jews in every land have adapted the liturgy for their own use, a variety of liturgical strands have come down to us. The standard liturgy has come to include poems written throughout the Middle Ages enhancing earlier prayers and expressing the religious sensibilities of their times. This *mahzor* follows the form customarily used by Ashkenazic Jewry — the Jews descended from Central and Eastern Europeans. Our manuscript sources show that while many *piyyutin*, liturgical poems, have been added or removed over time, the foundational texts have remained fairly consistent for the last several centuries, and we have tried to remain faithful to that longstanding tradition. To these basic texts we have added some prayers used only by Sephardic Jewry—Jews descended from those living in the Iberian peninsula and Arab lands—and by Italian Jewry. We have also added contemporary prayers, since the prayerbook must give voice to the needs of our own generation, as it did for those in the past.

The Translation

Several principles have guided this translation:

We believe the translation ought to reflect the Hebrew original as closely as possible, allowing the English reader to experience the text without a filter, and allowing the congregant who has some basic familiarity with Hebrew to find familiar words. When the Hebrew text is jarring, which it sometimes is, the English translation ought not to smooth over the difficulty.

The Hebrew prose frequently borders on the poetic, and the translation ought to convey some sense of that in its cadence, in its form, and in its use of language.

The translation ought to be prayerful; it ought to put the English reader in the mood of prayer.

Because each language has a distinct grammar, we have sometimes changed the word order, syntax, and sentence structure to create an appropriate English translation.

A contemporary American translation needs to be gender-neutral as far as possible, while conveying the intent and meaning of the original. Sometimes this has necessitated changing the third person in the original to the second person in this translation.

We have consulted previous translations, especially the most recent version of the *maḥzor* for the Conservative movement (1972), which was edited and translated by Rabbi Jules Harlow, as well as the re-edited Shabbat and Festival prayerbook, *Siddur Sim Shalom* (1998). We owe these sources a debt of gratitude—they were always our starting point, though the reader will readily recognize this as a new and original translation. For the Morning Blessings and P'sukei D'zimra (Verses of Song), we have for the most part used the translations found in *Siddur Sim Shalom*. And for the Torah and Haftarah readings, we have adapted David E. S. Stein's *The Contemporary Torah: A Gender-Sensitive Adaptation of the*

JPS *Translation* and the Jewish Publication Society's *TaNaKh: The Holy Scriptures*, respectively.

The formula with which a *b'rakhah* begins, *Barukh atah Adonai*, is often translated as "blessed are You" or "praised are You." We decided, however, not to translate these standard opening words, for we felt that neither "blessed" nor "praised" is an adequate translation of *barukh*, and that it was important to convey that these words in Jewish liturgy function primarily as the formal introduction of *b'rakhah*. A few other basic Jewish vocabulary words such as *mitzvah* lose all their deep overtones when translated, so most often they have simply been transliterated when they appear in English.

Running Commentary

We believe that a modern commentary ought to accompany the ancient texts to inform the reader of their history, to explain unusual vocabulary, to comment on difficult ideas and key concepts, and to explain why a particular prayer appears in a certain context and is recited at a particular moment in the service. The commentary generally appears in the right margin. . . .

Readings and Meditations

In the left margin, we have included *kavvanot*, meditational readings to help congregants focus at central moments, as well as readings that may be recited aloud. We have also provided some alternative renderings that offer a different approach to the theological ideas raised by the text. Some of these *kavvanot* and readings are drawn from classical sources, while others are new prayers and meditations related to the traditional context in which they are placed that we hope will resonate with contemporary Jews. These readings do not represent a particular point of view or consistent theological perspective. Rather, we have been conscious that a High Holy Day congregation is a diverse community and that what speaks to some will not resonate with others. We hope that among the different voices you will find something that inspires your prayer.

Feld, ed., *Maḥzor Lev Shalem* (2010), introduction, ix–xi

The Evolving Conservative Prayer Service

Just as Conservative prayer books changed over time, so too did Conservative prayer services.

In the 1930s, 1940s, and 1950s the second generation of American Jews of Eastern European descent wanted their services to resemble those of their Protestant coreligionists in order to help them blend into the American environment. This translated into formal prayer environments—ceremonial spaces, robed rabbis and cantors conducting full services, worshippers facing front, decorum emphasized.

Meanwhile, many of their children were participating in Ramah camps and/or United Synagogue Youth (USY) activities. There they conducted their own services, read from the Torah scroll, gave homilies, wore respectful yet casual clothing, and worshipped more joyously. When these young people became adults, they wanted services similar to the ones they had experienced growing up.

This is how the movement for alternative services began in the late 1960s and 1970s. It is also how some talented musicians, such as Craig Taubman, created new musical renditions of the traditional liturgy, encouraged by former Ramah campers and USYers who wanted to sing them in their synagogues.

Conservative congregations continued to host formal services in their sanctuaries, but many also began offering alternative services designed for their younger adults in another room. Not all synagogues enthusiastically adopted this "synaplex," as Rabbi Jacob Pressman of Temple Beth Am in Los Angeles called it, because then the most committed young adults were usually not in the "main" service, and so rabbis lost the opportunity to teach them and enjoy their participation in services. Still, as time went on, an increasing number of independent minyanim (prayer quorums running their own services) were established. Most met within the structure of an established synagogue, but some gathered elsewhere, often because of opposition from the synagogue leadership.

These services were highly participatory because both the worshippers wanted involvement and the logistics required it. While the synagogue's professional staff planned and led the "main" service, participants in alternative services had to plan (who would read from the Torah, lead which part of the service, give the homily, arrange for *Kiddush*, etc.) and lead their own worship. These worshippers felt both an obligation to and ownership of "their" service, all of which strengthened their prayer experience.

However, a problem emerged—quality control. Regular participants never knew how good the upcoming prayer leader's voice or Hebrew pronunciation would be, how accurate the Torah reading would be, or how thoughtful the homily would be.

As years passed, more congregations realized that their future lay with participants in these minyanim. Leaders increasingly integrated the minyanim into their synagogue offerings, and alternative services grew. At Temple Beth Am in Los Angeles, for example, the Library Minyan, which had begun with about thirty young adults in 1971, now regularly welcomes up to two hundred worshippers on Shabbat mornings, and minyan regulars comprise about one-third of the temple's board. These days, too, a third minyan meets every Shabbat in the synagogue. Participants lead the services and read the Torah and Haftorah, similar to the Library Minyan, but rather than a participant giving a homily, a congregational rabbi leads a discussion session about the Torah reading. Often there is also a fourth minyan (alternatively, a learners' service, a service for people thinking of converting to Judaism, or a service for families with young children), as well as children's services for different age groups happening simultaneously in the building.

These alternative services, and the Ramah camp and United Synagogue Youth experiences, influenced Conservative congregations' main prayer services as well. For example, while many Conservative services still are led by rabbis and cantors, they no longer resemble stage performances. Now they are communal acts of worship, singing, and learning. Moreover, when congregations redesign prayer spaces as part of a renovation, they often take the communal nature of prayer into account.

The Next Frontier in Conservative Worship

The next frontier in Conservative worship involves if and how to use instruments on the Sabbath.

Many Conservative Jews object to musical accompaniment for varying reasons. Older synagogue members tend to associate musical instrumentation on the Sabbath with the Reform movement. Others worry that loud instruments will drown out congregational singing and make worshippers more passive. Still others oppose using instruments because of halakhic (legal) prohibitions, such as disallowing carrying and fixing anything on Shabbat, connecting and disconnecting electronic instruments, and, for some, using electricity altogether on that day.

Halakhically, organs and pianos tend to be of less concern than other instruments because they are too heavy to carry, and those who play them do not know how to fix them. Some Conservative synagogues are therefore using piano or organ accompaniment.

Nowadays, though, more Conservative synagogues are experimenting with a variety of instruments, especially drums, which typically do not need to be fixed, but also guitars and other string instruments that do need periodic tuning and fixing (as when a string breaks), resolving the halakhic and aesthetic issues in differing ways.

Suggestions for Further Reading

ON THE NATURE AND GOALS OF PRAYER

Bradley Shavit Artson. *God of Becoming and Relationship: The Dynamic Nature of Process Theology*, chap. 14. Woodstock VT: Jewish Lights, 2013.

Elliot N. Dorff. *Knowing God: Jewish Journeys to the Unknowable.* Northvale NJ: Jason Aronson Press (now Lanham MD: Rowman and Littlefield), 1992, esp. chap. 6, which includes his full, thorough discourse on prayer goals (only listed at the end of the excerpt in this chapter) and why they count as goals in the first place.

Amy Eilberg. "The Siddur: A Guide to Jewish Spiritual Direction." In *Jewish Spiritual Direction*, edited by Howard Avruhm Addison and Barbara Eve Breitman, 197–208. Woodstock VT: Jewish Lights, 2006.

Robert Gordis. *A Faith for Moderns*, chap. 15. New York: Bloch, 1960.

Abraham Joshua Heschel. *Quest for God* (originally *Man's Quest for God*). New York: Charles Scribner's Sons, 1954.

Louis Jacobs. *A Jewish Theology*, chap. 13. New York: Behrman House, 1973.

Max Kadushin. *Worship and Ethics: A Study in Rabbinic Judaism*, chaps. 4–7, esp. chap. 7. Evanston IL: Northwestern University Press, 1964.

Mordecai M. Kaplan. *Judaism as a Civilization*, 345–49, 425–30. New York: Reconstructionist Press, 1957; 1st ed., New York: Macmillan, 1934.

Karen G. Reiss Medwed. "Prayer." In *The Observant Life: The Wisdom of Conservative Judaism for Contemporary Jews*, edited by Martin Cohen, 5–60. New York: Rabbinical Assembly, 2012.

ON CONSERVATIVE LITURGY

See the full introductions to the various Conservative prayer books described in this chapter.

ON NEW CONSERVATIVE FORMS AND CONTEXTS FOR PRAYER

Jack Wertheimer. *The American Synagogue: A Sanctuary Transformed*. New York: Cambridge University Press, 1987.

Ron Wolfson. *The Spirituality of Welcoming: How to Transform Your Congregation into a Sacred Community*. Woodstock VT: Jewish Lights, 2006.

PART TWO

Torah

CHAPTER THREE

Talmud Torah

Study

The Conservative movement began in Germany in the 1840s not as a group of synagogues but rather as a distinctive way to study the history and texts of Jewish tradition. This involved not only studying traditional Jewish interpretations of the Bible and Rabbinic literature but also using new study methods.

Already during the Middle Ages, some Jewish commentators were distinguishing between how a given verse of Torah was interpreted in the Rabbinic tradition in contrast to what it probably meant in its literary context. By the nineteenth century, the progenitors of the Conservative movement had begun to study the Torah and other classical Jewish texts in their historical context as well. From archaeological findings and cross-cultural studies of the languages, ideas, and laws of the peoples among whom Jews lived, early members of the Conservative movement gained insight into how Jews of biblical times were similar to or different from their neighbors.

Still to this day, an important distinction between Conservative and Orthodox study is one of method. Orthodox Jews understand classical Jewish texts only through the interpretations of past rabbis, whereas Conservative Jews also study Judaism's classical texts in their literary and historical contexts to help them discern what the texts originally meant and how they were applied in their day. To be able to distinguish when, why, and how Jews of antiquity and later times borrowed from other cultures requires us to study not only the Hebrew of the Bible but also the relevant languages, cultures, and practices of other peoples in their time and place.

Applying such historical methods has opened the Conservative movement to using sciences—paleontology, archaeology, biology, astronomy, astrophysics, chemistry, medicine, and more—to shed light on passages in Jewish classical and later texts. It has also led Conservative Judaism to accept the "Documentary Hypothesis"—the analysis of modern biblical scholars that the Torah is composed of documents from different times and places that were later edited together.

The vast majority of Orthodox Jews do not see the Bible, especially the Torah, that way out of fear that doing so would undermine the divine authority of those texts. Conservative Jews, by contrast, understand revelation and the various grounds of authority of Jewish law in a way that facilitates honesty about how Jewish foundational texts came to be and also gives them authority for shaping important parts of our lives.

Some Orthodox interpreters view the sciences as threats to their beliefs. For example, the last Lubavitcher (Chabad) Rebbe, Rabbi Menachem Mendel Schneerson, famously asserted that God placed fossils in the earth to mislead us into thinking the earth is much older than what the Torah says—and so Jews should ignore any science that dates the beginnings of the earth, lest they stop believing in the Torah.

Conservative Jews, in contrast, do not view the Torah as foundational for scientific analysis. They use scientific methods to resolve scientific questions. They rely on Torah instead for insights into the nature of who we are and who we ought to be, for how to repair the world (tikkun olam), and for a vision of the ideal world they and God might someday create together.

Furthermore, study in the Conservative movement requires a broader sweep of subjects than what is typical in the Orthodox world. An early Conservative (and later Reconstructionist) thinker, Rabbi Mordecai M. Kaplan, reconceived of Judaism not only as a religion, with particular beliefs and rituals, but as an entire civilization, with a distinctive language (Hebrew), land (Israel), theology, law, literature, music, art, and dance, as well as community. His influence led the Conservative movement to require studying not only classical Jewish texts but also all the other elements of Jewish civilization.

For modern Conservative/Masorti Jews, Jewish study therefore becomes a life-long endeavor. Jewish tradition is so rich—encompassing Bible, Mishnah, *Midrash Halakhah*, *Midrash Aggadah*, Talmud, responsa, and codes (if possible in their original forms and languages), as well as Jewish philosophy, history, literature, and all the arts—that even adults who devote their entire lives to studying the Jewish tradition will never know it all.

Emet Ve-Emunah on Jewish Study

Emet Ve-Emunah, the one official statement of Conservative Jewish belief, has this to say about Talmud Torah and creative Jewish study:

Lifelong Study

Talmud Torah (study of Torah, including all classical Jewish texts) is an essential value of Judaism. Virtually alone among all religious traditions, Judaism regards study as a cardinal commandment, the highest form of the worship of God. Talmud Torah is the obligation and the privilege of every Jew, male and female, young and old, no matter how much or how little one knows at present. Since following the precepts of Judaism requires that one know its beliefs and practices, and since it is impossible to exhaust the Torah's meaning, each individual Jew is commanded to be a *ben* or *bat Torah*, studying Torah throughout his or her life. According to talmudic legend, God Himself spends part of His day studying Torah.

Jewish education is not supposed to be restricted to childhood. On the contrary, the education of children must be understood as a preparation for lifelong Jewish study. From the outset, in the Conservative community this has applied to females as well as males. Formal and informal patterns of Jewish education in Conservative day schools, supplementary schools, youth groups, and summer camps are all dedicated to the goal of fashioning learned and learning Jewish adults.

This goal must also pervade the home, which should both support and enhance the work of educational institutions. Without reinforcement at home, the school cannot succeed. Jewish parents are duty-bound to teach the commandments and love of God to their children: "And you shall teach them diligently to your children" (Deut. 6:7). Jewish education in the home may consist of formal study, but it occurs even more pervasively and persuasively when parents demonstrate by their actions their own commitment to Jewish life. The numerous educational programs for parents, families, and other adults that are now available enable all Jews to fulfill this basic responsibility.

We of the Conservative community study the Jewish sources using the traditional mode of study at its best, utilizing methods both ancient and modern. This means that Jews must ideally study as many of the traditional sources as possible: Bible, Mishnah, Tosefta, Talmud, Midrash Halakhah, Midrash Aggadah, responsa, and codes. In this process, they must apply to their study their knowledge of science, philosophy, history, archaeology, literature, and all other relevant disciplines. We should not be restricted to questions and answers internal to the tradition itself; rather, we should look, as did our greatest scholars throughout time, both inside and outside the tradition to understand its history, practice, and beliefs. The Conservative approach to study thus combines traditional exegesis with modern historical methods. We believe this combination to be the most accurate, open, and penetrating way to understand Judaism and the Jews.

Aside from the intellectual honesty and fruitfulness of this approach, studying this way can be a genuinely spiritual experience. We are able to relate to the people of the classical texts with understanding and empathy when we come to know them in their full historical setting. Through the combination of traditional and modern methods of study, we come to recognize the variety and growth of the Jewish tradition over time, giving us a sense of its richness and dynamism. The whole tradition becomes more intelligible; we see the choices that we made and why our ancestors made them. We also face squarely those aspects of the tradition that are intellectually and morally problematic. By doing so, we come to appreciate even more the remarkable sensitivity, adaptability, and sheer wisdom of so much of the tradition. And we learn how our people, living in a variety of circumstances, sought and discovered God, helping us all to experience the Divine Presence in our own lives. The study of Torah offers every Jew, and not merely the intellectual elite, the privilege of thinking God's thoughts after Him.

An educated Jew must be at home in the religious texts of the Jewish tradition. Jewish knowledge, however, includes much more, and a learned Jew must therefore be familiar with Jewish literature, history, philosophy, and the arts. Study of these subjects enhances our understanding of Jewish history and religion. The aesthetic, emotional, and intellectual components of some of these subjects also help to initiate or reinforce Jewish commitment and add to the joy of being Jewish.

Creative Jewish Scholarship

Jewish study is not confined to a study of materials from our past; it also consists of the creative contribution to the heritage that we will pass on to the next generation. The Conservative community fosters such creativity in Jewish scholarship, literature, and the arts through the faculties of its educational institutions, its scholarly and pedagogic publications, its conferences, its museums, its artistic and theatrical productions, and its institutes and fellowships for the study of specific subjects. Creative work in all of these areas enters into the corpus of Torah to be studied by present and future generations of Jews.

No one can possibly master the entirety of the Jewish tradition. One of the goals of the Conservative movement, however, is to inspire each of its members to become a *ben Torah* or *bat Torah*, a learned and learning Jew, constantly growing in Jewish knowledge and thus coming ever closer to the presence of God.

Dr. Arnold Eisen on Conservative Jewish Learning

Jewish Theological Seminary chancellor Dr. Arnold Eisen wrote his own analysis of what makes Conservative Jewish learning distinctive. While reading the excerpt from his essay that follows, readers may wish to consider how his perspective on Talmud Torah adds, supports, and/or differs in emphasis, tone, and/or content from *Emet Ve-Emunah*.

Jewish Learning

The central questions facing every individual Jew and every generation of Jews are these: What role will we play in fulfilling the Covenant linking Jews to one another, to God, and to the world? What word will we say in the conversation begun at Sinai? What chapter will we write in the story that goes back to Abraham and Sarah?

It is impossible to answer these questions responsibly without serious Jewish learning. Our knowledge of how Jews have lived and taught Torah until now must be broad and deep enough to be adequate to the challenge of teaching and living Torah now and in the future. That challenge includes the momentous questions posed by every serious human being: How shall I use my time on earth well? How can I be a good person, a good friend, spouse, or parent? A good child to my own parents? How can I make sure I leave the world better than I found it? How should I think about and serve God? . . .

We need those answers. That, more than anything else, is what drives Jewish learning. Conservative Judaism at its best offers distinctive formulations of both the questions and the answers:

* It speaks forcefully, honestly, and authentically to contemporary dilemmas, in the conviction that the Torah, properly interpreted for changed conditions, offers the wisdom needed to guide us through present-day complexities in our private lives and our public lives, in the Jewish community and in society at large.

* Our Movement maintains that the diversity of voices sounding forth from the sacred texts of our tradition, and the variety of ways Jews in the past have applied the Torah's teachings to new circumstances, are essential to the Jewish future. We thrive on that connection to the Jewish teachings and practices handed down to us. We are enriched by responsibility not just to our contemporaries but to our ancestors and our descendants.

* Conservative Judaism believes as well that Jews cannot carry our tradition forward without appreciation for the rich encounter between learned and observant Jewish communities, past and present, and the larger societies and cultures in which Jews participate. "Who

is wise?" ask our sages in *Ethics of the Fathers*. "He who learns from every person."

And, Conservative Judaism adds, from every culture, every religion, every corner of ancient or modern human knowledge and experience. All of these elements shape Conservative Jewish learning. We believe that all of them are needed to make the world better by means of Torah.

Louis Finkelstein, the chancellor of The Jewish Theological Seminary from 1940 to 1972, . . . stressed that rigorous, intellectually honest learning of our tradition is often undertaken in love. "We are drawn to the Torah with the bonds of love for it and for its norms. We love its ceremonies, its commandments, its rules and its spirit. We delight in its study." I have found this to be true; Conservative Jews—if fortunate in their teachers and study partners—experience moments of excitement, joy, and real gratitude from active participation in the age-old conversation with Torah. Their experience of learning is heightened by the realization that everyone at the table—women and men, adults and teens, professionals and laypeople—has a great deal to contribute. . . .

There is a kind of knowledge—of love, for example, or of parenting—that cannot be had from the outside. There are things we learn—and learn to love—only through disciplined practice. Love of God and the commandments develops in this fashion. Communities of practice read Torah—*and follow its precepts*. They ponder the nature of commandment and commandedness—as they walk the path defined by mitzvah, submit to the curtailment of complete autonomy, and enjoy the higher freedom and responsibility that it makes possible.

The fact that Conservative Jews move comfortably in the larger world and know its attractions heightens our need to move to Jewish rhythms and norms as well, and to experience their attractions powerfully. Learning is greatly enhanced when communities of practice interweave the study of the Torah's words with observance of the Torah's precepts.

The important thing is that our learning be a matter of urgency for life. We want to be the best parents, partners, friends, and citizens that we can be; we need to think about God and the purpose of life as best we can; we have to figure out how best to serve God and leave God's world a better place than we found it. To that end, we mine our texts for wisdom and turn to ancestors and contemporaries for insights.

Recently, a group of rabbis, teachers, and leaders of the Conservative Movement joined with me in formulating principles for Jewish learning, many of them implicit or explicit in what I have already said on the subject. I briefly summarize them here; every principle stands in need of translation into curricula, programs, and activities designed with particular groups of learners and teachers in mind.

1. Torah is the foundation, method, and aim of Conservative Jewish learning (CJL), both in the narrow sense of the Five Books of Moses ("the Torah") and the broad sense ("Torah") that includes all the layers of teachings and lives built over the centuries around the core of the Torah. Text, the record of our ancestors' wrestlings with God and tradition, is primary for Conservative Jews. Learning begins with, and circles back again to, the primary texts of Judaism.

2. The history and ongoing life of the Jewish people constitute an integral part of CJL. We pay careful attention to both text and context as we study. Torah is revealed in the manifold attempts by Jewish communities and individuals over the centuries to live in accordance with its teaching. For the same reason, we want to understand Jewish communities, societies, and institutions today, whether in North America, in other Diaspora countries, or in Israel.

3. Conservative Jewish learning is honest, rational—"in the sunlight," as one colleague put it—ever encouraging students to ask questions and always seeking to understand reasons for believing and practicing as they do. At the same time, and to an equal degree, CJL is passionate, from the heart and touching the soul, partaking of deep emotion that bespeaks love for Torah, love for the Jewish people, love for life itself, and—at its best—love for God.

4. CJL flows from and to—is an integral part of—committed, joyful, and disciplined Jewish practice undertaken in fulfillment of Jews' role as partners to the Covenant. We are determined to increase justice and compassion in the world. Our study of Torah, therefore, includes Halakhah [Jewish law] as well as Aggadah [Jewish lore], takes both

seriously, and tries its best to link observance with meaning, ritual with ethics and social justice work, behavior that is unique to Judaism with universal strivings and concerns. Practice is a form of learning, a teacher of lessons that can be learned no other way. We learn Torah because we want to assist God in making the world more just and compassionate—and so to leave the world a better place than we found it.

5. CJL emphasizes Hebrew as much as possible, for two reasons: to maintain close connection to fellow Jews in Israel and around the world and to have immediate access to sacred texts, the siddur, and the record of previous Jewish study and living of Torah.

6. Shabbat and festivals are major occasions for, subjects of, and means to CJL. We set aside spaces and times that bring Jews together, reconnect them with their people and traditions, engage them in compelling ritual experiences of holiness, and provide traditional frameworks inside which Conservative Jews can seek to stand before God.

7. CJL serves the eternal human quest for wisdom. It seeks to improve our lives demonstrably and to foster our growth as Jewish human beings by providing guidance for marriage, friendship, raising children, and coping with sickness and tragedy. Learning under Conservative auspices should be a spiritual experience that addresses the deepest strivings of the self.

8. CJL values scholarship about Judaism and Jews, and exposes students to it, putting scholarship in the service of Torah. We resist a purely critical posture even while welcoming modern critical approaches to test—and history as an integral part of—our learning and our practice.

9. Conservative Jews regard Torah as what one participant in our gathering called "love letters from God to the Jewish people"; we regard engagement with Torah study over the centuries and in our generation as the love letters to God sent in response from the Jewish people. Our Movement has always recognized the diversity of Jewish belief about God over the centuries, differences that have never been more striking than in our own day. Many Conservative Jews are not and will not be "believers" in any traditional sense. Our communities remain committed to "God wrestling" and the quest for encounter with the Holy One.

10. For all these reasons, CJL studies and adds to what another participant in our gathering called the *daf* of Torah, a term borrowed from the Hebrew word for each page of talmudic text and commentary. The *daf* for Conservative Jews signifies the ever-growing revelation of God's will to the Jewish people that comes by means of our study and our practice. We are committed to expanding the *daf*, as our ancestors did, through new media, new questions, and new insights. . . .

Conservative Judaism Today and Tomorrow, 10–15

Suggestions for Further Reading

jps.org/books/modernconservativejudaism/. The Jewish Publication Society study materials published in conjunction with this volume showcase differences between traditional and contemporary Conservative interpretations of the same Torah passages, as well as differences between the Conservative movement's Torah commentary and three other relatively modern commentaries (Orthodox, Reform, and an earlier Conservative commentary) on the same four verses.

Martin S. Cohen, ed. *The Observant Life: The Wisdom of Conservative Judaism for Contemporary Jews*. New York: Rabbinical Assembly, 2012. The work includes rich essays on all of life from a Conservative perspective. With respect to the topic of this chapter, see especially "Torah Study" by Eliezer Diamond on pages 81–97.

David L. Lieber, ed. *Etz Hayim: Torah and Commentary*. New York: Rabbinical Assembly, 2001. In addition to reading the literal, midrashic, and legal commentaries on each page of Torah text, consult the essays at the back on many subjects. On the approach of Conservative Judaism to the study of the Torah and Rabbinic literature, see especially the essays by Lee Levine, Robert Wexler, and Gordon Freeman on pages 1339–52 dealing with, respectively, archaeology, mythology, and biblical society, and those by Benjamin Edidin Scolnic on traditional and modern methods of Bible study on pages 1494–1503.

United Synagogue of Conservative Judaism books, including its Department of Youth Activities source books, which are appropriate for study by teenagers and adults on twenty-eight different topics, are available at https://rowman.com/Action/BISAC /_/REL040050/Religion_Judaism_Conservative.

CHAPTER FOUR

Halakhah

Legal Theories

Many varied, vibrant discussions have ensued within the Conservative movement about how we understand the nature and authority of Jewish law and how it should be applied in our day. In this chapter, we explore two official Conservative texts that articulate theories of Jewish law and five Conservative rabbis' disparate legal theories.

1913 Preamble to the Constitution of the United Synagogue of America

The 1913 Preamble to the Constitution of the United Synagogue of America (renamed United Synagogue of Conservative Judaism in 1992) served as the Conservative movement's only official statement concerning Jewish law until *Emet Ve-Emunah* was published in 1988.

The document (reproduced here in full) is noteworthy for its commitment to Jewish practice in both the home and synagogue, its openness to considering change, and its affirmation of both Hebrew and Zionism as fundamental to Conservative Judaism at a time when Hebrew was just being renewed as a modern language and the First Zionist Congress had taken place just sixteen years earlier.

The purpose of this organization is as follows:

* The advancement of the cause of Judaism in America and the maintenance of Jewish tradition in its historical continuity,
* To assert and establish loyalty to the Torah and its historical exposition,
* To further the observance of the Sabbath and dietary laws,
* To preserve in the service the reference to Israel's past and the hopes for Israel's restoration,
* To maintain the traditional character of the liturgy with Hebrew as the language of prayer,
* To foster Jewish religious life in the home, as expressed in traditional observances,
* To encourage the establishment of Jewish religious schools, in the curricula of which the study of the Hebrew language and literature shall be given a prominent place, both as the key to the true understanding of Judaism, and as a bond holding together the scattered communities of Israel throughout the world.

It shall be the aim of the United Synagogue of America, while not endorsing the innovations introduced by any of its constituent bodies, to embrace all elements essentially loyal to traditional Judaism and in sympathy with the purposes outlined above.

Emet Ve-Emunah on Jewish Law (1988)

Interestingly, although *Emet Ve-Emunah*'s statement on Jewish law, published seventy-five years later, is considerably longer and more detailed, it expresses virtually the same stance. Jewish law is deemed "indispensable," meaning that Conservative Jews cannot imagine an authentic form of Judaism without it.

Why this is so is a matter of multiple motivations. The Bible articulates at least eight such motives for acting in accordance with Jewish law, and the Rabbis added four more.[1] Subsequent Jewish thinkers articulated others. Having multiple reasons to take an action increases the likelihood that a person will do it, for if one particular motive does not provoke action at a particular time, another might, and specific motives speak more compellingly to some people than to others.

Note that some of *Emet Ve-Emunah*'s assertions are made in the name of the whole commission, whereas elsewhere the text reads "Some say x, and some say y."[2] The former type of statement indicates where the movement is (more or less) at one on a given issue. Although the latter type of statement, indicating disagreement, may disturb our quest for certainty, authority, and unity, historically Judaism has not only tolerated but encouraged debate. On some matters of action, a decision has to be made within a given community so that people know what actions are expected of them and what they can expect of others. When that practical necessity is not present, however, as is true in most theological and in some legal matters, openness to debate and pluralism is both theologically and practically wiser, because no human being, no matter how learned or experienced, is omniscient.

The Indispensability of Halakhah

Halakhah consists of the norms taught by the Jewish tradition, how one is to live as a Jew. Most Jewish norms are embodied in the laws of the Bible and their rabbinic interpretation and expansion over the centuries, but some take the form of customs, and others are derived from the ethical ideals that inform the laws and customs and extend beyond them (*lifnim m'shurat hadin*). Since each age requires new interpretations and applications of the received norms, Halakhah is an ongoing process. It is thus both an ancient tradition, rooted in the experience and texts of our ancestors, and a contemporary way of life, giving value, shape, and direction to our lives.

For many Conservative Jews, Halakhah is indispensable first and foremost because it is what the Jewish community understands God's will to be. Moreover, it is a concrete expression of our ongoing encounter with God. This divine element of Jewish law is understood in varying ways within the Conservative community, but, however it is understood, it is for many the primary rationale for obeying Halakhah, the reason that undergirds all the rest.

Other considerations, however, complement the theological basis for Halakhah. It is a means of identifying and preserving the Jewish people and its traditions. It trains and sharpens the moral conscience of individuals and society by presenting cases for consideration and teaching Jews how to think about them morally. It establishes minimal standards of behavior and gives ideals concrete expression. In addition to shaping the content of moral standards in these ways, Halakhah helps to motivate obedience to them, not, as in generations past, through legal enforcement (except, in some measure, in Israel), but by establishing a set of goals that has both divine and social authority. Halakhah thus establishes a structure of rules to govern human interactions.

Halakhah shapes our relationship to God. It affords us symbols by which we together can learn and express piety, including linguistic symbols of prayer, specific forms of clothing, and the study of sacred texts. The religious base of Halakhah makes it a far more comprehensive guide for life than any secular system of rules. Ultimately, as the prayer book reminds us twice each day, Halakhah is God's gift to us, an expression of God's love. Similarly, our adherence to Halakhah is an act of love for God on our part. It is, in fact, the primary way in which God and the Jewish people exhibit their love for each other.

For all these reasons, Halakhah in its developing form is an indispensable element of a traditional Judaism that is vital and modern. Halakhah is not the entirety of our Jewish identity; Judaism includes the ethical and theological reflections embodied in its lore (*aggadah*), a history, a commitment to a specific land and language, art, music, literature, and more. Judaism is indeed a civilization in the fullest sense of the term. But Halakhah is fundamental to that civilization.

Tradition and Development in Halakhah

The sanctity and authority of Halakhah attaches to the body of the law, not to each law separately, for throughout Jewish history Halakhah has been subject to change. Reverence for the tradition and concern for its continuity prevented rash revision of the law, but Jewish practice was modified from time to time. Most often, new interpretation or application of existing precedents produced the needed development; but sometimes new ordinances were necessary. Sometimes, as in the education of girls and the creation of the Simḥat Torah festival, the changes occurred first in the conduct of the rabbis or the people and only then were confirmed in law.

The rabbis of the Mishnah, the Talmud, and the Midrash recognized that changes had occurred and that they themselves were instituting them. They took pains to justify the legitimacy of rabbis in each generation applying the law in new ways to meet the demands of the time. They pointed out that the Torah itself requires such judicial activity, a mandate that they interpreted broadly to include, at times, even outright revisions of the law. Each individual cannot be empowered to make changes in the law, for that would undermine its authority and coherence; only the rabbinic leaders of the community, because of their knowledge of the content, aims, and methods of Halakhah, are authorized by Jewish tradition to make the necessary changes, although they must keep the customs and needs of the community in mind as they deliberate.

We in the Conservative community are committed to carrying on the rabbinic tradition of preserving and enhancing Halakhah by making appropriate changes in it through rabbinic decision. This flows from our conviction that Halakhah is indispensable for each age. As in the past, the nature and number of adjustments of the law will vary with the degree of change in the environment in which Jews live. The rapid technological and social changes of our time, as well as new ethical insights and goals, have required new interpretations and applications of Halakhah to keep it vital for our lives; more adjustments will undoubtedly be necessary in the future. These include additions to the received tradition to deal with the new circumstances and, in some cases, modifications of the corpus of Halakhah.

While change is both a traditional and a necessary part of Halakhah, we, like our ancestors, are not committed to change for its own sake. Hence, the thrust of the Jewish tradition and the Conservative community is to maintain the law and practices of the past as much as possible, and the burden of proof is on the one who wants to alter them. Halakhah has responded and must continue to respond to changing conditions, sometimes through alteration of the law and sometimes by standing firm against passing fads and skewed values. Moreover, the necessity for change does not justify any particular proposal for revision. Each suggestion cannot be treated mechanically but must rather be judged on its own terms, a process that requires thorough knowledge of both Halakhah and the contemporary scene as well as carefully honed skills of judgment.

Following the example of our rabbinic predecessors over the ages, however, we consider instituting changes for a variety of reasons. Occasionally the integrity of the law must be maintained by adjusting it to conform to contemporary practice among observant Jews. Every legal system from time to time must adjust what is on the books to be in line with actual practice if the law is to be taken seriously as a guide to conduct. New technological, social, economic, or political realities sometimes require legal action. Some changes in law are designed to improve the material conditions of the Jewish people or society at large. The goal of others is to foster better relations among Jews or between Jews and the larger community. In some cases, changes are necessary to prevent or remove injustice, while in others they constitute a positive program to enhance the quality of Jewish life by elevating its moral standards or deepening its piety.

We affirm that the halakhic process has striven to embody the highest moral principles. Where changing conditions produce what seem to be immoral consequences and human anguish, varying approaches exist within our community to rectify the situation. Where it is deemed possible and desirable to solve the problem through the existing halakhic norms, we prefer to use them. If not, some within the Conservative community are prepared to amend the existing law by means of a formal procedure of legislation (*takkanah*). Some are willing to make a change only when they find it justified by sources in the halakhic literature. All of us, however, are committed to the indispensability of Halakhah for authentic Jewish living.

Our dedication to Halakhah flows from our deep awareness of the divine element and the positive values inherent in it. Every effort is made to conserve and enhance it. When changes are necessary, they are made with the express goal of ensuring that Halakhah remains an effective, viable, and moral guide for our lives.

Understanding Theories of Law

What is a theory of law, and why do theories matter? Most theories of law include these four elements:

1. The author's fundamental convictions about who we are as human beings and as a society (which gives us insight into why the author thinks the law should function in a certain way)
2. The place and roles that law should (and should not) have in our lives
3. The circumstances and methods in and by which the law may or should change
4. How the law is related to other facets of life, such as morality, custom, economics, politics, and culture

In principle, a full-fledged theory of law should also address these seven questions:

1. What are the nature and status of individual human beings and human communities—and, for religious theories of law, the nature and status of God and God's relationship to humans and the environment—and what should they strive to be?
2. What is the role of law in society? Why should we have law? What are its aims?
3. What is the scope of the law—what topics does it address, which topics (if any) are beyond its jurisdiction, and how does its scope follow from its purposes in a given society?
4. What gives the law authority?
5. How and why should the law be determined in a particular way?
6. How does the law maintain continuity and coherence while simultaneously allowing for change?
7. What is the relationship between law and morality, law and religion, law and economics, law and art, and law and custom—and how does this legal system handle conflicts of jurisdiction with another legal system?

Not all treatments of Jewish law discuss all these issues. Then it becomes the reader's task to unearth a given theory's unarticulated assumptions as part of assessing its individual strengths and weaknesses.

Theories of law matter because they shape the thinking, motivations, and decisions of people charged with determining and/or following the law. In many cases of legal disagreement, the dispute is not limited to the issue at hand; it stems from a much broader disagreement about one or more of the elements included in a theory of law. Therefore, people equally committed to Jewish law can disagree about what the law should be on a given issue, or they can agree on the law but for different reasons that may become important in deciding another related case. Studying theories of law helps in understanding the role and operation of law, as variously conceived, as well as why certain individuals decide particular legal questions as they do.

Some Conservative/Masorti Theories of Jewish Law

The following five Conservative theories of law, chosen from among at least fifteen articulated by Conservative thinkers, differ from one another in significant ways.[3] Joel Roth generally sees Jewish law as a deductive system that is similar to geometry, except that it allows "extralegal" factors to influence the system in some limited ways. Neil Gillman sees Jewish law as the way the Jewish community acts in response to our shared convictions as embodied in our communal myths. Elliot Dorff sees Jewish law as part of an organic system in which theology, moral values, prayer, history, economics, social and political realities, and law all influence each other, much as every system of a human body (respiratory, circulatory, gastrointestinal, neurological, etc.) influences every other system. Harold Kushner sees Jewish law not as law at all but as an opportunity to embody holiness in our lives, as articulating our aspiration to holiness without the need for, or the presence of, legal authority. Alana Suskin sees Jewish law as the product of an entire Jewish community of women and men and, as such, Jewish law requires new interpretations to acknowledge women's equality.

Despite their differences, all of these theories are distinctly within the realm of the Conservative movement. All uphold the official Conservative belief that Jewish law is binding, even as its content has developed over time and will continue to do so.

Rabbi Joel Roth on a Deductive Legal System

The Concept of the Basic Norm

The concept of the basic norm is complex, yet indispensable. Its complexity derives mainly from the fact that this *grundnorm* [basic norm] is at once "metalegal" and "legal," that is, while its validity is presupposed by the system, it functions *legally* as a norm of the system. Any attempt to prove the validity of the basic norm must belong to a realm other than the legal. To the extent that its validity can be proved at all, the proof must be theological, philosophical, or metaphysical. Yet it is this norm that serves as the ultimate basis of the legal system and has definite legal functions. Put succinctly, the orderly functioning of any legal order requires of its adherents a "leap of faith" concerning the validity of the basic norm of the system. Although leaps of faith do not fall within the realm of law, such a leap of faith is the ultimate validation of the legal system.

Furthermore, it is important to grasp that presupposing the existence of a *grundnorm* is an amoral and nonvaluative act. The fact that a tyrant may have promulgated a constitution, obedience to which is the basic norm of a particular legal system, does not affect its status as a *grundnorm*. A postulated *grundnorm* is the *sine qua non* of a legal system, not a statement of the desirability, morality, or positive nature of the system. In many instances, such considerations will vary with the perspective of the viewer. The *grundnorm* of the American legal system was created as the result of an act of rebellion against a legal sovereign. To some, it was a necessary and ethical rebellion; to others, it was an immoral act of rebellion against the British crown. But even to this latter group, the *grundnorm* is the basic norm of the American system. Presupposing the basic norm of the American system is necessary in order to comprehend the functioning of the system, but carries no valuational implications whatsoever concerning the rectitude of the framers of the Constitution in postulating it. Thus, every legal system—democracy, monarchy, dictatorship, benevolent despotism—presupposes a basic norm; that fact, however, is independent of any consideration of the desirability of the system itself.

How, then, shall the *grundnorm* of the halakhic system be formulated so as to express the presupposed axiom that validates the system *legally?* The following seems reasonable and correct: The document called the Torah embodies the word and will of God, which it behooves man to obey, and is, therefore, authoritative. Remembering that the basic norm is both "metalegal" and "legal," certain points follow. The first is that the individual legal statements of the Torah are legal sources of the system, i.e., they are norms the authority of which is accepted by and integral to the system. The second is that the concept conveyed by the rabbinic term *de-oraita* ([literally, "from the Torah"] norms having the authority of the *grundnorm* itself) is postulated by the system itself as a *sine qua non* of its functioning, and implies, as well, a distinction (as yet undefined) between itself and the concept *de-rabbanan* ([literally, "from the rabbis"] norms that are not *de-oraita*).

The third point is that any quest to establish the "truth" of the historical claims of the Torah is irrelevant to the halakhic process, since that quest seeks only clarification of the historical sources of the legal system, not its legal sources. Since in the halakhic system, as in all others, presupposing the existence of a *grundnorm* requires a "leap of faith," the truth or falsity of the historical claims of the *grundnorm* is legally irrelevant. Once norms are incorporated into the system as legal sources, the persuasive influence of the historical sources, originally so important, fades into legal insignificance.

Thus, it follows on one important level that the halakhic system *qua* system is independent of any considerations of the accuracy of the historical claims of its basic norm. Whether or not it is "true" that the Torah embodies the word and will of God is of great historical and theological significance, but of no legal significance. Even if one has traced the origins of the Torah to documents called J, E, P, and D, he may have uncovered the historical sources of the legal norms, but he has in no way abrogated the *grundnorm* of the halakhic system, which is *presupposed* by the system. As any number of observant scholars can attest, the system continues to function on the basis of its presupposed *grundnorm* regardless of the contention that the historical claims of the *grundnorm* may be inaccurate.

If one is so inclined, one may reformulate the *grundnorm* in the light of modern scholarship as follows: The document called the Torah embodies the word and the will of God, which it behooves man to obey, as mediated through the agency of J, E, P, and D, and is, therefore, authoritative. An alternative possible formulation might be: The document called the Torah embodies the constitution promulgated by J, E, P, and D, which it behooves man to obey, and is, therefore, authoritative. The first formulation has the advantage of incorporating God into the *grundnorm*. It is theologically self-evident that it behooves man to obey His will; thus, the "leap of faith" is simply in affirming that His word and will are mediated through J, E, P, and D. The second formulation obviates this "leap of faith" but replaces it with the presupposition that it behooves man to obey the will of J, E, P, and D. In either case, the halakhic system is ultimately predicated on a presupposition that it behooves man to obey the document called the Torah, regardless of the historical realities of its promulgation. Any discussion of the validity of the *grundnorm* must be nonlegal, i.e., philosophical, theological, or metaphysical. . . .

Extralegal Sources within Halakhah

We have thus far been dealing with the systemic machinery of the decision-making process and must now proceed to examine the factors that may legitimately be taken into account by *posekim* [rabbis who rule on matters under Jewish law] as they utilize the machinery. These factors constitute the extralegal sources of the halakhic system, which, although not themselves legal norms, nevertheless bear greatly on the determination of the law. Among these factors are some that are stated explicitly in the literature as well as others that are implicit.

Before we proceed, however, a crucial caveat is necessary. The fact that these factors are admissible as data in the decision-making process might lead to the idea that they are also, by themselves, capable of determining the law rather than merely affecting it. However, in truth, extralegal sources constitute only one among many kinds of information available for and subject to the arbiter's evaluation: It is *he* alone who determines the law. For example, ichthyologists may offer data concerning the nature of the fins and scales of swordfish, but the *posek* [rabbi] alone can determine whether or not they fulfill the requirements of *senappir* (fins) and *kaskeset* (scales) required by Leviticus 11:9. Sociologists, demographers, and ecologists may offer data concerning the ability of the earth to sustain increasing numbers of humans in the next thousand years, but only *posekim* [rabbis] can determine whether those data warrant overturning the precedent that advocates large families for Jews. Chemists may provide analyses of the changes in chemical composition resulting from various steps in the processing of foods, but only *posekim* can determine whether these chemical changes affect the status of the finished foodstuff in relation to the laws of *kashrut* [the Jewish dietary laws, "keeping kosher"].

Moreover, since extralegal sources, although admissible, are not determinative, it follows that two arbiters can disagree concerning the actual significance of specific extralegal data. But, it must be stressed, what they would *not* be in disagreement about is the potential significance (i.e., the admissibility) of extralegal sources in general. . . .

Extralegal sources can be divided into four basic categories. . . . We shall call these categories: (1) medical/scientific; (2) sociological/*realia*; (3) economic; (4) ethical/psychological.

The Halakhic Process, 7–10, 231–34

Rabbi Neil Gillman on Communal Responses to Shared Myths

Mitzvot and the Jewish Myth

Myths can "live" or "die," and they can be "broken"—these are commonly accepted terms in the language of the philosophy of religion. A live myth is a myth that continues to work; a dead myth is one that has ceased to function. A broken myth is one that is acknowledged as myth. When a myth is broken, one is tempted to respond in either of two ways: to proclaim it as dead, or to deny its brokenness and retreat to literalism. But neither response is necessary; a myth can be broken and still live.

[It can be so] because there is simply no alternative to myth making. The issue is never myth or no myth but which myth, for myths are the only means available to us for comprehending complex and elusive dimensions of our experience. Astronomers and psychoanalysts know this very well. If we abandon one myth, it can only be in favor of another. What we cannot endure, simply because we are human beings, is the utter confusion or chaos that results from the absence of a structure of meaning by which to read our experience.

Even more important, once we have accepted the inevitability of myth making, we begin to welcome the uncanny power that myths exercise over us. This post-literal or post-critical phase of the inquiry has been dubbed, by the French philosopher Paul Ricoeur, a state of "second" or "willed naïveté." We willfully accept the mythic structure precisely as myth and allow it to work for us as the poetic, dramatic, and imaginative creation that it is.

The mythic definition of Jewish identity as formed out of a covenant with God and concretized in a series of behavioral obligations remains alive, however broken it may be for many of us. Its vitality emerges in the palpable sense of a shared history and destiny that binds Jews everywhere, even those who are not formally "religious" or observant. . . . It may be expressed in some form of social action on behalf of Jewish causes, whether local or international, such as the State of Israel or Soviet Jewry. But it continues to manifest the sense of Jewish covenantedness, and it is frequently performed with the same strong sense of obligation that accompanies traditional Jewish observance.

Finally, note the very distinctive mood that accompanies the performance of the ritual of circumcision whereby the male child enters into the covenantal community. There is joy, but it is mingled with a sense of awe, a palpable tension that is felt by all, participants and onlookers alike. This is the most ancient ritual we have, dating back to Abraham and our very beginnings as a people. It is also a blood ritual, and the sign of the covenant imparted on the male child is indelible. Most of all it expresses the sheer fact of continuity, of another link in the chain of the generations.

At this moment, all of the features of Jewish identity come together: a shared destiny, an indelible bond, a commitment that defies historical forces, and a clear statement that that commitment has to be expressed behaviorally in the performance of a ritual that will forever transform the very body of the male Jew. There is no greater testimony to the power and efficacy of this ritual than the demand by many of our contemporaries for a parallel ritual celebrating the birth of a female child. In fact, many such rituals have emerged out of the community itself, frequently without official rabbinic sanction, simply as an expression of our impulse to celebrate another link in the chain of Jewish continuity.

Just as the sense of covenantedness is very much alive, so is the commitment to the fact of *mitzvot* [commandments], or more precisely, to the fact of *mitzvah* [commandment or being commanded]. For if God did not dictate the content of Torah, then He did not dictate the specific *mitzvot*. The immediate corollary of this conclusion is that it is not possible for us to speak of *the* body of *mitzvot* or of *the halakhah* as if it formed one clearly circumscribed, monolithic, internally consistent system. There never was such a system, and there surely cannot be one in our day.

We should, instead, view the community of caring, committed Jews as a series of overlapping mini-communities, each of which centers itself about a body of *mitzvot* that it accepts as binding. Institutionally, these mini-communities organize themselves into three major coalition movements, Orthodox, Conservative, and Reform, with right-wing Orthodoxy (or the Hasidic communities) and left-wing Reform forming the boundary positions. Reconstructionism, representing one modern attempt to reconceptualize the relationship between the Jewish religion and the sense of Jewish peoplehood, sharpens the Conservative and Reform thrust. It might even be arguable, as noted above, that Jews who do not formally affiliate with a synagogue or observe the rituals of Judaism, but work actively within the framework of what we call Jewish "civil religion," also belong in the picture, for they too feel a sense of coercion about their Jewish activity. It is not always clear, then, who is the "observant" Jew and who is not; the dividing line is not sharp and clean.

This view denies neither the existence of parameters for what constitutes authentic Jewish behavior nor the fact of authority. It does insist, however, that both the parameters and the authority emerge out of the community. . . . It is the community that decides for itself what will be considered *mitzvah*, and it does so on its own authority. The assumption, of course, is that this process is taken seriously, not casually. It is clearly not taken this way by the entire community; substantial numbers of Jews have no interest in any of it. But many Jews do. In the final analysis, all we can do is speak to and for them.

The position also makes two assumptions about the nature of Judaism that are very much part of the modern consciousness: pluralism and historical development. Much has been made of the diversity and divisiveness that characterize Jewish life today. But never in the long course of Jewish history did all Jews agree on what they should do as Jews. That diversity—even in the content of the body of *mitzvot*—was always understood as both inevitable and a mark of vitality. It is all the more so today. One of the reasons for pluralism is that various segments of the community differ on which of the *mitzvot* are still binding, which are no longer binding, which new ones should be adopted, on whose authority, and when. . . .

There is simply no religious authenticity in Judaism outside of a halakhic system—not necessarily *the* halakhic system that the traditionalists exalt, but a halakhic system that concretizes our sense of covenantedness as a community to God. For all of its inherent dangers, this commitment is axiomatic to Jewish religion. It stems from our earliest attempts at religious and communal self-definition. The challenge is to view *halakhah* as the means, not the end of Jewish piety, to welcome the opportunities it provides for worship and celebration, and then to strive for that elusive blend of structure and spontaneity that has been the hallmark of Jewish religious living from time immemorial.

Sacred Fragments, 54–60

Rabbi Elliot N. Dorff on an Organic System That Expresses Love and Addresses Morality

Jewish Law as a Living Organism

To capture both the ongoing, direct applications of previous Jewish law and its innovative, revisionary rulings over the ages and in our own time, we must abandon the deductive model and think of Jewish law instead as a living organism. . . . Every system within it will influence every other system, and sometimes one will be determinative and sometimes another will be. . . . And so, sometimes the law will override theology (or moral, economic, social, or political concerns), sometimes the reverse will happen, and sometimes (hopefully most of the time) they will pull in the same direction.

Jewish Law as an Expression of Love

Jewish law is . . . an important way in which we relate to both God and human beings. Specifically, I view Jewish law as an expression of the love that we Jews have for both God and other human beings. Like all forms of human love, our love of God and other human beings and God's love of us ideally involve all of our being—body, mind, emotions, will, and interactions with others. Putting this another way, our love is best expressed in both body and soul, for then it can be both physically active and intellectually and emotionally compelling.

To be a meaningful expression of both forms of love—the mutual love among people and that between God and us—Jewish law must, therefore, have both a body and a soul. I consequently see Jewish law very much like a human being. . . . Some of the features of Jewish law resemble a human body, and some are like a human soul—that is, the mind, emotions, will, and the ability to interact with others. Just as the body and soul of a person constantly interact and affect each other, so too do the body of the law (literally, in the Latin term for it, the *corpus juris*) and its beliefs, values, emotions, and goals continually interact and affect one another. . . . Furthermore, just as people are very much affected by the physical, political, economic, social, and moral environment in which they live, both the body and the soul of Jewish law are influenced by their ongoing interactions with God, with other peoples and cultures, and with the various aspects of the environment in which they function.[4]

Every human being has a body, and although each of our bodies is unique in some ways (for example, its DNA), we share a great deal—so much so, that a physician can treat people from widely varying genetic backgrounds. Analogously, in its bodily functions Jewish law resembles other legal systems . . . [though it] is different in some ways from other legal systems, just as we each walk and talk a bit differently. . . .

The same is true for the soul of Jewish law. The religious convictions at its heart make it markedly different from secular and other religious legal systems. At the same time, just as all people wrestle with some of the same emotional and psychological issues, and thus the disciplines of social work, psychology, and psychiatry can exist, so too Jewish law has some similarities in its assumptions and approaches to other legal systems. . . .

In general, the similarities between Jewish law and other legal systems will be more a function of the bodily features of all legal systems, the aspects of law that enable it to function in the world, while the uniqueness of Jewish law will be primarily a function of its soul. . . .

I view Jewish law as an expression of love for, and commitment to, both God and other people in part because I grew up in a warm, supportive home and I was influenced heavily by Camp Ramah. . . . Jewish law was the vehicle that enabled us to celebrate Shabbat with great joy and to mourn the tragedies of the Jewish people on Tisha b'Av with real sorrow. It also demanded that we think hard about the serious issues of life, behave with others in ways that respected their inherent dignity as human beings created in the image of God even if we did not like them or what they did, and act continuously to make human lives better. . . . [As a result,] I take Jewish law seriously and even see it as being authoritative for my life, but also think that we should apply our own sense of judgment to change it in the few places where the received law causes harm to people.

Legislating Morality in Jewish Law

How does one make moral decisions? If you are a Catholic, you ask your priest and, ultimately, the Pope. If you are a Protestant, you consult your conscience. Catholics also have room for individual conscience in their moral theology, and Protestants are to be guided in their use of conscience by the Bible and by policy statements of their denominations, but the emphasis among Catholics is on institutional authority, and among Protestants on individual conscience. The American, secular way of making moral decisions, from abortion to welfare programs for the poor, is by majority vote of legislatures and by courts.

Jewish tradition, in contrast, makes its moral decisions primarily through the instrumentality of Jewish law. It trusts the legal process to discern the moral path, teach it, and enforce it. Most Jews, like other Westerners, accept the Enlightenment view that "you cannot legislate morality." The Jewish tradition, however, believes not only that we can legislate morality, but that we should.

Why so? The basic reason Jewish tradition relies on law as the primary vehicle for discerning moral norms is because the law is seen as an expression of a moral God's call that we be moral and holy. "You shall be holy, for I, the Lord your God, am holy," Leviticus 19:2 proclaims, and what follows is a list of both ritual and moral commands that spell out what it means to be holy. "God is good to all, and His mercies extend to all His creatures," the Psalmist declares in a passage Jewish liturgy has us read three times daily,[5] and the Rabbis spell out the implications of that conviction for our own human behavior: "Just as God is gracious and compassionate, you too must be gracious and compassionate. . . . As the Holy One is faithful, you too must be faithful. . . . As the Holy one is loving, you too must be loving. . . ."[6] "As God clothes the naked, you should clothe the naked. . . . As God visited the sick, you too should visit the sick. . . . As the Holy Blessed One comforted those who mourned, you too should comfort those who mourn. . . . As the Holy Blessed One buried the dead, you too should bury the dead. . . ."[7] God thus calls us to morality and holiness and teaches us how to fulfill that call through Jewish law. Thus . . . Jewish law must be interpreted and shaped by moral considerations; to do otherwise would ignore and undermine both the roots of Jewish law in a moral God and the aims of both God and God's law to produce a moral society.

For the Love of God and People, 60, 45–48, 211–12

Rabbi Harold Kushner on Jewish Law as an Opportunity for Holiness

Responding to the Age of Individuality

My mentor, Mordecai Kaplan, taught me . . . [a] great truth: . . . The French Revolution of 1789 was as traumatic and paradigm-shattering for the Jewish people as was the destruction of the Temple in 70 CE. It ushered in an age of democracy and individualism, empowering people to make choices about their own lives. It defined people as individuals rather than as members of a group. Thus the formula by which equal rights were extended to the Jews of France: "to the Jews as a people, nothing; to the Jew as an individual, everything." . . .

When our movement was at its most creative and most relevant, our appeal was not to halakhah but to history, to the argument that the forms in which Jews lived their Jewishness had always changed as circumstances changed. We countenanced driving on Shabbat and invited women to share liturgical responsibilities, not as a concession to human frailty or political pressure but in recognition of suburban living patterns and the unprecedented involvement of women in all aspects of modern life.

But even that will not be enough of a response to an age of democracy and individuality, the era of the "sovereign self." A colleague recently lamented to me, "If you ask an Orthodox rabbi what Orthodoxy stands for, he will answer in two words: *Torah umitzvot* [Torah and commandments]. Ask a Reform rabbi what Reform stands for and he or she will answer in two words: social justice. Ask a Conservative rabbi what Conservative Judaism stands for, and he or she will hand you a 48-page brochure." I would venture to suggest a theological-behavioral foundation for Conservative Judaism that can be expressed in just three words and will do for Jews in the 21st century what the halakhic system did so effectively for our ancestors: *asher kid'shanu b'mitzvotav* [Who has sanctified us through His commandments], life as a quest for holiness and the Torah as our guide to bringing holiness into our lives. The mitzvot would be seen as holy, as commanding and deserving our loyalty, not only because of where they stem from but because of what they lead to.

Understanding Holiness

What is holiness? It is that dimension of life that human beings can experience but animals cannot. I understand the verse *na'aseh adam b'tzalmenu*, "Let *us* make a human being in *our* image" (Gen. 1:26), as having been spoken by God to the animals who had been created in the preceding verse. I picture God saying to the animals, "Between us, let us fashion a new kind of creature, one that will resemble you in some ways, needing to eat, sleep, procreate, and will resemble Me in some ways, capable of making moral distinctions, capable of rising to a level of self-consciousness and self-control that no animal could achieve. This new creature will have your body but My breath, My spirit. Unlike any other living thing, it will be able to recognize holiness and ultimately to create holiness itself. The purpose of its existence will be to transcend its animal origins and experience true humanity through the achievement of holiness. It will find holiness in a poem, a symphony, a sunset, in forgiveness and generosity, in love as a dimension of procreation, in exercising self-control over appetite in all of its manifestations. By tasting holiness, it will understand what it means to be a human being in the image of God and will introduce a moral dimension into a world that would otherwise be ruled by blind, amoral Nature."

Professor Max Kadushin coined the term "normal mysticism" to describe the ability of normative Jewish practices to invoke the presence of God without having to resort to drugs, fasting, or turning one's back on the everyday world the way mystics in other faith systems do. For Kadushin, performing a mitzvah summons up the presence of God, entitling us to say "Barukh Atah . . ." [Blessed are You], using the second person form of address because we sense God's presence in the moment. We don't find God in places; we find God in moments, and we have the power to transform an ordinary moment into one in which God is found. Abraham Joshua Heschel said something similar when he wrote that a religious Jew is never alone because God and the Jew meet in the performance of a mitzvah. If I had to define the essence of halakhah for today's Jews in a single sentence, I would describe it as the science of taking the ordinary and making it holy.

On Holiness and Mitzvot

I would even carry that idea a step further. When we perform a mitzvah, not only do we cause God to be present, we put ourselves in touch with the divine dimension in ourselves, our capacity to fashion holiness by our behavior. We say ". . . *asher kidshanu b'mitzvotav*," praising God for having shown us the way to fashion and experience holiness through the performance of mitzvot.

Extending that thought, I would understand mitzvah differently than our ancestors did. In the 21st century, it can no longer mean "commandment, obligation." I would prefer not to translate the word "mitzvah" at all, but I would understand it to mean "opportunity," the opportunity to be in touch with God by transforming the ordinary into the sacred.

"Conservative Judaism in an Age of Democracy," 3–13

Rabbi Alana Suskin on Investing Jewish Law with Egalitarian/Feminist Principles

Add Women and Stir Is Not Enough

There cannot just be more women's voices in the conversation; the voices of both women and men need to take egalitarian principles into account. . . .[8] For example, who has access to texts through access to day schools, summer camps, etc. . . . affects women disproportionately because we have to . . . make up for the past in which girls and women were not given the opportunity to study and, according to some, not even allowed to do so. . . .

So what are these egalitarian/feminist principles?

When there are two possible options, the one that makes women equal should not only be favored, but the other option needs to be recognized as not acceptable. This is much like the status of slavery: although slavery is halakhicly permitted, few would rule in its favor today, given the ethical implications of slavery. Those who did make such a ruling would be shunned from most communities as engaging in morally abhorrent practices.

a. This is the very minimum in a traditional community, but it is not enough. To live it, it is necessary to live by the rule of *loeg larash kheref osehu*—that one who mocks a pauper blasphemes his Maker. In B. *Berakhot* 18a this is cited against a person walking in a cemetery with *tefillin* on his head or while reading from a Torah scroll, or reciting the *Shema* within four *amot* [cubits] of a corpse. Surely if we must take such care with the dead, it should be equally incumbent to do no less for the living. Thus, for example, I know someone who has taken upon himself never to be counted in a minyan that does not count women; that I know of only one such Jewish man is sad. When honors and responsibilities are not available to women, men are obligated also to turn them down. Granted that this may cause a dilemma in communities where women are not counted in *minyanim* [prayer quorums], or for *aliyot* [the honor of saying blessings over the Torah during its reading in the synagogue], or the role of *shaliah* [leader of the service], but in all places that insist upon men having a role that women may not, men may not take them either. At the very least, men should understand that they are responsible not to take on such honors and responsibilities as respecting the principle of *kavod ha'briyyot* [honor due to all people] and in order to avoid *loeg larash*.

b. Jewish laws that exclude women must be revisited. Except for laws that deal specifically with reproductive matters, there should be no difference in treatment of men and women. This is the first step in establishing that broader, mutual feedback … in which change affects not only women, but also men.

c. On the other end, men must also be seen as needing to participate more in family life. Thus the idea that women were exempted from positive time-bound commandments because of family responsibilities should be used as the beginning of a discussion about reassessing family responsibilities. We no longer see women as chattel, subject to men's whims to the extent that women may not do positive *kavod* [honor] for their parents because their husband's desires take precedence. We would see that as abusive, which it is. Nor is it acceptable for women to be working the second shift (that is, doing all or most or even more than half the childcare and house cleaning in addition to working a full time job). This is not, as many social conservatives would have it, a mandate for taking away women's jobs; rather, it is a requirement that men share more of the responsibility for their family. When we say that women must be considered obligated publicly, the way men have been in the past, we must also say that men are obligated privately, as women have been in the past. Rabbis, then, as the judiciary, must not view the laws as a means to support the status quo; to the contrary, we must be an activist court to ensure that justice is done and the vulnerable are removed from their vulnerable position, not simply protected within it.

d. We must understand the enforcing of the equality of women as a *ḥumrah*, a stringency. We are not making a *kula*, a leniency, when we rule that women are obligated for all the *mitzvot* [commandments] that our tradition imposes on men; we are making a stringency.

Toward this end, we must address the arguments against giving women these responsibilities along the lines of "we don't want to increase the number of sinners." There is a strong response: to the contrary, … we are actually improving the chances of reducing the numbers of sinners. In secular life, we are accustomed to the ideology at least (even if it is not always quite borne out in practice) that women and men are equal in rights. Since in Judaism we speak not in the language of rights but of obligations, most American Jews view those obligations much in the way that in secular law we view rights. As a result, when Jewish men see that Jewish women seem to have a choice about whether or not to do certain things in Jewish practice, that they are not obligated, the men—perhaps unconsciously, and perhaps not—understand themselves also not to be obligated, that *halakhah* is a choice. What appears to be happening is that we are losing the sense that Jews are obligated. If we are more stringent about women being obligated, it is likely to have the effect of increasing men's participation in obligatory *mitzvot.*[9]

On the other side of the argument, it is condescending to give women a choice to obligate themselves or not. We Jews live in a system of obligation: choice about whether or not to obligate is the same as saying "you still really do not count."

Thus, contrary to the *teshuvah* (rabbinic ruling) by Rabbi Joel Roth,[10] we should assume that women are obligated *a priori*, that our community has developed to the point that the majority of women consider themselves the equal of men. Instead of requiring that women who wish to be considered equal in obligation take steps to make themselves such, as Roth stipulates, it should be the woman who does *not* wish to be considered equal who must speak up and say that she does not wish to be—and this should be a temporary measure: no more than 100 years. This would actually be more syntonic with how our communities already work; Rabbi Roth's *teshuvah*, as I understand he himself admits, simply does not happen. . . .

e. Finally—and this is a very radical step that I am not certain of yet, but I suggest as a possibility—it may be that in applying Jewish law, we should view *ishah* [woman] and *ish* [man] as empty terms. . . . It may be time for us all to be *adam*, simply human. . . .

Suggestions for Further Reading

Elliot N. Dorff. *For the Love of God and People: A Philosophy of Jewish Law.* Philadelphia: Jewish Publication Society, 2007.

———. *The Unfolding Tradition: Philosophies of Jewish Law.* New York: Rabbinical Assembly (Aviv Press), 2005; 2nd, rev. ed., 2011.

Neil Gillman. *Sacred Fragments: Recovering Theology for the Modern Jew*, esp. 44–60 and 224–36. Philadelphia: Jewish Publication Society, 1990.

Harold Kushner. "Conservative Judaism in an Age of Democracy." *Conservative Judaism* 59, no. 4 (Summer 2007): 3–13. Reprinted in Dorff, *The Unfolding Tradition*, 397–405 (2011 ed.).

Joel Roth. *The Halakhic Process: A Systematic Analysis*. New York: Jewish Theological Seminary of America, 1986.

Alana Suskin. "A Feminist Theory of Jewish Law." In Dorff, *The Unfolding Tradition*, 368–89 (2005 ed.), 357–78 (2011 ed.).

CHAPTER FIVE

P'sak Din

Determining Conservative Practice

To determine what Conservative Jews should practice, the Conservative/Masorti movement — committed to preserving Judaism as it developed historically — continues the views and methods of rabbis over the last two thousand years. Because acting in accordance with Jewish law and custom has always been key to what it means to be a Jew, Conservative Judaism requires observing the laws of classical Judaism, including the Jewish dietary laws (*kashrut*), the rituals of the Sabbath and festivals, daily worship, and the moral norms of the Torah, prophets, and sages.

This, in fact, accounts for why the movement is called "Conservative" (or, in Hebrew, "Masorti," meaning "traditional"). By studying and practicing Judaism, Conservative Judaism is intent upon conserving Jewish tradition.[1] Only through such observance can one identify authentically with what Judaism has stood for over the centuries. Consequently, the movement invests its talent and energy in all kinds of Jewish education, including schools, youth groups, camps, conventions, educational trips to Israel and other Jewish communities worldwide, adult education programs, publications, and more. The focus is always on motivating and enabling Jews to observe Jewish law, not upon changing that law.

Nonetheless, Conservative leaders recognize that sometimes laws and customs must change — just as they have historically — particularly when change is needed to engage people effectively in Jewish tradition. Deciding when such additions or modifications are necessary and how they should be made requires considerable judgment and risk; consequently, in contrast to the individual autonomy embraced by Reform Judaism, the Conservative movement has made the decision a *communal* matter for both rabbis and laypeople. Specifically, the movement evaluates possible changes in law and custom by using the same three mechanisms through which Jewish law traditionally developed: decisions of the local rabbi, decisions of a communal body, and custom.

The Local Rabbi

In the vast majority of cases, questions raised in Jewish law have been answered by the local rabbi, the *mara d'atra*, the "teacher of the place." Local rabbis are entrusted with the right to make such decisions, in effect, to interpret Jewish law for the people,[2] both by virtue of their Jewish education and commitment, symbolized by their ordination as rabbis, and by their election as a community's rabbi, marking the respect the community accords them to interpret Jewish law on the people's behalf.

Historically, most such questions and answers were communicated in person and orally. However, communities without rabbis would address their questions to a rabbi in another community and receive a response in writing. In addition, rabbis unable to answer particular questions of Jewish law would consult with a rabbi known to be expert in that area, who would then pen a response. Rabbis' responses to questions came to be called the responsa literature (singular, responsum)—in Hebrew, *she'elot u'teshuvot*, "questions and answers" or, simply, *teshuvot*, "answers."

Nowadays, legal consultation among rabbis continues, often by more modern means of communication. Even with such consultations, however, local rabbis remain the ultimate decision-makers for the vast majority of Jewish legal issues that arise in their communities.

A Central Communal Institution

A Central Agency in Jewish History

At certain places and times in Jewish history, though, a central agency made Jewish legal decisions for an entire region or community, for example:

* The Sanhedrin, sitting originally in Jerusalem and then, after 90 CE, in Yavneh from approximately the first century CE until 361 CE.
* The Geonim in Babylonia (650–1050 CE). These heads of academies of Jewish learning functioned both as the court of first inquiry for some Jewish communities and the court of last review for others worldwide.
* Rabbinic assemblies in Western and Central Europe from the eleventh to the early seventeenth century. While meeting at commercial fairs for business, they used the opportunity to meet in "synods" in the evenings to make legal decisions for the Jewish communities of the Rhineland and France.[3]
* The Council of Four Lands in Eastern Europe between approximately 1550 and 1764, which determined Jewish law and other matters of public policy for much of Eastern European (especially Polish) Jewry.

A Central Jewish Agency in Modern Nations

Similarly, today the Orthodox chief rabbinate in England, France, and Israel officially determines Jewish law for these Jewish communities. However, because all three nations guarantee religious freedom, the chief rabbinate cannot function as the sole religious authority for the Jewish populace. In these nations and other parts of the world, the Conservative and Reform movements are working to provide Jewish citizens with non-Orthodox options.

In Latin America, the Conservative movement is actually the dominant movement, with a rabbinical seminary in Buenos Aires and synagogues,

Ramah camps, and other Conservative institutions stretching from Mexico to Argentina and Chile. For these communities, the Conservative movement's Committee on Jewish Law and Standards serves as the central Jewish agency for determining Jewish law, as it does for the rest of the movement worldwide.

A Central Jewish Agency for the Modern Conservative Movement

In line with these precedents, the Committee on Jewish Law and Standards (CJLS, sometimes called the Law Committee) helps to determine Jewish law for the Conservative movement. Individual Jews with questions in Jewish law are referred to their local rabbi, but rabbis and arms of the movement may pose questions of halakhic policy pertaining to the wider movement to the CJLS. If a question requires an immediate answer, the CJLS chair or the chair of the relevant CJLS subcommittee will typically address it and record the exchange on the Committee on Jewish Law and Standards website (https://www.rabbinicalassembly.org/jewish-law /committee-jewish-law-and-standards) as an unofficial decision of the chair. For questions that can wait, the CJLS chair assigns a committee member to write a well-researched, thorough, formal rabbinical ruling on the question. In addition, any Conservative rabbi may write a *teshuvah* (an answer to an halakhic question) for the committee's consideration.[4]

Because the act of deciding upon legal additions or modifications requires considerable judgment and risk, the Conservative movement makes sure that every ruling emerges from considerable communal discussion. The Committee on Jewish Law and Standards consists of twenty-five Conservative rabbis, all of whom have full voting privileges, as well as five lay members and a cantor, who participate actively in discussions and may contribute to writing a *teshuvah* for consideration but who do not vote.[5] A *teshuvah* that receives six or more votes at a meeting (in which as few as thirteen or as many as all twenty-five voting members are in attendance) becomes what is called "a valid option" within the Conservative movement.

The CJLS *teshuvot* cover a wide range of topics, including ritual, moral, social, economic, and even aesthetic issues. Approved responsa from 1980 on appear on the CJLS website, http://www.rabbinicalassembly.org/jewish -law/committee-jewish-law-and-standards (and those approved before 1980 are being scanned and added to the site). The website is divided into four sections, following the organization of the Tur and the Shulḥan Arukh, two important medieval codes of Jewish law; alternatively, visitors can use the search engine at the upper right corner of the homepage. Given space constraints, this book only reproduces responsa excerpts and conclusions; readers can find the full responsa either by searching the CJLS website or by following the specific link supplied at the beginning of each responsum discussed.

The fact that only six votes are necessary to approve a rabbinical ruling as a valid option within the Conservative movement means, of course, that on any given issue, there may be more than one validated option within the movement. For the vast majority of issues, only one *teshuvah* has been approved, thereby articulating some of the many ways in which the movement is unified in its practice of Jewish law. On some matters, however, two or more options have been approved. In this way, the spectrum of religious practice within the Conservative community is made manifest, together with the legal reasoning that justified each validated position.

Even when the CJLS approves only one *teshuvah* on a given issue, the local rabbi has the authority to rule otherwise for his or her community. This indicates the power entrusted to the local rabbi in recognition that he or she knows best what will work in the local setting. Similarly, when two or more rulings are approved, the local rabbi decides which best fits his or her own understanding of Jewish law and the needs and nature of his or her particular community.

Rabbi Gordon Tucker points out in an essay (excerpted here) that this pluralistic approach is not only a pragmatic response to variations in Conservative thought and practice but also an adoption of the nonauthoritarianism side of a long-standing rabbinical debate. Specifically, when the majority of rabbis in any generation set common practice, the question arose: Was everyone else mandated to follow that ruling ("majoritarianism with authoritarianism"), or could individual rabbis rule otherwise for their communities ("majoritarianism without authoritarianism")?

Underlying these two positions were ideological differences regarding the human ability to know with certainty what God wants of us. From the authoritarianism vantage point, held by Rabban Gamliel and his intellectual successors, religious truth was definitive and determined by the court's majority. From the nonauthoritarian position, evinced by Rabbi Yehoshua in the Babylonian Talmud and Rabbi Ba in the Jerusalem Talmud, majority decisions were considered "best approximation to a truth which God has decided to leave indeterminate to humans, and are thus both the culminations of rounds of debate and dissension, and the preludes to further such rounds."[6] Local rabbis who followed this school of thought and adopted the majority position on any given legal issue could thereby rest assured that they were obeying God on the given issue as far as the majority of rabbis understood God's command. At the same time, local rabbis could also investigate legal issues on their own, come to their own conclusions, follow those conclusions in practice, and instruct their communities to do so likewise, even when their decisions differed from those of the rabbinical majority.

Today, the high tolerance for pluralism that marked this latter approach to rabbinical rulings in mishnaic and talmudic times is characteristic of the Conservative movement as well.[7] A nonauthoritarian structure, which holds both central and local authorities in tension, has the potential to facilitate creativity at the local level without risking major damage to the Conservative community as a whole.

This endorsement of pluralism notwithstanding, in three instances to date, matters of Conservative practice were deemed so important that the teshuvot became classified as Standards of Rabbinic Practice. A rabbi—and, by agreement with the United Synagogue of Conservative Judaism (USCJ), a synagogue—that violates any such standard is subject to dismissal from the Rabbinical Assembly or the USCJ.

Attainment of Standards of Rabbinic Practice status requires a vote of two-thirds of the CJLS to consider a rabbinical ruling as a potential Standard of Rabbinic Practice (for there have been many responsa approved by unanimous or close-to-unanimous votes of the CJLS that are simply validated rulings of the CJLS and not Standards), followed by approval by four-fifths of the Committee on Jewish Law and Standards polled by mail, and a majority of the members of the Rabbinical Assembly (specifically, 51 percent), also polled by mail.

Here are the three Standards of Rabbinic Practice to date:

1. No member of the Rabbinical Assembly may officiate at the marriage between a Jew and a non-Jew. (Based on unanimous decisions of the CJLS on October 28 and December 2, 1970 and reaffirmed by the CJLS as a binding Standard on December 21, 1971).

2. No rabbi shall perform a marriage for a divorced man or woman unless such a person has obtained a get [a Jewish writ of divorce] or hafka'at kiddushin [the marriage was annulled by the movement's Joint Bet Din]. (Resolution, Rabbinical Assembly Convention, 1975)

3. [After some "Whereas" clauses:]
   (a) ascription of Jewish lineage through a legal instrument or ceremonial act on the basis of anything other than matrilineal descent; or
   (b) supervision of a conversion that omits tevilah in the case of females, or tevilah and brit milah in the case of males
   shall continue to be regarded as violations of the halakhah of Conservative Judaism. They shall henceforth be violations of a Standard of Rabbinic Practice and be inconsistent with membership in the Rabbinical Assembly, it being understood that any member of the Rabbinical Assembly shall continue to possess the right to petition the Committee on Jewish Law and Standards for an opinion on any case of extraordinary circumstances. (Responsum of Rabbis Joel Roth and Akiba Lubow, adopted as a Standard

by the Committee on Jewish Law and Standards, May, 1985; Resolution, Rabbinical Assembly Convention, 1986).[8]

Meanwhile, a great many Jewish laws that the Conservative movement assumes and shares have not been made standards. No Conservative synagogue, for example, will intentionally have a nonkosher kitchen, and no Conservative synagogue will sponsor activities that involve writing or exchanging money on Shabbat. Conversely, Conservative prayer services will be primarily in Hebrew, every Conservative synagogue will offer Jewish education to Jews of all ages, and all Conservative institutions will strive in some way to improve the world (*tikkun olam*). Because no one in the movement has seriously challenged these and numerous other standards for living as Conservative Jews, they have not been established as Standards of Rabbinic Practice. Still (and regardless of whether individual Jews affiliated with the movement observe them to a greater or lesser degree), the movement itself stands for these broadly shared practices.

Movement Organizations and Local Institutions

Arms of the Conservative movement other than the Rabbinical Assembly have also created standards to address various movement issues. Although these standards of behavior have not been approved by a cJLS vote and therefore do not have the force of Jewish law, they are considered serious nonetheless, for example:

* The Solomon Schechter Day School Association has established religious and academic standards for schools interested in affiliating with the association. Similarly, the movement's schools of higher learning have all established religious and academic standards for students and faculty.
* The Federation of Jewish Men's Clubs and Women's League for Conservative Judaism have set criteria for becoming members of those organizations. Individual Conservative synagogues and schools have their own standards as well, which speak to such

issues as whether both or only the Jewish member of an interfaith couple will be considered organizational members and which activities are open to non-Jews.

* The Rabbinical Assembly's Commission on Human Sexuality has created "A Rabbinic Letter on Intimate Relations," and the Joint Social Action Committee of the Rabbinical Assembly and the United Synagogue of Conservative Judaism has published "The Rabbinic Letter on the Poor."[9] Both documents (excerpted later in this book) are statements of expectation, encouraging Conservative Jews to hold themselves to the moral standards of the Conservative community, with its God-given mission to be not only morally decent but holy.

Custom

Minhag (custom) also holds considerable power in Jewish law. In fact, Jewish law and practice have always been the product of an interaction between what the rabbis say and what the general Jewish community does. In line with this historical precedent, Conservative movement practice may be determined by custom.

Sometimes, Jewish law motivates Jews to create new customs to embellish Jewish life. For example, Jewish law requires that Jews pray the evening service, but the Jewish community of sixteenth-century Tsfat created *Kabbalat Shabbat*, a group of psalms, and a poem, *Lekha Dodi*, that Jews recite (often sing) before the Friday evening service to welcome the Sabbath beautifully and distinctly. Similarly, Jewish law mandates a Seder on Passover night, but varying Jewish communities and even individual families have created multiple customs about how the story of the Exodus is told and what foods are eaten.

Other times, the process is reversed, with custom being the primary root of the practice that then influences later rabbinical rulings. So, for example, when Conservative synagogues emerged in North America, it was customary for men and women to sit together at services. Decades later, the movement's Committee on Jewish Law and Standards confirmed:

"There is no specific prohibition in Jewish law of mixed seating (rather it is a custom), and therefore this question is to be decided by each congregation as guided by its rabbi."[10] Similarly, women's participation in services—specifically, the bat mitzvah ceremony, women being called to the Torah, and women becoming service leaders—all began as practices within some Conservative congregations. Over time, the Committee on Jewish Law and Standards examined these practices and ruled that they were legally justified.[11]

Emet Ve-Emunah on Authority for Jewish Practice

The following excerpt from *Emet Ve-Emunah* encapsulates the balance between the authority of the local rabbi and the Committee on Jewish Law and Standards in determining Conservative/Masorti practice:

Arriving at Halakhic Decisions

The Conservative method for arriving at halakhic decisions reflects our interest in pluralism and also exhibits the trait characteristic of Conservative Judaism, the melding of the traditional with the modern. The rich tradition that we possess depends upon the scholarship, integrity, and piety of our leadership and laity. For religious guidance, the Conservative movement looks to the scholars of the Jewish Theological Seminary of America and other institutions of higher learning. The United Synagogue of America, the Women's League for Conservative Judaism, and the Federation of Jewish Men's Clubs represent the human resources of laypeople of our community.

Authority for religious practice in each congregation resides in the rabbi (its *mara d'atra* [teacher of the place]). It derives from the rabbi's training in the Jewish tradition, attested by his or her ordination as a rabbi, and by the fact the congregation has chosen that rabbi to be its religious guide. In making decisions, rabbis may consult the Committee on Jewish Law and Standards, consisting of representatives of the Rabbinical Assembly, the Jewish Theological Seminary of America, and the United Synagogue of America. The Committee on Jewish Law and Standards issues rulings shaping the practice of the Conservative community. Parameters set by that Committee and at Rabbinical Assembly conventions govern all of the rabbis of the Rabbinical Assembly, but within those bounds there are variations of practice recognized as both legitimate and, in many cases, contributory to the richness of Jewish life. In this way the Conservative community preserves the traditional interactions between individual rabbis in their communities and the larger, central authority of the movement in making decisions in Jewish law. At the same time, Conservative Judaism responds to the needs of individual Jews and congregations. This assures us a clear sense of identity together with a vibrant, healthy pluralism.

Rabbi Gordon Tucker's Rationale for Pluralism in Jewish Law

Rabbi Gordon Tucker's 1991 paper, "A Principled Defense of the Current Structure and Status of the CJLS," illuminates the theological rationale for the Conservative movement's complex, overlapping, pluralistic system.[12] The CJLS discussed the paper in 1993 and accepted it into its record without a vote. Here is a short excerpt:

Majoritarianism without Authoritarianism

The late Robert Cover gave a principled defense of the jurisdictional complexities, redundancies, and rivalries in the American federal system against those who have argued for the desirability of a more uniform, linear flow of legal authority. It is an instructive defense for our purposes. For like those who have criticized the Conservative movement's legal structure (with local decisors somewhat beholden to, but still independent of, the CJLS) as incoherent and haphazard, there have always been those who have looked at concurrent and overlapping jurisdictions in the United States as "an accident of history and a . . . malformed jurisdictional anomaly that we have endured, but not loved, for so long."[13]

But there is another way to view such complexities, argued Cover . . . as a product of a coherent evolution, which persists because of its strong functionality . . . :

There may be with respect to many matters a potential for a unitary national norm. . . . However, more typically we rely upon a regime of polycentric norm articulation in which state organs and lower federal courts enjoy a great deal of legislative autonomy. This multiplicity of norm articulation sources provides opportunities for norm application over a limited domain without risking losses throughout the nation. This proliferation of norm-generating centers also makes it more likely that at least one such center will attempt any given, plausible innovation. . . . The multiplicity of centers means an innovation is more likely to be tried and correspondingly less likely to be wholly embraced. The two effects dampen both momentum and inertia.[14]

Stated in our terms, this argument means that, in addition to all the principled reasons we have given for maintaining the distinctive and delicate balance between the CJLS and the *mara d'atra* [local rabbi], our movement's structure allows for religious and halakhic creativity locally, where the need for it first arises, and where its authenticity can best be evaluated. This is a precious resource indeed, and it should not be lightly dismissed for the sake of an elusive "uniformity" which will disappoint tomorrow those whom it satisfies today.

Suggestions for Further Reading

Elliot N. Dorff. *Conservative Judaism: Our Ancestors to Our Descendants*, esp. chap. 3. New York: United Synagogue of Conservative Judaism, 1996.

Neil Gillman. *Conservative Judaism: The New Century*, esp. chaps. 6–8. West Orange NJ: Behrman House, 1993.

Gordon Tucker. "A Principled Defense of the Current Structure and Status of the CJLS." In *The Unfolding Tradition: Philosophies of Jewish Law*, edited by Elliot N. Dorff, 450–68. New York: Aviv Press (Rabbinical Assembly), 2011. There is an explanation and analysis of his essay on pages 424–28. The essay alone is also available at http://www.rabbinicalassembly.org/sites/default/files/public/halakhah/teshuvot/19912000/tucker_defense.pdf.

CHAPTER SIX

Nashim

Women in Jewish Life

Women's expanding roles in the Conservative movement happened first through local customs and only later by legal decisions.

From the very beginning of the twentieth century, men and women worshipped side by side in Conservative synagogues, and boys and girls, as well as men and women, studied together in the classroom. (To this day, in most Orthodox communities, after the third or fourth grade, learning occurs in gender-specific classes. Also, teenage boys often study Talmud, while teenage girls study Bible, commentaries, and laws governing Jewish practice.)

In 1922 Rabbi Mordecai Kaplan inaugurated the bat mitzvah ceremony for his daughter Judith, and by the middle of the century most Conservative synagogues were scheduling them for young women. The ceremonies varied, however. Some bat mitzvah girls did what most bar mitzvah boys did: recite *Kiddush* on Friday night, chant the Torah blessings and the haftarah on Saturday morning, and give a homily on the Torah reading. At other synagogues, the bat mitzvah only recited some readings and delivered a homily on Friday night.

Some Conservative synagogues were fully egalitarian by the late 1940s, but that was rare. Only in the 1970s did a significant number of Conservative synagogues move in that direction. In 1973 the Conservative movement's Committee on Jewish Law and Standards (CJLS) voted to authorize counting women as part of a minyan and to permit women's participation as worship leaders but without legal briefs to justify such policies, and so many rabbis were reticent to rely on those votes. In most congregations, it took until the 1980s or even later for a woman to be elected synagogue president.

Gradually, legal rulings were needed to justify the emerging customs and to augment them in areas that custom could not determine. This happened with the decision to ordain women in 1983 and with subsequent CJLS rulings that enabled women to count as part of a prayer quorum, to lead services, to act as witnesses on documents, and to serve in other capacities in Jewish life. Rabbi Pamela Barmash's responsum, approved in 2014 (and excerpted in this chapter), culminated this process by proclaiming as a matter of principle that, except in areas of Jewish law addressing biological differences (circumcision, family purity laws), men and women were to be treated as equals.

Emet Ve-Emunah's 1988 Stance

In 1988, however, when *Emet Ve-Emunah* was published, the movement's synagogues, schools, youth groups, and camps varied widely in accepting women's involvement in Jewish communal life. At that time, some congregations barred women from taking any roles in synagogue services, and others were fully egalitarian. In the middle, some "Torah egalitarian" congregations permitted women to read the week's Torah and haftarah selections, to recite blessings over the Torah, and to lead the parts of the services that were not legally required (such as *P'sukei D'zimra* in the morning service and *Kabbalat Shabbat* on Friday night). It would take until the 1990s for the vast majority of Conservative synagogues to become completely egalitarian (the exceptions were primarily in eastern Canada and New York's Long Island).

This excerpt from *Emet Ve-Emunah* articulates the range of positions then in effect:

Women's Roles and Rights

The dignity of every human being has always been central to Judaism. This fundamental premise is derived from the biblical assertions in Genesis 1:27 and 5:1 that God created humanity, both male and female, in the divine image.

The equality of the sexes is explicitly affirmed in the Conservative Prayerbook, in the blessing in which both men and women thank God for having been created in His image. Access to Jewish education for women has been a hallmark of Conservative Judaism since the days of Solomon Schechter. In almost all our synagogues, men and women are seated together. The *bat mitzvah* ceremony, now celebrated in virtually all synagogues, was originated in the Conservative movement by Professor Mordecai M. Kaplan. Over the years our movement has encouraged women to assume roles of communal service and leadership both in a professional and in a lay capacity. In recent days, the discussion of the role of women has rekindled interest in some quarters in areas as diverse as *tohorat ha-mishpahah* (the system of family purity revolving around the use of the *mikveh* [ritual bath]), the creation of naming ceremonies for girls, and special women's observances of *Rosh Ḥodesh*.

We are convinced that justice and dignity for each human being can be achieved within the framework of Halakhah, thus obviating the inequalities that lead to situations like that of *agunot* (women who cannot remarry without their husbands' initiating divorce). After years of research and trial by the Committee on Jewish Law and Standards, the Conservative movement has provided satisfactory practical solutions to many of the knotty problems in this area.

There is a wide spectrum of opinion within our movement with regard to the role of women in Jewish ritual. Many believe that women should assume the full rights and responsibilities of ritual participation, including serving as rabbis and cantors. Indeed, the Jewish Theological Seminary now ordains women as rabbis and certifies them as cantors, and the Rabbinical Assembly accepts women as members. On the other hand, many within the movement believe that women today can find religious fulfillment in the context of traditional practice.

All the various views on the specifics of women's roles and rights accept Halakhah as the governing framework for Jewish life.

The Report of the Commission on the Ordination of Women as Rabbis

Unlike other developments in women's Jewish rights that entered Conservative Jewish practice first by custom, the Conservative movement's ordination of women rabbis was a conscious decision grounded in extensive legal and moral reasoning. In 1977 the Jewish Theological Seminary of America (JTSA, or, more commonly now, JTS) and the Rabbinical Assembly (the Conservative movement's rabbinical association) formed the Commission on the Ordination of Women as Rabbis, consisting of four JTS professors, three synagogue rabbis, and seven lay Jews (including three women). Commission members traveled throughout North America to solicit input before reaching a decision.

The official commission report, issued on January 30, 1979, included both majority and minority reports and was written by Rabbi Gordon Tucker, secretary of the commission.

Upon its receipt, then JTS chancellor Gerson Cohen solicited papers from faculty members who wished to speak to the issue. These were subsequently collected and published in the book *The Ordination of Women as Rabbis*, edited by Rabbi Simon Greenberg.

Four years later, in 1983, JTS's faculty voted to approve women's admission to the Jewish Theological Seminary's rabbinical school. At present, about three hundred of the approximately seventeen hundred Rabbinical Assembly members are women.

As you will read in the following excerpts from the commission's official 1979 report, the majority of members believed that women could be ordained because most of the tasks rabbis do are not restricted to men in Jewish law. Since then, the Committee on Jewish Law and Standards has validated rabbinical rulings that open to women the few remaining rabbinical functions traditionally limited to men, such as leading services and serving as witnesses on documents. Even so, women rabbis can choose not to take advantage of these permissive rulings and ask men in their community to perform these tasks instead.

Parameters of Discussion

There are certain aspects . . . which it was at once established that there was unanimity among members of the Commission . . . the ability and willingness of women to perform rabbinic duties as well as men, the right to equal job opportunities, the right to pursue a career of one's choice. Indeed, it could be said that with respect to the context in which general feminist issues are discussed, there was never any serious dispute among Commission members, nor apparently within the community either. There were and are, for example, many men who fully accept the fact that their wives are pursuing careers, as well as women actually pursuing careers who nevertheless oppose the ordination of women.

It was therefore determined at the outset that this could not be treated solely as a feminist issue. From that point of view, there was plainly very little to discuss. The complexity of the issue at hand stemmed from the fact that, although there is general agreement concerning the questions that characterize general feminist debates, there is still a wide range of other considerations of which account must be taken. Those considerations include some peculiar to the rabbinate, to Jewish practice in general, and to Conservative Judaism in particular. It was about these special considerations that discussion and debate revolved.

Halakhic Considerations

. . . The Commission eventually adopted the classical position that had been embraced by the religious leadership of the Conservative Movement since its founding . . . that the body of Jewish law is not uniform in texture, but is rather composed of materials that fall into two main categories, usually referred to as *de-oraita* (biblically ordained) and *de-rabbanan* (rabbinically developed). That which is *de-oraita* can be considered to be the very core of the system, which holds it in place and provides a frame of reference. It therefore must be treated as inviolable. . . .

The much greater (that is, in terms of volume) overlay that is *de-rabbanan*, on the other hand, comes with procedures for change and development. What is *de-rabbanan* can develop, is in fact meant to develop, as the conditions of the Jewish community change. That is what ensures the vibrancy and the continuity of the *halakhah* as the coordinate system that roots all Jewish communities.

It is a commonplace among Conservative Jews that the recognition of the flexibility and fluidity of the *halakhah* is one of the hallmarks of Conservative Judaism, and this is certainly true. . . . Yet . . . it cannot be stressed too strongly that the strength of Conservative Judaism depends as much on its continuation as a movement devoted to tradition as it does on its continued devotion to *halakhic* development. The two are inseparable in classical terms, and the centrality of tradition expresses itself in the conditions under which development becomes acceptable. Those conditions include:

The core that is *de-oraita* may not be altered or displaced. The general principles of, for example, *kashrut* or *Shabbat* could never be displaced as central pillars of Conservative Judaism.

Development in the domain of *de-rabbanan* must not be abrupt or discontinuous, must be rooted in traditional exegetical methodologies, and above all, must be ratified by the community of the committed and the informed.

The impetus for development in what is *de-rabbanan* must come from *within* the community of the committed and the informed, and not be an external influence originating outside the concerned Jewish community.

. . . Once agreement was reached on the philosophical and theoretical level, the specific *halakhic* problems that arise were addressed. . . . A variety of *halakhic* criteria . . . have traditionally distinguished between men and women. Primary among these are the following:

1. According to some sources, women may be ineligible to be appointed to any office of communal responsibility in the Jewish community.
2. Women are exempted from the obligation to study Torah (except for the acquisition of knowledge concerning obligations they do have), although there is no problem presented by their voluntarily assuming that obligation.

3. Women are exempted from positive time-dependent commandments, with a few notable exceptions. The most relevant commandments under this category for purposes of this Commission are those relating to public worship, for exemption from performance raises problems concerning eligibility to discharge the obligation of another person who cannot claim exception.

4. Women are traditionally ineligible to serve as witnesses in judicial proceedings, including the execution of documents determining personal and familial status.

5. Women are, by virtue of (4) above, considered by most traditional authorities to be ineligible to serve as judges.

All of these sex-role distinctions of the *halakhah* were discussed and researched by members of the Commission. The results of those deliberations will now be summarized:

The role of the rabbi as we know it today is not one that is established in classical Jewish texts, but rather is one that has evolved through social need and custom. Consequently, there is no specifiable *halakhic* category that can be identified with the modern rabbinate, nor with the currently accepted mode of ordination. Ordination of the Jewish Theological Seminary of America is done in a way that is nearly indistinguishable from the granting of an academic degree at the successful completion of a course of study. Of course, it still has a profound religious and symbolic significance not shared by any academic degree. In other words, issues relating to ordination are not *halakhic* issues per se, though it is certainly true that there may be serious ramifications of decisions concerning ordination that can lead to a confrontation with certain *halakhic* principles. Strictly speaking, point (1) above is general enough to present an *halakhic* problem concerning ordination. That point has its origin in a passage in the *halakhic* midrash on the Book of Deuteronomy, the *Sifre*. On the verse in Deuteronomy 17:15, "You shall be free to set a king over yourself," the *Sifre* comments, "A king and not a queen." Extrapolating from this comment, Maimonides in *Laws Relating to Kings* 1:5 says, "Only men may be appointed [to positions of authority] in Israel."

Insufficient *Halakhic* Barrier

After considering the opinion of Maimonides on this matter, the Commission decided that it was beset by numerous ambiguities and uncertainties and should not be accounted as an immutable provision of the *halakhah*.

The modern rabbinate cannot be analogized to an appointment on the order of magnitude of the ancient monarchy. The many obvious high-level appointments of women in modern Jewish life indicate the passing of this principle from general Jewish usage. The Commission therefore determined that this *halakhah* as formulated by Maimonides was insufficient to pose an *halakhic* barrier to the ordination of women.

With respect to point (2) above, the Conservative Movement has already taken the strongest possible stand in favor of obligating women to study Torah on a basis equal to that of men. The Movement's introduction of *Bat Mitzvah* half a century ago, its educational programs in Camp Ramah, United Synagogue Youth, Leaders Training Fellowship, and last but not least, the schools of the Jewish Theological Seminary of America, all bear witness to that stand. Indeed, the history of the Conservative Movement on the issue of the religious education of women not only vitiates the force of point (2), but actually constitutes a consideration in favor of ordaining women, as will be noted below.

Points (3), (4), and (5) are a group in several respects. First, they have all been dealt with to some extent by a constituent arm of the Conservative Movement. Second, they are all *halakhic* sex-role distinctions that are secondary to the issue of ordination, as will be explained. Third, although they are secondary to the ordination issue *logically*, they are closely connected to the rabbinic role *practically*. These points accounted for most of the *halakhically* based discussions during the Commission's proceedings.

Matters of *halakhic* import in the Conservative Movement have always been channeled through the Rabbinical Assembly Committee on Jewish Law and Standards (hencefort: the Law Committee). That Committee's composition and rules of procedure have varied considerably over the years, but it has consistently defined itself as a panel that primarily makes recommendations on the basis of legal scholarship; its decisions have binding power on Movement leaders only when a very strong consensus condition is met. For the past several years, the operating rule has been that only a position held by all but two or fewer members of the Committee is binding; a minority position with three adherents on the Committee becomes a legitimate option for Conservative congregations and rabbis. [Editor's note: The minimum for a validated option was changed to six in the revisions of the Rabbinical Assembly Constitution in 1986. In accordance with those revisions, even a unanimous CJLS ruling is not binding on individual rabbis unless introduced and voted on as a Standard of Rabbinic Practice.]

Despite inevitable disagreements concerning one or another of the Law Committee's decisions, nearly universal respect has been accorded to the principle of legitimate option. Accordingly, in considering the proper course for the entire Conservative Movement on a matter such as the one under scrutiny, the history of the Law Committee's treatment of some of the related questions must be looked into.

The Law Committee published a majority decision in 1955 that allowed women the privilege of an *aliyah* at Torah-readings services. Although this practice is far from universal in Conservative congregations, it is a practice that is growing and that was legitimated by the 1955 decision. In 1973, the same committee issued a majority responsum that permitted congregations to count women as part of the *minyan* for public worship. This practice has likewise not nearly become universal, but the number of congregations that have been accepting it is steadily growing. Finally, a *minority* report in 1974 declared that women should be permitted to serve as witnesses in legal proceedings, including the signing of *ketubot* [marriage documents] and *gittin* [divorce documents]. Since that minority report was issued by six committee members, the rules of the Law Committee imply that it is a legitimate option for rabbis and congregations in the Conservative Movement. Thus, the Commission established that the practices referred to in points (3), (4), and (5) had already been declared by the Committee on Jewish Law and Standards of the Rabbinical Assembly to be *halakhically* acceptable options within the Conservative Movement. Hence the Commission determined that its resolution of the ordination issue could not lead to a possible contravention of a binding standard for the Conservative Movement.

More important than the foregoing observations was the fact that irrespective of what one's *halakhic* view is on the matter of a woman performing these practices, they are strictly secondary to the issue of ordination. A wide variety of functions are viewed as part of the role of the rabbi today. Among these are teaching, preaching, counseling, officiating at religious ceremonies, representing the Jewish community, etc. Leading a prayer service as the *shaliah tzibur* [leader of worship], receiving an *aliyah* [honored to recite blessings before and after a public Torah reading], or even signing a *ketubah* or *get* as a witness are not among these essential functions. A rabbi supervising divorce proceedings might be entitled to sign the *get* as a witness, and may on occasion do so as a matter of convenience, but surely it is not the rabbi's role qua rabbi to do so. Similar observations would apply to other forms of testimony and to the various roles associated with public worship that have been mentioned. The simple fact is that the rabbinate, as noted above, is not defined or circumscribed by *halakhic* strictures. Hence there can be no direct *halakhic* objection to the conferral of the title "rabbi" upon a woman, together with all the rights and responsibilities to perform the functions essentially connected to the office. In connection with this, the Commission noted that it is a commonplace to ordain *Kohanim* ["priests," that is, male rabbis who are descendants of Aaron], even though officiating at a funeral, which can pose *halakhic* problems for a *Kohen*, is popularly viewed as a rabbinic function. . . .

In closing this section on *halakhah*, the Commission notes that in the medieval period, the spiritual leadership of women was not unknown. One bit of evidence for this is to be found in the fourteenth-century work of a Spanish rabbi, known as *Sefer Hahinukh*, which assumes that a woman is eligible to perform the most basic of the classical rabbinic functions, viz., deciding specific matters of law. Section 152 of that treatise, which deals with the prohibition of deciding matters of ritual law while intoxicated, notes that the prohibition "applies to males, as well as to a knowledgeable woman who is eligible to give such instruction."

To summarize, then: The *halakhic* objections to the ordination of women center around disapproval of the performance by a woman of certain functions. Those functions, however, are not essentially rabbinic, nor are they universally disapproved, by the accepted rules governing the discussion of *halakhah* in the Conservative Movement. *There is no direct halakhic objection to the acts of training and ordaining a woman to be a rabbi, preacher, and teacher in Israel.*

The problems associated with ancillary functions were deemed by the Commission to be insufficient grounds for denying a considerable and growing group of highly talented and committed Jewish women the access they desire to the roles of spiritual and community leaders.

Ethical Considerations

. . . The most compelling ethical argument heard by the Commission was in favor of ordaining women, and it was heard from members of the Conservative laity in many different parts of North America. . . . The Conservative Movement has a proud history of educating females in Jewish Studies from the earliest ages on a perfect par with males. In fact, it is worth considering for a moment what it is like today for boys and girls to grow up in a committed Jewish home identified and affiliated with the Conservative Movement. Such a boy and girl would both be given the very same Hebrew or Day School education from the outset. Both would prepare for *Bar* or *Bat Mitzvah* ceremonies and in most cases perform the same functions in the service. Both would likely receive intense Judaic training at Camp Ramah. They would proceed to Hebrew High School, join LTF [Leaders' Training Fellowship, for high school students enrolled in Jewish studies courses for at least six hours a week], and/or United Synagogue Youth. In many congregations, they would participate in public worship equally through adolescence, building on their acquired Jewish skills. They would seek out the same reinforcement of their Jewish values while away at college, and form a more sophisticated intellectual commitment to Judaism. That commitment would in some cases be strong enough to generate a desire to study for the rabbinate at the Seminary of the Conservative Movement. Suddenly, discontinuously, at this point, the female is differentiated from the male in being unable to fulfill the education she was given and encouraged to pursue in the way she chose to fulfill it.

This scenario was not an abstract creation, but rather was the actual testimony of many parents who, confronted by the problem, were unable to explain the sudden differentiation to their daughters. In considering this increasingly common phenomenon, the Commission felt that it was morally wrong to maintain an educational structure that treats males and females equally up to the final stage, but distinguishes between them at that stage, *without a firm and clearly identifiable halakhic reason for doing so.* In such a case, the Commission felt that the secondary *halakhically* related issues dealt with in the previous section paled even further in significance. On balance, the ethical arguments *coupled with the absence of halakhic counter-argument* were considered by the Commission to constitute a strong case for the training and ordination of women as rabbis at the Jewish Theological Seminary of America.

Other Considerations

A good deal of other evidence came to the attention of the Commission and was discussed by it. Most of it tended to support a decision to recommend the training and ordination of women as Conservative rabbis. . . .

Preliminary data from the survey commissioned by this body indicated that, in absolute numbers, a majority of the laity of the Conservative Movement was ready to accept women in the role of congregational spiritual leader. . . .

The student body of the Seminary's Rabbinical School, when surveyed by the Student Government, expressed support for the admission of women to the Rabbinical School by an affirmative vote of 74 percent. . . .

It became clear as well that a decision not to ordain women would mean the neglect if not the rejection of a pool of talented, committed, and energetic women who could eventually represent 50 percent of the potential spiritual leaders, and who could play a major role in revitalizing Jewish tradition and values in the Conservative Movement. Indications are that the Movement cannot afford the cost of refusing to take advantage of that leadership talent at the present time.

There was one other major consideration that was voiced many times and could best be classified under the category of "symbolism." This point was raised by many persons who believed on substantive grounds that the ordination of women was both correct and defensible, but who feared what they termed the symbolic break with tradition that such a move would represent. For exponents of this argument, the symbolic result of admitting women to the rabbinate would be a blurring of the ideological lines that have divided Conservatism from more liberal Jewish movements. That, it is claimed, would destroy the main attraction of the Conservative Movement, to wit, the coexistence of authenticity of tradition with a critical view aimed at developing that tradition within the framework of *halakhic* norms.

The Commission took this argument most seriously, but concluded that it was insufficient to militate against ordaining women. The reason for this conclusion was that, by the Commission's own commitments and chosen procedures, a recommendation in favor of ordination would be based on a thorough and predominant commitment to *halakhah*. In a case such as this, where a recommended development is consistent with *halakhah*, and manifestly to the advantage of the community, symbolic considerations must not be allowed to block that development. To be sure, the symbolic considerations must be taken very seriously, but rather as a challenge to educate the community to the extent that it is evident to all that the development is in consonance with the historical ideological commitments of Conservative Judaism, and does not represent an ideological shift. It is hoped that this report will constitute a first step in that process of education.

Recommendations

Based on its overall commitment to *halakhic* authenticity and all of the evidence and reasoning that have been summarized or alluded to in this report, the signatories to this majority opinion recommend that qualified women be ordained as rabbis in the Conservative Movement. Specifically, the recommendations are:

> That the Rabbinical School of the Jewish Theological Seminary of America revise its admission procedures to allow for applications from female candidates and the processing thereof for the purpose of admission to the ordination program on a basis equal to that maintained heretofore for males.
>
> That this revision of policy be accomplished as quickly as possible,

preferably so as to allow applications from women for the academic year beginning in September 1979.

That the Jewish Theological Seminary of America take steps to set up appropriate apparatuses for the recruitment, orientation, and eventually, career placement of female rabbinical students.

That the major arms of the Conservative Movement immediately begin discussion of procedures to be followed to educate the community concerning issues raised in this report so as to ensure as smooth and as harmonious an adjustment to the new policy as possible....

In making these recommendations, the Commission is making no recommendation in regard to traditional practices relating to testimony, and no implications concerning such practices should be drawn on the basis of this report.

The following members of the Commission join in supporting the above majority report:

Rabbi Gerson D. Cohen, Chair of the Commission, JTS Chancellor; Victor Goodhill, MD, Professor of Otologic Research, UCLA; Marion Siner Gordon, attorney; Rivkah Harris, PhD, Assyriologist; Milton Himmelfarb, Editor, *American Jewish Yearbook*, American Jewish Committee; Francine Klagsbrun, author; Rabbi Fishel A. Pearlmutter, Toledo, Ohio; Harry M. Plotkin, attorney; Norman Redlich, Dean, New York University School of Law; Rabbi Seymour Siegel, Professor of Theology, JTS; Rabbi Gordon Tucker, Assistant to the Chancellor, JTS.

Minority Opinion

Although the signatories to this section are in sympathy with many of the arguments and sentiments expressed by our colleagues on the Commission, and embodied in the majority opinion given above, we remain opposed to the ordination of women as rabbis in the Conservative Movement. Since many of the reasons for this conclusion have already been discussed or at least mentioned earlier in this report, we shall simply list briefly our motivations for arriving at this recommendation.

(A) Our main thrust has to do with certain *halakhic* problems that cannot, in our opinion, be separated from the question of ordination but flow from it almost inexorably. Not all congregations accept the view that women may be counted in a *minyan*, receive *aliyot*, or lead the service in liturgical prayer as a surrogate for others. Many more congregations and many Jews outside our Movement may be affected by practices in connection with testimony relating to marriage and divorce, where the laws are restrictive in the case of women. You cannot, within the present climate of the Conservative Movement, ordain women and expect that they will not at some point infringe on these *halakhic* restrictions in the performance of their rabbinical duties.

(B) We fear the possible disruption of the unity of the Movement. One of the consequences of a decision to ordain women might very well be the violations of *halakhic* principles adhered to by others in the Movement, which in turn would result in the untenable position of individual rabbis being unable in good conscience to recognize the validity of marriages, divorces, and conversions supervised by one of their colleagues.

(C) A decision to ordain women would mark the first time in recent history that the Seminary had entered the arena of *halakhic* decision-making. The centrality and authority of the Seminary would perforce be a uniformizing influence that could have the unfortunate effect of foreclosing the options of minorities wishing to remain within the Movement.

(D) Finally, we are concerned that at a time when American Jewish youth seem to be turning more toward traditional values, and to an authentic *halakhic* life-style, this would seriously compromise the traditional image of the Conservative Movement, and the Jewish Theological Seminary of America as an authentic *halakhic* institution. We feel strongly that such matters of symbolism must be taken as seriously as possible, for a wrong decision on an issue of this magnitude will, in our opinion, alienate many more *halakhically* committed people than it will attract.

For these reasons, we recommend to the leaders of the Conservative Movement that appropriate roles be created for Jewish women short of ordination so that their commitment and talents may be a source of blessing and not of unnecessary controversy.

The following members of the Commission join in supporting the above minority opinion: Rabbi Haim Z. Dimitrovsky, Professor of Talmud, JTS; Rabbi Elijah J. Schochet, Canoga Park, CA; Rabbi Wilfred Shuchat, Westmont, Quebec.

Aftermath of the Commission Report

In 1983, four years after the Report of the Commission on the Ordination of Women as Rabbis, the Jewish Theological Seminary of America (JTS) began admitting women to rabbinical school. The University of Judaism (later American Jewish University) rabbinical program in Los Angeles, which was then part of JTS's rabbinical program, admitted women to rabbinical school at the same time. Rabbi Amy Eilberg, JTS class of 1985, became the first woman to be ordained in the Conservative movement. (She had taken numerous JTS classes as a graduate student before the decision; afterward, the administration counted all those classes toward her rabbinical school requirements, enabling her to be ordained just two years later.)

In Israel, the Schechter Institute of Jewish Studies, established by JTS and the Masorti movement, began admitting women in 1984, the first year of its operation.

The Seminario Rabínico Latinoamericano in Buenos Aires first ordained a woman in 1994 and has ordained about a dozen women since then.

Responsa on Women's Issues

From the 1980s to the present, various CJLS responsa went on to address specific women's issues. In the late 1980s and 1990s, these encompassed calling a woman to the Torah for the *Kohen* or Levi reading of the Torah if her father had that status (1989); adding the names of the Matriarchs to the opening line of the *Amidah* (1990); creating a special ceremony, parallel to *pidyon ha-ben*, for first-born female children (1993); participating in the Priestly Blessing of the congregation if a woman is the daughter of a *Kohen* (1994); and women tying tzitzit knots (1997).

By the twenty-first century, Conservative responsa had set guidelines for women acting as witnesses to documents (2001); counting in a minyan

(2002); breastfeeding in public (2005); and observing the laws of family purity (2006).

In addition, the CJLS produced many responsa on medical issues with special meaning for women: abortion (1983); prenatal testing and abortion (1983); using surrogate mothers for gestating a baby (1997 and 1984); miscarriage (1987 and 1991); artificial insemination, egg donation, and adoption (1994); in vitro fertilization (1995); communal and liturgical responses to a stillbirth (1996); maternal identity and the status of a child born to a surrogate mother (1997); partial-birth abortion and the question of when life begins (2001); the commandment to procreate in our day (2005); preimplantation genetic diagnosis (2008); and contraception (2010).

The section of the Rabbinical Assembly website on its Committee of Jewish Law and Standards, http://www.rabbinicalassembly.org/jewish-law /committee-jewish-law-and-standards includes all of these full responsa. Excerpts of some of the ones addressing medical issues appear in chapter 7 of this volume, and excerpts of others addressing sex and family life are presented in chapter 11.

Rabbi Pamela Barmash's Responsum on Women's Equality

As a culmination of this legal work, Rabbi Pamela Barmash, professor of Hebrew Bible and biblical Hebrew at Washington University in St. Louis, wrote a responsum stating that women should be considered equal to men in both their privileges and their responsibilities. Specifically, she asked: Are Jewish women responsible for observing the mitzvot from which they have traditionally been exempted? She concluded that women do bear the exact same responsibilities as men, except with regard to following commandments specific to male and female anatomy, such as circumcision and family purity laws after menstruation.

Most of the CJLS discussion about her responsum revolved around whether this meant that women should now consider themselves obligated to put on tefillin (phylacteries) for daily morning prayers, as Jewish law has required men to do from the time of the Torah. Some women, often the most traditional, see the black boxes and leather straps that constitute tefillin as a man's form of liturgical dress, given both its history and its hard feel to the skin. On the other hand, Rabbi Barmash noted that most teenage boys wear tefillin in camp and youth group services only because they are required to do so; if the Conservative movement did not require teenage girls to do likewise, she asserted, women would never take this on.

Ultimately, the committee adopted Rabbi Barmash's responsum on April 29, 2014, by a vote of fifteen in favor, three against, and three abstaining (15–3–3). Excerpts follow; to read the full responsum and its notes, visit http://rabbinicalassembly.org/sites/default/files/public/halakhah/teshuvot /2011-2020/womenandhiyyuvfinal.pdf.

Understanding Egalitarianism

... Egalitarianism, the equality of women in the observance of mitzvot, is not just about the participation of women: it is about fostering the fulfillment of mitzvot by all Jews. ...

> Rabbi Hananyah ben Aqashya said: The Holy One, blessed is he, wanted to grant merit to Israel. Therefore, he gave them Torah and mitzvot in abundance, as it is written, "It pleased the Lord for the sake of (Israel's) righteousness to magnify the Torah and make it glorious" (Isaiah 42:21).
> —m. Makkot 3:16

> The halakhah develops. In regard to the status of women, the development of halakhah has shown phenomenal creativity and urgency in the adaptation of its sources and principles to the needs of time and place.
> —Justice Menachem Elon

Observing mitzvot is the primary way Jews live a religious life. We express our search for God and our quest to live in holiness through the observance of mitzvot. The mitzvot inspire us by focusing our thoughts and elevating our feelings: they guide us toward behavior imbued with certain values and goals. The observance of mitzvot shapes our actions and sanctifies our behavior. We make ourselves open to the spirit through the act of fulfilling mitzvot.

Women have always been responsible to observe mitzvot, but women were exempted from many ritual mitzvot that men were required to observe. In many (and perhaps most) cases, the exemption of women from a specific mitzvah was extended erroneously to mean that women were forbidden from observing it. Most significantly, women were exempted from the study of Torah and, thereby, played a greatly limited role in the process of transmitting and interpreting Torah.

Throughout the ages, a small number of women sought to fulfill the mitzvot from which women were exempted, and women were educated mostly in domestic matters. However, in the past century, accelerated in recent decades, women have sought to suffuse their lives with greater Torah and more mitzvot. By integrating more mitzvot to their lives, women have enriched themselves by the daily routines of Torah and of seeking God both in public and private. At the same time, cultural attitudes have shifted dramatically in society in general, and doors into business and the professions formerly closed to women are now open.... Women are now seen as equal to men, in social status, in political and legal rights, and in intellectual ability by both men and women. A new world-view has resulted in new roles for women.

For many Jewish women, the pathway of observance that Judaism has traditionally assigned to women is no longer sufficient. They want to observe more mitzvot and participate equally in the public life of Jewish liturgy and community. They want to study Torah in the same depth and breadth that Jewish men have enjoyed. Jewish women are seeking to grow in their religious lives, in seeking God, in integrating the daily routines of Torah into everyday living, and in availing themselves of a public role in Jewish communal life.

This development has happened in most, if not all, Jewish communities, and the Conservative movement has been at the forefront of this development. Conservative Jews, both lay-people and rabbis, educators and ḥazzanim [cantors], have demonstrated leadership in increasing access to Torah for women. Indeed, they have championed equality in Jewish life. The Conservative movement started educating women, often on an equal or near equal basis with men. In Conservative synagogues, schools, and camps, opening mitzvot to women has led to the implicit assumption that women are equally obligated to observe the mitzvot as men have been and that mitzvot from which women have traditionally been exempted are not only open to them but are required of them. The Conservative movement has for almost a century moved toward egalitarianism, the equality of women in the observance of mitzvot, but this principle has not yet been articulated clearly by the Committee on Jewish Law and Standards.

An essential concept in Jewish thought is the link between responsibility for the mitzvot and how an individual is esteemed, for being responsible for the mitzvot expresses the high esteem in which those who were responsible for mitzvot were held. While the exemption of women from specific mitzvot never meant that women were forbidden from them, merely allowing women to perform those mitzvot relegates women to a lower status. Those who are not obligated are considered as lesser, even when they observe the same mitzvot as those who are. A rabbinic statement expresses the importance of being obligated:

גדול מצווה ועושה ממי שאינו מצווה ועושה

Greater is the one who is commanded [to observe a mitzvah] and does [it] than the one who is not commanded [to do it and yet] does [it]. (b. *Kiddushin* 31a)

Being permitted to perform a mitzvah is not the same as being required to perform a mitzvah, and women want to express their commitment to their lives as Jews by performing mitzvot on an equal basis with men. From a profoundly Jewish perspective, the highest rank and esteem is for those who are required to fulfill mitzvot. By requiring women to observe mitzvot in the same way men are required to, we are putting into effect the principle that women are created in equal status with men. . . .

Women observing more mitzvot is at once both deeply conservative and profoundly innovative. While extending women's observance to include the mitzvot from which they have traditionally been exempted (and often excluded) may seem radical to some, it demonstrates our profound love for tradition: we want more Jews to observe more mitzvot.

We are aware that our tradition has developed historically, and at times there have been dramatic transformations. We find ourselves in a period of the reinvention of tradition, and we are seeking to preserve tradition by modifying it. . . . Establishing the equality of women in the observance of mitzvot expresses our love for Jewish tradition, and it exemplifies how our knowledge of the historical development of our tradition inspires us. We are on a spiritual quest with a modern heart and mind. . . .

Women and Mitzvot

The Committee on Jewish Law and Standards . . . rules that women are now held equally responsible for the mitzvot as men have been. Women are responsible for the mitzvot of reciting the *Shema* and the *Shemoneh Esreh*, wearing *tzitzit* and donning *tefillin*, residing in a *sukkah*, taking up the *lulav*, hearing the *shofar*, counting the *omer*, and studying Torah. Mothers are equally responsible for the circumcision of their sons and the covenantal naming of their daughters and the redemption of their first-born sons and daughters as fathers are. The Committee on Jewish Law and Standards recognizes that the social status of women entitles them to participate in public ritual and may fulfill mitzvot on behalf of others.

It must be stated clearly that while we rule that men and women are equally responsible for the mitzvot because women are no longer subordinate to men, there are anatomical differences between men and women. Gender differences are socially constituted, but the sexual organs of human beings do determine certain behavior. The mitzvah of *brit milah* (circumcision) applies only to males. The mitzvah of *niddah* (menstrual separation) is primarily observed by women, although it does affect their sexual partners. The mitzvah of procreation applies to men and not to women because of the health risks of pregnancy and labor to women. Requiring women to become pregnant would subject them to dangers to their health. Even today, when the risks have decreased substantially, the risks inherent in pregnancy and labor for women still remain far greater than the risks of intercourse for procreation for men.

The spirit of egalitarianism has created a number of issues left unpondered in our tradition. . . . One of the traditional reasons offered for the exemption of women, that women needed to serve the domestic needs of their husbands, has been transformed in modern times to one less offensive to contemporary sensitivities, that the reason for the exemption of women was that fulfilling time-bound positive mitzvot interfered with a woman's domestic responsibilities in caring for her children. While this was not the reason why women were exempted, it does raise a significant issue. If (some) women are occupied with caring for infants and young children, who need intensive daily care, perhaps an exemption in part might be appropriate. The same would be true for men who bear those duties. If fathers are now taking more responsibility for infants and young children, and men are now assuming a greater commitment for taking care of frail relatives and friends, it may be that their domestic responsibilities mean that they should be released from the mitzvot that interfere with caregiving for the duration in which they bear those duties.

An exemption for care-givers has ample precedents in halakhah. The tradition has always made realistic adjustments, such as for the minimum in daily prayer. Furthermore, an essential principle of rabbinic tradition has been that an individual who is busy with one mitzvah is exempt from another (b. *Sukkah* 25a). Caring for the young and the elderly and frail are tasks with religious significance, and if a person is busy fulfilling the need to care for those in need of care, that person ought to be released from certain religious tasks, such as prayer, that might interfere. Since this exemption is limited to that particular span of time when an individual care-giver is occupied with responsibilities, that care-giver would retain the responsibilities and privileges that he/she would otherwise have. Care-givers may, for example, be included in the minyan because they still are obligated for prayer, even if at times they may be exempted. This exemption applies only to individuals during the time they are fulfilling a mitzvah and would not be applied across the board to them as a class. The exemption would be granted case-by-case, as conflicts in care-giving tasks interfere with fulfilling a specific opportunity to fulfill a mitzvah. This understanding of care-giving duties may also raise awareness of their value, a powerful statement to counteract the negative value that society oftentimes assigns to care-giving.

We aim to guide our people into lives suffused with more Torah and more holiness. We pray that our people will enrich their lives with mitzvot and with seeking God both in public and private. Therefore, we rule that women and men are equally obligated to observe the mitzvot. Those ritual mitzvot required and expected of men are now to be required and expected of women (except for those mitzvot that are determined by sexual anatomy).

A Special Note

... For many women who grew up in a different atmosphere regarding women's roles, the call to observe mitzvot heretofore closed to them will be inspiring and deeply spiritual. They will feel ready to fulfill many mitzvot, and they will eagerly learn new habits. But for some women who were raised in a non-egalitarian or not-completely egalitarian atmosphere, it is understandable that they may be hesitant to take on new mitzvot. Learning new mitzvot may be challenging, and some women may find certain mitzvot daunting for a significant span of time. However, it is the calling of our communities, synagogues, schools, and camps to teach men and women to consider themselves equally obligated to fulfill mitzvot and to educate them equally in mitzvot. ...

Ruling

Women and men are equally obligated to observe the mitzvot, with the exception of those mitzvot that are determined by sexual anatomy.

Egalitarianism in Practice Worldwide

Today, the vast majority of North American Conservative synagogues are egalitarian. The exceptions are primarily synagogues in eastern Canada, as well as a few on Long Island and in New Jersey.

In the United Kingdom, by contrast, only three or four of the twelve Masorti synagogues are egalitarian, according to Rabbi Tzvi Graetz, executive director of Masorti Olami, the World Council of Masorti/Conservative Synagogues. Generally in the UK, women do not participate in leading services, and some synagogues even have separate seating. That said, Noam UK, the United Kingdom's Conservative youth movement, is fully egalitarian—an indication of where the movement in England is heading.

In the rest of Europe, about fifteen out of the twenty Masorti synagogues are mostly egalitarian, but most congregations prefer male rabbis. Latin America varies: In Argentina, most of the forty congregations are egalitarian, but in Chile that is true of only one of the six and in Brazil of only two of the twelve. Australia has two Masorti congregations, both egalitarian.

Notably, in Israel, 95 percent of the more than fifty Masorti congregations are fully egalitarian.

Suggestions for Further Reading

Amy Eilberg. "'Where Is God for You?': A Jewish Feminist Faith." In *Lifecycles, Volume 2: Jewish Women on Biblical Themes in Contemporary Life*, edited by Debra Orenstein and Jane Rachel Litman, 104–12. Woodstock VT: Jewish Lights, 1997.

Neil Gillman. *Conservative Judaism: The New Century*, esp. chap. 8. West Orange NJ: Behrman House, 1993.

Simon Greenberg, ed. *The Ordination of Women as Rabbis*. New York: Jewish Theological Seminary of America, 1988.

Susan Grossman and Rivka Haut, eds. *Daughters of the King: Women and the Synagogue*. Philadelphia: Jewish Publication Society, 1992.

Danya Ruttenberg. *Surprised by God: How I Learned to Stop Worrying and Love Religion*. Boston: Beacon Press, 2008.

CHAPTER SEVEN

Ḥayyim u'Mavet

Rulings on Bioethics

When the authors of classical Jewish law weighed ethical issues in medicine many hundreds of years ago, they could never have imagined today's incredible medical advances. As a result, whereas the conditions and therefore also the rules for building a sukkah have not changed much in more than two thousand years, the medical rulings of yore offer few straightforward answers to most of today's bioethical questions.

Modern Conservative movement thinkers have consequently approached new medical realities by applying traditional Jewish perceptions and values to the new circumstances. Sometimes that may mean trying to balance conflicting goals. For example, one responsum permits contraception and yet encourages couples not to wait too long to have children and then to have three or more if they can.

Because of the radically new medical realities of our times, it should not be surprising that different Conservative rabbis who endeavor to strike the right balance in applying the tradition to contemporary circumstances sometimes arrive at different conclusions. (This is true in the Orthodox and Reform movements as well.) So, for example, in this chapter, Rabbis Elliot Dorff and Avram Israel Reisner agree on most end-of-life issues but differ on whether it is legitimate to withhold or withdraw artificial nutrition and hydration from a dying patient and the amount of morphine that may be used in quelling pain.

Responsum on Contraception

The following responsum asks: When is contraception permitted within
Jewish law, and what classical teachings should guide the decision to
employ it? When contraception is permitted, does Jewish law determine
which contraceptive method is preferable? Does Jewish law distinguish
between contraceptive methods initiated prior to intercourse and "emergency" or other contraception introduced only after intercourse? What
does Jewish tradition teach about an adolescent obtaining contraception
without a parent's consent?

Authors and Rabbis Miriam Berkowitz and Mark Popovsky identify four
Jewish legal issues involved in using contraception, some of which may
surprise the modern reader, and explain why these issues, at least according
to some readings, do not prohibit couples from using contraceptives for
family planning purposes. Then they rank-order available contraceptives
from those that least infringe on Jewish legal concerns to those that do so
most—but that, in some circumstances, may still be permissible.

The CJLS unanimously approved the responsum (excerpted here)
on December 14, 2010, by a vote of seventeen in favor, none against,
and none abstaining (17–0–0). To read the full ruling, see http://www
.rabbinicalassembly.org/sites/default/files/public/halakhah/teshuvot
/20052010/Contraception%20Berkowitz%20and%20Popovsky.pdf.

Relevant Halakhic Principles/Concerns

The Jewish discourse on contraception has identified four possible concerns that might incline against the unrestricted use of contraception: (1)
the prohibition forbidding the unnecessary destruction of seed; (2) the
prohibition against castration; (3) the mitzvah to be fruitful and multiply;
and (4) the reluctance to encourage sexual activity outside of normative
Jewish bounds. A ruling permitting the use of contraception first must
show that efforts to prevent pregnancy do not raise any of these concerns
or that the concern raised is outweighed by an even greater Jewish principle that is upheld through the use of contraception. . . .

Our analysis will show that [the first two concerns] both factor heavily in determining which particular forms of contraception are preferable over others, but neither one can serve as a basis to prohibit the use of contraception generally. It will further show that [the second two] direct committed Jews to make decisions about contraception cautiously with an eye towards fulfilling the mitzvah of procreation; however, within the bounds specified, neither one of these concerns is sufficient to prohibit the use of contraception altogether. . . . We will evaluate the most common contemporary contraceptive methods and discuss which most successfully avoid any of the concerns listed above. Finally, we will turn our attention to Jewish teachings that might inform our approach to issues of parental consent for the use of contraception by adolescents. . . .

Ruling

Jewish law enjoins those who are physically and mentally able to procreate and raise children to have a minimum of two offspring. A recent opinion of the CJLS has increased this to three whenever possible.[1]

Contraception may be used before, after, and in between pregnancies if there is a compelling physical or emotional well-being justification. However financial concerns that go beyond obtaining basic necessities and other issues of convenience are not generally considered sufficient reasons [to avoid procreating through the use of contraceptives].

Safety and efficacy are the primary criteria for determining the most halakhically preferable means of contraception. Because the medical and behavioral issues affecting safety and efficacy will vary for each couple, it is a decision that should be made with a healthcare professional, and blanket halakhic generalizations should be eschewed.

Assuming that all aspects of safety and efficacy with respect to more than one contraceptive method are equal for a particular couple, the couple is advised to follow the order set out in this teshuvah from most to least preferable means:

* Hormonal contraception (the pill, implants, vaginal insertion, trans-dermal patch)
* Intrauterine device — copper or hormonal (IUD)
* Diaphragm, cervical cap

* Sponge, including spermicidal gel; spermicidal gel in combination with another method
* Condoms
* Emergency contraception ("the morning after pill") — only after the fact and not for regular use

If a woman elects to employ a method of contraception farther down the list for reasons of health, safety or efficacy specific to her circumstances, she may rest assured that such a choice represents a halakhically valid decision, fully justified within normative Jewish practice.

Birth control of any means is far preferable to abortion. Every effort should be made to ensure access to and accurate information about contraception for all who might engage in sexual intercourse. The concern that such measures will encourage risky sexual activity or promiscuity is unsupported by scientific evidence and insufficient to warrant the increased health risks borne by those in communities where access to contraception is limited. . . .

Jewish tradition places great value on consistent, direct communication between parents and children. Parents should be actively involved in the major life decisions made by adolescents. However, Jewish law does not mandate parental consent or notification for access to contraception. Where there is concern for the safety of the adolescent or the threat of domestic abuse, care should be taken to be particularly lenient in this area.

Responsum on Procreation

Even though some readings of the tradition permit contraception for family planning purposes, Jewish tradition wants those who can have children to procreate. In their responsum on this subject, "Mitzvah Children," Rabbis Kassel Abelson and Elliot Dorff ask: How many children should a young married Jewish couple seek to have? What are the duties of the Jewish community to make it possible for them to have more than two?

The authors note that the question of how many children a fertile couple should aim to have does not apply to people who cannot conceive or bear them, for Jewish law can never be properly construed to require people to do what they cannot. They encourage the Jewish community to support these people as they grapple with the medical procedures, anxieties, and expenses of trying to have children and the disappointments when they cannot. For these individuals, adoption is an encouraged option.

For fertile couples, however, Rabbis Abelson and Dorff expand their thinking beyond considerations of Jewish law to encompass today's Jewish demographic crisis. For the sake of the Jewish people, they suggest that couples produce one more child in addition to the two-child minimum required by early Jewish law—or one additional child beyond the three or more children the couple had planned to have.

The CJLS approved the responsum (excerpted here) on December 12, 2007, by a vote of 15–3–3, fifteen in favor, three opposed, and three abstaining. To read it in full, see https://www.rabbinicalassembly.org/sites/default /files/assets/public/halakhah/teshuvot/20052010/mitzvah_children.pdf.

Introduction

The Torah includes two positive commandments with regard to sexual relations, one for the companionship, pleasure, and mutual bonding of the couple (Exodus 21:10), and the other for procreation (Genesis 1:28). Although this responsum focuses only on the latter, an extensive discussion of the former can be found in the Rabbinical Assembly's *Rabbinic Letter on Human Intimacy*.[2]

Those Unable to Have Children and Those
Who Can Produce Only One or Two

... There is no obligation to procreate when the couple is unable to have any children or when they cannot have any more children than they have already produced. ...

The Commandment to Procreate

For those able to procreate, there is no specific limit on the number of children that would constitute a Jewish family. However there is a minimum number that the early *halakhah* requires and an additional recommendation that each couple should carefully consider when they discuss their ideal family size. ...

Children are considered not only a blessing, but also an obligation. The Torah tells us that God blessed the first man and woman and commanded them:

פרו ורבו ומלאו את הארץ וכבשה

"Be fertile and increase, fill the earth and conquer it. . . ."[3]

A Shared Obligation

. . . It is possible that the Rabbis chose to make only the male responsible [for procreation] out of concern for the woman's health, and today, despite the egalitarian view in the Conservative movement, it does not seem to be wise to give up the right the woman was granted to practice birth control. Nonetheless, in our day, when we have accepted the equality of men and women, and when we know that women contribute genetically to the creation of a child just as men do, and when effective contraceptive methods for both sexes are available, we should recognize that both the husband and the wife should together decide the number of children they would like to have and the timing and methods they choose to achieve their goal. Indeed, as Rabbis Dorff, Nevins, and Reisner asserted in their paper on the subject, homosexual Jews should also see it as their duty to procreate or adopt, if they can, to convert their children according to Jewish law, if necessary, and to raise them as Jews.

This will mean that a Jewish couple may use birth control at various points in their child-bearing years as part of their family planning. Further, in accordance with Jewish law and previous CJLS rulings, the woman must arrange to abort a fetus that is causing imminent danger to her, and she may arrange to abort it if she will be at greater risk than is normal in pregnancy (e.g., if she has diabetes), if the fetus poses a grave risk to her mental health, or if the fetus will suffer from a significant genetic disease.[4] . . .

The Number and Gender of Children

The Torah commands us to have children, but it does not specify the number that we are to have. The Rabbis debated this question in the

Mishnah, and determined that the commandment of the Torah was fulfilled by having two children . . . :

> A man should not give up having sexual relations unless he has children. The House of Shammai say, "Two boys." The House of Hillel say, "A boy and a girl, since it is said, 'Male and female God created them' (Genesis 5:2)."[5]

In the *Mishneh Torah*, Maimonides endorsed the position of Hillel and held that the command to have children requires producing a boy and a girl: "How many children must a man have to fulfill the command [to have children]? A boy and a girl."[6]

In the *Shulḥan Arukh*, R. Joseph Qaro agrees that having two children, specifically a boy and a girl, is required, and he adds a further requirement that to fulfill the commandment both children must themselves be able to procreate: "When a person has a male and a female, he has fulfilled the command to 'be fruitful and multiply.' This applies when the son is not a eunuch and the daughter is not barren."[7]

. . . Rabbi Qaro [also] voices an age-old concern that the number of Jews in the world not diminish and that each couple replace itself: "If a male and a female were born to him and they died but they left children, he fulfilled the command to procreate. When does this apply? When the [grand]children were male and female and they came from male and female. Even if the male is descended from his daughter and the female from his son, he fulfilled the command to procreate. . . ."

A family with a boy and a girl would literally replace the father and mother in the world. However the *Shulhan Arukah* suggests that when one views the number of males and females over a generation or two, the number of males and females will probably balance. Based on this broader view it is the number of children, two, that is the key. With the passage of a generation or two, the children of this marriage together with the children of other marriages will statistically reproduce and approximately balance the number of males and females needed to populate the world.[8] Knowing even more now about the statistical probabilities of producing children of both genders in the general population, and wanting to express in law that we cherish each and every Jew, regardless of gender, we rule that the gender of the children need not be a consideration; rather, a young couple ready to start a family should seek to have at least two children.[9]

More Than Two Children?

Although the minimum number to fulfill the obligation to reproduce is two, the tradition encourages couples to have larger numbers, and Jewish history made it necessary to go beyond the acceptable minimum. Thus the Talmud (B. *Yevamot* 62b) asserts that a man who has had two children should continue to have as many children as he can. It bases this on two verses, Isaiah 45:18 ("Not for void did God create the world, but for habitation [*lashevet*]") and Ecclesiastes 11:6 ("In the morning sow your seed, and in the evening [*la'erev*] do not withhold your hand," where "morning" is understood to refer to a person's youth and "evening" to a person's older years). Maimonides later codifies this as law: "Even after a person has fulfilled the [biblical] command to 'be fruitful and multiply,' he is still commanded by the Sages 'to be fruitful and multiply' all the time that he has the strength, for one who adds a soul to Israel is as though he built a whole world."[10]

Why did encouraging the birth of as many Jewish children as possible become the dominant view in the Halakhah? Rabbi Robert Gordis helps us understand the reason the Halakhah developed in this direction. "... The answer lies in the history of the Jewish people, for whom the Middle Ages lasted from the sixth to the eighteenth century and beyond. Over and above the natural calamities of famine and disease to which medieval men generally were exposed, Jews suffered decimation through frequent and violent expulsions, massacres, and forced conversions."[11] ...

The Situation Today

The world Jewish community has not recovered numerically from the devastating losses during the Nazi era. There were over 18 million Jews in the world before World War II, we lost six million in the Holocaust, and now, counting everyone who identifies as a Jew, we are between 13 and 14 million. ...

The Jewish population of the United States is estimated to be around

5.5 million. Despite the influx in the past 50 years of at least a half-million Jewish immigrants, that number has remained static because Jews living here are not reproducing themselves. Furthermore, the median age of Jews is approximately seven years older than other Americans, and at least half of all marriages involving a Jew are to non-Jews, with few of the resulting children being raised as Jews. Among all segments of the American population, moreover, Jews have the fewest number of siblings, the smallest household size, and the second lowest number of children under eighteen at home. Jewish women marry later and are therefore less fertile than their gentile counterparts. Jewish families have fewer children than needed to replace themselves.[12]

In part, this can be explained by the high rates of achievement in education and jobs among Jewish men and women, who spend more time than most other subsets of the American population in universities and then in advancing their careers before marrying and trying to have children. . . .

If current trends continue, [the demographic effect] will be more pronounced as time goes by. The total Jewish population of the United States will drop in numbers and in influence. . . . There will also be a drop in the number of Jewish children who will attend Jewish schools, camps and other institutions for the young, fewer Jews to belong to and to attend synagogues, and fewer Jews to engage in the acts of *tikkun olam* (fixing the world) that our tradition demands.[13] . . . Substantial education is necessary to transform a child into a learned and practicing Jew, but one cannot educate someone who is not there. Thus *both* higher reproductive rates *and* deeper and wider Jewish educational efforts are necessary for Judaism and the Jewish people to survive, let alone thrive.

The Present Challenge

. . . Today the challenge is one of seduction into the general, secular culture through assimilation, intermarriage, and a commitment to work over family. . . . How shall we meet this challenge?

Upholding the legal norm imposed by the later Rabbis on the male member of the couple of unlimited reproduction is neither practical nor desirable. Nor does it seem right or wise to say to the female member of the family, "Give up higher education and a career to have a large family."

Rather, a reasonable course would be to encourage a fertile couple to have at least two children in compliance with the early Halakhah and at least one additional child to help the Jewish people replace those lost in the Holocaust and maintain its numbers in the modern world. The first two children that a couple produces are *mitzvah* children in the sense that they enable the couple (specifically, the man) to fulfill the command to procreate. We would like to suggest that the third child (and any further children) also be designated *"mitzvah* children," not only in the sense that classical Jewish law requires us to have as many children as we can, but also in the sense that having three or more children helps the Jewish people maintain its numbers and even regain a bit of the numbers we lost in the Holocaust. Another way to think of this is that the couple should have, if possible, at least one more child than they were planning for the sake of the Jewish people, with a minimum of three.[14]

Are there any limits to this? Yes, the limits that Jewish law's ongoing concern for health and safety would impose. Thus if the couple is already in their late thirties or beyond, when the probability of both infertility and genetic defects rises, they may decide, in consultation with their doctor, that they have had as many children as it is safe for them to have. . . . On the other hand, if they are young and healthy enough to have more . . . children, then any further children would also be *mitzvah* children. . . . Even then, concerns for the physical and psychological health of the parents (especially the woman) and the other children should play an important role in determining the limit of the number of children a couple should have. The practice in some parts of the Orthodox community of having ten or twelve children is clearly done in violation of these concerns. . . .

Encourage Larger Families

In accord with the Rabbinical Assembly's *Rabbinic Letter on Intimate Relations,* the Jewish community's interest in enabling Jewish young people to find Jewish mates "requires energetic communal planning and action to help Jews meet each other when college will no longer provide a convenient place for that to happen."[15] So, for example, synagogues and other Jewish institutions might fund the efforts of the young Jews in their midst to meet through online Jewish dating services, and they may and should create social, intellectual, religious, and social action programs specifically designated for that age group, not only for the value of the programs themselves, but also so that young people have a comfortable venue in which to meet each other.

Every rabbi who meets with a young couple should include in premarital counselling a discussion of family planning that warns the couple not to wait too long to begin having children to avoid problems of infertility as much as possible and that stresses that having a third child or more is a *mitzvah* that each fertile couple should feel responsible to fulfill.

It is also a responsibility of grandparents, the synagogue, and the Jewish community to ease the financial cost of raising Jewish children and educating them Jewishly.[16] Grandparents, who often have more discretionary income than young couples do, should understand that it is their halakhic duty to contribute to the Jewish education of their grandchildren: As the Rabbis taught: "And you shall teach your children (Deuteronomy 11:19), from this I know only [that you should teach] your children. How do I know [that you should teach] your children's children? Because the Torah says: And you shall inform your children and your children's children" (Deuteronomy 4:9).[17]

Indeed, grandparents should do this not only as their Jewish legal obligation, but as their distinct privilege and an act of love. If they live close by, grandparents should also help with child care and babysitting, not only as a duty but as a joy.

Keeping the cost of tuition reasonable in Jewish nursery schools, in Hebrew schools, and in Jewish day schools is also an obligation of our synagogues and of our community federations. Raising funds for scholarships to help young families send their children to Jewish schools and to Jewish camps is a critical part of reversing our diminishing birthrate, for couples will produce more than two children and educate them in Judaism only if they can manage financially to do that.[18] Several Jewish communities (e.g., Spokane and Seattle, Washington) have undertaken to do just that, and others should follow their example.

Furthermore, many of us live far away from our extended families, and it is difficult to raise children in an isolated family unit. To ease the burden on young parents and to encourage them to have three or more children, Jewish institutions should provide work environments with flexible hours for their employees, day care options, reasonable school schedules that do not leave parents without day care for any more days during the school year than absolutely necessary, and volunteer networks to help with babysitting and day care. All of these are all the more necessary for the many single parents in our midst. . . .

Adopting children, converting them to Judaism, if necessary, and raising them as Jews helps in this effort as well. . . .

Rulings

1) Every couple who can produce children is commanded to have at least two children. If the couple is infertile, they are no longer bound by this commandment, but may explore alternative ways to have children such as adoption or assisted reproductive techniques.

2) The gender of the children is not a consideration in the fulfillment of this commandment because over time the number of boys and girls will balance out in the Jewish population.

3) Although the Jewish legal duty to produce at least two children technically applies to men alone, both men and women should see procreation as their duty (for men their Jewish legal duty, and for both men and women their moral duty to the Jewish people) and should participate together in the decision of how many children the couple will have beyond the minimum of two set by Jewish law.

4) Rabbis should discuss the desirability of having more than two children with young couples as part of pre-marital counseling and in other settings. They should inform them that every couple who has a third child or more, whether through sexual intercourse, any of the artificial reproductive techniques, or adoption, may rightly feel that such children are *mitzvah* children not only in the sense that they fulfill the Jewish legal duty to have as many children as one can, but also in the sense that they have done a good deed in contributing, beyond replacement of themselves, to ensuring the future of Judaism and the Jewish people. The limit of this good deed—this *mitzvah* in this second sense—is the number of children that it is physically and psychologically safe for the couple (especially the woman) and the other children to have.

5) Jewish institutions should take steps to encourage young adult Jews to have three or more children. They can do that through methods such as these: funding and programs to enable young Jewish singles to meet a Jewish mate; flexible work schedules for the institution's own employees who are parents of young children; pricing policies that award tuition relief for families with multiple children; day care options; school schedules that do not leave parents without day care for any more days during the school year than absolutely necessary; and volunteer networks to help with babysitting and day care.

Responsa on Birth Surrogates

What is the Conservative movement's response to couples who cannot have a child on their own and therefore employ a female "birth surrogate" to carry their child?

In some instances, when the woman cannot produce viable eggs, the couple will hire a woman whose viable eggs can be inseminated with the man's sperm. This is called "traditional" surrogacy because it has been used ever since Sarah had Abraham have sexual intercourse with her handmaid, Hagar, to produce a child (Genesis 16:1–4). In addition, both Rachel (Genesis 30:1–7) and Leah (Genesis 30:9–13) used this technique in hopes of producing children to win the love of their husband, Jacob.

In modern times, however, most traditional surrogates are inseminated not through sexual intercourse with a man who is not their husband but rather through techniques of artificial insemination. In these cases, because surrogate women supply the egg, they are now more commonly called "ovum surrogates."

Sometimes, though, both the man and the woman can produce viable sperm and eggs, but something else prevents the woman from carrying the baby. In such instances, the couple's gametes (sperm and egg) are joined together in a petri dish, and the resulting embryos are implanted artificially in the birth surrogate, who carries the baby (babies) to term. With the exception of some mitochondrial DNA, all of the baby's biological makeup then comes from the couple. This is called "gestational surrogacy," because the woman carries ("gestates") the baby but does not contribute an ovum to create it.

The CJLS approved two responsa on the use of birth surrogates, one by Rabbi Elie Spitz and the second by Rabbi Aaron Mackler, on September 17, 1997. Rabbi Spitz is more sanguine about using birth surrogates, but Rabbi Mackler permits their use when a couple has no other reproductive choice. Both insist on precautions to protect the welfare of the birth surrogate, the child that results, and any of the surrogate's own children. Together, the two rabbis wrote the following summary of where they agree and disagree. To read the rabbis' full paper explaining their commonalities and differences in approach to this issue, see http://www.rabbinicalassembly .org/sites/default/files/public/halakhah/teshuvot/19912000/macklerspitz _surrogates.pdf. To read Rabbi Spitz's full responsum, see http://www .rabbinicalassembly.org/sites/default/files/public/halakhah/teshuvot /19912000/spitz_surrogate.pdf. For Rabbi Mackler's full responsum, see http://www.rabbinicalassembly.org/sites/default/files/public/halakhah /teshuvot/19912000/mackler_surrogate.pdf.

Overview

The practice of surrogacy involves powerful and sometimes conflicting Jewish concerns, including the value of procreation, respect for persons, and concern for the well-being of all of the vulnerable people involved. The Rabbinical Assembly's Committee on Jewish Law and Standards has approved two different papers on this sensitive subject, by Rabbis Aaron L. Mackler and Elie Kaplan Spitz. Both agree that, on one hand, traditional Jewish law does not mandate an absolute prohibition of surrogacy in all cases. On the other hand, surrogacy entails serious potential problems that would make it inappropriate in at least some cases. The two papers differ, however, both in their general evaluation of surrogacy and on some more particular points.

General Evaluation

For Rabbi Spitz, the great benefit of providing a child to an infertile couple is decisive. Concerns with avoiding exploitation of the surrogate, and harm to children born of the procedure, are real but manageable. These must be addressed by couples considering surrogacy, and ideally would be dealt with at the policy level by civil legislation. At the same time, the data of the last fifteen years indicate that problems as a result of these risks occur only in a small number of cases, and that the vast majority of surrogacies have resulted in offering the couple the joy of parenthood without harming or exploiting the surrogate or others. "From a Jewish perspective, it would be wrong to outlaw a procedure that has the potential to help so many couples overcome infertility and that works smoothly in the overwhelming majority of cases."

Rabbi Mackler expresses greater concern with potential harms and exploitation. There is a danger of treating people as commodities, and in some extreme cases, contracting/intended parents have sought to refuse custody of a child born with birth defects or of the undesired gender. When the surrogate has other children, those children face the potential psychological harm of seeing their mother go through pregnancy and give birth to a child who is given to others. The risk of exploitation of surrogates is real as well. While such harms have been documented in some cases, their extent is debated and difficult to ascertain precisely. Still, these have been enough to lead secular groups such as the Ethics Committee of the American Fertility Society, which generally supports reproductive technologies, to express "serious ethical reservations," and "not to recommend widespread clinical application of clinical surrogate motherhood at this time." From a Jewish perspective, "surrogacy cannot be halakhically recommended, and in at least most cases would be forbidden by Jewish law and ethics."

Particular Guidelines

Whether surrogacy agreements might be appropriate in most cases or only in exceptional cases, both rabbis agree on some important guidelines:

1. Couples contemplating the use of a surrogate should consider the halakhic and personal concerns involved, receive thorough counseling, and seriously investigate alternatives, including adoption. Either member of the couple would be fully justified in a decision not to proceed with surrogacy, and such refusal must be fully respected.

2. The surrogate should be protected from pressure to continue pregnancy when she judges abortion to be required to avoid serious threat to her health, and conversely she should be protected from pressure to abort.

3. In the formulation of surrogacy agreements and all actions taken with regard to surrogacy, greatest concern must be given to the well-being and rights of the child to be born of the procedure, as well as any other children who might be affected. Concern must be given to avoid exploitation of other vulnerable parties, including the surrogate, as well.

4. Both Rabbi Spitz and Rabbi Mackler agree that a surrogate may receive reimbursement for her expenses and that any money the surrogate receives cannot be contingent on her giving up custody of the child. For Rabbi Spitz, it is appropriate that a surrogate be paid a reasonable sum for her services, which is separate and distinct from payment for a child. This payment is compensation for time engaged in the medical, psychological, and legal procedures; physical restrictions due to pregnancy; medical risk; and the use of her womb. The permissibility of payment is rooted in the reality that not everyone has a volunteer family member or friend to assist in the much wanted blessing of a child. For Rabbi Mackler, any payment to a surrogate mother beyond reimbursement of expenses would be discouraged as dangerously close to babyselling, or minimally the selling and purchase of parental relationships, which are inconsistent with halakhah.

5. Both Rabbi Spitz and Rabbi Mackler address the possibility of a dispute arising over the custody of the child. . . . For Rabbi Spitz, during the pregnancy a surrogate has the right to withdraw from the agreement, an extension of her freedom of choice. Upon birth to a gestational surrogate the surrogate should have no right to challenge custody. In contrast, an ovum surrogate may assert her maternal rights, but the burden of proof is on her to show cause why the original intent should not be honored. For Rabbi Mackler, the surrogate mother, as gestational and birth mother, is halakhically recognized as mother, and should have the right to contest the assumption of custody by the intended parents (one of whom would be halakhically recognized as the child's father). This right would be held by both ovum surrogates

and gestational surrogates. Custody of the child, in these as in other cases, should be determined on the basis of the child's best interest, as required by Jewish ethical values as well as halakhic precedent. The views of Rabbi Spitz and Rabbi Mackler on this matter are not necessarily offered as decisive halakhic rulings, however, and both rabbis recognize that in practice custody likely would be determined by general civil law.

6. The sole position approved by the Committee on Jewish Law and Standards is that the religious status of a child follows that of the gestational/birth mother, in cases involving surrogacy and in all other cases. Children born to a non-Jewish surrogate (whether a gestational or ovum surrogate) would require conversion to be halakhically recognized as Jewish. Rabbis should display personal and pastoral sensitivity in such cases. Any individuals considering surrogacy, as well as other interested readers, are strongly advised to read the full papers.

Responsum on Abortion

Conservative Judaism's stance on abortion is in between that of the United States Supreme Court's 1973 *Roe v. Wade* decision and the Roman Catholic Church's view. In *Roe*, the Supreme Court asserted that until the fetus is viable outside the womb, it is part of its mother, and therefore it is totally within that mother's capacity to decide whether or not to abort the fetus as a function of the Constitutional right of privacy. On the other end of the spectrum, the Roman Catholic Church holds that as soon as an egg is fertilized, it is a full human being—even if it is fertilized in a petri dish and never inserted into a woman's uterus for gestation, thereby never having the chance to become a human being. Destruction of any fertilized egg cell is therefore considered murder.

The Jewish position is not only in between these two extremes but also much more nuanced. Based on the verses in Exodus 21:22–25 requiring monetary compensation for destroying a fetus but "life for life, eye for an eye" for harming the mother, the Rabbis saw a fetus as less than a full human being. Most likely based on their witnessing miscarriages, the

Rabbis deemed a fetus "merely liquid" (*b. Yevamot* 69b) during the first forty days of gestation and "the thigh of its mother" (*b. Yevamot* 78a) thereafter.

But because in Judaism our bodies belong to God, and therefore men and women may not intentionally harm any part of themselves, Jewish law generally forbids abortion — not as an act of murder but rather as an act of self-harm. A clear exception arises when the mother's life or health is at stake, at which point abortion is not only permitted but required — even if it is at the moment of birth.

Although Jewish law therefore usually forbids abortion but requires it if the mother's life or health is at stake, there are cases where abortion is permitted but not required. This would apply if the risks to the woman are greater than those normally incurred in pregnancy (e.g., if she has diabetes) or if the fetus has a lethal or devastating genetic problem.

Conservative rabbis disagree, however, as to the severity of risk needed to justify an abortion. Furthermore, although Conservative rabbis as a group also accept mental health justifications for aborting a fetus, rabbis disagree on what psychological issues warrant an abortion and whether the father's mental health should also be taken into account, especially in cases where the fetus is abnormal. (See the several CJLS rulings spanning the spectrum by Rabbis David Feldman, Robert Gordis, Kassel Abelson, and Isaac Klein cited in the endnotes.)[19]

Nonetheless, the CJLS adopted a consensus statement by Rabbis Ben Zion Bokser and Kassel Abelson, "A Statement on the Permissibility of Abortion" (reproduced here in its entirety), on November 21, 1983, by a vote of 16-1-1, sixteen in favor, one against, and one abstention. The statement is also available online: http://www.rabbinicalassembly.org/sites/default/files/public/halakhah/teshuvot/20012004/07.pdf.

A Statement on the Permissibility of Abortion

Jewish tradition is sensitive to the sanctity of life, and does not permit abortion on demand. However, it sanctions abortion under some circumstances because it does not regard the fetus as an autonomous person. This is based partly on the Bible (Exodus 21:22–23), which prescribes monetary damages where a person injures a pregnant woman, causing a miscarriage. The Mishnah (Ohalot 7:6) explicitly indicates that one is to abort a fetus if the continuation of pregnancy might imperil the life of the mother. Later authorities have differed as to how far we might go in defining the peril to the mother in order to justify an abortion. The Rabbinical Assembly Committee on Jewish Law and Standards takes the view that an abortion is justifiable if a continuation of pregnancy might cause the mother severe physical or psychological harm, or when the fetus is judged by competent medical opinion as severely defective. The fetus is a life in the process of development, and the decision to abort it should never be taken lightly. Before reaching her final decision, the mother should consult with the father, other members of her family, her physician, her spiritual leader, and any other person who can help her in assessing the many grave legal and moral issues involved.

Responsum on Stem Cell Research and Cloning

Determining when stem cell research and cloning may be appropriate requires some understanding of terms and procedures. Stem cells are cells that can change into several different kinds of more specialized cells that stem from them. Considered "undifferentiated" (i.e., not yet specifically one kind of cell), some kinds of stem cells can produce any kind of cell in the human body, while other types of stem cells can produce only certain kinds of cells.

All living creatures begin as one cell. In people this is the fertilized human egg, just after the sperm cell has entered the ovum.

The most flexible stem cells are known as "embryonic stem (ES) cells," as they appear in the early embryo, formed five to eight days after a sperm and an egg combine. These one hundred to two hundred cells, produced in the first few days after fertilization, ultimately mature into every kind of cell in the complex human organism. That is, they "differentiate"— specialize—into specific kinds of cells (heart, brain, lung, etc.), each cell group doing its part to enable the human body to function.

At about five days of gestation, the form we call an early embryo looks like a small circle (the perimeter of which, later in pregnancy, becomes the placenta). Together, the clump of cells inside that circle is known as the "inner cell mass." The large circle that surrounds it, together with the inner cell mass inside it, is called a "blastocyst," which is also the embryo's name at this stage.

Extracting the inner cells for embryonic stem cell research destroys the blastocyst. When those extracted cells are placed in chemical solutions that facilitate their development, they are called "human embryonic stem cells in culture." As of this writing, sixteen years after the first human embryonic stem cells were cultivated, these cells are still replicating, which is why they are sometimes called "immortal" cell lines.

Both children and adults have what are called "somatic stem cells," from the Greek word *soma*, meaning "body." That is, they come from the body of a living, fully developed person. Unlike embryonic stem cells, somatic cells can change only into a few kinds of cells; for example, they are used to renew our blood, skin, and hair throughout our lives. They are, however, more differentiated than embryonic stem cells and therefore unable to produce other types of cells. So, for example, skin stem cells can produce all three kinds of skin cells but not cells for any other part of the body unless they are "wound back" to their undifferentiated state (a procedure that scientists are trying out). Somatic stem cells are also not immortal; they lose their ability to produce new cells after a period of time. In other words, somatic stem cells are less pliable and less durable than embryonic stem cells. Still, they have two advantages that support continued advancement in somatic stem cell research: (1) they do not raise moral questions about harming the source of the cells, because taking a few skin or blood cells from a person does not significantly injure that person, in contrast to destroying a blastocyst; and (2) using a person's somatic cells to cure his or her own disease would free that person from having to take immunosuppressive drugs for the rest of his or her life, since his or her immune system would not react to the new cells as foreign and attack them.

Stem cell research can also be performed with embryonic germ (EG) cells (i.e., cells taken from the ovaries or testes of aborted fetuses). This, however, involves at least some sticky questions: (1) When is an abortion acceptable? (2) Even if the fetus is aborted for what Jewish law considers an unacceptable reason (at least according to some interpretations), may it be used to advance medicine in curing diseases? This raises a more general question: (3) May one use parts of any dead body, even for the sake of developing cures for diseases?

Biologists have long sought to understand how a single cell created from a sperm and egg can create a complex human being. How does the DNA program in the nucleus interact and signal the cell to duplicate and differentiate? How does the small, microscopic mass of identical cells produced approximately five days after fertilization ultimately form a human fetus?[20] And if each of these cells in that early embryo has the capacity to develop into all cells of the human body, can scientists use them to create new cells that repair damaged cells and heal disease?

Furthermore, at some point stem cells turn off, so that most of us have two legs, not five. If scientists understood how these cells "decide" to turn off, they might be able to apply the discovery to curing cancer, because cancer cells reproduce uncontrollably.

In essence, through stem cell research, scientists hope to learn how to replace damaged cells (from a stroke, heart attack, burn, spinal cord injury, and the like), to replace full organs (such as kidneys), and potentially to find a cure for cancer. If stem cell research can accomplish even some of these goals, it would be as dramatic a breakthrough in curing disease as antibiotics were in the mid-twentieth century.

To engage in research on embryonic stem cells or to use them to cure diseases, however, means destroying the blastocyst. Whether that is permissible depends on the status of the fetus at five or six days of gestation. The same range of views on the status of the fetus with regard to abortion—from Roe v. Wade on one end to Roman Catholics on the other—affects the discussion of embryonic stem cell research as well.

In his responsum on Stem Cell Research (excerpted here), Rabbi Elliot N. Dorff asked two questions: (1) May embryonic stem cells from frozen embryos originally created for purposes of procreation or embryonic germ cells from aborted fetuses be used for research? (2) May embryonic stem cells from embryos created specifically for research, either by combining donated sperm and eggs in a petri dish or by cloning, be used for research? On March 13, 2002, the CJLS approved his response to question 1 by a vote of fifteen in favor and one abstention (15–0–1) and to question 2 by fourteen in favor, one against, and one abstention (14–1–1). For the full responsum, see http://www.rabbinicalassembly.org/sites/default/files /public/halakhah/teshuvot/19912000/dorff_stemcell.pdf.

General Summary

1. We both may and should take the steps necessary to advance stem cell research and its applications in an effort to take advantage of its great potential for human healing . . . for two reasons: First, we have a duty to heal and, as a corollary to that, to develop our means to heal; and second, genetic materials, including embryos, lack the status of a person or even part of a person (e.g., a thigh): within the womb, the Talmud declares that before forty days of gestation they are "simply water," and outside the womb they are certainly not any more to be protected than pre-embryos and embryos are within the womb. Embryos and even gametes themselves deserve our respect, for they are the materials that have the potential of creating human beings, but that status is outweighed by the duty to seek to cure.

2. In accordance with Jewish law, stem cells may be procured from all of the following sources, but the following list ranks sources from the most desirable to the least desirable:

   a. Aborted fetuses.

   b. Frozen embryos originally created for overcoming infertility that the couple has now decided to discard but has instead agreed to donate for stem cell research.

   In both (a) and (b), researchers are not responsible for the abortion itself or for creating the frozen embryos, and they are using materials that would otherwise just be discarded, but (a) avoids legal fights over frozen embryos as well as the frequent unwillingness of couples to donate their frozen embryos. Still, it may be the case that more can be done with ES cells than with EG cells because the latter have already differentiated into reproductive cells. . . . If ES cells indeed turn out to be more malleable, then the order of these two options may be reversed, or it may be that both sources are equally acceptable, each with its advantages and disadvantages.

c. A cell taken from an embryo and grown independently. This technique would avoid the extra dangers to the woman involved in the methods listed in (d) below, but it does not have the advantage of using materials that would otherwise be discarded, as in (a) and (b), and it has not yet proven to be successful in producing stem cells.

d. Embryos created specifically for medical research by combining sperm and eggs donated for that purpose, by cloning (SCNT), or by parthenogenesis. These are the least desirable because of the increased danger to the woman donating her eggs, but they are permissible sources of stem cells if the woman donates eggs for this purpose only once or twice after being prescreened to insure that it is safe for her to do this. A man does not violate any laws by masturbating to contribute to stem cell research. The use of cloning poses the additional risks raised by our inexperience with the technique and our current inability to assure good results, but if and when cloning technology improves, cloning will become more desirable than any of the other methods to produce stem cells because the patient's immune system will not reject the therapy taken from his/her own tissues and will not need to be subjected to immunosuppressive drugs for the rest of his/her life.

3. We should also pursue healing methods that can be developed from adult stem cells, but such efforts must not replace nor even slow down our attempts to develop healing methods from embryonic stem cells, for the latter hold out much more promise than the former.

4. We should pursue this research, though, with restrictions to enable access to its applications to all who need it.

5. This responsum deals only with stem cell research conducted for purposes of curing diseases. Applications of this or any other technique to the goal of enhancement must be considered in another paper.

Answer to Question 1

After scientists have accomplished all that they can toward a given goal through animal experiments, (1) human embryonic germ cells from aborted fetuses and embryonic stem cells from (2) frozen human embryos originally created for purposes of procreation not only may, but should be aggressively used for research into creating cures for a number of human ailments. Toward that end, just as we need to educate our laity about the importance of organ donation, so too we should educate them to know that those who have aborted a fetus or created frozen embryos that they are not going to use should donate such materials to scientists pursuing stem cell research. As difficult as the distinction between therapy and enhancement is to define, and as much as the line may change over time, this responsum deals only with stem cell research for purposes of therapy; another paper is required to consider the possible use of this and other techniques for purposes of enhancement.

Answer to Question 2

Embryonic stem cells from embryos created specifically for research, either by (3) combining donated sperm and eggs in a petri dish, (4) by cloning, or (5) by extracting a cell from an early embryo, may also be used for research to provide therapies for diseases, but only if the woman donating the eggs does so only once or twice and is pre-screened to avoid undue risks to her own health.

Responsa on End-of-Life Care

In December 1990 the CJLS approved two rabbinical rulings on end-of-life care. Both rulings used different legal categories to address the relevant issues and yet agreed on most (but not all) of the policies to be followed in practice.

Rabbi Avram Israel Reisner utilized the Jewish legal category of *goses*, a moribund person, defined in a post-talmudic work as "like a flickering candle"; just as moving the candle may extinguish it, so too one may not even move a *goses* for fear that doing so will bring about the patient's death. He expanded this category to encompass anyone expected to die within a year. For the full responsum, see http://www.rabbinicalassembly.org /sites/default/files/public/halakhah/teshuvot/19861990/reisner_care.pdf.

In contrast, Rabbi Elliot Dorff used the Jewish legal category of *terayfah*, a person with an incurable, lethal disease. For the full responsum, see http://www.rabbinicalassembly.org/sites/default/files/public/halakhah /teshuvot/19861990/dorff_care.pdf.

Each category offers advantages and disadvantages when it comes to considering if seriously ill patients who are unlikely to recover should be sustained by technological innovations such as heart-lung machines, kidney dialysis machines, and artificial nutrition and hydration. Neither category fits exactly, in large part because of what medicine has taught us about the dying process since those categories were created in the Talmud.

An important dispute between the two rabbis concerns the status of artificial nutrition and hydration—that is, nutrients and liquids administered through tubes to patients who can no longer eat on their own. To Reisner, this intervention is the functional equivalent of the food and liquids we all need to survive, and so intubations (inserting tubes into the patient) to provide artificial nutrition and hydration (in contrast to medicines or machines) must always be done and may never be withdrawn until death.

To Dorff, in contrast, artificial nutrition and hydration constitute medicine because they do not enter the body the usual way and they lack the typical taste, temperature, texture, and other characteristics of food and liquids. Furthermore, intubating likely involves discomfort and often involves risks. Therefore, for Dorff, decisions to intubate and, if done, to extubate (remove the tubes) must be decided on the basis of the patient's best interests, as determined by his or her own stated will (if the patient is mentally competent to express this), advance directive, or, lacking those, a surrogate decision maker.

Dorff and Reisner also disagreed on the amount of morphine that may be used to quell pain and how to treat a person in a vegetative state.

In the end, though, Reisner and Dorff agreed on most end-of-life practices. They concurred, for example, that medicines and machines may be withheld or withdrawn if they are not benefitting the patient. They also agreed that hospice care is permissible; that is, when there is no reasonable hope for a cure, we should accept that diagnosis rather than subject the person to the pain and suffering of trying extraordinary and unproved methods to keep the body alive. Then the goal of medicine should be to keep the person physically and psychologically comfortable.

After the CJLS approved both rulings, Reisner summarized their differences in a paper entitled "Mai Beinaihu: What Is the Practical Difference between Them," excerpted here and available at http://www .rabbinicalassembly.org/sites/default/files/public/halakhah/teshuvot /19861990/maibeinaihu.pdf. In addition, Rabbi Aaron Mackler subsequently created an Advance Directive for Health Care, based on those two rulings; see http://www.rabbinicalassembly.org/sites/default/files /public/halakhah/teshuvot/19861990/mackler_care.pdf.

What Is the Practical Difference?

In the spirit of the Talmudic interrogative "mai beinaihu?" ("What is the practical difference?"), the Subcommittee on Biomedical Ethics of the CJLS undertook a careful consideration of the practical differences of law that remain between the presentations of Rabbi Reisner and Rabbi Dorff. It was felt that, although the legal reasoning differs strongly, both papers tend toward a consensus of treatment in most areas, which would perhaps obviate the need to fight it out on theoretical grounds. The following are our conclusions:

The primary difference in theory between the positions of Rabbi Reisner and Rabbi Dorff may be summarized by their key phrases, "neither the quality of life nor its likely short duration are admitted as mitigating circumstances" [Rabbi Reisner] as against Rabbi Dorff, "The fetus and the terayfah are both cases of human beings whose blood is indeed judged to be 'less red' than that of viable people." Rabbi Reisner insists on the inviolability of the principle of protecting even hayyei sha'ah, life of short duration, whereas Rabbi Dorff maintains that that principle is made moot by the status of terayfah and the need to consider the patient's best interests (avdinan l'tovato). Rabbi Dorff might center his objection to Rabbi Reisner's paper in the comment that it is too literalist and not sufficiently alert to the real emotional needs of patients and their families. Rabbi Reisner might frame his objection to Rabbi Dorff's paper in the comment that it arrives at its sensitivity to patients by degrading the status of their God-given lives, which we are constrained not to do.

Nevertheless, both agree in principle and practice on the large area of autonomy that the patient holds with regard to his or her own treatment where risk and prognostic uncertainty exist, as they almost always do. Thus both would allow patients to rule certain treatment options off limits, to choose hospice care as a treatment option, [and] to draft advance directive documents but only within the parameters established to be in accord with Jewish law. Both permit withdrawal of mechanical life support where unsupported life has been shown to be impossible, under the primary precedent of removing impediments to the death of a goses. Both are in agreement concerning the use of CPR [cardiopulmonary resuscitation] and DNR [do not resuscitate] orders, though for fundamentally different reasons. They agree that CPR need not be done where it is unlikely to succeed in restoring the patient to a meaningfully healthy life. That is perforce a medical judgment call. It is not clear that they would adjudge all cases equally, but on a case-by-case basis this judgment will fall neither to Rabbi Dorff nor to Rabbi Reisner, but to the family, attending physician, and any member of the clergy advising them.

[As explained below,] the points on which they differ are few, but significant.

Medication and Artificial Nutrition/Hydration to Treat a Terminally Ill Patient

Rabbi Dorff would permit withholding or withdrawing such medication, since the patient is categorized as a terayfah, whose life does not require our full protection. Rabbi Dorff would assimilate artificial nutrition/hydration to medication in such a case.

Rabbi Reisner would prohibit withholding medication, nutrition, or hydration as long as they are believed to be beneficial, since we are obligated to maintain even "hayyei sha'ah" (N.B. [nota bene, that is, note well] and as long as the patient has not ruled out said treatment in a valid treatment directive).

The Patient in a Persistent Vegetative State

Rabbi Dorff would permit withholding/withdrawal of artificial nutrition and hydration, viewing this patient, like the terayfah, as an impaired life (N.B. after due tests and time, of course).

Rabbi Reisner finds no grounds for denying even this limited life, and therefore requires full maintenance pending God's own determination.

Pain Relief

Both Rabbis Dorff and Reisner regard treatment for pain as medical treatment to be pursued. They differ on the question of "double effect"—of whether pain medication must be capped at that point at which its probable effect would be to hasten the patient's death.

Rabbi Dorff argues that the intent to alleviate pain controls, Rabbi Reisner that the probable result controls. Although they do not argue this point clearly in terms of the primary premises of their papers, it appears clear that Rabbi Reisner's concern for "hayyei sha'ah" and Rabbi Dorff's vacating of that principle inform their rulings here.

Both Rabbis Dorff and Reisner point out, however, that the best medicine available today should permit sufficient relief of pain without approaching this dilemma; both hope that it quickly recedes to a footnote about antiquated medical ethical problems. . . .

In Summary

We believe both [points of view] represent cogent, Conservative responses to the demands of God's Torah and our times, and commend them, as such, to the attention of the full Committee on Jewish Law and Standards.

Responsum on the Distribution of Health Care

Canada, Israel, and most European nations hold their governments responsible for providing health care for all citizens—and, sometimes, for noncitizen legal residents and even visitors. Inherent in this "single payer system," also known as "socialized medicine," are high government taxes (to pay for health care), less cutting-edge research and slower adoption of new medical procedures (both of which would increase the government's health care costs), and treatment delays for almost all procedures (except for routine or emergency care). As a result, wealthier citizens frequently take out private insurance, thereby creating a two-tier health care system. (Canada prohibits such additional insurance, so its wealthy residents generally expedite their care by crossing the U.S. border to get it.)

In contrast, the United States, grounded in an ethos of individual rights and responsibilities, has adopted government health care programs more slowly and reluctantly. Before World War II, most citizens paid for their own health care. After World War II, an increasing number of employers provided health care insurance to lure well-trained employees, eventually resulting in today's standard of employer-furnished health insurance.

In the mid-1960s President Lyndon Baines Johnson convinced Congress to approve Medicare, providing health care to people age sixty-five and older, and Medicaid, providing health care for people living below the poverty line. In 1993 President Bill Clinton and his wife, Hillary, attempted (unsuccessfully) to create a new health care system for everyone else.

The health care issue gained even more momentum in 2010 after Congress approved President Barack Obama's Affordable Care Act ("Obamacare") by the narrowest of margins. Quite a few states—almost all with Republican legislatures and governors—refused to take part in the program, thereby leaving it to the federal government to administer their states' program.

Obamacare also had to survive a number of court challenges, including three U.S. Supreme Court cases. One questioned whether it was constitutional for the government to mandate that every American citizen have health care insurance; the Court ruled, 5–4, that it was a valid exercise of the government's ability to tax. The second case, *Burwell v. Hobby Lobby Stores, Inc.*, asked whether the mandate to employers to provide contraception as part of health insurance applied to private companies whose owners objected to contraception on religious grounds; the Court ruled, again 5–4, that privately held companies whose owners objected to contraception on religious grounds were exempt from the law's mandate. The third case, again decided on a 5–4 split, determined that the language of the act that speaks of state health insurance exchanges nevertheless applies to those states that refuse to create such exchanges and that therefore, under the act, defer to the federal government to do so. Furthermore, the Republican-controlled House of Representatives has voted numerous times to repeal the Affordable Care Act altogether, and the Republican-controlled Congress in 2017, with a Republican president in office, is, as of this writing, trying to "repeal and replace" it.

In all these cases, Republicans maintain that the government should not take away citizens' right to refuse to buy health insurance and should not fine citizens who do not purchase insurance. Democrats, on the other hand, argue that citizens are all in this together, for if an uninsured citizen goes to a hospital emergency room, where treatment is much more expensive—and where that person's health issue might have been nipped in the bud much earlier with a routine doctor's visit—the U.S. taxpayers ultimately foot the escalated bill.

Rabbis Elliot N. Dorff and Aaron L. Mackler's responsum, "Responsibilities for the Provision of Health Care," began by asking three questions: (1) To what extent are individual patients and their family members responsible for providing health care? (2) To what extent are physicians and other health care providers responsible for providing health care? (3) What is the extent of the community's responsibilities to provide health care? In contemporary countries such as the United States and Canada, to what extent are these responsibilities of the Jewish community? Of the general society?

Until recently, most of these questions did not exist in Jewish law, because curative health care was both inexpensive and ineffective. Given considerable medical advances, however, health care costs have ballooned. Now, only the very rich can pay for long hospital stays as well as sophisticated procedures such as stem cell and organ transplants.

Seeking applicable precedents, Dorff and Mackler looked to sources in the tradition in which questions arose about how to distribute scarce resources. Discovering relevant models in the laws requiring Jewish communities to support the poor and redeem the captive, they then applied those laws to health care while taking due note of the similarities and differences inherent in the different contexts and time periods.

Rather than mandate a particular form of health care, the responsum establishes parameters of responsibilities for individuals, health care providers, and communities. The authors conclude that any system that fits within these parameters would fulfill the requirements of Jewish law.

On September 9, 1998, committee members voted to approve the responsum's introduction and part 1 by a vote of sixteen in favor and four abstaining (16–0–4). Part 2 passed by a vote of fourteen in favor and six abstaining (14–0–6), and part 3 by a vote of twelve in favor, one opposed, and seven abstaining (12–1–7). Excerpts of the conclusions follow; for the full responsum, see http://www.rabbinicalassembly.org/sites/default/files /public/halakhah/teshuvot/19912000/dorffmackler_care.pdf.

Conclusions

1. Jewish law requires that people be provided with needed health care, at least a "decent minimum" that preserves life and meets other basic needs, including some amount of preventive care. The responsibility to assure this provision is shared among individuals and families, physicians and other health care providers, and the community.

2. Individuals and family members have the responsibility to care for their own health, and the primary responsibility to pay (directly or through insurance) for health care needed by themselves or by family members. When they cannot do so, they may and should avail themselves of publicly funded programs to acquire the health care they need. In any case, one should seek to prevent illness rather than wait to cure an illness that has already occurred.

3. Physicians and other health care professionals must treat patients in case of emergency, and they have some responsibility more generally to make health care available to those who cannot afford their normal fees. At the same time, health care professionals legitimately may expect compensation for their efforts and expenses, and should be able to earn a living.

4. The community bears ultimate responsibility to assure provision of needed health care for individuals who cannot afford it, as a matter of justice as well as a specific halakhic obligation. The "community" that bears that responsibility in our day is the national society, through its government, health care institutions, insurance companies, and private enterprise. Jewish citizens should support (by lobbying and other means) general societal institutions that will fulfill this responsibility. The Jewish community, through its federations, synagogues, and other institutions, must assess whether and to what extent it should support hospitals and other forms of health care. It should balance that purpose against its commitment to other important Jewish needs, such as Jewish education and social services, in light of contemporary patterns of funding health care.

5. The guarantee of provision of needed health care does not extend to all treatment that is desired, or even all that might provide some benefit. Even needed treatment might be limited when it is so extraordinarily expensive that its provision would deprive other patients of needed care. Still, possible limits to interventions must be weighed against the value of human life and healing, and the injunction that a physician who fails to provide needed health care is considered as one who sheds blood.

Suggestions for Further Reading

Elliot N. Dorff. "Artificial Insemination, Egg Donation, and Adoption." http://www.rabbinicalassembly.org/sites/default/files/assets/public/halakhah/teshuvot/19912000/dorff_artificial.pdf.

———. *Matters of Life and Death: A Jewish Approach to Modern Medical Ethics.* Philadelphia: Jewish Publication Society, 1998.

Elliot N. Dorff and Louis E. Newman, eds. *Jewish Choices, Jewish Voices: Body.* Philadelphia: Jewish Publication Society, 2008.

Aaron L. Mackler. "In Vitro Fertilization." http://www.rabbinicalassembly.org/sites/default/files/assets/public/halakhah/teshuvot/19912000/mackler_ivf.pdf.

———, ed. *Life and Death Responsibilities in Jewish Biomedical Ethics.* New York: Finklestein Institute of the Jewish Theological Seminary of America, 2000.

Avram Israel Reisner. "Medical Ethics." In *The Observant Life: The Wisdom of Conservative Judaism for Contemporary Jews,* edited by Martin S. Cohen, 751–805. New York: Rabbinical Assembly, 2012.

CHAPTER EIGHT

Masa u'Mattan

Legal Rulings on Business Ethics

Jewish law gives Jews rules governing social and medical issues, such as the role of women in society (see chapter 6) and biomedical issues from the point of conception to end-of-life care (see chapter 7). Jewish laws also regulate criminal and civil behavior. The Torah's first law code, in fact, includes rules governing murder, assault, damage to property, negligence, bailments, loans, and court procedures (Exodus 21–23). Laws in subsequent chapters require honest weights and measures (Leviticus 19:34–36; Deuteronomy 25:13–16) and explicate other matters, such as the ethics of war (Deuteronomy 20–21), kidnapping (Deuteronomy 24:7), loan collection (Deuteronomy 24:10–13), and workers' rights (Deuteronomy 24:14–15). Jewish law, in other words, was intended to be a full-service legal system.

That said, practically speaking, ever since the destruction of the First Temple and Jewish Commonwealth in 586 BCE, Jews have almost always lived under the rule of non-Jewish governments. There have been only two exceptions to that reality: Jews living in Israel during the Hasmonean period (ca. 165–63 BCE) and Jews living in the modern State of Israel.

Still, even when beholden to other governments, Jewish law has, by and large, remained authoritative for Jews until modern times. Beginning with the Romans, most regimes allowed Jews to govern their own communities so long as they paid taxes to the government and provided men for the army when called upon to do so. Internally, then, Jews remained governed by Jewish laws and courts, even on some criminal matters.

There was, however, one unvarying exception to this rule: Jews' business transactions with non-Jews. Jews had to adopt the rules and customs established by the presiding government and marketplace. Thus, as early as the third century CE, Samuel announced the rule that in business matters, "The law of the land is the law," *dina d'malkhuta dina* (*b. Nedarim* 28a; *b. Gittin* 10b; *b. Bava Kamma* 113a; *b. Bava Batra* 54b–55a). (Whether the government's laws also governed Jews' business dealings with other Jews varied by time and place.)

The pattern of communal, internal rule by Jewish law changed with the Enlightenment. Seventeenth-century thinkers such as John Locke and Baruch Spinoza and eighteenth-century thinkers such as Jean-Jacques Rousseau and Claude Montesquieu made it clear that each person was to be treated legally as an individual, not as a member of a group within the nation. For Jews, who had endured centuries of persecution, in part owing to their inferior communal status, in which they were at best tolerated and second class, this was a major, welcome change. When this theory realized political expressions in Germany in the 1760s, in America in 1776, and in France in 1789, Jews found themselves, at least in principle, full citizens of their nations. (In actuality, full realization of this theory in most countries took several centuries to complete.)

To be treated as equal citizens of the realm, however, Jews had to pay a price, one perhaps best articulated by Napoleon. In 1806–7 he convened "the French Sanhedrin," a group of Jewish leaders, to respond to twelve questions:

1. Is it lawful for Jews to have more than one wife?
2. Is divorce allowed by the Jewish religion? Is divorce valid, although pronounced not by courts of justice but by virtue of laws in contradiction to the French code?
3. May a Jewess marry a Christian, or [may] a Jew [marry] a Christian woman? Or does Jewish law order that the Jews should only intermarry among themselves?

4. In the eyes of Jews, are Frenchmen not of the Jewish religion considered as brethren or as strangers?
5. What conduct does Jewish law prescribe toward Frenchmen not of the Jewish religion?
6. Do the Jews born in France, and treated by the law as French citizens, acknowledge France as their country? Are they bound to defend it? Are they bound to obey the laws and follow the directions of the civil code?
7. Who elects the rabbis?
8. What kind of police jurisdiction do the rabbis exercise over the Jews? What judicial power do they exercise over them?
9. Are the police jurisdiction of the rabbis and the forms of the election regulated by Jewish law, or are they only sanctioned by custom?
10. Are there professions from which the Jews are excluded by their law?
11. Does Jewish law forbid the Jews to take usury from their brethren?
12. Does it forbid, or does it allow, usury in dealings with strangers?[1]

The French Sanhedrin struggled to answer Napoleon's penetrating questions about whether Jews would assimilate into French society or insist on their separate status as Jews (questions many Jews continue to wrestle with to this day). One can see this struggle in their responses, in which they frankly bent Jewish law in a number of places in order to please Napoleon and benefit from the new status and rights he offered:

1. That, in conformity with the decree of R. Gershom ben Judah, polygamy is forbidden to the Israelites;
2. That divorce by the Jewish law is valid only after previous decision of the civil authorities;
3. That the religious act of marriage must be preceded by a civil contract;
4. That marriages contracted between Israelites and Christians are binding, although they cannot be celebrated with religious forms;
5. That every Israelite is religiously bound to consider his non-Jewish fellow citizens as brothers, and to aid, protect, and love them as though they were coreligionists;

6. That the Israelite is required to consider the land of his birth or adoption as his fatherland, and shall love and defend it when called upon;

7. That Judaism does not forbid any kind of handicraft or occupation;

8. That it is commendable for Israelites to engage in agriculture, manual labor, and the arts, as their ancestors in Palestine were wont to do;

9. That, finally, Israelites are forbidden to exact usury from Jew or Christian.

In their answers to questions 2 and 3, the Jewish communal representatives were inventing a wholly new requirement, because until the Enlightenment, marriage in Christian and Muslim countries was entirely a religious matter, with no state involvement whatsoever. That is why, for example, Henry VIII could not, as head of state, simply declare that his divorce from his first wife and his second and subsequent weddings and divorces were legally binding; instead, he had to create a whole new church, the Anglican Church, to authorize his divorces and weddings.

Contrary to the French Sanhedrin's answer to question 4, a marriage between a Jew and a non-Jew is not legally recognized in Jewish law. So in saying that interfaith marriages were "binding," the Jewish representatives could only have meant that they recognized that such marriages were binding in the laws of France.

Their answer to question 5 hides the fact that in Jewish law, Jews' obligations to their fellow Jews take precedence over their duties to non-Jews.[2] The classical Rabbis do say, however, that Jews also have the following duties to non-Jews: to visit them when they are sick, aid their poor, bury their dead, and comfort their mourners.[3] Here, the French Jewish leaders chose to overstate their duty to help the non-Jews of their nation and to conceal that the foremost recipients of their care would be other Jews.

Finally, the French Sanhedrin's answer to question 9 blatantly misstates Jewish law. The Torah and all subsequent developments of Jewish law through the Middle Ages forbid Jews to charge interest on loans to fellow Jews but allowed Jews to charge interest on loans to non-Jews. So if one wants to see the Sanhedrin's answer charitably, one could suppose they were saying that from now on, under the new status Jews were attaining, that part of Jewish law would not be used.

Two centuries later, Jews living in Western countries regularly take their disputes to civil venues of mediation, arbitration, or law and consider themselves bound by the government's civil and criminal law. This raises the question: Can Jewish law pertaining to business matters be of any benefit?

As you would imagine, the answer is yes. Given civil law's authority on such matters, though, rabbinical responsa in all modern Jewish movements on business issues are not intended to challenge or replace the laws of the land. Rather, they perform one or more of three functions: (1) show Jews how Jewish values may be realized within civil law; (2) give Jewish motivations for obeying civil laws on business matters beyond the fact that these constitute the law; and (3) augment the demands of civil law with Jewish sensitivities that require more of Jews than what the civil law does. In essence, Jews are to pay attention to these rulings not because they will be enforced in a Jewish court, as was true in times of old, but instead in order to know the kinds of behaviors in business dealings that Jewish tradition demands of them as Jews.

Responsum on Intellectual Property

Article 1, section 8, clause 8 of the U.S. Constitution grants Congress the authority to establish copyrights and patents "to promote the progress of science and useful arts, by securing for limited times to authors and inventors the exclusive right to their respective writings and discoveries." Until the advent of the Internet, this was a fairly easy right to define and enforce. Today, though, with technological advances facilitating quick dissemination of all kinds of materials worldwide, theft of intellectual property for personal benefit, including financial profit, is proliferating. Napster, for example, enabled people to listen to copyrighted music without paying for it until the courts shut it down. New ways were then developed to buy music legally, and the law is still trying to catch up to determine exactly what constitutes a legal use of Internet material.

In the responsum that follows, Rabbi Barry Leff, a Conservative rabbi who earned a doctorate in business administration and has run several businesses, explores "whether it is ethically wrong, within a halakhic framework, to download, swap, or otherwise use music, videos, software, or other forms of intellectual property without paying. In places where secular law may allow—or at least turns a blind eye to—copying intellectual property without the author's permission, would Jewish law still prohibit the practice?"

In his response, Leff notes that if that intellectual property is essentially a new Torah commentary, Jewish tradition views expansions of Torah learning not as the intellectual property of their creators but rather as part of the public domain of the Jewish people. After all, according to the Torah itself, the Torah is "the inheritance of the Congregation of Jacob" (Deuteronomy 33:4), and thus the Torah and all its interpretations and applications belong to the Jewish people as a whole. Nonetheless, Leff points out, the Talmud proclaims that "someone who quotes something in the name of the person who said it brings redemption to the world" (b. Megillah 15a), indicating that even with regard to new applications of Jewish tradition, one has at least a moral duty to cite the author of a comment and thereby not pretend it is one's own. (In upholding his own component of this moral duty, when Leff presented the responsum to the CJLS, he mentioned that his wife, a lawyer specializing in American intellectual property law, helped him with that aspect of the responsum.) Leff also offers guidelines for Jewish institutions—and, by extension, all Jews—to follow when using other people's intellectual property.

The CJLS approved the responsum (excerpted here, with the original Hebrew phrases replaced by transliterations and translations) on December 12, 2007, by a vote of eighteen in favor, one opposed, and two abstaining (18–1–2). To read the original responsum in full, see http://www.rabbinicalassembly.org/sites/default/files/public/halakhah/teshuvot/20052010/leff_IP.pdf.

Overview

. . . Copying, downloading or otherwise using music, videos, software or other forms of intellectual property such as patents or trademarks without paying for them is theft, not only under secular law, but under halakhah as well, and it is wrong for a Jew to engage in such behavior. . . .

Background and Discussion

Copying of software and music is a rampant problem. The Business Software Alliance estimates that worldwide 35% of all software is pirated—representing a cost to the software industry of over $34 Billion.[4] In 2005, for every $2 worth of PC software purchased legally, $1 worth was procured illegally. While the problem is greater in developing countries, even in America 22% of software in use is in the form of illegal copies.[5] . . .

Why is intellectual property theft so rampant? Perhaps because many people have a hard time seeing it as theft. Many people who would never walk into a store and slip a CD into their pocket and walk out without paying have no problem doing effectively the same thing by making a copy of a friend's CD or downloading music files. Many people who would never sneak into a movie theater to see a movie for free have no problem doing the same thing by means of a computer. . . .

Despite all of the rationalizations that Intellectual Property pirates might use, the costs are real, and the harm to businesses, individuals, and society is very real. The RIAA website lists several ways in which harm is done through music piracy:[6]

* Consumers lose out because the shortcut savings enjoyed by pirates drive up the costs of legitimate product for everyone. . . .
* Honest retailers (who back up the products they sell) lose because they cannot compete with the prices offered by illegal vendors. Less business means fewer jobs. . . .
* Record companies lose. Eighty-five percent of recordings released do not even generate enough revenue to cover their costs. Record companies depend heavily on the profitable fifteen percent of recordings to subsidize the less profitable types of music, to cover the costs of developing new artists, and to keep their businesses operational. . . .

* Finally, and perhaps most importantly, the creative artists lose. Musicians, singers, songwriters and producers do not get the royalties and fees they have earned. Virtually all artists (95%) depend on these fees to make a living. The artists also depend on their reputations, which are damaged by the inferior quality of pirated copies sold to the public. . . .

. . . Similar arguments . . . apply to pirating movies or software. If piracy is rampant, in addition to lost revenue to the rightful owners of the property, incentives to develop new product offerings go down, and costs to the people who buy legitimate products go up.

Similar issues are found in the business world, relating to misuse of patents or trade secrets. Protection of the intellectual property found in patents has been a major contributor to many . . . technological advances. . . . What drug company would invest hundreds of millions of dollars in developing a new medicine if as soon as they put it on the market other people could sell the exact same thing at a cost of pennies per pill with nothing invested in research? What high-tech company would invest tens of millions of dollars in developing a new product if others could immediately copy all the fruits of their research?

A further reason to condemn casual intellectual property theft such as music or video file swapping is that it contributes to a general weakening of the moral fiber of society. If people see this form of "cheating" as being OK, other forms of cheating are also likely to be taken more lightly. The Talmud forbids us to steal, even from a thief.[7] . . .

The Status of Intellectual Property under Halakhah

. . . In addition to the principle that "The law of the land is the law," there are three major justifications for copyright protection we find in the sources:

1. *Haskamot* (Approbations)
2. *Hasagat g'vul* (Unfair competition)
3. *Shi'ur b'kinyan* (Limited sale) . . .

Haskamot (Approbations): *Haskamot* [constitute] . . . an early form of copyright protection for authors/publishers of works of Torah. Going back to the 17th century, when respected rabbis would write a letter of introduction for a book, praising the virtues of the book and the author, they would often add a statement prohibiting the reprinting of the book for a specified period of time in order to allow the publishers time to print and sell enough copies of the book to recoup their costs and make a profit. The Ḥatam Sofer [Rabbi Moses Schreiber (Sofer, in Hebrew), 1762–1839, Slovakia] speculates that this practice goes back to the 16th century, when two competing publishers were offering Rambam's *Mishneh Torah*.[8]

Originally, the approbations were put in place to protect the publisher, not the author. Hundreds of years ago, typesetting a book was a very labor-intensive process. The Ḥatam Sofer points out that if publishers were not assured of a monopoly in the publication for a fixed period of time so they would be able to recoup their costs, they would not want to publish works of Torah—and the community would be spiritually impoverished:

> If we were not to close the door in the face of other publishers [i.e., prohibit competition], which fool would [undertake the publication of Judaica and] risk a heavy financial loss [literally, a loss of several thousands]? The publication [of Jewish works] will cease, God forbid, and Torah [study] will be weakened. Therefore, for the benefit of the Jewish people and for the sake of the exaltation of the Torah, our early sages have enacted [prohibitions banning publication of a given book by other publishers for a fixed period of time]. . . .[9]

The communal benefit argument advanced by R. Sofer is very similar to the economic justification model, cited earlier, which is the basis for IP protection in the United States: protecting creative people is good for society.

Most early approbations warned that a person making copies would be placed under the ban [that is, excommunicated]. An interesting case where a rabbi not only invoked a ban, but also invoked a curse is found in Jewish-Italian composer Salamone Rossi's 1623 publication of a collection of sheet music:

> We have agreed to the reasonable and proper request of the worthy and honored Master Salamone Rossi of Mantua . . . who has become by his painstaking labors the first man to print Hebrew music. He has laid out a large disbursement that has not been provided for, and it is not proper

that anyone should harm him by reprinting similar copies or purchasing them from a source other than himself. Therefore ... we the undersigned decree by the authority of the angels and the word of the holy ones, invoking the curse of the serpent's bite, that no Israelite, wherever he may be, may print the music contained in this work in any manner, in whole or in part, without the permission of the abovementioned author. . . . Let every Israelite hearken and stand in fear of being entrapped by this ban and curse. And those who hearken will dwell in confidence and ease, abiding in blessing under the shelter of the Almighty. Amen.[10]

Rabbi Mordecai Benet [1753–1829, Moravia] argues against the rabbinical bans on publication, believing that restricting competition drives up the prices and therefore limits Torah study. This cost is also noted in secular sources: "Granting authors and inventors the right to exclude others from using their ideas necessarily limits the diffusion of those ideas and so prevents many people from benefiting from them."[11] This is why there are time limits put on intellectual property protection in American law, to balance the costs and benefits. . . . Between 1499 and 1850, 3,662 letters of approbation were written and attached to books or other religious works.[12] . . .

Hasagat g'vul (unfair competition): *Hasagat g'vul* literally means "moving a boundary," and the concept is rooted in a prohibition found in the Torah: "Do not move your neighbor's boundary."[13] In other words, do not steal his land by moving the landmarks used to delineate the boundaries of his field.

The Talmud extends this concept to tradespeople and competition. In the Babylonian Talmud, Bava Batra 21b, we find the following teaching: "If a resident of a cul de sac sets up a mill to grind grain for others, and then a fellow resident of the cul de sac comes and sets up a mill in the same street, the law is the first one can stop the second one, for he can say to him 'You are cutting off my livelihood!'"[14] The same discussion in the Talmud brings another example showing that fishermen have to respect each other's fishing areas, even though the fish themselves are ownerless: "Fishing nets must be kept away from [the hiding place of] a fish [that has been spotted by another fisherman] the full length of the fish's swim."[15]

The rabbis did, however, recognize that competition can be a good thing, bringing lower prices, and other people—competitors—are entitled to make a living as well. Several examples of limits to the ability to argue "you are interfering with my livelihood" are stated as well, for example: "Certain basket-sellers brought baskets to Babylon [to sell]. The townspeople came and stopped them (because they did not want the competition), so they (the basket sellers) appealed to Rabina. He said, 'They have come from outside, and they can sell to the people from outside.' This restriction, however, applied only to the market day, but not to other days; and even on the market day only for selling in the market, but not for going round to the houses."

The Ḥatam Sofer specifically applies *hasagat g'vul* to copyrights. After a lengthy discussion regarding protecting the rights of printers, he turns to the rights of authors: "If the case is so [that limited protection is granted] for printers of other texts [already in the public domain], so much more so for one who created a new entity . . . for example, the consummate scholar, Rabbi Wolf Heidenheim, . . . spent countless hours . . . editing and translating the *piyutim* [medieval religious poems] . . . and why should others profit from his creativity? It [our case] can be compared to the case of the fisherman who by means of his actions caused the gathering of the fish."[16]

Rabbi Sofer is relying on a teaching brought in Tosafot that the reason the fishermen are afforded protection is because they bait the area with dead fish, drawing the fish to the area, so they deserve protection lest others profit from their labors: "For thus is the way of fishermen—to put dead fish in their traps, and the fish gather there."[17]

We see in this series of teachings an interesting development from the commandment "Do not move your neighbor's boundary marker" to a prohibition on unfair competition as in the case of the placing of the fishermen's nets, to a protection for the fruits of one's labor, as R. Sofer interprets the justification given in Tosafot.

This is similar to one of the arguments advanced by the RIAA, cited earlier: "Finally, and perhaps most importantly, the creative artists lose [from illegal copying of their music]. Musicians, singers, songwriters and producers do not get the royalties and fees they have earned. Virtually all artists (95%) depend on these fees to make a living."

The same arguments relating to *hasagat g'vul* apply equally to other forms of intellectual property. In one of the rare *teshuvot* [responsa] that specifically reference patents, R. Ovadiah Yosef [1920–2013, Israel] says, "When a person invents new technology and patents a particular subject, no one is permitted to distribute it without permission of the inventor, because of *hasagat g'vul*."[18]

Shi'ur b'kinyan (limited sale): Rabbi Zalman Nechemia Goldberg (b. 1931, Israel) suggests a novel theory for protecting the rights of an author in his paper "Copying a Cassette Without the Owner's Permission" . . . that a seller can put limits (a *shi'ur*) when he sells an item to a purchaser—in other words, he can retain certain rights for himself.[19] He brings support for this argument from the Talmud, where in a debate over a retroactive sale and whether the purchaser should be entitled to shearings and offspring of the animal from the time the sale became effective to the present, R. Zera says, "Consider it like a case where [the seller] said 'Except its shearings and offsprings.'"[20] No one argues with R. Zera's proposition that the sale could be limited in this way.

A similar argument is used elsewhere in [the Talmud's tractate] *Bava Metzia*: "R. Simeon b. Eleazar said on R. Meir's authority: If one gives a denar [unit of money] to a poor man to buy a shirt, he may not buy a cloak therewith; to buy a cloak, he must not buy a shirt, because he disregards the donor's desire . . . and he who disregards the owner's desire is called a robber."[21]

Rabbi Goldberg's reasoning is that by calling the poor man a thief, the Talmud's implication is that he took something that was owned by the giver. He reasons that the owner did not give the whole coin to the poor man: rather he held back for himself the right to determine what the coin would be spent on. He argues that similarly, when a publisher of a book or the producer of a cassette of software sells his product, he can expressly reserve the right to copy it and not grant that right to the purchaser. . . .

The concept of *shi'ur b'kinyan* is similar to the idea in secular law that the sale of copyrighted products includes some rights (fair use) but excludes other rights (making copies for sale). . . .

Even if one concedes that intellectual property is protected under halakhah, one might argue whether its misappropriation constitutes theft.

Since there is nothing that has been "taken" that the owner will miss in this case, even if one were to argue that it is not stealing, the situation could be seen as analogous to borrowing someone's property without permission, which is also forbidden. The losses from making unauthorized copies, or using a patent without permission stem not from the fact that the music or technology itself is missing (it is not), but rather from the fact that someone borrowed it without permission. According to the Shulhan Arukh, "Even one who takes something as a borrower, if it is without the knowledge of the owners, is called a thief."[22]

R. Moshe Feinstein also states that someone making copies of cassette tapes of Torah lectures without permission is stealing: "It is forbidden to make from one's tape additional tapes, and it is certainly forbidden because the subject [the tape] has monetary value, and [the author] made the tape to profit from it, that if others want it, they have to pay him.... [T]o make another tape from one tape without permission is forbidden as theft."[23] ...

Guidelines on the Usage of Intellectual Property in Jewish Institutions

Jewish institutions such as synagogues, day schools, and Jewish-oriented non-profit organizations all encounter issues surrounding the use and protection of intellectual property on a daily basis.... Many issues ... arise regarding making photocopies of printed materials for classes, showing movies or clips from movies, playing recorded music, and using software on office or school computers.... This section does not give specific legal advice regarding particular situations — rather it is intended to highlight issues that institutions should be aware of. It is incumbent on the Jewish community that our communal institutions should have the highest standards of ethical and legal conduct so as to be a good role model and example for the people with whom we interact....

Books, music, movies, software and other forms of intellectual property are all sold with a bundle of rights known as "fair use" that defines what the buyer may and may not do with that intellectual property....

While this section is written from the perspective of U.S. law, copyright protection is relatively standard worldwide due to international treaties, especially the Berne Convention. More than 100 countries have signed the Berne Convention, which says that each nation must provide copyright protection to authors who are nationals of any other country that has signed the convention.[24]

Computer software: Software is generally sold with what in the trade is known as a "shrink-wrap license."[25] By opening the packaging on a piece of software, the purchaser consents to the conditions under which the software is sold. Nowadays, a lot of software is sold over the internet, through downloading the program. Prior to downloading a program, the user generally has to click that he agrees to the conditions of sale. This is usually a large section of legalistic text that many people skip over and simply click on "accept." It is advisable actually to take the time to read the agreement, because the rights being conveyed often vary from vendor to vendor and from program to program. Some programs give you a license to install the software on one computer for whoever uses that computer; others license a user for as many computers as he uses; others specify a particular number of computers, with the idea being one user can load the program on both a desktop computer and a laptop. Whatever restrictions the vendor puts into the license, the user is obligated to follow, both under secular law, and under halakhah following the principle of *shi'ur b'kinyan*. . . .

A synagogue or other non-profit organization is subject to the same restrictions as for-profit enterprises. There are no blanket exemptions from the laws of making copies of software for schools or synagogues.

Books and other printed materials: A comprehensive treatment of fair use of printed materials would be very involved, confusing, and far beyond the scope of this paper. This section presents a few broad guidelines. . . .

Judgment is required in determining how much material one can legitimately copy. To copy an entire book, even if done one chapter at a time to give to a class, even without charge, would not be allowed as it would potentially affect the sales of the copied material: the students should be asked to buy a copy of the book. To copy a portion of a chapter of a book for a one-time non-profit use in a class would generally be considered fair use and permissible. To make copies of an article in a magazine for a class would be permissible; to copy a whole magazine, or most of a magazine, would not. . . .

There are some additional fair use rights granted to libraries, primarily to provide for copies made for preservation and security.[26]

Movies/videos: Many people never think about whether they need a special license to show a video in the synagogue; they assume as long as no admission is charged, it is permissible. This is not correct. If you read the fine print on a DVD box, you will generally see the following statement or something very similar: "WARNING: For private home use only. Federal law provides severe civil and criminal penalties for the unauthorized reproduction, distribution, or exhibition of copyrighted motion pictures and video formats."

Note that the statement reads "private home use only." And that is exactly what it means. You may invite a dozen friends over to watch a copy of "Raiders of the Lost Ark" that you rented. . . . You may not, however, show it to five people at the synagogue without a license.

There is a specific exemption for schools when the video is being shown for educational purposes. However, to be in compliance with this educational exemption, ALL of the following conditions must be met:

* A teacher or instructor must be present.
* The showing must take place in a classroom setting with only the enrolled students attending.
* The movie is used as an essential part of the curriculum—the instructor should be able to demonstrate how it is relevant to the course.
* The movie being used is a legitimate copy, purchased or rented. It may not be a copy of a legitimate copy, or taped from TV.[27]

If a synagogue wishes to show a movie as part of a program—for example, showing movies before a *seliḥot* service is popular with many congregations—the synagogue must have a public performance license.

Fortunately, it is relatively easy to acquire an annual license that will allow a synagogue or other non-profit organization to show all the movies they want for one simple licensing fee, typically a few hundred dollars a year. There are clearinghouse organizations that work out licensing deals with all the major studios and include them as part of one annual license. CVLI (Christian Video Licensing International) provides annual licenses to religious institutions on a sliding scale, depending on the size of the congregation.[28] The Motion Picture Licensing Corporation provides licenses to other non-profit organizations.[29] Note that both the CVLI and

MPLC licenses do not allow charging admission beyond what would be needed to recover direct costs (if you rent a big-screen TV for $100 and one hundred people show up, you may charge only $1/person).

Music: As previously mentioned, the DMCA does not allow circumventing copyright restrictions even for permitted purposes. However, a lot of music is available that is not technologically protected. What usage and copying is permissible?

It is permissible to make a copy for backup protection for yourself, or to copy music to a different media. For example, if you purchase a CD, it is OK to download it to your computer so you can either listen to it from your computer or to further download it to an iPod or other MP3 player. . . .

It is NOT permissible to make a copy of a CD and give it to someone else, or to download the contents of a CD to your computer and/or MP3 player, and then sell the CD; from the perspective of the copyright holder, that is the same as making a duplicate CD and keeping it. . . . Downloading copyrighted music using file sharing software is forbidden even if the intended use is personal or for a non-profit organization.

Playing recorded music in public, like showing movies in public, can create a situation where a public performance license is required. Fortunately for synagogues, there is a blanket exemption for playing music that does not exist for showing videos. "The Fairness in Music Licensing Act of 1998" provides a blanket exemption for religious use of music:

> Notwithstanding the provisions of section 106, the following are not infringements of copyright: . . . (3) performance of a nondramatic literary or musical work or of a dramatico-musical work of a religious nature, or display of a work, in the course of services at a place of worship or other religious assembly.[30]

Note that the exemption is for use of music during services; to perform copyrighted music, or to play recorded copyrighted music during a concert could require a performance license. No license is required if the following three conditions are ALL met:

1. there is no purpose of direct or indirect commercial advantage; and

2. there is no payment for the performance to the performers, promoters or organizers; and

3. there is no direct or indirect admission charge or, alternatively, if there is an admission charge, the net proceeds are used exclusively for educational, religious or charitable purposes.[31]

If a performance will not meet those criteria, a public performance license should be obtained from either the publisher of the music, or one of the licensing clearinghouses such as ASCAP (the American Society of Composers, Authors, and Publishers). More information can be found on the ASCAP website at www.ascap.com. ASCAP licenses include permission both to play recorded music such as CDs, or to do live performances with musicians of copyrighted music.

And of course printed sheet music is also subject to copyright as would be books or other printed matter. Making a copy of a few pages so that a pianist does not have to flip pages during a performance is permissible; making multiple copies of a complete work for a choir is not. Even making a single photocopy for an accompanist is technically not permitted without the permission of the copyright holder. It is not onerous to get permission to make a small number of copies; many music publishers will even grant permission over the phone if the time is short. . . .

Piskei Halakhah (Legal Findings)

Based on our study of halakhic precedent and the applicability of secular law we rule as follows:

1. The concept of *dina d'malkhuta dina*, the law of the land is the law, is applicable to issues surrounding intellectual property, and we are obligated halakhically to follow the laws of the country we live in or do business with as regards protection of intellectual property. Even if certain forms of copying or otherwise reproducing intellectual property are permitted halakhically, if secular law forbids the practice, we are still obligated to obey the law of the land.

2. Halakhah affords protection of intellectual property that can in some cases go beyond what secular law affords. Even in countries such as

Russia or China, which may have lax laws and laxer enforcement, ample halakhic precedent calls on us to protect the intellectual property of others.

3. Ignorance of the law is no excuse. Our communal institutions such as synagogues, schools, etc., are obligated to learn about proper use and protection of intellectual property and to make sure they serve as role models in complying with the law.

Simply put, even though it may at times be burdensome, we are obligated to follow the stricter of secular law or halakhah when it comes to ethical issues. As citizens, residents, or visitors to a country, we are obligated under the principle of *dina d'malkhuta dina* to follow the local laws. As Jews living lives faithful to the ethical teachings of our tradition, we are obligated to follow the halakhah even if it is stricter than the secular law. . . .

Responsum on Whistle-Blowing

In the following responsum, Rabbi Barry Leff addresses the ticklish question of whistle-blowing: To what extent does an employee have an obligation to report wrongdoing on the part of his or her employer? What if it will cost the employee his or her job?

Leff takes into account two Jewish values that seem to go in opposite directions: On the one hand, the Torah says, "Do not stand idly by the blood of your brother" (Leviticus 19:16), which the Rabbis (b. *Sanhedrin* 73a) interpret to mean that we have a duty to rescue people from danger. The Torah also requires us to rebuke a neighbor who has done something wrong (Leviticus 19:17). On the other, we also have a duty to refrain from *lashon ha-ra*, speaking ill of a person, even if what one says is true. How, then, do we balance these duties in the employer-employee context?

The CJLS approved this responsum (excerpted below) on December 12, 2007, by a vote of seventeen in favor, one opposed, and three abstaining (17–1–3). To read it in full, see http://www.rabbinicalassembly.org/sites/default/files/public/halakhah/teshuvot/20052010/leff_whistleblowing.pdf.

Whistle-Blowing and *Lashon Hara*

Engaging in *lashon hara*—broadly speaking, all forms of "improper speech," including gossip, slander, etc.—is considered a very serious violation under halakhah. The Ḥofetz Ḥaim, Rabbi Yisrael Meir HaCohen Kagen [1839–1933, Belarus], lists 17 negative commandments and 14 positive commandments that can be violated through improper speech.[32]

The first major work that detailed the laws relating to *lashon hara* was Ḥofetz Ḥaim. In general principle 10, the Ḥofetz Ḥaim says, "If someone stole from someone, or defrauded him, or cursed him—in what manner is it permissible to reveal the matter to people?"[33]

It is interesting to note the language the Ḥofetz Ḥaim uses: "In what manner is it permitted to reveal the matter to people?"—not "In what manner is it REQUIRED to reveal the matter to people?" The language reflects a common bias against speaking out. Ḥofetz Ḥaim goes on to state that if someone sees someone doing something wicked to another, like stealing from him, and it is known to him that the goods have not been returned, etc., it is permissible to tell people to help those who have been transgressed against. He lists seven conditions that should be met before conveying the information to others:

1. It should be something he saw himself, not based on hearsay;
2. He should reflect carefully that he is certain the behavior he saw met the requirements of being considered theft or damage;
3. He should first gently rebuke the wrongdoer;
4. He should not make the transgression greater than what it really was—do not exaggerate;
5. He should be clear about his motives—that this is being done to benefit the one who was sinned against, and that the one who is reporting the matter is not going to benefit from the damage he is about to inflict on another, or that he is doing it because he hates the transgressor;
6. If he is able to accomplish the effect through some other means without having to engage in *lashon hara*, he should do so, and not speak of the matter;
7. His speaking about this should not result in greater damage to the transgressor than if the matter had come before a *bet din* [rabbinical court].[34]

Most of these principles are equally applicable in situations of whistleblowing against an employer as they are in situations of informing an individual regarding a transgression another made against him. The important point here is that the rules about *lashon hara* do not provide an excuse or a barrier NOT to report employer wrongdoing. . . .

The Responsibility to Rebuke

The Torah charges us with an obligation to rebuke our neighbor when we see him doing something wrong: Leviticus 19:17 commands us: "You shall not hate your brother in your heart, you shall surely rebuke your neighbor, and not bear sin on his account."

In his commentary on this verse, Naḥmanides says the way to understand the whole verse is as saying that you should rebuke your neighbor, because if you do not, you will end up hating him for his sin, and then you will be a sinner, hating your neighbor in your heart. Naḥmanides also brings an indication that we should apply this to non-Jews as well: the example he uses is Abraham reproving the non-Jew Avimelech.[35]

When we see something wrong being done, we have a responsibility to speak up. The Talmud both reinforces and limits this principle. It is reinforced in a teaching brought in *Bava Metzia*, which relates that the repetition of the word *hokhe'ah* [rebuke in Leviticus 19:17] comes to tell us that you should rebuke your neighbor not just once, but even a hundred times; furthermore, we learn that from the repetition that not only is a master obligated to rebuke a disciple, but a disciple is obligated to rebuke his master.[36] Since a teacher is to be accorded more respect than just about anyone else, even including a parent, we could make an *a fortiori* argument that if one is obligated to rebuke one's master, all the more so one would be obligated to rebuke someone else, like an employer.

The Talmud limits this principle of "rebuke your neighbor" in the following passage from *Yevamot*:

R. Ile'a further stated in the name of R. Eleazar, son of R. Simeon: "As one is commanded to say that which will be obeyed, so is one commanded not to say that which will not be obeyed." R. Abba stated: "It is a duty; for it is said in Scripture, 'Reprove not a scorner, lest he hate thee; reprove a wise man and he will love thee.'"[37]

One factor in determining whether or not there is an expectation that the rebuke would be listened to is the culture of the corporation. Some companies make a real effort to solicit input from employees and to be responsive to that input. Other companies follow a much more rigidly hierarchical model, or have a CEO who is known NOT to take criticism well.

However, a mere general sense that a rebuke will not be listened to is not sufficient to relieve a person of the responsibility to rebuke a wrong-doer. In the Mishneh Torah, Maimonides not only brings rebuking a wrong-doer as a commandment, but he says:

> If [the rebuke] is accepted from him, fine, and if not, he rebukes him a second and third time, and the obligation to rebuke continues until the sinner hits him and says I am not listening. Anyone who has the opportunity to protest and does not protest, he is found a transgressor of these sins, since he has the possibility to protest.[38]

From Rambam's statement, we would infer that if there is doubt whether a rebuke will or will not be listened to, there is an obligation to rebuke. Furthermore, in general a high level executive is not only responsible for his particular department, but he is part of a team leading the corporation, and the expectation is that his advice will at least be listened to, even if it will not always be followed. Therefore, unless there were truly unusual circumstances, an executive would be expected to rebuke his employer (tactfully, of course), whereas a lower level employee could argue that the CEO would not listen to criticism coming from someone lower down in the organization.

A lower level worker might also be afraid that rebuking the CEO could harm his career, which might also argue against an obligation to rebuke.... However, if a lower level employee refrains from rebuking his employer because he does not believe he will be listened to, there may still be an obligation to report the wrongdoing to others....

We learn from the Talmud that we are each responsible to correct others who are within our sphere of influence. In tractate *Shabbat* we learn:

Whoever has the ability to protest against the members of his household when they are doing something wrong but does not protest, is punished for the transgressions of the members of his household. One who can protest against the people of the town but does not do so is punished for the transgressions of the people of his town. Further, one who can protest against the entire world but does not is punished for the transgressions of the entire world. . . .[39]

If the prospective whistleblower is himself personally engaged in an inappropriate act, he could be held accountable halakhically because of the principle "There is no agency in sin." An individual who commits a sin—like theft—is guilty of theft, even if he is doing it at someone else's direction.[40] And under secular law, violating the law on behalf of your employer can land you in jail.[41] . . .

The obligation to rebuke someone doing wrong extends to the person doing the wrongdoing, not to others. In *Hilkhot De'ot*, Rambam says, "He who rebukes another, whether for offenses against the rebuker himself or for sins against God, should administer the rebuke in private, speak to the offender gently and tenderly, and point out that he is only speaking for the wrongdoer's own good, to bring him to eternal life."[42] Note Rambam specifies that the rebuke is administered privately. . . .

Pesak Halakhah (Legal Ruling)

1. In any case of wrongdoing, there is an obligation to rebuke the person doing wrong if it can be assumed there is a reasonable chance the rebuke will be listened to, and the rebuke can be administered without substantial cost.
2. In cases of *pikuah nefesh* [saving a life], where there is a certainty or substantial likelihood of loss of life if information is withheld, one is obligated to report the information to appropriate authorities, even at substantial personal cost.
3. In cases of financial loss, if wrongdoing can be reported at no cost to the reporter, there is a positive obligation to do so. If wrongdoing would jeopardize the reporter's money or livelihood, there is no strict obligation to report wrongdoing. It is, however, appropriate to

consider proportionality. It is appropriate to demur from reporting minor wrongdoing that would have a major cost to the reporter. On the other hand, in the event of major wrongdoing, it is appropriate to go *lifnim m'shurat ha-din*, beyond the minimum requirement of the law, and report it even at substantial personal cost.

Responsum on Employers and Employees

Rabbi Jill Jacobs's responsum, "Work, Workers and the Jewish Owner," considers what Jewish law requires of Jewish owners vis-à-vis their employees.[43] What are the obligations of Jewish owners to workers paid by the hour? Specifically, are employers obligated to pay these workers a living wage? Are employers obligated to provide health care and other benefits? Are employers obligated to permit workers to organize and to join unions? Do employers' obligations change if workers take additional jobs?

Although employment conditions are governed by civil law, Jacobs asks whether Jewish law requires even more of Jewish employers. Here, she has to analyze what was meant by the dominant principle of Jewish employment law that "everything is according to local custom," because "local custom" might conceivably justify employers stipulating unlivable employee wages and oppressive working conditions. She cites later Jewish materials that interpret "the local custom" to be binding only when it requires a livable salary and safe and reasonable working conditions. She also addresses the question of whether such employer obligations beyond those required by contemporary American law are unrealistic or unfair to Jewish owners in putting them at a competitive disadvantage with non-Jewish businesses. (Her responsum was approved in 2008, two years before the U.S. Congress enacted the Affordable Health Care Act, so her comments about health care need to be adjusted to take account of the additional health care insurance options provided by that law.)

Jacobs also examines the specific case of minimum-wage workers' duties toward their employers. Although she does not discuss whether and how all her conclusions would apply to people earning a living wage, certain sections, such as those on the dignity of work and the duties of employers and employees to each other, would seem to pertain to all workers.

The CJLS approved the responsum (excerpted here with Hebrew and Aramaic words translated) on May 28, 2008, by a vote of thirteen in favor, one opposed, and three abstaining (13–1–3). To access the original, see http://www.rabbinicalassembly.org/sites/default/files/public/halakhah /teshuvot/20052010/jacobs-living-wage.pdf. Readers may also wish to review the opinion of Marc Gary, a CJLS lay representative and lawyer specializing in employment law, who concurred with the overall ruling but dissented from parts of it; six rabbis on the CJLS joined in his opinion: http://www.rabbinicalassembly.org/sites/default/files/assets/public /halakhah/teshuvot/20052010/gary_final_worker%27s.pdf.

We Cannot Make Halakhah in a Vacuum

For the past nine years, Aurelio Minaya, an immigrant from the Dominican Republic, has worked full time cleaning a large office building in Franklin Lakes, NJ. In that time, his salary has risen only 25 cents—to $6.55/hour. On these wages, Minaya supports three children. He receives no health benefits.[44]

In many ways, Minaya is lucky. Other office cleaning jobs in New Jersey pay as little as $5.25/hour, and few offer full-time work. As a result, most janitors take on second, and even third, jobs in order to make ends meet. In contrast, in New York City, janitors working on union contracts earn up to $16/hour, work full time, and receive family health benefits and a pension.[45] . . .

We cannot make halakhah in a vacuum, but must consider the real-life experience of those whom our decisions will affect. Addressing the interplay between the "texts" of workers' lives and the texts of our tradition yields a richer understanding of appropriate Jewish labor practice. . . .

The Place of Work in Jewish Tradition

. . . [There is] a deep rabbinic ambivalence about the value of work. On the one hand, the rabbis do not always view work as inherently valuable; on the other hand, they recognize that individuals must earn a living, and that the life of the community depends on certain types of work and workers. One text, *Pirkei Avot* 2:2, even suggests that work is not only economically necessary, but also a means of guaranteeing one's own moral well-being: "Great is Talmud Torah [study of the Torah] that is combined with work, as the two together will lead to the abandonment of sin. All Talmud Torah that is not combined with work will, in the end, be nullified and will lead to sin." . . .

Employers' Obligations to Create a Dignified Workplace Environment

The story of the Exodus and its associated commentary offers the most extensive insight into traditional Jewish understandings about work and about work conditions. While the biblical account of the Israelites' slavery in Egypt focuses on the difficulty of the imposed physical labor, midrash and other rabbinic commentaries understand the difficulties of slavery to arise primarily from spiritual, rather than physical, oppression. In rabbinic expansions of the slavery narrative, the Egyptians prevent Israelite husbands and wives from seeing one another, and view the Israelites as "thorns," rather than as human beings (*Sh'mot Rabbah* 1:12, 1:11). According to one well-known midrash, "The Egyptians placed a heavy burden on a child and a light burden on an adult; a man's burden on a woman and a woman's burden on a man; the burden of an elderly person on a youth, and the burden of a youth on an elderly person" (*Sh'mot Rabbah* 1:27).[46]

The emphasis in these texts on the loss of dignity as the primary condition of slavery mirrors the experience of the low-wage workers I know who, when asked to describe their working conditions, invariably reply "They don't respect us" even before mentioning more concrete concerns such as low wages, long hours, or the lack of health care. In the words of Marie Pierre, a nursing home assistant interviewed by Human Rights Watch (HRW), "We know our job, we love our job, we love our patients, but management does not respect us." Although Pierre and her co-workers twice voted to accept a union, HRW reports, the company has refused to accept the union and fired Pierre for speaking Creole with other employees.[47] . . .

If we understand the biblical and rabbinic account of Egyptian slavery to present the primary example of unacceptable working conditions, we can assume a general prohibition against mimicking the practices of

Pharaoh and his taskmasters. This assumption gains support from the repeated biblical assertion that the memory of slavery creates an obligation not to subject others to the conditions the Egyptians imposed on the Israelites.[48] ... Thus, in contrast to the Israelite workers described by the midrashim discussed above, the workers we hire should be permitted to continue regular family relations, and should perform jobs suited to their abilities.

Traditional sources also indicate an awareness of the unclear boundaries between work and slavery. Workers are specifically permitted to quit a job in the middle of the day because "The children of Israel are [God's] servants and not servants to servants" (B. *Bava Kamma* 117b).[49]

Likewise, a person may not accept employment in the household of another for more than three years, as such a position may take on the appearance of servitude (Rema, Hoshen Mishpat 333:3). Today, when the institution of slavery is illegal, it is unlikely that anyone would confuse long-term employment, even for domestic servants, with slavery. Even so, we should be aware that some low-wage employment situations become, de facto, slavery. In my own organizing work in New Jersey, I was shocked to encounter a nursing home that employed Filipino nurses who were brought to the United States illegally and forced to work as indentured servants to pay off their transportation costs. The nurses lived in the nursing home and were on call twenty-four hours a day. Without documentation, the nurses could not take the risk of leaving the home. When the local health care union sent Tagalog-speaking organizers to speak with the nurses, nursing home administrators prevented these organizers from entering.

While midrashim on Egypt offer insight into unhealthy workplaces, one biblical episode offers us a more positive workplace model. The second chapter of the book of Ruth begins with Boaz, a wealthy field owner, visiting his fields to speak to the workers. This interaction offers a few insights into appropriate employer-employee relations. First, it is clear that Boaz visits the field often. He is familiar with the workers, and even notices the appearance of a new gleaner. Second, Boaz invokes God's name in greeting his workers. The Talmud understands the interaction between Boaz and his workers as the precedent for always invoking God's name in asking about the well-being of another (B. *Berakhot* 54a). It is significant that the initial use of God's name as a greeting appears in a workplace situation, and not in a religious context. Perhaps it becomes even more important to introduce God into a situation in which one might not expect to sense God's presence. . . .

The rabbis . . . push us toward the conclusion that work, when necessary, should confer dignity upon the worker. Employers should, like Boaz, maintain close contact with their workers. Most importantly, the rabbis insist that divinity manifest itself in the workplace. One's work environment should offer the same kind of dignity and honor we associate with religious spaces such as the Beit Midrash [place of study].

Employers' Financial Obligations toward Workers Paid by the Hour

. . . Most Jewish employment law revolves around the concept of *minhag hamakom* — that the custom of the place determines workers' salaries, as well as other working conditions.[50] This principle is laid out most clearly in Mishnah *Bava Metzia* 7:1:

> One who hires workers and instructs them to begin work early and to stay late — in a place in which it is not the custom to begin work early and to stay late, the employer may not force them to do so. In a place in which it is the custom to feed the workers, he must do so. In a place in which it is the custom to distribute sweets, he must do so. Everything goes according to the custom of the land.
>
> A story [is told] about Rabbi Yohanan ben Matya, who told his son, "Go, hire us workers." His son went and promised them food (without specifying what kind, or how much). When he returned, his father said to him, "My son! Even if you gave them a feast like that of King Solomon, you would not have fulfilled your obligation toward them, for they are the children of Abraham, Isaac and Jacob. However, as they have not yet begun to work, go back and say to them that their employment is conditional on their not demanding more than bread and vegetables." Rabbi Shimon ben Gamliel said, "It is not necessary to make such a stipulation. Everything goes according to the custom of the place." . . .

The gemara [Talmud] notices the expansive nature of the mishnah and questions the necessity of specifying that an employer may not force workers to begin early and stay late. The Talmud responds:

> We need [this statement] for the case in which the employer raises the workers' wages. In the case in which he says to them, "I raised your wages in order that you would begin work early and stay late," they may reply, "You raised our wages in order that we would do better work." (B. *Bava Metzia* 83a)

With these words, the gemara establishes wages and hours, and presumably other working conditions, as categories that are not inherently dependent on one another. Raising a worker's salary does not necessarily obligate this worker to work longer hours, or to accept new responsibilities. Employers and workers presumably may stipulate longer hours when they negotiate a contract, but an employer who fails to make such a stipulation before raising wages may not, post facto, demand a longer workday.

The Talmud is also surprising in its suggestion that workers may adjust their production rate to salary levels. The gemara implicitly permits an employee who earns low wages to work less hard than one who earns a higher salary. In this allowance, the text calls to mind the common labor tactic of a "work to rule" strike, in which workers refuse to exceed the precise job requirements. In first encountering this talmudic text, I also read it as a personal chastisement for the many times I have complained about slow cashiers in grocery stores and other establishments. Instead of blaming cashiers for working slowly, we can perhaps say that these employees perform as well as might be expected of those who earn $6 or $7/hour. I am also reminded of historian Robin Kelley's description of himself and his friends as teenagers, quietly challenging the management of the McDonald's where they worked by conducting work slowdowns, or by finding other ways to compensate for the indignity of their jobs.[51]

When we pay people minimum wage, we can expect a low level of production. To increase work quality, we must also increase wages and improve other working conditions.

In the mishnaic story of Rabbi Yoḥanan ben Matya, we find a challenge to the idea that the local *minhag* [custom] governs all workplace conditions. Rabbi Yoḥanan assumes not only that the employer must stipulate the exact working conditions, but also that vague statements should be interpreted in favor of the worker. . . .

The talmudic texts we have thus examined therefore leave us with questions and paradoxes. On the one hand, some textual evidence points to a bias in favor of workers. On the other hand . . . the text instructs us to follow the *minhag* of the place in all areas of labor law. . . . To sort out these issues, we must expand our inquiry into the *assumptions* of labor law.

We will first examine the two biblical verses that provide the basis for much of Jewish labor law: "Do not oppress your neighbor and do not rob him. Do not keep the wages of the worker with you until morning" (Leviticus 19:13). "Do not oppress the hired laborer who is poor and needy, whether he is one of your people or one of the sojourners in your land within your gates. Give him his wages in the daytime, and do not let the sun set on them, for he is poor, and his life depends on them, lest he cry out to God about you, for this will be counted as a sin for you" (Deuteronomy 24:14–15).

These biblical verses are significant in their acknowledgment of the essential power and wealth imbalance between employer and employee. The texts understand both the employer's power to rob the employee and the employee's dependence on the wages. From these verses, we understand workers to be a protected category, perhaps similar to widows, orphans, and sojourners. The Deuteronomy verses further include sojourners among the protected workers, thereby prohibiting us from distinguishing between Jewish and non-Jewish workers.

From the biblical text, we therefore derive a few general principles. First, workers are understood to be poor and deserving of our protection. Second, both Jews and non-Jews are considered to be included in the category of protected workers. Third, the texts assert the need for specific legislation to prevent the oppression of workers.

Still, these biblical verses offer little assistance in determining appropriate wages or other labor conditions. . . . We must explore further to determine a Jewish response to these modern-day concerns.

Two rabbinic texts do explicitly legislate against the gross underpayment of workers. One *mishnah* forbids an employer from telling an employee paid to handle straw, "Take the result of your labor as your wages" (M. *Bava Metzia* 10:5). The Tosefta considers a case in which an employer hires someone to bring fruit to a sick person. If the employee goes to the home of the sick person and finds that this person has died or gotten better, the employer must pay the worker's wages in full and cannot say, "Take what you are carrying as payment" (T. *Bava Metzia* 7:4). . . .

Rabbinic commentary on the biblical verse helps us to understand the emphasis on prompt payment of wages, rather than on the amount of the wages themselves. In interpreting the phrase, "His life depends on [the wages]," the Talmud explains,

> Why does he climb a ladder or hang from a tree or risk death? Is it not for his wages? Another interpretation—"His life depends on them" indicates that anyone who denies a hired laborer his wages, it is as though he takes his life from him. (B. *Bava Metzia* 112a)

This reading is surprising in its suggestion that the employer assumes responsibility for the health and well-being of his workers. Even more radical is the statement of Jonah Gerondi [d. 1263, Spain], the medieval author of the *Sefer HaYirah*: "Be careful not to afflict a living creature, whether animal or fowl, and even more so not to afflict a human being, who is created in God's image. If you want to hire workers and you find that they are poor, they should become like poor members of your household. You should not disgrace them, for you are commanded to behave respectfully toward them and to pay their wages."

Given this emphasis on the employer's responsibilities toward the worker, we are puzzled by the absence of specific legislation about appropriate wages . . . [though the] text hints at an assumption that wages, when paid on time, will be sufficient to lift a person out of poverty.

This point becomes even clearer in Nahmanides' commentary to Deuteronomy 24:15. He writes: "For he is poor—like the majority of hired laborers, and he depends on the wages to buy food by which to live. . . . [I]f he does not collect the wages right away as he is leaving work, he will go home, and his wages will remain with you until the morning, and he will die of hunger that night." Like Gerondi, Nahmanides holds the employer responsible for the health and sustenance of the worker. If the worker and/or his family die of hunger as a result of nonpayment of wages, Naḥmanides implies, fault for the death lies with the employer.

In commenting that a person who does not receive wages on time will "die of hunger that night," Naḥmanides takes for granted that a person who *does* receive payment on time *will* be able to provide sufficiently for himself and his family and will not die of hunger. This assumption also forms the premise for Maimonides' designation of the highest level of *tzedakah* [charity] as "the one who strengthens the hand of his fellow Jew by giving him a gift or a loan or entering into partnership with him or finding him work in order to strengthen his hand so that he will not need to ask in the future."[52] For Maimonides, a person who has permanent employment or a share in a business will never find it necessary to ask for *tzedakah*.

The assumption that an employed person will be able to support himself or herself and a family may respond to the reality of the medieval world, but does not reflect the current situation. In a time when 20% of homeless people and 37% of those who apply for emergency food relief are employed, we can no longer assume that providing jobs will eradicate poverty.[53] . . .

We therefore find ourselves in a difficult position. As discussed earlier, traditional *halakhah* remains relevant for many areas of employment law. However, in regard to wages, the rabbinic premise does not correspond with our current reality. This discrepancy suggests that the application of traditional *halakhah* to present-day labor issues first requires raising wages to a level at which rabbinic assumptions hold true.

Employers' Obligations When Workers Take Additional Jobs

Traditional sources compel employees to work diligently, to be precise in their work, and to avoid wasting the employer's time. Workers may even recite abbreviated prayers and excuse themselves from certain religious obligations in order not to detract from their work (B. *Berakhot* 17a, 46a). According to Maimonides:

> Just as the employer must be careful not to steal the salary of the poor [worker], so too must the poor person be careful not to steal the work

of the owner by wasting a little time here and there until the entire day is filled with trickery. Rather, he should be careful about time. For this reason, the rabbis specified that workers do not need to recite the fourth blessing of *Birkat HaMazon* [Blessings after Meals]. Similarly, the worker is obligated to work with all of his strength, for behold, Jacob the righteous said [to Laban,] "I have served your father with all my might" (Genesis 31:6). (Mishneh Torah, *Hilkhot Skhirut [Laws of Hiring]* 13:7)[54]

Workers are also prohibited from working both during the day and at night, as taking on a second job interferes with one's ability to perform the first job well (T. *Bava Metzia* 8:2).[55] Furthermore, workers must care for their own health. According to the Tosefta, "[A worker] may not starve or afflict himself in order to feed his children, as this is considered stealing work from the employer" [T. *Bava Metzia* 8:2].[56]

In theory, these regulations offer the employer reasonable guarantees that workers will be efficient and productive. However, as in the above discussion of appropriate wages, the assumptions that generate these laws do not reflect our current reality. For many Americans, holding multiple jobs is an economic necessity, particularly for low-wage workers. The Bureau of Labor Statistics estimates that 5.6% of Americans (7,556,000) hold multiple jobs, with 300,000 working two full-time jobs.[57] Some have suggested that the actual rate may be closer to 15 or 20%.[58] . . . Anecdotal evidence suggests that a high percentage of the lowest paid workers supplement their primary jobs with weekend and evening work. One union organizer reports coming to grips with the frequency of this phenomenon only when she asked a janitor what he planned to do with the higher wages promised by a new contract. His reply? "Quit my third job."

A strict reading of the *Mishneh Torah* and other sources might suggest that these workers cheat their employers when accepting second and third jobs. However, given the virtual impossibility of supporting a family on a few hundred dollars a week, we cannot reasonably expect low-wage workers to confine themselves to a single, forty-hour/week job. . . .

The lack of adequate health benefits for many workers makes it particularly difficult to fulfill the Tosefta's requirement that workers maintain their health. Without health benefits, workers forgo regular doctors' visits and instead use the emergency room as their first line of medical care. The lack of adequate health care leads to missed work days, and also constitutes a drain on the public, as communal funds pay for the workers' emergency medical care.[59]

Given the discrepancy between *halakhic* obligations on workers and the contemporary reality, we find ourselves with two possibilities. We can either reconsider the *halakhic* prohibition against taking multiple jobs and the requirement that employees work at full capacity, or we can accept the current reality as a challenge to traditional *halakhah* and, in turn, use *halakhah* to critique the present-day situation. In his analysis of Jewish labor issues, David Schnall takes the former approach. He suggests that in American society, multiple employment may have assumed the status of *minhag hamakom*, the custom of the community, and therefore may be acceptable.[60] He also cites evidence that those who work second jobs "appear no more likely to underperform or to behave in an undesirable fashion [than those who work only one job]." Furthermore, Schnall classifies as "substantial" the argument that permitting multiple employment "is a means of retaining and satisfying talented workers when an employer cannot continue to raise salary or benefits."[61]

Schnall's analysis may appropriately respond to certain instances of multiple employment, including the examples he cites of teachers who tutor after school or during the summer, and professionals who consult in their free time.[62] Within certain professions, such additional part-time work may be a reasonable and accepted practice. Teachers who take on one or two weekend or after-school tutoring jobs will not necessarily be less effective in their full-time jobs. However, it does seem reasonable to assume that a low-wage worker holding more than one *full-time* job will not be as effective as a person working a single job. . . . We can therefore suggest that the *halakhic* requirements that the employee maintain his/her health, eat properly, and work only one job implicitly obligate the employer to enable the worker to fulfill these conditions. . . .

In the current situation, then . . . applying Jewish labor laws to contemporary America requires first creating a system that mirrors the ideal upon which traditional sources are based. Most importantly, we need to ensure that even the lowest paid workers earn enough to provide their families with food, shelter, health care, and other basic necessities. Only then can employers sufficiently fulfill their obligations toward the workers simply by paying salaries on time; and only then can we expect employees to work a single job, and to perform this job to the best of their abilities. . . .

Interfering with Market-Determined Wages

Having established that our current *minhagim* [customs]—including the minimum wage of $5.15/hour and the failure to grant health benefits to all employees—do not enable employers or employees to fulfill their *halakhic* obligations toward one another, we must ask whether there is precedent for changing the *minhag hamakom* [local custom] in response to new economic realities.

A few texts do indicate a need to adapt employment laws to changing conditions. The laws concerning a worker's right to quit a job in the middle of the day, as enumerated in the Talmud and later codes of law, change according to the availability of other workers. The principle that "the children of Israel are [God's] servants and not servants to servants" theoretically grants the worker permission to quit midday without penalty. However, in a case in which the work in question will be lost if not completed immediately and in which no other workers are available, a worker may not be able to quit early, or may face penalties for doing so (B. *Bava Metzia* 86b).[63] Here, the texts stipulate one law for an ideal situation and then offer alternate laws for different economic conditions. These laws further establish a general principle that the law should favor the person in the more precarious position. Most commonly, the law protects the worker, who stands in danger of becoming like a servant to the employer. However, when economic conditions favor the worker, the law benefits the employer.

Other texts more explicitly allow communities, and even groups of workers, to change the *minhag hamakom*. The Tosefta permits the "people of the city" to stipulate workers' wages, as well as prices and measurements (T. *Bava Metzia* 11:23). Here, we have an explicit break with the controlled free market system that some other texts describe. In granting individual communities the authority to determine wages, the rabbis indicate an understanding of the failures of a free market system. While certain economic conditions might enable such a system to succeed, other conditions will make this system unworkable. To maintain stability, the local authority must have the power to adjust wage rates as necessary.

Some traditional texts extend to members of a trade this ability to set wages and regulate work. The clearest statement of this allowance appears in Tosefta *Bava Metzia* 11:24–26:

> The wool workers and the dyers are permitted to say, "We will all be partners in any business that comes to the city."
>
> The bakers are permitted to establish work shifts among themselves. Donkey drivers are permitted to say, "We will provide another donkey for anyone whose donkey dies." If it dies through negligence, they do not need to provide a new one; if not through negligence, they do need to provide him with another donkey. And if he says, "Give me the money, and I will purchase one myself," they should not listen to him, but should buy a donkey and give it to him.
>
> Merchants are permitted to say, "We will provide another ship for anyone whose ship is destroyed." If it is destroyed through negligence, they do not need to provide another one; if it is not destroyed through negligence, they do need to provide another. And if he departs for a place to which people do not go, they do not need to provide him with another ship.

Interpreting this Tosefta, the Rashba comments, "All members of an organization are, unto themselves, like the people of a city in regard to these things. Similarly, every community is permitted to make enactments for itself and to establish fines and punishments beyond those mandated by the Torah" (*She'elot u'Teshuvot* 4:185). This opinion also appears in the Mishneh Torah[64] and in the Shulhan Arukh.[65]

Permissibility of Labor Unions and Worker Strikes

Early rabbinic discussions of stipulations among members of a single trade allow a few twentieth-century scholars, notably [Rabbis] Eliezer Waldenburg and Moshe Feinstein, to permit labor unions. According to Waldenburg, the people of a town, or their elected officials, may enact labor laws, which then become the *minhag hamakom*, incumbent on employers and employees (*She'elot u'Teshuvot* of the Tzitz Eliezer 2:23). If a particular employer fails to comply with these regulations, workers may strike in order to force the employer to adhere to the established *minhag*. As justification for the permissibility of striking, Waldenburg takes the radical step of invoking Maimonides' statement that "a person who is able to do so may take the law into his own hands" (Mishneh Torah, *Hilkhot Sanhedrin* [*Laws of Courts*] 2:12).

Furthermore, Waldenburg says, there is no need for workers to bring the employer to a *beit din* [a rabbinic court], as the workers are acting in accordance with *halakhah*. In this, Waldenburg differs from Rav Kook, who permits striking only in a case in which the employer refuses to go before a *beit din* to resolve the conflict.[66] The question of the necessity of a *beit din* may be relevant in Israel, where both Waldenburg and Kook wrote, but it is less important in America, where it is rare that both owners and workers are Jewish. When—as in most cases in contemporary America—there is no possibility of taking the case before a *beit din*, it is likely that Kook, like Waldenburg, would permit employees to strike. . . .

Feinstein further permits union members to prevent non-union members from working during a strike. As a basis for this ruling, he invokes the principle of *"ka pasakta l'ḥayuti"*—that one person may not take away the livelihood of another. He also compares the union to a *m'arupiya*, a person with whom one has an exclusive, and binding, business agreement. A company that has agreed to hire union workers may not, during a strike, contract with other, non-union workers. . . .

Feinstein is more cautious about teachers' strikes, which he permits only if the teachers "do not have enough for their needs, so that as a result, it becomes difficult for them to teach the students well, and if it is clear that if they do not teach for a day or two that the employers will pay them on time or raise their salaries . . ." (*Iggerot Moshe, Ḥoshen Mishpat* 58–59).

Jewish Employers' Obligations to Hire Union Workers

. . . Though both [Waldenburg and Feinstein] obligate workers to comply with union rules and employers to follow established *minhagim*, neither takes the additional step of requiring owners to hire only unionized workers.

An oral statement by Rav Kook begins to lead us toward taking this next step of obligating employers to hire unionized workers. Kook says:

> Within the workers' organization, which is formed for the purpose of guarding and protecting the work conditions, there is an aspect of righteousness and uprightness and *tikkun olam* [repairing the world]. The workers' organization may sue both the employer and the worker who causes this problem, for unorganized labor brings damage and loss of money to workers. For the unorganized worker works under worse conditions—both in regard to wages and in regard to working hours, etc. And this is likely to make working conditions worse in general.[67] ...

With this understanding of the phrase *"tikkun olam"* [that is, a moral requirement beyond the letter of the law], we can now understand Rav Kook to indicate that unions, though perhaps not specifically mandated by *halakhah*, help to preserve the *halakhic* system as a whole. As we have argued, traditional *halakhah* governing the relationship between employers and employees cannot work in a market in which workers do not earn enough money to provide their families with basic necessities, and in which workers may not be able to fulfill their obligations toward their employers. As Rav Kook suggests, unions may provide the only means of rectifying this situation. While legislation, including "living wage" laws and the institution of national health care, may eventually create a market in which employers and employees can fulfill their obligations to one another, it is unlikely that such legislation will be in place soon. In the meantime, unions appear to be the most efficient means of guaranteeing that workers can live on their salaries, care for their health, and avoid taking second and third jobs.

In industries such as office cleaning, there is an even greater imperative to hire unionized workers. As discussed earlier, cleaning companies engage in constant bidding wars for business, and thus are reluctant to pay workers higher wages. Therefore, the unions working in this industry generally agree not to hold companies to a union contract until the majority of companies in the region also agree to sign. The decision of each individual company thus has an impact on all other companies in the area, and on all of the associated workers. For the sake of *tikkun ha'olam*, as we have defined the term, we may insist that Jewish employers allow workers to unionize, in order to help all workers in the industry attain higher wages and benefits. To maintain the halakhically-desired equality in the employer-employee relationship, we may also insist that Jewish employees and union leaders endeavor to provide employers with the highest possible quality of work.

Rulings

1. The *halakhic* system supports a controlled free-market wage system *only* when the market produces wages on which one can support oneself and one's family.
2. Jewish employers are obligated to pay workers wages that will allow these workers to support their families without taking on additional employment or compromising their own health. Jews should work toward legislation that mandates such wages.
3. Unions offer the most effective means of collective bargaining and of ensuring that workers are treated with dignity and paid sufficiently. Therefore, Jewish employers should, when possible, hire union workers.
4. Jewish union leaders should, insofar as they are able, ensure that workers uphold the *halakhic* obligations of employees to employers. When paid enough to support themselves and their families, employees can be expected to provide employers with the best work possible. . . .

Suggestions for Further Reading

The following essays in Martin Cohen, ed. *The Observant Life: The Wisdom of Conservative Judaism for Contemporary Jews.* New York: Rabbinical Assembly, 2012:

Jacob Blumenthal. "Commerce," 491–507.
Cheryl Peretz. "Between Employers and Employees," 508–28.
Barry Leff. "Among Co-workers," 529–39.
Jane Kanarek. "Contracts," 540–50.
David Fine. "Taxation," 551–55.
Tracee L. Rosen. "Loans and Lending," 556–70.
Martin S. Cohen. "Intellectual Property," 571–81.
Martin S. Cohen. "Bequests and Inheritance," 590–605.

Elliot N. Dorff and Louis E. Newman, eds. *Jewish Choices, Jewish Voices: Money.* Philadelphia: Jewish Publication Society, 2008.

———. *Jewish Choices, Jewish Voices: Power.* Philadelphia: Jewish Publication Society, 2009.

Barry Leff. "Jewish Business Ethics." In *The Oxford Handbook of Jewish Ethics and Morality*, edited by Elliot N. Dorff and Jonathan K. Crane, 367–82. New York: Oxford University Press, 2012.

Seymour Siegel. "A Jewish View of Economic Justice." In *Contemporary Jewish Ethics and Morality: A Reader*, edited by Elliot N. Dorff and Louis E. Newman, 336–43. New York: Oxford University Press, 1995.

David A. Teutsch. *Organizational Ethics and Economic Justice.* Wyncote PA: Reconstructionist Rabbinical College Press, 2007. Reprinted as part of his *Guide to Jewish Practice: Volume 1 — Everyday Living*, 315–402. Wyncote PA: Reconstructionist Rabbinical College Press, 2011.

CHAPTER NINE

Bein Adam LaMakom

Rulings on Ritual Observance

In Conservative/Masorti Judaism, rituals are integral to Jewish living. To be sure that they are understood and performed correctly, the Conservative movement's Committee on Jewish Law and Standards has published more than two hundred responsa on prayer, the Sabbath, festivals, High Holy Days, fasts, dietary laws, and life cycle events. You can find them in the first two sections (*Orah Ḥyyim* and *Yoreh De'ah*) of the committee's website, https://www.rabbinicalassembly.org/jewish-law/committee-jewish-law-and-standards.

Why are Jewish rituals—and the particulars of their practice—considered so important? The traditional answer is that God commanded the Jewish people to observe these rituals, just as God commanded the moral parts of Jewish tradition. For some Jews, including some Conservative Jews, that is enough.

Other Conservative Jews, however, are motivated by the power of ritual to identify community. For them, eating kosher foods exclusively identifies them as Jewish. The dietary laws and other Jewish rituals tie Jews to their tradition and community, present, past, and future.

Still others appreciate the power of rituals to mark off moments in time. When certain moments are marked as different from others, the days of our lives become different as well—and, for that matter, the morning of one day is different from that day's afternoon and evening. Prayers that identify the parts of the day, week, and year and rituals that articulate different themes for the weekday, Sabbath, festivals, High Holy Days, and fasts help us to invest these times with varying meanings. They also join us with family, friends, and community for prayer, meals, singing, and conversation, helping us nurture kinship and connectedness.

Finally, rituals help to make an art of life. Songs, foods, artwork, special events (participating in a seder on Passover, blowing the shofar on Rosh Hashanah, eating in a sukkah on Sukkot), blessings, and liturgy sung to distinctive melodies give life character and flavor. Under the glow of Sabbath candles, parents may bless their children. A husband may sing "A Woman of Valor" (*Eishet Hayyil*, Proverbs 31) to his wife. A wife may sing Psalm 15 or Psalm 112 to her husband. Together the family may sing the blessings over the wine (*Kiddush*) and recite the blessings over washing one's hands and bread. Everyone may join in singing Shabbat songs and the Blessings after Meals (*Birkat ha-Mazon*).

Responsum on Tattooing and Body Piercing

Sometimes Conservative responsa address contemporary rituals. As one example, given the high percentage of young Jews getting "inked" or piercing their bodies to accommodate jewelry, the CJLS adopted a responsum on tattooing and body piercing.

In his responsum, Rabbi Alan Lucas asked these questions: "Is either body piercing (nose, navel, etc.) or tattooing permitted? Does doing either one preclude taking part in synagogue rituals or being buried in a Jewish cemetery?" In response, he explains that from the vantage point of Jewish law, tattooing is not allowed, but body piercing is permitted when done safely and modestly. (For a defense of tattooing and a rabbi's reactions to her daughter's tattoo, see this chapter's suggestions for further reading.)

The CJLS adopted his paper (excerpted here), on March 11, 1997, by a vote of seventeen in favor and four abstaining (17-0-4). To read the full responsum, see http://www.rabbinicalassembly.org/sites/default/files /public/halakhah/teshuvot/19912000/lucas_tattooing.pdf.

Tattooing

The prohibition of tattooing is found in the Torah: "You shall not make gashes in your flesh for the dead, nor incise any marks on yourselves: I am the Lord."[1]

It is the second part of this verse from which we derive the general prohibition against tattooing. From the outset there is disagreement about what precisely makes tattooing a prohibited act. The anonymous author of a mishnah states that it is the lasting and permanent nature of tattooing that makes it a culpable act: "If a man wrote [on his skin] pricked-in writing [he is culpable] . . . but only if he writes it and pricks it in with ink or eye-paint or anything that leaves a lasting mark."[2]

But Rabbi Simeon b. Judah disagrees and says that it is the inclusion of God's name that makes it a culpable act: "Rabbi Simeon b. Judah says in the name of Rabbi Simeon: He is not culpable unless he writes there the name [of a god], for it is written, *'Or incise any marks on yourselves: I am the Lord.'*"[3]

The Gemara [Talmud] goes on to debate whether it is the inclusion of God's name or that of a pagan deity that makes it a culpable act. The Rambam [Maimonides] clearly sees the origin of this prohibition as an act of idolatry. He includes it in his section concerning idolatry and then explicitly states: "This was a custom among the pagans who marked themselves for idolatry."[4] But the Rambam concludes that regardless of intent, the act of tattooing is prohibited.[5]

Aaron Demsky of Bar Ilan University, in an article in the *Encyclopaedia Judaica*,[6] goes even further to suggest that non-idolatrous tattooing may have been permitted in Biblical times. He cites the following Biblical references:

One shall say, "I am the Lord's," another shall use the name of "Jacob," another shall mark his arm "of the Lord's" and adopt the name of "Israel."[7]

See, I have engraved you on the palms of My hands.[8]

Like a sign on every man's hand that all men may know His doings.[9]

While these verses may be purely metaphoric, Demsky suggests they could be taken literally as instances of tattooing that were acceptable in Biblical times. He goes on to add that A. Cowley showed that in Elephantine, slaves of Jews were marked with the name of their owners as was the general practice.[10]

Regardless of the exact limits of this prohibition, over time the Rabbis clearly extended the prohibition to include all tattooing.[11]

In our day, the prohibition against all forms of tattooing, regardless of their intent, should be maintained. In addition to the fact that Judaism has a long history of distaste for tattoos, tattooing becomes even more distasteful when confronted with a contemporary secular society that is constantly challenging the Jewish concept that we are created "in the Image of God," and that our bodies are to be viewed as a precious gift on loan from God, to be entrusted into our care and not our personal property to do with as we choose. Voluntary tattooing, even if not done for idolatrous purposes, expresses a negation of this fundamental Jewish perspective. As tattoos become more popular in contemporary society, there is a need to reinforce the prohibition against tattooing in our communities and counterbalance it with education regarding the traditional concept that we are created "in the Image of God."

However distasteful we may find the practice, though, there is no basis for restricting burial to a Jew who violates this prohibition or even limiting [his or her] participation in synagogue ritual. The fact that someone may have violated the laws of kashrut at some point in his or her life or violated the laws of Shabbat would not merit such sanctions; the prohibition against tattooing is certainly no worse. It is only because of the permanent nature of the tattoo that the transgression is still visible.

New laser technology has raised the possibility of removing what was once irremovable. To date, this procedure is painful, long, and very expensive. However, it will probably not be long before the process is refined to the point where it will not be painful, overly involved, or very expensive. At such time it might be appropriate for the CJLS to consider whether removal of tattoos should become a requirement of conversion or burial.

The prohibition of tattooing throughout the halakhic literature deals only with personal, voluntary tattooing. With respect to the reprehensible practice of the Nazis who marked the arms of Jews with tattooed numbers and letters during the Shoah, the *Shulḥan Arukh* makes it clear that those who bear these tattoos are blameless: "If it [the tattoo] was done in the flesh of another, the one to whom it was done is blameless."[12]

Tattoos that are used in cancer treatment or any similar medical procedure to permanently mark the body for necessary lifesaving treatment are also not included in the prohibition against tattooing.[13]

The prohibition against tattoos applies only to permanent marks to the skin. Therefore hand stamps or other popular children's decorations that mimic tattoos and paint the skin in a nonpermanent manner cannot be included under the prohibition of tattooing. However, for the purpose of education it might be appropriate for parents to make the distinction clear to their children. These also present an excellent opportunity to introduce young children to the concept that we are created "in God's Image," and the implications of that concept.

Body Piercing

. . . What has long been an issue only of "ear piercing" and limited to women has now been extended to men and to almost every imaginable part of the body capable of being pierced.[14] While many of us may not understand why anyone would want to pierce some of the parts of the body, the question before us asks if such acts render one unfit for ritual inclusion or burial.

Ear-piercing is mentioned in the Bible in several contexts. The most familiar is with reference to a Hebrew slave who was to be freed in the seventh year of servitude but in declaring his love for his master might refuse to go free: "His master shall take him before God. He shall be brought to the door or the doorpost, and his master shall pierce his ear with an awl; and he shall then remain his slave for life."[15]

There is some disagreement in the Gemara as to how permanent this piercing of the slave's ear was supposed to be.[16] But our piercing is clearly of a non-permanent nature and its intent is purely decorative. This type of piercing was also known in the Bible:

I inquired of her, "Whose daughter are you?" . . . And I put the ring on her nose and the bands on her arm.[17]

Aaron said to them, "Take off the gold rings that are on the ears of your wives. . . ."[18]

I decked you out in finery. . . . I put a ring in your nose, and earrings in your ears.[19]

This is also well documented in Rabbinic times: "Small girls may go out [on Shabbat] with threads or even chips in their ears."[20]
. . . There may be references to male ear piercing in the Talmud as well. In a discussion regarding the wearing of jewelry on Shabbat, the Gemara states: "A tailor must not go out with a needle stuck in his garment, nor a carpenter with a chip in his ear."[21] Rashi refers to a custom in his day for men to wear earrings that were signs of their respective trades.[22] While Rashi seems to understand this chip as being tucked behind the ear, Jacob Lauterbach understands it as an example of piercing.[23] The same expression is found in the above cited mishnah of Shabbat and clearly refers to piercing.[24] It was also an established custom in European countries well into the Middle Ages for tradesmen to wear pierced earrings of the symbol of their trade.

The surgical process of piercing both the ear and the nose seems to be well documented in the Bible and the Talmud. While there are many today who would find the Biblical custom of nose piercing unacceptable, there are apparently many young people today who find it attractive. And while some are uncomfortable with men having their ears pierced, even this has a precedent in traditional literature. The only issue that seems to direct this matter is the fashions of the day. It is hard to argue from a halakhic perspective that there is a substantive difference between the non-permanent piercing of the ear for fashion purposes and the non-permanent piercing of the eyebrow, navel or even nipple. The lack of aesthetic appeal to many of us is hardly a halakhic consideration.

There are, however, some legitimate concerns that could and should be raised. There is a concern that an inappropriate procedure or lack of proper hygiene involved in the piercing of a clitoris, nipple, or scrotum, for example, could lead to an infection with significant consequences. Piercing should only be done by those medically qualified to address these concerns.

In addition there is the issue of "in God's Image" and modesty. With respect to the traditional Jewish value, one has to wonder if private parts of the body are being pierced for fashion purposes if the intent is to keep that private part private. While there may be no prohibition against such body piercings, they must be placed in the larger context that values privacy for private parts of the body, for that remains an important Jewish value.

And, while ear piercing seems to be a fairly benign practice, there comes some point at which multiple piercings of the body, however fashionable, begin to challenge our concept that we are created in God's image. It seems to me that Jews sufficiently educated and sensitive to the concepts of modesty, and being created in God's image, will limit themselves appropriately regarding body piercing.

I am reminded of a lecture that Rabbi David Weiss Halivni once gave at the Seminary regarding the permissibility of animal hunting for pleasure by Jews. He quoted Rabbi Ezekiel ben Judah Landau.[25] After taking some time to explain why it was indeed permitted by the Torah, he concluded by saying, "Yes, it is permitted, but what kind of a Jew would want to hunt for pleasure?" While not nearly as serious an issue as hunting, one can only wonder what questions about body piercing and tattooing tell us about our contemporary community.

Ultimately this seems to be a matter of fashion that may pass with time. But until then, we should strengthen the sense of modesty, which should guide our fashion choices and underscore our belief that we are created "in God's Image" in an attempt to balance contemporary pressures. But I see no basis for any sanctions against those who engage in such fashions, certainly not of the magnitude of refusing burial in a Jewish cemetery or refraining from including them in any synagogue practices.

Conclusion

Tattooing is an explicit prohibition in the Torah. However, those who violate this prohibition may be buried in a Jewish cemetery and participate fully in all synagogue ritual. While no sanctions are imposed, the practice should continue to be discouraged as a violation of the Torah. Body piercing is not prohibited, although legitimate concerns regarding safety and modesty and other traditional Jewish values should be taken into consideration to guide one's choices. At all times a Jew should remember that we are created "in God's Image." We are called upon to incorporate this understanding in all our decisions.

Responsum on Forming a Minyan on the Internet

Can one form a prayer quorum of ten adults (minyan) over the Internet? Although this may be especially important for people who live in rural areas or cannot leave their homes for medical reasons, presumably it also applies to employees who wish to participate in a minyan for the afternoon service (*Minḥah*) but cannot take the time to travel to a synagogue, pray, and then travel back again. In addition, certain prayers, such as the *Kedushah* and mourner's *Kaddish*, may only be recited in the context of a minyan. Consequently, this issue is relevant for Jews who wish to be able to recite particular prayers.

Rabbi Avram Israel Reisner's responsum, "Wired to the Kadosh Barukh Hu: Minyan through the Internet," asked: "May one pray over the Internet? Constitute a minyan over the Internet? Through e-mail, in chat rooms, only with a real-time audio or video connection? Is this permissible in telephone or video conferences? If it is not now permissible, is there some foreseeable technological advance that would make it so?"

The CJLS approved his paper on March 13, 2001, by a vote of eighteen in favor, two opposed, and one abstaining (18–2–1). At the time, video conferencing was not available, but the responsum's principles would apply to that as well. To read the full responsum, see https://www.rabbinicalassembly .org/sites/default/files/assets/public/halakhah/teshuvot/19912000/reisner _internetminyan.pdf.

Considering Virtual Assembly

. . . God, by divine nature, does not need our ingenuity of wire or wave in order to hear our prayers. But in order for us to get together for prayer, which is an essential requirement of Jewish communal prayer, we might wish to consider technological solutions. Particularly for Jews in far-flung communities, where a minyan is not possible, could virtual assembly serve the purpose of allowing communal prayer? Clearly, there is unlikely to be an unequivocal ruling on this question in our ancient sources; these technological developments were largely undreamed of even earlier in our own generation. We need to seek precedents that will establish principles that can guide our inference and extrapolation to present realities and beyond.

What Constitutes a Minyan?

The guiding precedent in the matter of constituting a minyan is found in Shulḥan Arukh, *Oraḥ Ḥayyim* 55. The text considers several cases, standing us in good stead to extrapolate the operant principles. I cite the relevant numbers in full: . . .

13] The ten [who constitute the minyan] must be in one place and the leader with them. If one stands in the doorway, . . . from the point where the interior face of the door rests and outward is treated as outside.

14] If a person is standing outside the synagogue and there is a window, even if it is several stories high and smaller than four cubits [six feet] wide, if he shows his face [in the window] he may be counted. (Note: Roofs and upper floors are not considered to be in the house. One who stands there is not counted.)

15] If a few of them [that is, the potential minyan] are inside and a few are outside, and the leader is positioned in the entryway—he connects them [to form one minyan]. . . .

18] If part of the ten were in the synagogue and part were in the courtyard, they do not connect [to form a minyan].

What Constitutes the Same Place?

Clearly the model that the sages had in mind was a physical model of place. May we extend that notion into hyper-space? . . .

The essential dilemma that might cause us to wish to allow Internet minyanim has an altogether other solution. The problem is that some individual Jews, far from an organized community, would wish — need at times — to participate in communal prayers. For that, we need not offer to count them in the minyan at all, but only to allow them to participate.

The solution grows from Tosafot's solution of the disagreement between Rav and R. Yehoshua ben Levi. The conclusion there was that Rav's dictum maintaining that the rules of the quorum require real physical proximity are true for constituting the quorum, but that once a duly constituted quorum is formed, anyone may respond to its prayers. At issue, then, is not whether one may constitute a quorum over the Internet; one may not. But the issue is rather whether one may respond and fulfill one's obligations from outside the quorum site, if one has heard the prayer of the minyan. Here, the precedents suggest that one may, indeed, do so. Thus, a person needing to hear the Megillah but unable to read it alone and unable to attend a minyan might hook up by telephone or modem to a site that is holding a minyan and fulfill their obligations thereby. . . .

As a matter of policy, should we allow this? To allow accessing of the minyan from remote locations, even though some minyan must yet convene, is to reduce the need of individuals to go out of their way to attend the minyan. Jan Urbach, a rabbinical student and attorney, asked whether busy attorneys that are currently making time for attendance at minyan will not be seduced into the easier route of connecting by video wall to their minyan. Indeed, some threat of such a phenomenon is present, but to rule against this distance rule would also be a hardship with regard to shut-ins and nursing-home patients for whom we would want to be able to offer distant connections to functioning services. . . .

The crux of the matter lies here. We have not permitted convening a minyan through long-distance connection. Will even the lesser technology of long distance audio connection threaten the drawing power of our synagogues? While much that is in modern culture does indeed compete with our synagogues for the attention of our members, it is hard to imagine that as a large scale phenomenon our members will stay home from synagogue and connect to it by means of a computer. It is the social aspect of the service that will remain our greatest attraction. Only in rare or exigent cases, with regard to shut-ins and hospital patients, those traveling or simply resident in distant parts, in hurricane or blizzard conditions, is the advantage of this use of distant-connection to the minyan compelling. Indeed, such use is already assumed by this body (Teshuva, CJLS 1989 by R. Gordon Tucker). It is only in those extraordinary conditions that we imagine its use.

Wherever possible in such cases, it is clearly desirable to establish a two-way audio-video connection to the whole minyan, since it is the minyan that enables the communal prayers to be held at all, and this best approximates being present given our current technology, now and in the foreseeable future. However, since the individual connected electronically is in the position of one overhearing from outside the room, it would be sufficient for the *shali'ah tzibbur* [the one leading the service] to have voice contact with the individual who wishes to respond, or, indeed, for the contact to be exclusively one way.

Kaddish

. . . Whereas *kaddish* is only to be recited in the presence of a minyan, the individual reciting *kaddish* at home along with a duly constituted minyan, but unheard by that minyan, is in a materially similar position to one muttering softly within the minyan among louder recitations [and therefore permissible]. It is necessary to reiterate, however, that comfort finds its greatest expression in tactile contact and human warmth. By a distant connection to a minyan, where no other connection is possible, one may fulfill one's obligations as a mourner to honor the deceased, but the corollary value of the minyan as a source of comfort cannot be found in a distant connection that does not, at least, have two-way capability, and will be found best in the proximate contact with a minyan. As Leon Wieseltier wrote simply in his recent, extended meditation on the personal meaning of saying *kaddish*, "I am here for them, and they are here for me."

The Issue of Time Zones

It was pointed out to me that distant participation in the minyan might entail the attempt to fulfill an obligation outside of its proper time, for instance, to hear the reading of the Megillah that is being done in Israel on

Purim night while it is yet the previous afternoon in the location wherein the listener resides, or to fulfill the requirement of reciting Sh'ma and its blessings in *Shaḥarit* [the morning prayers] while it is yet dark. It is apparent to me that to fulfill any time-bound obligation this way, the listener would need to do so by connecting to a minyan functioning within the relevant time-frame of the one wishing to fulfill the obligation. . . .

Conclusions

1. A minyan may not be constituted over the Internet, an audio- or video-conference, or any other medium of long distance communication. Only physical proximity, as defined, that is being in the same room with the *shaliaḥ tzibbur*, allows a quorum to be constituted.

2. Once a quorum has been duly constituted, anyone hearing the prayers being offered in that minyan may respond and fulfill their obligations thereby, even over long distance communications of whatever sort. . . . Some would refrain from fulfilling the specific requirement to hear the shofar in this way, due to its specific nature, but others permit this as well. This committee is on record among those who would allow even the hearing of Shofar in this way.

3. This specifically refers to hearing. A real-time audio connection is necessary. A two-way connection to the whole minyan is preferable, though connection to the *shali'aḥ tzibbur* alone or a one way connection linking the minyan to the individual are sufficient. E-mail and chat room or other typewritten connections do not suffice. Video connections are not necessary, and in the absence of audio would not suffice.

4. A clear hierarchy of preference is discernible here. It is preferable by far to attend a minyan, for the full social and communal effect of minyan, for which it was established, is only possible in that way. Less desirable, but closest to attendance at a minyan proper, is real-time two-way audio-video connection, wherein the individual, though unable to reach the other people in the minyan, is able to converse with them and see and be seen by them. Only in rare or exigent circumstances should one enact the third, and least desirable method, of fulfilling one's obligation to pray with a minyan by attaching oneself to that minyan

through a one-way audio vehicle, essentially overhearing them as one standing outside the synagogue.

5. With regard to Mourner's Kaddish, some member of the minyan must recite the *Kaddish*, but a participant at a distant location may recite it along with them, as this is not considered a superfluous blessing (*berakhah l'vatalah*). There is no obligation to pursue additional opportunities to recite *Kaddish*, and this should be discouraged.

6. To fulfill one's time-bound obligation, the prayer must be offered during the requisite period in the frame of reference of the one whose obligation is to be fulfilled.

Responsum on Playing Sports on Shabbat

Conservative leaders have engaged in extensive deliberations about what constitutes appropriate practice on the Sabbath. One such example is Rabbi Jonathan Lubliner's responsum, "Recreational Sports on Shabbat," asking, "May one exercise or play recreational sports on Shabbat? If so, what kinds of sports and exercise are compatible with Shabbat observance and what kinds are not?"

The CJLS voted on its sections individually. The general conclusions (excerpted here) were approved on May 13, 2015, by a vote of thirteen in favor, one against, and four abstaining (13–1–4). Other sections (which also follow) were approved by different votes, as follows: "Is it Permissible to Ride a Bicycle or a Skateboard on Shabbat?" by 10–5–3; "Riding a Bicycle for the Performance of a Mitzvah" by 14–4–0; "Non-motorized Scooters, Tricycles, Skates and Skateboards" by 17–1–0; "Playing Court and Field Sports on Shabbat" by 17–0–1; "Ice Skating on Shabbat" by 11–6–1; "Running on Shabbat" by 16–1–1; "Skiing on Shabbat" by 9–1–8; "Swimming on Shabbat" by 18–0–0; "Weight Lifting and Body Building" by 11–2–5; "Yoga on Shabbat" by 15–1–2; and "Bathing after Exercise on Shabbat" by 11–2–5. To read the full seventy-seven-page responsum, see https://www.rabbinicalassembly.org/sites/default/files/assets/public/halakhah/teshuvot/2011-2020/lubliner-recreation-sports-shabbat.pdf.

Exercising or Playing Sports on Shabbat: General Conclusions

Oneg Shabbat [joy on the Sabbath] is a *mitzvah* [a positive commandment]. Although the Torah does not explicitly mention it, numerous authorities sought to accord the enjoyment of Shabbat *d'oraita*-like status [that is, as if it came from the Torah directly], legally and homiletically.

Traditional *halakhic* sources tend to prohibit exercise generally on the basis of *shevut* [a Rabbinically enacted prohibition]; even when permissible, they do not perceive it as a vehicle in and of itself for *oneg Shabbat*. Given important changes in our cultural perceptions and the importance they play in framing a meaningful protective framework for Shabbat observance, it is no longer tenable to maintain a blanket prohibition of all exercise as *tirḥa yetirta* (superfluous exertion) or *u'vdin d'ḥol* [a weekday activity]. In our time many types of exercise can and do serve as permissible — even praiseworthy — activities for the pursuit of *oneg Shabbat*.

The halakhic literature points to a recognition that subjective enjoyment plays an important, if not ultimate, role in determining whether or not an activity is a matter of *oneg Shabbat* or *shevut* for the individual. This may mean that while one person may be permitted to engage in a certain activity because he finds it Shabbat-enhancing, another may be prohibited from doing so because it diminishes his enjoyment of Shabbat.

For those who engage regularly in exercise during the week, but do not actually enjoy the experience, or are training in pursuit of specific goals, exercise on Shabbat does not constitute *oneg Shabbat*; on the contrary, it remains *u'vdin d'ḥol* [a weekday activity]. With the exception of medical reasons (see below), the only permissible rationale for engaging in recreational sports or exercise activity on Shabbat is for the sake of enhancing one's experience of Shabbat itself.

For those in good health, the general benefits of exercise do not automatically override the issue of *shevut*. Those with skeleto-muscular issues, however, who need to follow therapeutic routines for the sake of mobility or relief from pain must do so on Shabbat — not because it yields them pleasure, but because it is a medical necessity.

Organized league sports, competitive racing against a clock or others for the sake of recognition, attainment of a prize, or first place within a league remain subject to the prohibition of *shevut* because their purpose is primarily goal oriented. They may be very enjoyable, especially for the victors, but this does not constitute *oneg Shabbat*.

Synagogues, Jewish schools, and other institutions within the Jewish community should neither sponsor nor participate in charity races or other sporting events to benefit not-for-profit causes when such events take place on Shabbat. Aside from the likelihood of violating myriad proscriptions of Toraitic law, the purpose of such events, no matter how worthy the cause, has nothing to do with the concept of *oneg Shabbat*.

No type of recreational sport or exercise may trump a *melakhah* [one of the thirty-nine categories of work that, according to Rabbinic interpretation, are prohibited by the Torah on the Sabbath] or its derivative categories. Any activity requiring prohibited types of carrying, travel beyond Shabbat boundaries, or the recording of data are forbidden as *d'oraita* [Torah] injunctions and not simply as matters of *shevut* [Rabbinic injunctions].

Beyond the broad parameters of the *oneg Shabbat* and *shevut*, the permissibility of individual types of exercise or sports and their compatibility with Shabbat will depend on the equipment they require, their respective characters, and the venues where they take place.

Is It Permissible to Ride a Bicycle or a Skateboard on Shabbat?

Riding a bicycle on Shabbat for the sake of *oneg* [joy] is not permitted, even within an *eruv* [a boundary marker, usually a wire or a natural barrier such as a river, that designates an area as a private domain within which a Jew may carry or travel on Shabbat just as one may do in one's home], because of *shema yitaken*, the concern that the rider may repair a flat tire or fix a derailed chain, especially if the breakdown occurs at some distance from one's destination.

Is It Permissible to Bicycle on Shabbat for the Performance of a Mitzvah?

For the performance of a mitzvah that takes place on Shabbat, it is permitted to ride a bicycle to/from one's destination, as long as doing so enables one to bike instead of drive because it is too far to walk; and so long as such travel takes place entirely within the boundaries of an *eruv*.

Are Non-motorized Scooters, Tricycles, Skates, and Skateboards Permissible?

Non-motorized scooters, tricycles, in-line skates, and skateboards are permissible on Shabbat within an *eruv* or private spaces.

Is It Permissible to Play Court and Field Sports on Shabbat?

... Recreational games such as baseball, softball, soccer, basketball, tennis, and other racquet sports, touch or flag football are permitted on Shabbat within an *eruv*.

Tackle football is not permitted on Shabbat.

Golf is not permitted on Shabbat because of the creation of divots [pieces of turf cut out of the ground by a golf club when a golfer makes a stroke]. Those who wish to hit golf balls from a non-grass mat on Shabbat may do so within an *eruv*.

Is Ice Skating Permissible on Shabbat?

Ice skating is permissible on Shabbat when it does not entail violations of Shabbat including, but not limited to, driving to/from a rink, paying to rent skates or for admission, or carrying outside of an *eruv*. Outdoor skating must take place within an *eruv*. Competitive skating of all types is impermissible on Shabbat.

Is Running Permissible on Shabbat?

Jogging or running at a leisurely pace constitutes a legitimate form of *oneg Shabbat*, if pursued for its own enjoyment, rather than for the purpose of training or racing.

Organized races remain prohibited as a matter of *shevut*. Similarly, running against one's own watch to beat a particular personal best is incompatible with the spirit of Shabbat.

The limits of *Teḥum Shabbat* [the distance from one's home on Shabbat, even if it is not one's permanent home, beyond which one may not go on Shabbat] apply to the distance and routes that runners may take.

Is It Permissible to Ski on Shabbat?

Downhill skiing and cross-country skiing are permissible on Shabbat only within an *eruv*. . . .

It is a violation of Shabbat to purchase lift tickets on Shabbat.

The limits of *Teḥum Shabbat* apply to the distance and routes that skiers may take.

Is Swimming Permissible on Shabbat?

Swimming in a pool or a natural body of water is permitted on Shabbat.

Contemporary flotation devices and pool toys may be used within an *eruv*. The same would apply to the carrying of towels or robes.

Care should be taken on Shabbat not to wring one's hair or bathing suit after swimming. One may rub one's hair with a towel, but should not wring out the towel after use.

Are Weight Lifting and Body Building Permitted on Shabbat?

Weight lifting and body building with free weights or machines are not permitted on Shabbat. Light stretching and mild calisthenics that do not require excessive exertion are permissible.

Is Yoga Permitted on Shabbat?

Yoga is permitted on Shabbat, with the sole exception of Bikram, which requires exercise in a highly heated room to induce heavy perspiration for therapeutic reasons.

Is Bathing after Exercise on Shabbat Permissible?

Bathing or showering one's entire body on Shabbat is permissible. Those living in large apartment complexes with multiple non-Jewish residents and large boilers for common use and those who own solar water heaters may take warm showers on Shabbat, but should not use water hot enough to qualify as *yad soledet bo* [one would flinch upon putting one's hand in it]. For those with conventional water heaters, the heating of water for bathing on Shabbat constitutes an act of *bishul* [cooking] and is therefore impermissible.

Shampoo, liquid and bar soap are permitted for Shabbat use.

Care should be taken on Shabbat not to wring out one's towel or hair after washing.

Responsa on the Dietary Laws (*Kashrut*)

The CJLS has passed many responsa regarding the dietary laws, including how food is procured, prepared, and served.

Rabbis Elliot N. Dorff and Joel Roth's responsum, "Is Shackling and Hoisting Animals during Slaughter a Violation of Jewish Laws Prohibiting Inflicting Pain to Animals?" (excerpted here), was accepted on September 20, 2000, by a vote of 21–0–0. To read the full responsum, see http://www.rabbinicalassembly.org/sites/default/files/public/halakhah/teshuvot/19912000/dorffroth_shackling.pdf.

Next, Rabbi Avram Israel Reisner's responsum asked "Are Genetically Engineered Foodstuffs Kosher?" Specifically, "If a genetic sequence is adapted from a non-kosher species and implanted in a new strain of a kosher foodstuff—for example, if a gene for swine growth hormone is introduced into a potato to induce larger growth, or if a gene from an insect is introduced into a tomato plant in order to give it unusual qualities of pest resistance—is that new strain rendered non-kosher?" The CJLS approved his responsum on December 10, 1997, by a vote of 16–0–0. To read it in full, see http://www.rabbinicalassembly.org/sites/default/files/public/halakhah/teshuvot/19912000/reisner_curiouser.pdf.

Shackling and Hoisting Animals during Slaughter

Now that kosher, humane slaughter using upright pens is both possible and widespread, we find shackling and hoisting to be a violation of Jewish laws forbidding cruelty to animals (*tza'ar ba'alei ḥayyim*) and requiring that we avoid unnecessary dangers to human life. As the CJLS, then, we rule that shackling and hoisting should be stopped.

The Kashrut of Genetically Engineered Foodstuffs

The kashrut laws of prohibited admixtures do not apply to the submicro-scopic manipulation of genetic material. The laws of *kilayim* [intermixing species of seeds or animals—Leviticus 19:19, Deuteronomy 22:9–11], which might apply, show an extraordinary tendency toward leniency. Natural *kilayim* products, though the fruit of an illicit operation of *kilayim*, have nonetheless been permitted as early as the Tosefta [second century CE], and the rationale tying the laws of *kilayim* to the Creation, while often tempting exegetes, has not become the dominant law.

Of genetically engineered foodstuffs it should be minimally said that even if genetic engineering is to be prohibited, the products thereof are permissible.

Of the process of genetic engineering itself, moreover, I think there is ample reason to permit it even to the Jew. (1) The process of genetic engineering bears only a very minimal resemblance to the sexual and grafting processes that the Torah bans. If, indeed, we are enjoined to treat the Torah's ban as a *ḥukkah* [a law commanded by God but without clear rationale]—a *ukase*—and not to expand its parameters beyond the parameters given, then it seems that no extension to genetic techniques is warranted. (2) Although the question was formulated to focus on commercial use of genetic engineering, a fuller review of those very commercial considerations would find that most commercial considerations have a ramification that could be life-saving. Thus, for instance, increased pest resistance, though useful to the food conglomerates in terms of their efficiency, will also prove useful in the endeavor to feed the world's starving population. Already such reports are mixed in among the early results of genetic engineering. Nothing appears more crassly commercial than engineering for greater shelf-life, but this, too, can facilitate distribution of foodstuffs to the needy. Given the law's tendency to limit the scope of the prohibition of *kilayim*, this would appear to be sufficient reason to permit genetic engineering to continue. (3) On the matter of gross changes in the characteristics by which species are recognized, it remains necessary to engage in further study and consideration.

Magen Tzedek (Shield of Justice)

To advance ethical food procurement, preparation, and serving, the Rabbinical Assembly's Magen Tzedek program, initiated by Rabbi Morris Allen, awards the Shield of Justice to establishments that observe not only kosher laws but also Jewish laws regarding five related areas of concern: worker, animal, consumer, and environmental welfare, as well as corporate integrity.

Rabbi Joshua Ratner's report detailing Magen Tzedek's standards (excerpted here) was published in September 2011. To read the full report, see http://www.rabbinicalassembly.org/sites/default/files/public/social _action/magen_tzedek/magen-tzedek-sources.pdf. To read Rabbi Avram Reisner's *Al Pi Din* (According to law), the background paper that provides the halakhic grounding for these stances, see this chapter's suggestions for further reading.

Standards and Religious Underpinnings

. . . As we have sought to develop Magen Tzedek and introduce it to the North American marketplace, we have found that we, too, must balance between competing tensions and interests, between our ideals and the pragmatics of the business world. Magen Tzedek is a ground-breaking endeavor, attempting to create something that has never before been done either within Judaism or American industry—creating a simultaneous set of comprehensive standards governing labor, health, corporate integrity, environment, and animal welfare. As with the adoption of any system of standards, there are those who might wish that an individual standard be more robust than it appears. But it is important to understand both the holistic and the developmental nature of the Magen Tzedek enterprise. What we have done by insisting that every certified product must meet all of our standards is to raise the bar of industry practice in five different categories concurrently. This approach enables us to push further regarding labor rights, where fairly advanced norms and standards already have been accepted by industries.

With regard to animal welfare, however, our effort to improve industry practice must begin at a more rudimentary level. Kashrut supervision rarely extends to the farm where animals are raised. Yet even at the level of kosher meat-packing plants, basic standards of animal welfare are not yet being routinely met. We have chosen to address the animal welfare issues at the level of the kashrut supervision and/or meat-packing plant first and allow producers a phase-in period to encourage suppliers to meet Magen Tzedek's broader standards. This will allow for more robust standards to be implemented in future years. The result is that the Magen Tzedek seal will advance substantially our desire for more ethical industry conduct within each of the five areas, bringing the Jewish commitment to ethics and social justice directly into the marketplace and the home. This is an accomplishment for which we, as Conservative rabbis, should be proud.

Labor Practices and Healthy Workplace Requirements

Any entity seeking Magen Tzedek certification must meet or exceed stringent labor practices requirements for all employees who are subject to U.S. federal wage and hour laws. To qualify, an entity must, among other things, (1) respect an employee's right to earn a living wage by paying all employees at least 15% more than the highest mandated U.S., federal, state or local minimum wage; (2) limit the maximum hours an employee can work to comply with federal and state law; (3) pay overtime salary in accordance with the most beneficial of all applicable federal and state labor laws and limit overtime obligations to no more than 20% of normal working hours per week; (4) provide clearly defined benefits of at least 35% of the base wage for all nonexempt employees; (5) allow for maternity/ paternity leave that comports with the most favorable applicable state or federal law; (6) allow for unpaid bereavement leave of at least three days for local leave or five days for out-of-state leave for the death of a family member as defined by Jewish law as well as for the death of other family members; (7) provide child care arrangements for employees; (8) provide for at least a minimum 20-minute unpaid lunch break and two 10-minute paid breaks, one before and one after the lunch break; (9) permit the right of employees to organize into unions; (10) provide a safe and healthy workplace environment and take effective steps to prevent potential accidents and injury to workers' health; and (11) promote gender diversity and avoid discrimination based on race, national or social origin, immigration status, caste, birth, religion, disability, gender, sexual orientation, family responsibilities, marital status, union membership, political opinions, or age in hiring, salary, promotion, or firing. Additionally, any Magen Tzedek entity shall employ only documented workers and shall not employ child or forced labor.

These robust labor standards are in keeping with Judaism's rich history of protecting the well-being of workers. The Torah in particular takes pains to prohibit exploitation of employees by their employer. The Torah insists, for example, that employers pay employees on the day of their labor (Lev. 19:13). Additionally, the standard's insistence on paying workers a living wage and its endorsement of the right to collective bargaining builds upon the values undergirding the . . . CJLS teshuvah, . . . Rabbi Jill Jacobs' "Work, Workers and the Jewish Owner." Moreover, medieval and modern halakhists have found that Judaism endorses a variety of work-related benefits. . . . Jewish legal authorities have held that, under Jewish law, employees are entitled to paid sick leave, employees limited by a disability are entitled to full wages, and employees are entitled to retirement benefits. . . . Magen Tzedek–certified entities will embrace these employee protections, adopting the type of equitable workplace relationship that halakhah calls on us to enact.

Magen Tzedek–certified products will also require companies to adhere to robust health and safety standards. Any company producing a Magen Tzedek–certified product must take affirmative steps to prevent potential accidents and injuries; conduct an annual independent health and safety inspection; publicly maintain inspection records; participate in a worker-management safety program to proactively discuss health and safety issues; appoint a senior management representative to be responsible for ensuring a safe and healthy workplace; provide appropriate safety training to personnel on a regular basis and in languages that employees understand; provide appropriate safety equipment; and establish systems to detect, avoid, or respond to potential threats to the health and safety of personnel. Additionally, all personnel shall have the right to remove themselves from imminent serious danger without seeking permission from the company and shall have on-site emergency healthcare access.

The halakhah has long required an employer to protect the safety and welfare of its employees. The general obligation of an individual to protect another from harm is encapsulated in the Shulḥan Arukh, in the very last section of Ḥoshen Mishpat (427), in which the Meḥaber [Joseph Karo, its author] states: "It is a positive commandment to remove any stumbling-block that might endanger life."

But, as Rabbi Avram Reisner points out in *Al Pi Din*, an employer's obligations toward his workers are greater than this standard obligation because, based on BT *Bava Metzia* 80b, employees delegate their judgment on health and safety workplace matters to their employer, who, in turn, is entrusted to provide safe working conditions. . . .

Animal Welfare

Magen Tzedek certification also requires an entity to participate in and comply with a Magen Tzedek–approved protective animal welfare audit program. Such a program will address an entity's facilities, veterinary care, human oversight, humane conditions, and appropriate diets on-site. Additionally, all slaughtered animal products shall come from a plant meeting a Magen Tzedek–approved audit program for both kosher and non-kosher slaughter processes, no matter where that process falls in the supply chain. Each entity must also develop, document, implement, and have management periodically review a traceability plan to ensure that key ingredients provided by their supply chain are sourced in compliance with Magen Tzedek requirements. This animal welfare standard applies a developmental approach to animal welfare requirements in which the entity must define specific conditions for improvement, document these improvements, and show progress in carrying out these improvements at each of three certification cycles. The plan shall define specific conditions to be achieved within a clearly articulated timeline.

Concern for animal welfare has animated Judaism from the Bible to the present day. As explicated in Rabbi Reisner's *Al Pi Din*, the ninth verse of Psalm 145 announces that since God is concerned with the well-being of all God's creatures, we too should be. In fact, numerous sources within the Bible command us to be concerned about the welfare of animals. The early [R]abbis likewise called for the consideration of animal welfare in one's daily conduct. For example, *Berakhot* 40a mandates that before one may sit down to eat, one must attend to the needs of one's animals. Moreover, the [R]abbis extracted the principle that it is forbidden to cause suffering to living things, and utilized this as a test of the propriety of various actions throughout the Talmud. In fact, the Rabbis saw individuals' treatment of animals to be so important that such treatment had direct causal ramifications for human welfare. Of course, concern for animal welfare did not lead to a ban on meat consumption. Yet even where animal killing was permitted, the laws of ritual slaughter were seen as derived in part so as to mitigate animal suffering by requiring that such killing was only to be done in the most humane, painless way possible. By shattering the modern, unwelcome dichotomy between animal welfare and ritual slaughter that has come to characterize the kosher meat marketplace, Magen Tzedek certification will restore harmony to the ritual and ethical dimensions of meat consumption. It will ensure that the principle of avoiding gratuitous animal suffering, both prior to and during slaughter, becomes concretized through explicit, reviewable practices. This would be a revolutionary development within the kashrut marketplace that we, as Conservative Jews, ought to feel proud of.

Consumer Safety and Reliability

Consumers purchasing Magen Tzedek–certified products will be able to rest assured that the products they purchase both are safe to consume and live up to their advertised qualities. Each entity shall have a food safety audit conducted by an outside auditor; shall substantiate with appropriate documentation any special product attributes such as organic or Fair Trade; and shall maintain all records of any health, kosher, and/or halal recall.

There are several halakhic issues that are associated with consumer safety and reliability. First, the halakhah has long been concerned with preventing commercial deception. For example, in Mishnah Bava Metzia 4:11–12, we are instructed:

Produce may not be mixed with other produce. . . . One does not mix the sediment of wine with wine. . . . If one's wine was diluted with water, one must not sell it in a shop unless one informs [the customer], nor to a merchant, even if one informs him, because [the latter buys it] only in order to deceive others. . . . People, cattle, and utensils may not be made up.

This focus on ensuring that producers actually sell to customers what customers think they are purchasing is also codified in the Shulḥan Arukh [S.A. Ḥoshen Mishpat 228:9]. Trickery, dishonesty, or chicanery in sales is categorically prohibited halakhically.

Jewish consumers therefore have a right to expect honesty and forthrightness from the producers of products they buy. The Magen Tzedek certification will provide this critical assurance by mandating that Magen Tzedek–certified entities sell only products that both are safe to consume and live up to their advertised qualities.

Corporate Integrity

Companies receiving Magen Tzedek certification also must adhere to strict standards of corporate integrity. These include adoption of anti-bribery and whistle-blower policies and a commitment to avoiding any association with wrongdoing, corruption, kickbacks, bribery, financial impropriety, or other illegal acts. Magen Tzedek companies must also report any notice of governmental investigations into alleged wrongdoing, and shall take prompt and firm action whenever wrongdoing of any kind is found among its employees. Finally, a Magen Tzedek entity should commit to participating in charitable giving, or tzedakah, to the extent of its ability to do so.

The halakhah prohibits the type of illegal conduct that would impugn a corporation's integrity. First, as set forth in Shulḥan Arukh, Ḥoshen Mishpat 356:1, it is impermissible for a consumer to purchase an item that is the product of thievery: "It is forbidden to purchase a stolen article from a thief. This is a great sin, for one supports the hands of sinners and causes him to steal other things, for if he does not find a buyer, he will not steal."

Second, and more broadly, the halakhah proscribes usurious or otherwise crooked business practices: "Hoarders, usurers, short-changers, and profiteers are the subject of the verse: 'Saying: when will the New Moon pass so that we may sell grain, [when will] the Sabbath [pass] so that we may set forth wheat, shorting the measure, overcharging, and falsifying with crooked weights' (Amos 8:5)" [*b. Bava Batra* 90a]. Indeed, the Talmud (in *Yoma* 86a) relates that dishonesty in business is one of the two types of sin by a Jew that causes God's name to be defiled. Likewise, in *Shabbat* 31a, the Talmud instructs: "When a person is judged, s/he will be asked: Did you do business with integrity? . . ."

Despite the fact that the halakhah so clearly prohibits corporate (or any other type of business) malfeasance, the Jewish community to date has focused little scrutiny upon the business practices of purveyors of kosher products. We should therefore feel proud that Magen Tzedek, by insisting on strict corporate integrity, will provide the kosher market-place with this important public service. Purchasers, for the first time, will be able to rest assured that not only are the products they consume halakhically permissible, but also that the way those products come to market comports with halakhic strictures.

Environmental Impact

Magen Tzedek certification will require entities to comply with compre-hensive environmental programs. For example, an entity must adopt an environmental management plan to reduce energy and water consumption, reduce solid and hazardous waste, and reduce air and water pollution. Additionally, entities must establish programs to promote recovery, reuse, and recycling. Entities must also undertake a carbon footprint and water footprint analysis. Finally, each entity must maintain records of any U.S. federal, state, or local violations that have led to fines or other legal action for environmental law violations.

Judaism has a rich history of concern for the welfare of the environ-ment and humanity's role as stewards of nature. From virtually the very beginning of Genesis, in Gen. 2:15, we are commanded "to work and to protect" our environment. Indeed, our tradition is rich with texts extolling us to care for the natural world. Most specific to Magen Tzedek, though, is the principle that each of us is responsible for the damage that we do to others in the common domain. The halakhah developed a robust body of laws prohibiting what, in modern legal parlance, is deemed a public nuisance. For example, it is prohibited to introduce pollutants to public water sources (Tosefta *Bava Metzia* 11:31) or to allow one's private septic system to leach into a neighbor's well (Shulḥan Arukh, *Ḥoshen Mishpat* 155:21). Various zoning laws (e.g., Mishnah *Bava Batra* chapter 2) are specifically concerned with the damage that may be caused by one's licit activity upon adjacent areas through various runoff and pollution. We therefore have an affirmative duty, as Rabbi Reisner points out in *Al Pi Din*, to avoid causing such damage, whether through toxic emissions, hazardous waste, or, as we are only now becoming aware, through the release of greenhouse gases into the atmosphere. Indeed, pollution damages are halakhically deemed so egregious that they cannot be waived (Shulhan Arukh, *Ḥoshen Mishpat* 155:36). As Maimonides succinctly put it: "One is not permitted to cause damage, planning to pay for the damage. Even to cause the damage is prohibited" [*Hilkhot Nizkei Mamon* 5:1].

In addition, efforts to reduce waste and promote recycling comport with the halakhic principle of *bal tashḥit*, "Do not destroy (wantonly)" [Deuteronomy 20:19]. As perhaps best reflected in *Kiddushin* 32a, the Rabbis warned that anyone who wantonly breaks vessels, tears garments, destroys a building, clogs a well, or does away with food in a destructive manner violates the negative mitzvah of *bal tashḥit*. Thus, we have a halakhic imperative to ensure that the entities that produce our kosher food do so in a manner that does not abrogate our collective responsibility to till and to tend the precious natural world around us. We therefore should celebrate Magen Tzedek's requirement that all certified companies adopt comprehensive environmental programs to reduce waste, reduce pollution, and increase recycling.

. . . We have created, for the first time, comprehensive ethical standards that will elevate labor, health, corporate integrity, environment, and animal welfare practices for entities producing kosher products. Magen Tzedek will be a tool for Jewish consumers to be able to make previously unavailable righteous choices about their kosher eating. This is a significant step toward concretizing the goals that God and the Torah have set for the Jewish people, and is therefore an achievement that all

Jews—Conservative or otherwise—should feel proud of and embrace within the kosher marketplace.

Suggestions for Further Reading

The responsa of the CJLS on ritual matters, primarily in the Oraḥ Ḥayyim and Yoreh De'ah sections of the CJLS website, are at https://www.rabbinicalassembly.org /jewish-law/committee-jewish-law-and-standards/orah-hayyim and https://www .rabbinicalassembly.org/jewish-law/committee-jewish-law-and-standards/yoreh-deah.

The responsa of the Va'ad Halakhah of the Conservative/Masorti movement in Israel are at http://www.responsafortoday.com.

A defense of tattooing and a rabbi's reactions to her daughter's tattoo are in essays by Andy Abrams and Rebecca Alpert within *Jewish Choices, Jewish Voices: Body*, edited by Elliot Dorff and Louis E. Newman, 93–104. Philadelphia: Jewish Publication Society, 2008.

Martin S. Cohen. *The Observant Life*. New York: Rabbinical Assembly, 2012, especially the following chapters:

> Karen G. Reiss Medwed. "Prayer," 5–60.
> Craig T. Sheff. "Synagogue Life," 61–80.
> Michael Katz and Gershom Schwartz. "Shabbat," 98–136.
> Alan B. Lucas. "Holy Days and Holidays," 137–238.
> Carl N. Astor. "The Jewish Life Cycle," 239–304.
> Paul S. Drazen. "The Dietary Laws," 305–38.

Rabbi Avram Israel Reisner, *Al Pi Din* (According to law), http://magentzedek.org/wp -content/uploads/2009/05/hekhsher_tzedek_al_pi_din_july_2009.pdf.

CHAPTER TEN

Tikkun Olam
Moral Guidance on Social Issues

Conservative Judaism seeks to guide Jews morally in both thought and action. From time to time the national movement or an arm of the movement issues documents addressing moral issues both to help Conservative Jews understand the movement's perspective and, hopefully, to turn that understanding into action.

Traditional Means of Inculcating Morality

This approach is faithful to Jewish tradition. Traditionally through the ages, a variety of Jewish resources have encouraged the Jewish people to make moral choices. Some of the most influential ways to cultivate that morality have been the moral values articulated in the Torah and later Jewish literature; the moral courage—and the failure of living morally—demonstrated in Jewish stories; and the moral and theological foundations, applications, and motivations articulated in Jewish theology, prayer, text study, and law.

Moral Values in the Torah and Later Jewish Literature

The Torah urges us to perform many actions grounded in moral values, such as pursuing formal and substantive justice, saving lives, caring for the needy, demonstrating respect for parents and elders, acting honestly in business and in personal relations, telling the truth while being tactful, and educating both children and adults.

Other ancient reservoirs of Jewish moral precepts include the biblical book of Proverbs and *Pirke Avot / Ethics of the Fathers* (a tractate of the Mishnah, ca. 200 CE), which describe different ideal types of living morally, together with concrete instructions about how to attain those ideals. Medieval and modern Jewish writers have produced other such works. For example, Moses Hayyim Luzzato's *Mesillat Yesharim / Paths of the Righteous* (1738) is widely studied in rabbinical academies to augment study of Jewish law with a deep consideration of how to acquire moral traits, following this statement of Pinchas ben Yair in the Talmud (*b. Avodah Zarah* 20b): "Torah leads to watchfulness; watchfulness leads to alacrity; alacrity leads to cleanliness; cleanliness leads to abstention; abstention leads to purity; purity leads to piety; piety leads to humility; humility leads to fear of sin; fear of sin leads to holiness; holiness leads to prophecy; prophecy leads to the resurrection of the dead." Luzzato explains what can aid, and what can impede, each step of Pinchas ben Yair's description of moral development.

Over the centuries, other Jewish thinkers have had very different concepts of the ideal person and how to accomplish that ideal. Hence, there have been a variety of works on morality, ethics, spirituality, and social justice from the Bible to our own time.

Morals in Stories

Stories are concrete, so they tend to be easier to remember than rules or maxims. So when stories portray real-life situations — including what can happen when moral norms are broken — they can effectively educate and motivate people to act morally.

For example, the core Jewish story encompassing the Exodus from Egypt, the revelation at Mount Sinai, and the trek to the Promised Land proclaims that the Jewish people can and must work together with God to redeem ourselves and others from slavery of all sorts. It also teaches us to live our lives in accordance with the moral norms revealed at Sinai and to continue to work for the real promised land, the State of Israel, as well as the Promised Land of the Messianic age.

Theology: Aspiring to Be Like God

In Judaism, God is central to morality by defining the good and the right, by enforcing those norms, and by serving as a model for us. Although the Bible itself raises questions about God's morality—at times God appears to act arbitrarily and even cruelly—nonetheless, Jewish texts trust that God is good.[1] We, then, should aspire to be like God: "As God clothes the naked,... so you should clothe the naked; as God visited the sick,... so you should visit the sick; as God comforted those who mourned,... so you should comfort those who mourn; as God buries the dead,... so you should bury the dead."[2]

Even more so, God serves to shape moral character by entering into a loving relationship with us. Just as we hopefully treat our beloved life partner by performing whatever the norms of morality require and more, "beyond the letter of the law" (*lifnim m'shurat ha-din*), we are asked to do as much for God.[3]

In moral terms, then, we become the kind of people who seek to do both the right and the good, not out of hope for reward but simply because that is the kind of people we strive to be and the kind of relationships we try to have, reflecting God as our model and our covenantal partner.

Prayer

The fixed liturgy draws our attention to Jewish values, including knowledge, forgiveness, health, justice, hope, and peace. It can reorient our focus from everyday distractions onto the fundamental, important things in life.

Prayer can help us muster the courage to recognize what we have done wrong and go through the process of *teshuvah*, returning to the proper path, repairing whatever harm we have done, and taking steps to act justly in the future.

Study

One evident goal of text study is to inform us about what constitutes right and wrong. Beyond this, when done correctly—when study enables us to understand Judaism's deeper philosophy as embedded in its moral rules—it can guide us ethically in new situations not covered by existing laws.

In real-life encounters, values often clash, making good judgment in resolving conflicts a necessary asset. Studying dialectic texts that themselves demonstrate moral argumentation helps to sharpen our ability to navigate these moral challenges.

Studying within a community of learners to which we want to belong can also give us a communal reason to sacrifice our immediate, perhaps immoral wants for Judaism's long-term ends. Learning with others reminds us that we are part of a community to whom we have moral obligations.

Then there are the moral values attached to study itself. They include responsibility, care, self-control, punctuality, exactitude, circumspection, sociability, friendliness, and team spirit.

Law

At the basic level, a minimal moral standard enacted into law enables everyone to know what is expected of each person and what each person can expect of others. This provides a level of security for everyone (contrast Kafka's depiction in *The Trial* of the absolute terror that ensues when you do not know this), and it also enables society to secure cooperation for that standard. Sometimes, too, law can impel us toward higher levels of morality by requiring us to uphold higher standards of behavior. And when the law requires us to do good, the hope is that ultimately, once educated, we will do good for its own sake.[4]

On the communal level, a goal of law is social peace. When disputes arise, law provides a forum for weighing conflicting moral values, adjudicating disputes, and setting moral priorities. A system such as Jewish law also delivers ways to make amends, repair moral damage, and reconcile with God and community.

Emet Ve-Emunah on Building a Moral and Just World

In addressing matters of moral and social justice, *Emet Ve-Emunah* instructs us to attend first to our own welfare as individuals, then to that of our family members, then to fellow Jewish community members, and then to members of a worldwide Jewish community. From there, our moral duties extend to concern and action on behalf of everyone in the world and our local and global environment.

The Talmud (*b. Nedarim* 80b; *b. Bava Metz'ia* 71a) explicitly articulates this view: our moral duties exist within concentric circles, beginning with ourselves and ultimately encompassing the entire world.

By its very nature, this central moral tenet of Conservative Judaism remains forever unfinished. It gives us an ongoing mission to repair the world, to realize, as close as possible, the ideal one, expressed theologically as "the Kingdom of God."

Universalism and Particularism

From its earliest beginnings, Judaism has sought to balance universalistic and particularistic elements. Jews were naturally concerned with Jewish needs and with the fate and the faith of the Jewish people. Our cult and ritual were important in our lives; our nation and its sovereignty were of utmost significance; Jewish interests and needs were paramount.

At the same time, we were enjoined never to turn our backs on the problems of others. The Prophets fought vigorously against any attempt to limit Jewish faith to the sacral or cultic domain. While not denying the beauty and significance of Jewish ritual, they also pointed to the world outside and to God's demand that we carry our faith beyond the Temple and incorporate it in our relationships with our fellow human beings. Our imperative was clear: "Justice, justice shall you pursue" (Deuteronomy 16:20). The Prophets never tired of calling on us to loose the bonds of the oppressed, to feed the hungry, clothe the naked, and shelter the homeless. They cried out against those who crushed the poor into dust; they urged justice and compassion for widows and orphans, for foreigners and the impoverished (e.g., Amos 2:7, Isaiah 10:2). Their vision was that of the just and humane society intended by God as the goal of creation.

While internal Jewish interests were the primary concern of the rabbis of the Talmud, they did not live in isolation, nor did they urge us to turn our backs on the outside world. Involvement in this world as expressed in the prayer *Aleinu* reflects our concern for all people and our impulse "to mend and improve the world under God's Kingship." In keeping with this approach, the sages ruled that we must give charity to needy non-Jews as well as Jews. The prophetic ideal of social justice found ample expression and concretization in the corpus of the Halakhah that sought to create a society concerned with the welfare of the homeless, the impoverished, and the alien. Halakhah insisted that no human being had the right to ignore the spectacle of injustice in order to engage exclusively in a search for God. Similarly, the medieval teachers and the later Hasidic and Musar movements, while stressing piety and ritual, never failed to urge us to behave honestly and compassionately towards our fellow creatures.

Conservative Judaism and Social Justice

The Conservative movement has a long and honorable history of concern for social justice for Jews and non-Jews alike. Sabato Morais, first president of the Jewish Theological Seminary, jeopardized his own position as a rabbi in Philadelphia when he publicly preached on Yom Kippur on behalf of striking shirtmakers. In more recent times, Dr. Abraham Joshua Heschel became the conscience of the nation, recognized for his concern for the aged, children, the ill and helpless, and above all for his passionate espousal of the cause of black Americans in their struggle for civil rights. Heschel denounced racism as "an eye disease, a cancer of the soul" and he and numerous Conservative rabbis and lay people marched arm-in-arm with Dr. Martin Luther King, Jr., in demanding basic human rights.

Over the years, the United Synagogue, the Rabbinical Assembly, and the other arms of the Conservative movement have issued significant statements on the need to deal with the injustices and tragedies of our times. These social justice pronouncements have urged our nation to work for nuclear disarmament, to eliminate poverty and homelessness, to create a national health plan as well as other measures to aid the impoverished. The Conservative movement reaffirms its commitment to social justice and freedom for men and women of all faiths and ethnic origins.

The Unfinished Agenda

An ancient Midrash suggests that the world remained unfinished during the Six Days of Creation so that we, as partners of God, might complete it. There is an unfinished agenda before us: *le-takken olam be-malkhut Shaddai,* "to mend and improve the world under God's Kingship." It is appropriate that Jews pay attention to internal issues of Jewish survival and continuity. Nevertheless, it is of the highest importance that both as a movement and as individuals we take action to fulfill the call of our tradition to advance the cause of justice, freedom and peace. Even as we speak out for Jews who are oppressed or persecuted in the Soviet Union, Arab lands, Ethiopia, and elsewhere, so must we speak out on the dangers of nuclear annihilation, racism, hunger, and poverty throughout the world, as well as the threats to our environment. We must work together with our fellow citizens of all faiths and take political action, if necessary, to achieve these goals. We must remember that we are descendants of Abraham, who demanded justice from God Himself on behalf of pagan sinners, and Moses, who turned his back on the luxury of the Egyptian court to serve his people. We must never forget that we were once strangers in the land of Egypt, and it behooves us to direct our energies to alleviating distress and helping set free those who do not yet know the blessings of liberty.

In addressing these issues, there are legitimate differences of option and approach. Some are willing to compromise in the interests of peace. Others are uncompromising in their demand of justice. Each approach requires both accommodation and cooperation in order to achieve its goals.

Above all, we must not succumb to apathy, cynicism or defeatism. By our active commitment to the ideals of justice found in biblical and rabbinic law and lore, we shall fulfill our obligation to be *shutafo shel ha-Kadosh Barukh Hu be-ma'aseh bereshit,* partners with God in the creation of a more perfect world.

The Rabbinic Letter on the Poor

In 1999 the Joint Social Action Commission of the Rabbinical Assembly and the United Synagogue of Conservative Judaism copublished Rabbi Elliot Dorff's "The Rabbinic Letter on the Poor" (excerpted here) to articulate Conservative Jews' moral obligations on behalf of people living in poverty. See the suggestions for further reading to access the full document, which, in its text and notes, elucidates how and where biblical and rabbinical literature demand that Jews take care of the downtrodden.

Overview

Civilized societies have confronted poverty for millennia. Some have seen it as a moral fault, and some have even imprisoned debtors who could not pay their bills. Jewish ideology, ethics, and law instead affirm that it is an obligation of both the individual and the community to care for the poor and ultimately to bring them out of poverty.

Traditional sources on the subject of poverty are not merely hortatory. Many of the rules were enforced as law. . . . The way we Jews have interpreted and met our obligations to the poor has changed over the years with our shifting economic and political fortunes and the varying political, social, and economic conditions of the countries in which we lived. Nevertheless, responsibility to the poor has endured as an essential ingredient in Jewish values and practice.

Jews generally know that our heritage manifests great concern for the poor. Some even identify as Jews primarily through efforts to take care of the downtrodden. Equating Judaism with social action alone is a mistake, for Judaism is much richer than that; but Judaism does concentrate a large portion of its attention on the care of those in need. Few Jews know, however, what Judaism specifically requires of its adherents in this area, and why. Likewise, too few Jews draw on traditional religious ideals and instructions in making practical political decisions about minimum wage, unemployment, or welfare reform.

Both vision and action are necessary. Without an over-arching framework to justify and motivate our efforts to help the poor, we devote less time and energy to the task, carry it out less well, and ultimately lose interest in it. On the other hand, pious theories about the need to provide such aid are useless without appropriate policies and action to effectuate them. By including, then, both the theoretical framework for a Jewish approach to poverty and some specific guidelines for action to combat it, this Rabbinic Letter provides a structure for Jewish thought, feeling, programming, and action.

Biblical Provisions for the Poor

. . . Ongoing biblical aid took several forms. Farmers were to leave for the poor the corners of the fields (*pe'ah*), sheaves or fruit forgotten while harvesting (*shekhihah*), the stalks that by chance fall aside from the edge of the farmer's sickle (*leket*), grapes separated from their clusters (*peret*), and defective clusters of grapes or olives (*olelot*). During the Sabbatical year (*shevi'it*), when fields were to lie fallow, the poor had first rights to the Sabbatical fruits. In addition, during the third and sixth years of the Sabbatical cycle, a tithe of all of one's crops was to be designated for the poor (*ma'aser oni*, "the tithe of the poor"). During the Sabbatical year, everyone had an open privilege to eat their fill from a neighboring vineyard or field. The first tithe (*ma'aser rishon*), given yearly to the Levites, was also a form of aid to the poor, since the Levites had no other income. Finally, the Bible provides that every fifty years, during the Jubilee year, all land reverts to its original owners; this was intended to prevent permanent impoverishment.

In addition to these agricultural gifts, several other provisions of biblical law helped to prevent poverty. Specifically, workers were to be paid promptly, and those who had money were to extend loans without usury to their fellow Israelites in need. On the Sabbatical year, debts are to be canceled altogether; despite that, Israelites are not to "harbor the base thought" (Deuteronomy 15:9) of refusing to loan money to needy Israelites when the Sabbatical year is near. Clothing taken as a pledge for a loan had to be returned each evening for use by the poor person at night. When collecting such a pledge, the creditor had to stand outside the poor person's home, thus reinforcing that person's abiding dignity despite his or her poverty. It was the duty of the judge to protect the rights of the downtrodden, although not at the price of fairness.

It is not at all surprising that biblical provisions for the poor focus primarily on agricultural gifts, for most Jews of that time earned their living through farming. A monetary economy was not well established until later times.

What is surprising is that there is any provision for the poor at all. No other ancient law code stipulates gifts for the poor based on each year's crops, as the Torah does. Until modern times, in fact, most law codes make the assumption that poor people were not just unfortunate; their poverty was caused by some moral fault of theirs, and they therefore did not deserve to be helped. On the contrary, in many legal systems the poor were to be punished. In England and the United States, for example, debtors' prisons were common until the nineteenth century, and even when they were theoretically abandoned at that time, imprisonment on other charges, such as concealment of assets or vagrancy, continued some of the substance of the idea that debtors should be imprisoned for their wrongdoing. Thus these biblical laws proclaiming that the poor are not to be blamed but rather helped are truly unprecedented and innovative, and they can be explained only on the basis of the Israelites' theological convictions described in the previous section [of the full Rabbinic Letter].

Rabbinic Poverty Law

By the time of the Talmud, Jews had become involved in commerce and trades, and so Rabbinic law provides for the urban, as well as the rural, poor. This included a number of curative and preventative measures. . . .

Forms of assistance. There were three Rabbinic forms of relief: the soup-kitchen (*tamḥui*), medical attention (*rippui*), and the charity fund (*kuppah*). . . .

Hierarchy of recipients. Jewish law provides that, as a general rule, women are to be aided before men—assuming that there is not enough for both—because "it is not unusual for a man to go begging, but it is unusual for a woman to do so." This assumed gender differentiation probably is based on, or combined with, fear for the physical safety of a begging woman.

Family members (especially women) are to be aided first, then close friends, then the poor of one's own community, and then the poor of other communities. In light of that list of priorities, the record of medieval Jewish communities who put themselves out for refugees fleeing persecution and expulsion is truly amazing. The historian S. D. Goitein estimates that in 1160 in the Cairo (Fustat) Jewish community, there was one relief recipient to every four contributors.

Redeeming captives (*pidyon shevu'im*), though, takes precedence over helping any other Jew in need, for those in captivity, even more than the homeless and destitute, are in danger of sexual violation and, ultimately, of losing their lives. . . .

Jewish law required Jews to support the non-Jewish poor as well "for the sake of peace." One must remember that until the twentieth century most Jews lived in societies that . . . [made them] second-class citizens [and the dominant sectors of society certainly did not worry about the Jewish poor]. . . . That Jewish law should require Jews to give charity to non-Jews at all—even if it is only for the political motive of maintaining peace—is therefore remarkable. . . .

Extent of assistance. . . . Throughout history, most Jewish communities were themselves poor. . . . The limited resources of Jewish communities made it especially imperative that they balance the individual needs of each poor person with due regard for their obligation to aid *all* the needy. No wonder the Talmud says that the distribution of charitable funds is more onerous than the collection!

The hierarchy of needs embedded in the sources, then, is this: (i) Redemption from captivity—especially for women—for captives were at risk of loss of life and physical violation. (ii) Medical care for people who need it, for . . . life and health take precedence over all other communal priorities, in accordance with the value of *piqqu'aḥ nefesh* [saving a life]. (iii) Food for those without it. (iv) Clothing and housing. Starvation was seen as more of a risk to a person's life than clothing or housing, at least in the Middle Eastern countries where the Tanna'itic and Amoraic sources were written. In America's northern states during the winter, though, clothing and housing may become more urgent than food. (v) Dowries and other necessities for indigent brides. (vi) Whatever is necessary to sustain a person's dignity. . . .

Preventive measures. Jewish family law is one mechanism by which the classical Rabbis sought to prevent poverty. According to Jewish law, fathers are obligated to teach their sons not only the Torah, but a trade as well. A father may delegate this responsibility to a teacher who is paid for taking the boy as an apprentice, but the father remained responsible to make sure that the son acquired a remunerative skill. As Rabbi Judah put it, failure to do that is effectively teaching your son to steal.

Jewish law requires Jewish communities to supply indigent young women with a dowry. Historically that insured that there would be few unmarried women and therefore, hopefully, few women who would need to go begging.

The Rabbis also used their power over the marketplace to prevent poverty. They imposed a profit limit of one sixth for merchants selling foodstuffs and other commodities essential to human life (e.g., clothing, rent). . . .

Rabbinic law also seeks to prevent poverty through making loans easily available to the poor. The Bible demands that Jews lend money interest-free to a needy fellow Jew. . . . The Rabbis altered the court's procedural rules "so as not to lock a door in front of potential borrowers."

Another important way to prevent poverty is to provide job opportunities for all.

Historically, the extended family, as the basic social unit within the community, took primary responsibility for affording employment to those of its members who were out of work or unskilled, but if that failed, the community as a whole became responsible. . . . This obligation was often not easy to fulfill. One historian estimates that between the fifteenth and eighteenth centuries approximately 20% of the Jewish community were unemployed or paupers. In trying first to secure employment for these people, the Jewish community was helping the poor to help themselves, the highest form of charity on Maimonides' famous list (M.T. Laws of Gifts to the Poor 10:7):

> The highest merit in giving charity is attained by the person who comes to the aid of another in bad circumstances before he reaches the stage of actual poverty. Such aid may be in the form of a substantial gift presented in an honorable manner, or a loan, or the forming of a partnership with him for the transaction of some business enterprise, or assistance in obtaining some employment for him, so that he will not be forced to seek charity from his fellow men. Concerning this Scripture says, "You shall strengthen him" (Leviticus 25:35), that is, you shall assist him so that he does not fall. . . .

Responsibilities of the poor. If, according to Jewish law, donors and distributors have obligations, so do the poor. The goal of Jewish charity is to help the poor become self-supporting. This objective is based on the assumption that the poor will work diligently to earn themselves out of poverty in order to avoid the disgrace inherent in begging. Jewish law does not require the poor to sell their homes or tools, nor does it force them to sell their fields at a substantial loss. Poor people are, however, obligated to work and to sell off any of their luxurious possessions in a good-faith effort to become independent of public assistance. . . .

The law could make this assumption in part because respect for labor runs deep within the Jewish tradition. In sharp contrast to many in the ancient world—including the Greek philosophers—Jews were not to disdain labor or the working classes but were rather to "love work and hate lordship." Jews certainly were not permitted to wage war or engage in robbery or piracy to earn a living, as many other peoples did. It was also forbidden simply to rely upon God to provide. . . .

The ideal for a human being, according to the Rabbis, is "Torah with gainful employment"—i.e., knowledge and continuing study of the tradition combined with constructive work. People should work not only for their own livelihood, but also for the inherent dignity of labor and the ongoing effects of work on generations to come. . . .

In addition to these moral, theological, and historical dimensions of labor, the Rabbis were sensitive to its psychological effects: "Great is work, for it honors the workers." They thus did not see work as a human punishment inherited from Adam in the Garden of Eden; it is instead our path to respect and self-worth. . . .

This work ethic in the Jewish tradition is a strong factor in explaining why Jewish sources do not express the worry, as American writers and lawmakers do, that providing too much in welfare will serve as a disincentive for the poor to become self-sustaining. Another factor, of course, is that those on welfare in Jewish communities were not richly provided for, and so there was little to recommend staying on the dole. . . .

Translating from Then to Now

. . . Our contemporary situation presents a new set of challenges and circumstances that did not exist when most Jewish laws and customs of charity distribution were established. . . . In the United States, [poverty] is spreading. Increasing numbers of previously stable families find themselves among the newly poor . . . [and] people from formerly "protected" geographic and economic backgrounds are in jeopardy. . . . Since the 1960s many . . . [poor] people received benefits—such as housing subsidies, food stamps, Aid to Families with Dependent Children, and direct cash payments—that enabled them to achieve a minimal standard of living, but in the 1996 Welfare Reform Act, Congress put many of these programs in jeopardy.

Increasingly today, we speak also of the "working poor." As a result of rising costs and lower-paying jobs, an increasing number of families are at, or perilously near, the poverty-line even though at least one member of the family is employed. . . .

In addition, some Americans have developed a "culture of poverty," in which it is acceptable or even honorable to be poor for generation after generation within a family. . . .

Who is responsible to provide for the poor? Today, we try to accomplish that task through massive and far-reaching social and governmental institutions. Thus . . . do our taxes, or a portion of them, fulfill part of our religious obligations to provide for the poor? If so, do we now have a religious as well as a civic duty to get involved in government to insure that the funds are equitably, honestly, and wisely apportioned?

The answer to both questions is "yes." Some of the poverty provisions in the Torah's laws are, after all, nothing less than taxes on a person's income. Since a percentage of taxes in the United States is used for aiding the poor, parallel to the use of some biblical taxes, one can legitimately argue that at least part of the duty to care for the poor is fulfilled through paying current taxes. At the same time, American social policy specifically presumes that the safety net for the poor will *not* be created by government alone; private charity must also play a significant role in this effort. Tax provisions permitting deductions for charity make this intention explicit. Jews therefore can fulfill only a *part* of their obligations to the poor through their taxes; they must, in addition, contribute some of their income to the charities of their choice. And, indeed, it is a mark of pride for Jews to be among the most generous segments of the general population, an ethic that all Jews should adopt and foster through their own giving.

Jewish law's preference for the poor near-at-hand over those far away is much harder to define and justify in a world of instant communications. . . . Some of the most pressing and costly needs concern Jews in places as distant as Israel and the former Soviet Union. Both morally and strategically, Western powers must be concerned with Third World poverty. We may still have primary responsibility for the poor who are near and dear, but it is not as simple to apply that criterion as it was when people knew little of conditions far away from home. "To increase learning is to increase heartache," as Ecclesiastes says. . . .

Many of the details described in the law for collection and distribution of aid are out of place in the modern world. Designating three people to decide how to distribute the community's charitable resources, as Jewish law does, seems blatantly autocratic to us; thirty is even too small a number for the boards of directors of many of our larger charitable organizations, to say nothing of governmental agencies. Moreover, delivery of the aid is much more efficiently and honorably done through the mail or through direct deposits in bank accounts rather than by delegations traveling door-to-door. This is . . . very much in keeping with Maimonides' ladder of charity that prefers gifts given and received anonymously over those where the giver and/or the recipient know the identity of the other. . . .

Jewish law gives the court legal power to force people to give an amount commensurate with their income and the community's needs, and it also assigns the court legal authority to seize the property of those who renege on a pledge. . . . [Today], Jewish communal officials no longer have such power. Government agents do. . . .

Despite these differences . . . the imperative to guarantee both the survival and the dignity of the impoverished, derived as it is from the fundamental concepts and values discussed in the first section of this Rabbinic Letter, remains just as strong now as it was in the past. . . .

Responsum on Capital Punishment

On October 15, 2013, the CJLS passed a responsum that addresses the ethical issues surrounding participation—as a prosecutor, judge, or juror—in the process of condemning a person to death.

Rabbi Jeremy Kalmanofsky's "Participating in the American Death Penalty" (excerpted here) begins by asking: "May a Jew participate in capital criminal cases in the American legal system? May a Jew serve as judge in a capital trial? Or serve as prosecutor seeking the death penalty? May a Jew testify in a trial in which the defendant could be sentenced to execution? May a Jew serve on the jury that could sentence a defendant to death?"

The Committee on Jewish Law and Standards adopted it by a vote of twenty in favor, none opposed, and none abstaining (20-0-0). To read the full responsum, see https://www.rabbinicalassembly.org/sites/default/files/assets/public/halakhah/teshuvot/2011-2020/cjls-onesh-mavet.pdf.

Overview

Jewish tradition is ambivalent regarding the death penalty. On one hand, Torah is replete with capital punishments. Maimonides lists 36 biblical violations carrying the death penalty, covering violent attacks like murder and kidnapping, as well as social, ritual and ethical evils like adultery, idolatry and contempt of court [MT *Sanhedrin* 15:10–13].

On the other hand, rabbinic tradition is generally averse to capital punishment. The Sages construed rules of evidence so strictly and stacked criminal procedure so strongly in favor of acquittal that the death penalty was almost never applied. Talmudic lore [*b. Avodah Zarah* 8b] records that 40 years before the Temple was destroyed, the Sanhedrin ceased to try capital cases, since society had collapsed into such chaos it would have had to impose too many death penalties. According to this view, there has been no official, judicial execution within the Torah legal system since the early 1st century CE.

There is yet a third side to the argument, however. Despite its general aversion to the death penalty, the Talmud [*b. Sanhedrin* 46a] recognized that desperate times can call for desperate measures, ruling that exigent circumstances sometimes required executions to maintain social order, to deter future crime, and to punish the guilty, even for crimes that would not otherwise deserve death, even in cases that did not conform to proper rabbinic criminal procedure.

The classic Mishnah [*m. Makko* 1:10] on capital punishment captures this ambivalence: . . .

A Sanhedrin that executes once in seven years is called bloodthirsty. R. Elazar b. Azariah said: Even once in 70 years. R. Akiba and R. Tarfon said: Had we been in the Sanhedrin, none would ever have been put to death. Rabban Shimon ben Gamaliel said: Then these sages would have created more murderers in Israel.

In good rabbinic fashion, this dispute remains unresolved. It seems that each side has a point, both Rabbi Akiva's and Rabbi Tarfon's inclination toward abolition and Rabban Shimon ben Gamliel's claim for a deterrence effect. More than 50 years ago, the CJLS affirmed its opposition to the death penalty, in this 1960 statement by Rabbi Ben Zion Bokser:

Only God has the right to take life. When the state allows itself to take life, it sets an example which the criminal distorts to his own ends. It proves to him that man may take into his own hands the disposition of another man's life. The elimination of capital punishment would help to establish a climate in which life will be held sacred. The sense of the sanctity of life needs to be bolstered in our time, and it will be perhaps the greatest contribution toward deterring crime and violence. . . . The abolition of capital punishment will be an important step forward in the direction of a more humane justice. It will free America from a black spot of barbarism, which still disfigures the good name of our country.[5]

We re-affirm that position today. We consider the contemporary death penalty a needlessly bloody measure, applied inconsistently and, all too often, wielded against those wrongfully convicted. We believe that in virtually all cases, even the worst murderers should be imprisoned rather than executed. We endorse the 1999 resolution of the Rabbinical Assembly that existing death penalty laws should be abolished and no new ones be enacted. Our religious community would contribute to American moral culture by opposing capital punishment in the name of our reverence for life. Moreover, we should express that view actively, for any who might protest a social wrong—even if their words are unlikely to be heeded—are nonetheless responsible if they fail to raise their voices [*b. Shabbat* 55a].

Jews Playing Roles in Capital Cases

However, we are asked not only about an ideal penal system, but about the one we actually have in the United States (the only country with significant Jewish population that applies capital punishment today). Given that the death penalty exists at the federal level and in 32 states, what should Jewish citizens do when called to play roles in capital cases? Should Jewish judges and prosecutors refuse to play their parts in what [U.S. Supreme Court] Justice Harry Blackmun called "the machinery of death"? Should Jewish citizens refuse to serve on juries that might send a person to execution? Should witnesses withhold testimony that might help send someone to death row? Or, alternatively, does Halakhah consider it within a government's legitimate authority to execute criminals, though based on our values we would argue that they should elect not to exercise that power? If this is the case, then Jewish citizens could take part in capital cases, albeit reluctantly or under protest. Certainly Jews are generally bound to obey the laws of the land, even those laws they oppose. Yet some laws may be so incompatible with our norms that Jews should refuse to follow them, by civil disobedience or conscientious objection. In which category does capital punishment belong? Is it beyond the bounds of what Judaism can tolerate? Or might it be bad policy, but not *prima facie* illegitimate? . . .

Conclusion

. . . Some moral and halakhic factors strengthen the argument for participating in death penalty trials as jurors and judges. A leading capital defense attorney, Marshall Dayan, argues that it is "tremendously injurious" to defendants when those who object to the death penalty recuse themselves. Studies show that such "death qualified" juries—that is, jurors who have asserted during jury selection that they would be willing to impose the death penalty—are more likely to convict even for lesser penalties than are juries taken from the general population. . . . The conscientious refusal to participate in capital trials, which seemed at first glance to be a good moral instinct, turns out to risk harming American justice by leaving these cases only in the hands of those already committed to the death penalty. Instead, it might practically enhance criminal justice for morally scrupulous Jews to serve as judges, prosecutors, jurors and witnesses, to try to mitigate the problems that compromise American capital punishment. Such service would not prevent Jews from using other venues to advocate against the death penalty. Let us consider each of these roles Jewish citizens might play in the criminal process.

Witnesses. This is the least morally freighted of the roles. . . . A witness merely conveys to the court the information for judges and jurors to evaluate. Even if that testimony proves decisive, it is not the witness who decided. If one has first-hand, accurate information about a crime, as a matter of public safety, one should speak to the police and testify in court, regardless of one's moral objection to whatever penalty may ensue. There is no halakhic basis to withhold information from investigators or testimony from court. In fact it would constitute a transgression to fail to give testimony in such a case. "One who is a witness, who sees or knows, but does not testify, will bear his guilt" [Leviticus 5:1]. Withholding testimony might help a violent criminal escape and expose others to future harm. Therefore, according to Maimonides [MT *Rotzeaḥ* 1:14], withholding testimony violates one of the Torah's major ethical mandates: "Do not stand idly by the blood of your neighbor" [Leviticus 19:16].

Jurors. . . . It can . . . accord with halakhic and ethical norms for death penalty opponents to sit on such juries. The Supreme Court has rendered several relevant rulings on this topic. In Witherspoon v. Illinois [1968], the court ruled that jurors cannot be removed for cause simply because they express general ethical or religious reservations about capital punishment. Later rulings in Adams v. Texas [1980] and Lockhart v. Mcree [1986] qualified this view, holding that jurors can be excused or excluded when their views are so strong that they would substantially impair them from performing the duties of the role. But as long as a person can perform a juror's duty within the law, such a person cannot be stricken for cause.

To determine whether they can follow the law, prospective jurors are typically asked something like: Would you always vote for life without the possibility of parole over the death penalty, regardless of the circumstances of the case? Even observant Jews who oppose the death penalty could answer that question in the negative. Let us remember that jury service is part of a citizen's general duty to fight crime in a society where "the law of the land is the law." Since, by any honest report, Halakhah recognizes that the death penalty is warranted in extreme cases, there is no halakhic reason why jurors should assert absolutely that they could never impose capital punishment. Observant Jewish jurors could promise to keep an open mind and vote for the death penalty if prosecutors could convince them execution was "the morally appropriate punishment," even if that applied only to a tiny class of cases.

Some might balk at this advice, considering it deceptive, if not an outright lie. I do not agree. In this case, I concur with a recent judgment of Chuck Klosterman, the *New York Times* Ethicist columnist, who took up this very problem. Prospective jurors should not misrepresent their views, Klosterman said, but should say honestly during jury vetting something like this: "I personally disagree with the state of Missouri's position on capital punishment, but—if selected—I will perform my duty to the best of my abilities, within the framework of my own conscience."

Judges and prosecutors. The foregoing applies equally and more strongly to prosecutors and judges. Their work helps keep society safe, and so, in its way, is holy work. When the law requires a capital sentence, or when one's superiors assign one to a capital case, a Jew may fulfill those tasks, albeit reluctantly. Prosecutors have virtually unfettered discretion over when to seek the death penalty or long-term imprisonment. In many jurisdictions, judges are not bound to follow juries' sentencing determinations; in others, judges have discretion to modify those determinations. Jewish values argue that, in the vast majority of cases, except in the greatest exigencies, prosecutors and judges should choose imprisonment over execution. But even in cases where American law dictates a capital punishment, Jewish prosecutors and judges can fulfill their professional duties without transgressing the Torah and the decrees of our Sages.

Prison guards and medical technicians. . . . We must confront the possibility that a Jewish guard may have to strap a prisoner to a gurney, or a Jewish medical aide may be called upon to administer a lethal injection. Such a prospect is genuinely ugly, and we feel a reflex to say that this is no job for a nice Jewish boy or girl. But given everything we have said heretofore, there is no escaping the conclusion that when these employees of the state—like Rabbi Elazar ben Rabbi Shimon, as recorded by the Talmud and Midrash—carry out their duties, they are not murderers, but duly authorized public servants.

Of course, no one has to work in a prison. A person who cannot imagine ending another person's life should seek another line of work. . . . [In a case where] it would be extremely difficult for a prison employee to end the life of someone that he or she believed was genuinely innocent . . . any prison employee—Jewish or gentile—might wish to petition to be excused from that assignment. . . .

Nonetheless, judicial executions, carried out in accordance with criminal justice laws and proper trials, do not constitute murder, any more than a court-imposed fine constitutes theft. The judges, prosecutors, jurors and witnesses who play their roles in reaching and executing a capital sentence would not be halakhically guilty of causing an unjust homicide.

Ruling

We urge the American federal and state governments to renounce capital punishment except in the rarest cases. Religious Jews should advocate for that position as the superior moral stance and best public policy. But given the weight of precedent, it would be false to assert that Jewish law forbids capital punishment. Halakhah confers on secular governments the legitimate power to punish criminals to protect the innocent, including the right to impose death, when needed, God forbid. Objection to the death penalty is not halakhic grounds to refuse to participate as judge, prosecutor, juror, police or witness in capital trials.

Suggestions for Further Reading

ON JUDAISM'S MULTIPLE WAYS OF CONTRIBUTING TO OUR MORALITY

Elliot N. Dorff. *Love Your Neighbor and Yourself: A Jewish Approach to Modern Personal Ethics*, 311–44. Philadelphia: Jewish Publication Society, 2003.

———. *The Way into Tikkun Olam (Repairing the World)*. Woodstock VT: Jewish Lights, 2005.

David Teutsch. *A Guide to Jewish Practice: Volume I: Everyday Living*, especially "Making Decisions," 551–636. Wyncote PA: Reconstructionist Rabbinical College Press, 2011.

ON RELIEVING POVERTY

The full "Rabbinic Letter on the Poor" is in Elliot N. Dorff, *To Do the Right and the Good: A Jewish Approach to Modern Social Ethics*, chap. 6. Philadelphia PA: Jewish Publication Society, 2002.

Jill Jacobs. *There Shall Be No Needy: Pursuing Social Justice through Jewish Law and Tradition.* Woodstock VT: Jewish Lights, 2009.

———. *Where Justice Dwells: A Hands-On Guide to Doing Social Justice in Your Jewish Community.* Woodstock VT: Jewish Lights, 2011.

ON CAPITAL PUNISHMENT

The full responsum on capital punishment by Jeremy Kalmanofsky is at http://www.rabbinicalassembly.org/sites/default/files/public/halakhah/teshuvot/2011-2020/cjls-onesh-mavet.pdf.

Laurie Levenson. "Judaism and Criminal Justice." In *The Oxford Handbook of Jewish Ethics and Morality*, edited by Elliot N. Dorff and Jonathan Crane, 472–86. New York: Oxford University Press, 2013.

Abagail N. Sosland. "Crime and Punishment." In *The Observant Life: The Wisdom of Conservative Judaism for Contemporary Jews*, edited by Martin S. Cohen, 458–75. New York: Rabbinical Assembly, 2012.

Elie Spitz. "The Jewish Tradition and Capital Punishment." In *Contemporary Jewish Ethics and Morality: A Reader*, edited by Elliot N. Dorff and Louis E. Newman, 344–49. New York: Oxford University Press, 1995.

CHAPTER ELEVEN

Ḥayyei Min u'Mishpaḥah

Moral Guidance on Sex and Family Life

Jewish law has often been described as "sex-positive." It does not view sex as a low expression of our animal nature, as many Western (Plato, Aristotle) and Christian (Augustine, Luther) thinkers have pronounced. Instead, it recognizes sexuality as an integrated part of the gift of life God has given us. In fact, as described below, the Torah and later Rabbinic law require us to engage in sexual activity for procreation and the mutual pleasure and bonding of the couple. At the same time, however, the Torah places numerous restrictions on sexual activity outside the confines of a marital relationship.

Judaism's directives about sex are thus consistent with its directives concerning all the other human appetites. We are to channel our energies to good purpose—in this case, to express deep love and to procreate.

On the whole, modern Western people have been exposed to very different understandings of the body and sexuality from what Jewish tradition upholds. It then becomes all the more important for us to learn the concepts and values behind Judaism's approach to sexuality. When we comprehend why it says what it does, it enables us to ask how traditional Jewish norms might need to change in order to honor Judaism's underlying concepts and values about sex in our times.

A Rabbinic Letter on Intimate Relations

In 1996 the Rabbinical Assembly's Commission on Human Sexuality published "A Rabbinic Letter on Intimate Relations" (excerpted here), cocreated by Rabbi Elliot Dorff and the commission. It is self-described as "an effort on the part of the Conservative rabbinate to talk openly about matters of human sexuality and intimacy with the members of our movement. Although sex is certainly not the whole of life, it is an important part of it, and so it should be part of the discussion that we Jews have about the norms by which we live." To read the full letter, which includes expanded commentary and references to biblical and rabbinical sources, see this chapter's suggestions for further reading.

Prologue

... Judaism has a distinctly positive view toward sexuality as the gift of God, and it articulates values and rules for this area of life that make it the pleasurable, yet holy, activity it was meant to be.

In times past, great rabbinic authorities wrote letters to the Jews of their generation to convey Judaism's message concerning human sexuality and intimate relations. Probably the most famous is *Iggeret Ha-Kodesh*, attributed to Rabbi Moses ben Nahman (Nahmanides, 1194–1270), but we also have manuals on these matters written by, or attributed to, Rabbi Moses ben Maimon (Maimonides, 1135–1204), Rabbi Abraham ben David of Posquieres (1125–1198), and others. They used the format of a letter (*iggeret*) or a manual rather than a rabbinic responsum (*teshuvah*) because in these essays they were not called upon to rule on a specific question in Jewish law but rather to educate their readers to the accepted rules of Jewish law on the subject and the concepts and values that underlie them. Their audience, then, was not primarily other rabbis, but the entire Jewish community. Moreover, they used the form of a letter or a manual, rather than a responsum, because they wanted to be personal in tone as well as in content regarding this most personal of areas.

This letter, then, follows a traditional form for discussing these matters. . . .

Sex to Express Marital Companionship

Sex is one of the ways in which [marital] companionship is expressed. The Torah recognizes the sexual desires of women as well as those of men; while we might take that for granted, other societies in the ancient—and, for that matter, in the medieval and the modern—world assume that only men have sexual appetites, and women tolerate them because they want financial support and children. Instead, the Torah and the Rabbis who later interpret it, in recognition of the couple's mutual desires, structure the laws of marriage such that both spouses have rights to sex with regularity within marriage. Moreover, while the husband may never force himself upon his wife, Jewish law permits couples, within the bounds of modesty, to have sex in any way they want. The Torah and the Rabbis thus went quite far to affirm the rights of both members of the couple to the pleasures of each other's sexual company. . . .

Marital companionship is, in part, sexual, but it is more than that. In the Jewish marriage ceremony, the only explicit reference to the couple being married describes them as *re'im ha-ahuvim*, the loving friends. This description appropriately indicates that the companionship of marriage should extend over a wide scope such that the husband and wife are not only lovers, but friends. They should take time to enjoy many things together. They should talk with each other about what is going on in their lives and what they are thinking and feeling. They should be, as the marriage ceremony says, loving friends, where the friendship is as strong an element in their relationship as their romantic love.

The Importance of Marriage and Children

The opening chapters of Genesis suggest an additional purpose for marriage. Once having created the first man and woman, God commands, "Be fruitful and multiply" (Genesis 1:28). Marriage is thus theologically important both to relieve human loneliness and to produce children.

This dual approach to marriage is reflected in Jewish law. In addition to the commandment to procreate, the Torah includes another verse (Exodus 21:10) commanding us to have sex to afford each other pleasure and companionship.

The Rabbis later determined that the command to procreate is fulfilled when the couple has had two children. If a couple cannot have children, the commandment to procreate no longer applies, for one can logically be commanded to do only what one can do. Nevertheless, such couples should seriously consider adoption, converting the child to Judaism if he or she was not born to a Jewish woman. The Talmud states that adopting and raising a child is "as if one has given birth to him/her," and that adoptive parents "follow the Lord at all times."

Those who can bear children or adopt them should see it as a *mitzvah* of the highest order to have more than the minimal number of two, for nothing less than the future of the Jewish community and of Judaism depends upon that. The Jewish community, after all, has lost a third of its members in the Holocaust, and contemporary Jews are not producing enough children even to maintain our present numbers. Add to these factors the high rate of intermarriage and assimilation among Jews today, and it becomes clear that we are in serious demographic trouble as a people. One needs a Jewish education to become an informed, practicing Jew, of course, but people can be educated only if they exist in the first place. The *mitzvah* of procreation, like all other commandments, does not apply to those who cannot fulfill it; but for those who can, procreation is literally a matter of life and death for us not only as individuals and as families, but as a people.

Children are not only an obligation: they are a blessing. . . . Moreover, children are our destiny, perhaps our strongest tie to the future. . . .

Both during and after the time that a couple is having their children, the duty to have conjugal relations for the sake of companionship continues. . . .

The importance of marriage for the Jewish tradition is not only for reasons of propagation and companionship, as important as they are; it is also to educate children in the Jewish tradition so it can continue across the generations. . . . This includes the children's education in sexual behavior. Children learn what it is to be a husband or wife first and foremost from their own parents. . . .

Many, however, do not or cannot get married, and others cannot have children. Unfortunately, the Jewish emphasis on marriage and children all too often amplifies the pain that such people feel. It is therefore important in this context to reaffirm the divine significance of everyone's life; we are all created in the image of God, and we all retain divine worth as individuals, whether or not we are married and whether or not we produce biological children of our own. . . .

In contemporary society, marriage and family are often balanced against the values of work. Judaism prizes work . . . for what it contributes to society as a whole, for the psychological health and self-worth of the individual, and for the support it affords to oneself and to one's family. For some people, though, the secular work ethic prevalent in contemporary society has made work the sole value, a virtual idol. . . .

Achieving a proper balance of work and family, of course, is not easy. Since most parents in our day do not live with an extended family nearby, the full burden of supporting themselves and also of rearing the children falls directly on them. Still, years from now, when we look back on our lives, most of us will not feel bad that we could not spend more time working; we will instead regret the time that we did not spend with our children, particularly when they were young and readily available for interaction. That long-term vision should help us keep our priorities straight when we are young.

Preparation for Marriage

. . . The goal of marriage preparation, whether in a course or in premarital counseling, is to give couples the skills to talk to each other about important aspects of their relationship. Adequate preparation might include issues of sexual concern, children, parents, friends, jobs, money, and communal commitments. It might also teach people to quarrel in healthy and loving ways so that they emerge stronger as a couple, and, more generally, it should help people learn how to communicate with each other. A couple should also discuss how they are going to express their Jewish commitments in their new home, and how Judaism can help them with some or all of the issues mentioned above. . . .

Preventive care for marriage does not end with the wedding. On the contrary, successful marriages are unions in which both spouses are mindful on an ongoing basis not only of their own needs but also of the needs of their mate. . . .

Non-marital Sex

Judaism posits marriage as the appropriate context for sexual intercourse. We recognize, though, that many Jews are engaging in sexual relations outside the marital bond. Some of these sexual acts are adulterous, incestuous, or involuntary, and we resoundingly condemn them as a gross violation of Jewish law. . . . We also condemn casual and promiscuous sexual encounters since they involve little or no love or commitment.

The non-marital relations that this section addresses, then, are . . . between two unmarried adults that take place in the context of an ongoing, loving relationship. . . .

According to the Mishnah, a man was supposed to marry at age 18, presumably a woman of 16 or 17. That does not presume high school education, let alone college or graduate school, and so the tradition must be read and applied understanding the major changes in context from that time to our own, where marriage is likely to take place at least ten years after puberty and often later than that.

. . . It is perfectly natural and healthy for unmarried people to hug and kiss each other as signs of friendship and warmth. . . . Unmarried . . . [people] should engage in these practices as they build and strengthen the loving relationships that make them distinctly human. . . .

Why does Judaism posit marriage as the appropriate context for sexual intercourse? . . . Because in that setting the couple can attain the three-fold purposes for marital sex described above—namely, companionship, procreation, and the education of the next generation. While non-marital sex can provide companionship as well as physical release, especially in the context of a long-term relationship, unmarried couples generally do not want to undertake the responsibilities of having and educating children. . . .

Jewish norms in sexual matters, like Jewish norms in other arenas, are not an "all or nothing" thing. Certainly, failing to abide by Judaism's command that we restrict sexual relations to marriage does not excuse one from trying to live by the concepts and values Judaism would have us use in all of our relationships, including our intimate ones. In fact, in the context of non-marital relationships, some of them take on new significance:

Seeing oneself and one's partner as the creatures of God. We are not machines; we are integrated wholes created by, and in the image of, God. As such, our sexual activity must reflect our value system and the personhood of the other....

Respect for others. This means, minimally, that we must avoid coercive sex.... Unmarried people must take special care to do this, if only because they know each other less well and are therefore more likely to misunderstand each other's cues.

Modesty. The demand that one be modest in one's sexual activities — as well as in one's speech and dress — is another corollary of seeing oneself in the image of God. For singles it is especially important to note that modesty requires that one's sexual activities be conducted in private and that they not be discussed with others.

Honesty. ... Unmarried sexual partners must ... openly and honestly confront what their sexual activity means for the length and depth of their relationship.

Fidelity. ... One should avoid short-term sexual encounters and seek, instead, long-term relationships to which one remains faithful for the duration of the relationship....

Health and safety. ... Most sexually transmitted diseases are contracted in non-marital, sexual liaisons. In our time, this includes not only recurring infections like syphilis but potentially fatal diseases like AIDS....

The possibility of a child. Unmarried couples should recognize that, even with the use of contraceptives, an unplanned pregnancy is always a possibility....

The Jewish quality of the relationship. Unmarried people who live together should discuss the Jewish character of their relationship just as much as newlyweds need to do. That ranges across the gamut of ritual commandments, such as the dietary laws and Sabbath and Festival observance, and it also involves all of the theological and moral issues [discussed above]....

Moreover, single Jews should date Jews exclusively so as not to incur the problems of intermarriage for themselves and for the Jewish people as a whole. Intermarriage is a major problem for the contemporary Jewish community, for studies indicate that some 90% of the children of intermarried couples are not raised as Jews. Furthermore, intermarriage is a problem for the people themselves. Marriage is hard enough as it is, involving, as it does, many adjustments of the couple to each other; it is even harder if they come from different religious backgrounds. It is no wonder, then, that as high as the divorce rate is among couples of the same religion, it is almost double that among couples consisting of a Jew and a non-Jew. Consequently, single Jews should date Jews exclusively if they want to enhance their chances of staying together and of having Jewish children and grandchildren. . . .

Divorce

. . . The Torah provides for divorce (Deuteronomy 24:1–4), and so from our earliest texts the Jewish tradition has not considered divorce to be a sin. On the contrary, at times divorce may be appropriate and possibly even a Jewish and moral good. That would be true, for example, when the marital bond includes abuse or when it causes severe harm to the self-esteem of one or both spouses such that they cannot live life fully in the image of God. . . .

Even when clearly indicated, divorce in most cases is nevertheless a profoundly sad event, shattering the hopes and dreams of both spouses and the sense of continuity in their lives, often destabilizing their self-image and self-confidence, and always requiring a radical change of their lives from within and from without. . . .

If a couple decides to be divorced, it is imperative that they secure a Jewish writ of divorce (a *get*) in addition to whatever procedures are demanded by civil law. . . .

Responsum on Family Violence

Historically, much of Jewish tradition presumed that violent acts did not happen within Jewish families. Now we know that this is a Jewish problem as well. Some Jewish adults abuse their spouses (usually men against women, but sometimes the reverse), and sometimes gay men or lesbians abuse their partners. Some parents abuse their young children, and some adult children abuse their elderly parents.

Jewish Family Service (JFS) has developed programs to give people susceptible to such behavior the help they need to learn to avoid it and established shelters in many cities to serve as safe havens for battered women and children. In addition, in states such as California, where rabbis and teachers are mandated reporters of abuse against children, JFS teaches rabbis and educators what the law requires if they witness or even suspect abuse.

The Committee on Jewish Law and Standards has also addressed this issue. On September 13, 1995, the CJLS approved Rabbi Elliot Dorff's responsum on the topic. The committee approved part 1, on physical, sexual, and verbal abuse, by a vote of sixteen in favor, one opposed, and no abstentions (16–1–0). CJLS approved parts 2 and 3, on witnesses to abuse and the abused party, by 17–0–0, and part 4, on the abuser, by 20–0–0. All four parts have been excerpted here; to read the full responsum, see http://www.rabbinicalassembly.org/sites/default/files/public/halakhah/teshuvot/19912000/dorff_violence.pdf or chapter 5 of Dorff's book *Love Your Neighbor and Yourself.*

Part I: Physical, Sexual, Verbal Abuse

Beating wives, husbands, or anyone else, and other forms of physical abuse, such as sexual abuse, are absolutely forbidden by Jewish law as we Conservative rabbis understand it.

Parents are obligated to discipline their children but should use means that do not in and of themselves teach children that physical assault is a right of parents or anyone in authority. For most people, this means *no use of any form of hitting at all.* For those who do use spanking or other forms of physical beating as a mode of discipline, it is difficult to draw definitive lines as to what is permissible and what is prohibited, but some guidelines can be stipulated.

Specifically, a light smack on the buttocks (a "potch") or a slap with an open hand is permissible, but any strike that causes bleeding or bruises, or blows administered with a rod, belt, or other weapon are forbidden. All the more so, any assault that causes severe, permanent damage to the child is clearly and emphatically forbidden. In addition, since discipline of the child is the only acceptable justification, random or unbridled beating or any beating unrelated to discipline of the child would also be forbidden. In general, discipline is better done without beating of any kind.

Children may not beat their parents, even when parents were formerly abusive themselves. Adult children may designate others to care for their parents if the emotional or physical conditions make that necessary. . . .

Verbal abuse is also forbidden. One may and should criticize others, including one's family members, when criticism is called for, but that must be done constructively and, if possible, in private.

Part II: Witnesses to the Act or Results of Abuse

It is *not* a violation of Jewish laws prohibiting defamatory speech (*leshon ha-ra*) or shaming another (*boshet*) for an abused party or, for that matter, for anyone who witnesses the abuse, to report it to civil authorities. On the contrary, the requirement that one preserve not only oneself (*pikku'aḥ nefesh*) but others as well, demanded by the laws of the pursuer (*rodef*) and of not standing idly by when another is in danger (*lo ta'amod 'al dam ray'ekha*), not only permit, but require others who discover spousal, filial, or parental abuse to help the victim report the abuse and take steps to prevent repetition of it.

It is *not* a violation of Jewish law to hand over Jews suspected of abusing others to civil authorities for trial and, if found guilty, for punishment. On the contrary, because Jewish courts have no power to invoke civil and criminal penalties, and because courts in Western countries can be assumed to be fair in treating individual Jews and not punish the entire Jewish community for their transgressions, and because most, if not all, civil jurisdictions now require that such abuse be reported (at least when it is done to children), it is the Jewish, and often the civil, duty of Jews to report abusers to governmental authorities. . . .

Jews who suspect that children are being abused must report such abuse to the civil authorities, even if that may mean that the child will be taken from the custody of one or both parents, and even if, in the extreme, it will mean that the child will be raised by non-Jews. Saving a life takes precedence over the presumption that parental custody is usually best for the child and even over the duty to raise the child as a Jew.

Part III: The Abused Party

It is *not* a violation of Jewish law prohibiting defamatory speech or shaming another for the victim of abuse to seek help to stop the abuse or to extricate oneself from the abusive relationship altogether. . . . On the contrary, it is a positive obligation of the most authoritative sort for victims to contact others to help them save their own lives by freeing them from the context and the relationships in which the abuse is taking place.

Part IV: The Abuser

Jewish institutions, and Jews individually, must take every precaution from jumping to conclusions of guilt merely because someone is accused of perpetuating abuse. Jewish law ascribes a strong presumption of innocence to each person, and so the burden of proof is on the accuser. Furthermore, any and all evidence must be carefully weighed by communal authorities and a formal determination of guilt must be reached before any action against the alleged abuser is taken. Allegations alone are not sufficient to justify that.

The process of return (*teshuvah*) described in our sources for other offenders is open to a person engaged in family violence too, but it must be complete to warrant reinstatement in the community. Where full *teshuvah* does occur, Jews are not permitted even to mention the former abuse in general conversation, but they may use that information in making practical decisions about what may tempt the abuser and/or pose a danger to others.

Where full *teshuvah* does not occur, synagogues may deem it appropriate to use the religious and communal power at their disposal to express their disgust at the abusive behavior and to motivate the abuser to change his or her ways. This may include suspension or refusal of membership and denial of honors in worship and in leadership. The rabbi may also use theological as well as communal language in explaining to the abuser why her or his behavior is unacceptable. The specific sanctions should be tailored by the rabbi and lay leaders in charge to the particular situation with the goals of preventing future abuse and of motivating the abuser to make amends and to change his or her ways. In some cases, full *teshuvah* may be impossible for the abuser because of the community's decision to protect itself from future abuse of the same nature by the perpetrator; in such circumstances, the community should reinstate the abuser, even absent full *teshuvah*, once she or he has completed all the steps of *teshuvah* that the community will allow him or her to do.

Jewish professionals and institutions can prevent and ameliorate cases of abuse by learning to recognize the signs of abuse [and] bringing in other professionals within the community who have expertise in this area to help the institution take steps to avoid abuse, identify likely instances of abuse, and heal it when it occurs. . . .

Addressing Interfaith Marriage

In 1970–71 the Conservative movement enacted its first Standard of Rabbinic Practice—incumbent on every Conservative rabbi—prohibiting rabbis from officiating at interfaith marriages. It reads: "A member of the Rabbinical Assembly may not officiate at an intermarriage."[1]

Since then, interfaith marriages have become increasingly common. Moreover, many interfaith couples where the Jewish partner grew up Conservative have since joined Reform synagogues, perhaps because a Reform rabbi has officiated at their wedding or because they otherwise felt more comfortable in that congregation. (In the Reform movement, rabbis are discouraged from officiating at interfaith weddings, but they are not forbidden to do so. Each rabbi is free to make a personal decision on the matter. Those rabbis who agree to officiate often require the couple or non-Jewish partner to learn about Judaism and commit both to creating a Jewish home and giving their children a Jewish education.)

As a result, Conservative rabbis and congregations have struggled with how best to welcome interfaith couples into the Conservative community (*keruv*, "bringing close") while still upholding the standard. In 1982 the CJLS approved five differing responsa on how, if at all, to involve the non-Jewish spouse in the synagogue and the movement. In June 2011 the newly formed Commission on Keruv, Conversion, and Jewish Peoplehood began reaching out to colleagues to deepen Conservative thinking on the matter.[2] Subsequently, a multisession discussion took place at the 2012 Rabbinical Assembly convention. As the call to the sessions put it,

> Rabbis throughout the Movement are constantly faced with one of the most difficult challenges of rabbinic practice: "How can I show you that I care for you even when I have to say no [to your request to officiate at our wedding]?"
>
> Our ideology of upholding tradition while remaining fully engaged in a changing world requires a constant balancing act. Conservative rabbis are finding language to convey the welcome in our hearts while we continue to uphold the values and commitments of our tradition. Most importantly, we need to support each other. In looking at the work being done by our rabbis, the Commission appreciated that this convention could be an opportunity for rabbis to speak openly and candidly with one another.[3]

In 2014 the Rabbinical Assembly went on to approve a resolution reaffirming that non-Jews, including those with a Jewish father and a non-Jewish mother, must convert to Judaism for the couple to be considered a fully Jewish couple and that Conservative rabbis stand ready to help in this process. The resolution stressed: "Members of the Rabbinical Assembly continue to welcome, counsel, dialogue, and engage with interfaith couples consistent with halakhah as interpreted by the Rabbinical Assembly's Committee on Jewish Law and Standards."[4]

Discussion continues within all the arms of the movement as to how to handle this increasingly common reality. Many synagogues have restructured their membership categories to offer only single and family memberships, with the latter including everyone in the family, Jewish or not. Then, rabbis, working with their lay leaders, have determined for their individual synagogues the parameters of what non-Jewish adults and children may and may not do within the synagogue in such areas as education, life-cycle events, worship, and membership (board of directors, Sisterhood or Men's Club, youth group, etc.). Tensions over these issues can be understandably strong, as the decisions affect the particular individuals, family, and friends in personal ways and simultaneously affect the character and reputation of the larger synagogue community.

Addressing Gays and Lesbians

The Conservative movement first took up the topic of gay men and lesbians in January 1989, when two differing responsa on the issue were presented to its Committee on Jewish Law and Standards. In one, Rabbi Steven Saltzman argued that even though Conservative Judaism believes that Jewish law evolves over time, Conservative rabbis should not change Jewish law on this issue because the Jewish community has a vested interest in procreation, especially after losing a third of our numbers during the Holocaust. In the other, Rabbi Bradley Shavit Artson argued on the basis of David F. Greenberg's book on the history of homosexuality, *The Construction of Homosexuality*, that the only kinds of homosexual relations that the ancients knew were coercive (master-slave), cultic, or licentious.[5] Monogamous, loving homosexual sex did not exist in the ancient world. Therefore, we should understand the Torah's bans on gay male sex in Leviticus 18:22 and 20:13 to refer to the types of homosexual sex people of that time knew and treat gay sex by loving partners as falling under the same moral values that "A Rabbinic Letter on Intimate Relations" delineated. After a four-hour discussion of both responsa, the CJLS tabled them both and asked the then CJLS chair, Rabbi Joel Roth, to find someone to articulate an intermediate position.

Ultimately, Rabbi Roth himself wrote an extensive responsum expressing a position that was, if anything, to the right of Rabbi Saltzman's. It included the directives that gay men and lesbians should not be rabbis or cantors and that a local rabbi should determine whether or not they might serve as educators.

This engendered four additional CJLS meetings during the fall of 1991 and the spring of 1992 devoted solely to this topic. In the process, Rabbis Reuven Kimmelman and Mayer Rabinowitz wrote opinions concurring with Rabbi Roth's result but for different reasons. Rabbi Elliot Dorff wrote a fourth responsum maintaining in part that the CJLS rabbis did not know enough yet about homosexuality to issue any official rulings about it. He recommended that the Rabbinical Assembly, Jewish Theological Seminary of America, and United Synagogue of Conservative Judaism establish the Commission on Human Sexuality, which would (among other things) thoroughly examine what was scientifically known about homosexuality to date. While the proposed commission was doing its work, he asserted, the movement should retain the status quo. In other words, gay and lesbian Jews could not be admitted to rabbinical school, and Conservative rabbis could not officiate at same-sex weddings. At the same time, gays and lesbians were to be fully welcomed in Conservative congregations, youth groups, camps, and schools; and the movement supported their full civic equality in society (per the Rabbinical Assembly resolution of May 1990, which follows, and the similar United Synagogue of Conservative Judaism resolution, passed in November 1991).

On March 15, 1992, the CJLS approved not only all of the four different responsa on this topic but also the Consensus Statement on Homosexuality (which follows), this by a vote of nineteen in favor, three opposed, and one abstention.

Behind the scenes, the nineteen CJLS members who voiced agreement on the Consensus Statement had wanted the movement to appear less splintered over this issue than it then was. In fact, although they had voted in seeming agreement with the Consensus Statement, they did not understand its application in the same way. Rabbis Roth, Rabinowitz, and Kimmelman, authors of three of the approved responsa, as well as the committee members who had voted for the three rabbis' responsa, intended for these positions to become the Conservative movement's permanent stance on homosexuality. However, the Consensus Statement language, taken from Rabbi Dorff's responsum, specifically noted that all of the status quo provisions of the Consensus Statement would apply only so long as the proposed Commission on Human Sexuality did its work, after which the CJLS was to revisit its policies.

Consensus Statement on Homosexuality

The Committee on Jewish Law and Standards of The Rabbinical Assembly affirms the following policies:

We will not perform commitment ceremonies for gays or lesbians.

We will not knowingly admit avowed homosexuals to our rabbinical or cantorial schools or to the Rabbinical Assembly or the Cantors' Assembly. At the same time, we will not instigate witch hunts against those who are already members or students.

Whether homosexuals may function as teachers or youth leaders in our congregations and schools will be left to the rabbi authorized to make halakhic decisions for a given institution within the Conservative Movement. Presumably, in this as in all other matters, the rabbi will make such decisions taking into account the sensitivities of the people of his or her particular congregation or school. The rabbi's own reading of Jewish law on these issues, informed by the responsa written for the Committee on Jewish Law and Standards to date, will also be a determinative factor in these decisions.

Similarly, the rabbi of each Conservative institution, in consultation with its lay leaders, will be entrusted to formulate policies regarding the eligibility of homosexuals for honors within worship and for lay leadership positions.

In any case, in accordance with The Rabbinical Assembly and United Synagogue resolutions, we hereby affirm that gays and lesbians are welcome in our congregations, youth groups, camps, and schools.

The Rabbinical Assembly Resolution

WHEREAS Judaism affirms that the Divine image reflected by every human being must always be cherished and affirmed, and

WHEREAS Jews have always been sensitive to the impact of official and unofficial prejudice and discrimination, wherever directed, and

WHEREAS gay and lesbian Jews have experienced not only the constant threats of physical violence and homophobic rejection, but also the pains of anti-Semitism known to all Jews and, additionally, a sense of painful alienation from our own religious institutions, and

WHEREAS the extended families of gay and lesbian Jews are often members of our congregations who live with concern for the safety, health, and well-being of their children, and

WHEREAS the AIDS crisis has deeply exacerbated the anxiety and suffering of this community of Jews who need in their lives the compassionate concern and support mandated by Jewish tradition,

THEREFORE BE IT RESOLVED that we, The Rabbinical Assembly, while affirming our tradition's prescription for heterosexuality,

Support full civil equality for gays and lesbians in our national life, and

Deplore the violence against gays and lesbians in our society, and

Reiterate that, as are all Jews, gay men and lesbians are welcome as members in our congregations, and

Call upon our synagogues and the arms of our movement to increase our awareness, understanding and concern for our fellow Jews who are gay and lesbian.[6]

Civil versus Religious Rights

On the whole, the Conservative movement was united in officially welcoming gay and lesbian Jews to Conservative congregations and in supporting civil rights for gays and lesbians. Both the RA and USCJ had voted for "full civil equality for gays and lesbians in our national life." The respective resolutions, however, never defined what civil rights those encompassed. Those who wrote and voted for them likely intended to voice support for equality in jobs, housing, health care, and inheritance and possibly also for equality in insurance, adoption, custody, and visitation rights. Civil marriage for gay men and lesbians had not yet become part of the national conversation. (It was not until April 2000 that Vermont became the first state to create civil unions for gay men and lesbians and until November 2003 that Massachusetts became the first state to legally recognize gay and lesbian marriage, per a Massachusetts Supreme Judicial Court ruling that the state's constitution required it.)

Despite these important areas of agreement, serious disagreement continued within the movement on admission of gays and lesbians to

Conservative rabbinical and cantorial schools and on gay and lesbian couples having a Jewish commitment ceremony or wedding. Even the name
of such a ceremony was a matter at issue. Options discussed included
"commitment ceremony"; *brit re'im* (covenant of friends) or *brit re'im
ha-ahuvim* (covenant of loving friends), based on the description of the
couple in the seven blessings for a heterosexual marriage; and marriage
or the Hebrew equivalents, *kiddushin* (betrothal) and *nisu'in* (marriage).

The liturgy for such a ceremony, if used at all, was also at issue. Possibilities ranged from ceremonies that were very close to Jewish marriage
rites to others that were considerably different.

Revisiting the Responsa

Ultimately, in December 2003 the then Rabbinical Assembly president,
Rabbi Reuven Hammer, and the United Synagogue of Conservative Judaism
president, Judy Yudoff, jointly asked the CJLS to reconsider its position on
both these issues. This provoked three more years of CJLS deliberations
on the topic, during which CJLS members interviewed experts on the
current science of sexual orientation and heard from representatives of
various positions within the movement.

CJLS procedures normally allowed any Rabbinical Assembly member
to submit a responsum for CJLS consideration. Making an exception,
the then CJLS chair, Rabbi Kassel Abelson, ruled that only CJLS members
were allowed to submit responsa on this one issue. Otherwise, given the
contention within the movement and within American society generally,
the CJLS was liable to be inundated with responsa and the equivalent of
amicus curiae opinion papers. His concern was well warranted, for in June
2005, nine of the twenty-five CJLS rabbis had already written responsa
on the topic for consideration. Rabbi Abelson asked whether some of the
authors, now seeing what others had written, could find a way to combine
their work. That is how Rabbis Elliot Dorff, Daniel Nevins, and Avram
Reisner came to write a joint responsum and how Rabbis Robert Fine,
David Fine, and Myron Geller did so as well.

In the end, on December 6, 2006, the CJLS voted on five responsa. Two of them argued for maintaining the bans on ordaining gay men or lesbians and on performing Jewish commitment ceremonies. Reaching that conclusion, Rabbi Joel Roth included and updated his 1992 responsum. From his perspective, closely tied to his theory of law (see chapter 4 of this volume), "extra-halakhic" factors such as new scientific understandings about sexual orientation and the suffering homosexuals endured as a result of societal discrimination were not sufficient to remove a prohibition rooted in the Torah and maintained by Rabbinic tradition ever since.

Rabbi Leonard Levy arrived at the same conclusion for a different reason. Although all the relevant professional organizations opposed attempts to convert homosexuals into heterosexuals, two psychiatrists nonetheless maintained that some forms of treatment could transform a homosexual into a heterosexual. Levy asserted that gay men and lesbians should try this.

On the other end of the spectrum, Rabbis Myron Geller, Robert Fine, and David Fine argued on historical grounds for removing the bans on both ordaining gay men or lesbians and performing Jewish commitment ceremonies. In the past, they stated, same-sex relations had been prohibited because they were considered an abomination (the English translation of *to'evah*, the Torah's descriptive word for men having sex with men in Leviticus 18:22). But now that this was no longer the case, Conservative Judaism should utilize the legal method of *mi'ut*, restricting a law to a specific case, to interpret the Torah's verse. From this perspective, men today should not have sex with each other when such activity would be considered an abomination—specifically, when such sexual activity would be deemed licentious or oppressive. Gay men and lesbians may and should, however, seek to create loving bonds of marriage, celebrated through public Jewish (and, where possible, civil) ceremonies, and otherwise qualified gay men and lesbians should be admitted to rabbinical school and ultimately ordained.

Rabbi Gordon Tucker also argued (in his case philosophically rather than historically) for dissolving the ban on homosexual relations. Jewish law, he said, must also accommodate unusual situations in which contemporary science and people's own testimony, a modern form of *aggadah*, justify abandoning precedent and striking out in new directions. Homosexual relations, he believed, are just such an instance.

The Dorff-Nevins-Reisner responsum took a middle stance. It argued, first on the basis of scientific evidence, that homosexuality, just like heterosexuality, is embedded in people. All society's attempts to change homosexuals into heterosexuals had not only failed but led to high levels of depression and suicide. Moreover, because of a highly discriminatory—and sometimes violent—environment, gay teenagers were committing suicide at three to four times the rate of heterosexual teens, and they were smoking and abusing alcohol considerably more as well. These alarming realities demonstrated that failure to permit homosexuals to have legitimate outlets for their sexual desires in society had undermined their dignity.

The Talmud asserted multiple times that *kevod ha-briyyot*, the honor due to all human beings, trumped any Rabbinic enactments.[7] Based on that precedent, Rabbis Dorff, Nevins, and Reisner ruled that the Torah's ban in Leviticus 18:22 and 20:13, interpreted by the Rabbis to prohibit gay anal sex, would stand, but all the prohibitions the Rabbis had added to that activity, such as oral sex or stroking each other's bodies to produce pleasure and sexual climaxes, would be removed in the name of restoring dignity to gay men and lesbians. This, then, meant that seminaries affiliated with the movement were at liberty to admit otherwise qualified gay men and lesbians to their rabbinical and cantorial schools and that Conservative/Masorti rabbis could officiate at Jewish commitment/marriage ceremonies to celebrate such unions.

In the appendix to the Dorff-Nevins-Reisner responsum, psychologist Dr. Judith Glassgold listed more than sixty studies in the fields of psychiatry, psychology, and social work on homosexuality and cited the research results as articulated in official statements of the American Psychiatric Association, the American Psychological Association, the American Association of Social Work, and the American Medical Association. Among the organizations' conclusions were these: homosexuality was not a psychological disease; homosexuals could not be changed into heterosexuals; efforts to do so were harmful; without discrimination, homosexuals would be able to live perfectly normal lives; the children of homosexuals, whether biological or adopted, were no more likely to be homosexual than the children of heterosexual parents; children raised by homosexuals had no special difficulties in forming their own gender identity; and homosexuals could be just as good at parenting as heterosexuals.

When on December 6, 2006, the CJLS finally convened to vote on the five responsa on the table, all twenty-five CJLS voting members were in attendance, one mark of the contentiousness that had continued, unabated, around this issue. A second mark was the CJLS's simultaneous approval of three diverging perspectives. Both Rabbi Joel Roth's responsum, which banned gay and lesbian ordination and Conservative rabbis officiating at same-sex commitment ceremonies, and the Rabbis Dorff, Nevins, and Reisner responsum, which permitted ordination and officiation, were adopted by votes of thirteen in favor and twelve against. Notably, one member voted for them both in order to strengthen the movement's pluralism on this issue. In addition, the CJLS adopted Rabbi Leonard Levy's responsum by a vote of six in favor, eight opposed, and eleven abstaining—six votes being the minimum necessary for a responsum to become a validated option within the movement.

Meanwhile, the Fine-Fine-Geller responsum vote was six in favor, seventeen opposed, and two abstaining, and the Tucker responsum vote was seven in favor, fourteen opposed, and four abstaining. By the rules then in operation, however, both of these responsa were declared *takkanot* (legislative changes in the law rather than judicial interpretations) and, as such, required a minimum of thirteen votes for acceptance. Thus, even though both had received the same or more yes votes than Rabbi Levy's, neither became an official CJLS position. Instead, to this date both responsa appear on the Rabbinical Assembly website as dissents to the three validated responsa.

Ironically, a few months after the meeting, the Rabbinical Assembly's Executive Council removed CJLS's jurisdiction to enact *takkanot* altogether.

Had that rule, which has held to date, been in place at the time of the vote, the Fine-Fine-Geller and the Tucker responsa would have been adopted, each having been endorsed by the six-vote minimum required to make a rabbinical ruling a validated option within the Conservative movement.

Many years later, one of the two researchers cited in Rabbi Levy's responsum recanted his conclusion that homosexuality could be cured, prompting some CJLS members to ask that this responsum be removed from the official list of validated Conservative responsa. Eradicating a responsum, however, requires an affirmative vote by twenty of the twenty-five voting members, and this has not happened to date, probably because the movement's positions on gay and lesbian Jews shifted dramatically in subsequent years, precluding the need to revisit the issue.

Ordaining Gay and Lesbian Rabbis

The Dorff-Nevins-Reisner responsum quickly paved the way for a newfound openness to gay and lesbian Jews as spiritual leaders within the Conservative movement. Immediately after the December 6, 2006, decision, the Ziegler School of Rabbinic Studies at American Jewish University in Los Angeles opened its doors to qualified gay men and lesbians, and a few months later the Rabbinical School of the Jewish Theological Seminary did likewise.

Although some movement leaders predicted that the December decision would tear the movement apart, that did not happen. Instead, gay and lesbian rabbis largely found acceptance and good positions within the movement, and those opposed to ordaining gay men or lesbians as rabbis have simply hired heterosexual rabbis. Just as it took some time for Conservative synagogues and other institutions to get used to women rabbis, it will probably take time for a number of Conservative institutions to get used to gay and lesbian rabbis, and here too societal developments are likely to play an influential role in this process.

It took nearly a decade after the December 2006 responsum for the Conservative/Masorti rabbinical school in Israel to admit openly gay and lesbian students. In 2014 the Schechter Institute of Jewish Studies in

Jerusalem consented to do so after an agreement was reached that the Rabbinical Assembly's Israel Region, rather than the school itself, would henceforth ordain all students, including gay men and lesbians. The Seminario Rabínico Latinoamericano in Buenos Aires also admits gay men and lesbians to its rabbinical school. The newest rabbinical school affiliated with the movement, the Zacharias Frankel College in Potsdam, Germany, is a branch of the Ziegler School in Los Angeles, and so it too is open to admitting and ordaining gay men and lesbians.

Officiating at Same-Sex Unions

After their responsum was approved, Rabbis Dorff, Nevins, and Reisner anticipated that rabbis would create ceremonies and documents celebrating gay or lesbian unions. Once vetted, these materials could subsequently be shared with the movement, probably within a new appendix to their responsum.

This did not happen. Rather, rabbis were asking Rabbis Dorff, Nevins, and Reisner to create a template or two that could be used for gay and lesbian unions. And so, in consultation with a number of gay and lesbian rabbinical students and rabbis, the three authors proceeded to create those ceremonies and documents. The CJLS approved their new responsum, "Rituals and Documents of Marriage and Divorce for Same-Sex Couples," on May 31, 2012, by a vote of fifteen in favor, none opposed, and one abstaining (15–0–1).

In this document, officially an appendix to their 2006 responsum, the authors called the union of gay and lesbian couples "marriage," as contemporary society was now doing as well. However, they did not use the standard Hebrew terms *kiddushin* (betrothal) and *ni'su'in* (marriage) for heterosexual betrothal and marriage, because, as they explained, those categories and their legal implications did not fit same-sex couples.

For example, in a traditional heterosexual ceremony, the man "acquires" his bride, but who would "acquire" whom in a same-sex union? In fact, many Conservative rabbis today find it difficult to use the legal category of acquisition (*kinyan*) even in heterosexual marriage. Those who still utilize it do so in the name of preserving the tradition and often modify it so that each member of the couple "acquires" the other. Nonetheless, the responsum authors did not want to expand this way of thinking about marriage to same-sex couples, where no precedent existed.

A similar problem affected divorce. Because in Jewish law only the husband can divorce his wife, it was unclear who in gay and lesbian marriages would have the right to divorce the other. Moreover, the provision in traditional Jewish marriage law that enables only the husband to initiate a divorce has led to many problems; the three rabbis did not want same-sex married couples to incur those problems as well.

As a result, to describe gay and lesbian unions, Rabbis Dorff, Nevins, and Reisner used the Hebrew term *brit re-im ahuvim*, "Covenant of Loving Companions." These are the only words in the traditional wedding ceremony that describe the couple and thereby indicate that marriage constitutes a covenant between them.

The parameters of Jewish same-sex marriage ceremonies and documents were also issues of discussion. The gay men and lesbians consulting with the three rabbis were themselves divided on whether these new rituals and forms should be very close to or different from those used for Jewish heterosexual marriage and divorce. Ultimately, the three rabbis presented templates for both options.

What follows are excerpts from the 2006 responsum, "Homosexuality, Human Dignity, and Halakhah," by Rabbis Elliot N. Dorff, Daniel S. Nevins, and Avram I. Reisner, which precipitated significant change in Conservative movement practice, and from its 2012 appendix, which included ceremonies and documents for gay and lesbian unions. To read the full responsum, see http://www.rabbinicalassembly.org/sites/default/files/public/halakhah/teshuvot/20052010/dorff_nevins_reisner_dignity.pdf. To read the other CJLS responsa from both 1992 and 2006 about the status of gay and lesbian unions and ordinations, see https://www.rabbinicalassembly.org/practical-rabbinics/committee-jewish-law-and-standards/even-haezer.

Following this responsum are portions of the same-sex marriage ceremony that are similar to the traditional Jewish wedding rite for heterosexuals and the "Covenant of Loving Partners," similar to a *ketub-bah*. To see the full ceremonies and documents from the 2012 responsum appendix for both creating and dissolving same-sex unions, see https://www.rabbinicalassembly.org/sites/default/files/assets/public/halakhah/teshuvot/2011-2020/same-sex-marriage-and-divorce-appendix.pdf.

Homosexuality, Human Dignity, and Halakhah
Responsum Conclusions (2006)

Based upon our study of halakhic precedents regarding both sexual norms and human dignity, we reach the following conclusions:

The explicit biblical ban on anal sex between men remains in effect. Gay men are instructed to refrain from anal sex.

Heterosexual marriage between two Jews remains the halakhic ideal. For homosexuals who are incapable of maintaining a heterosexual relationship, the rabbinic prohibitions that have been associated with other gay and lesbian intimate acts are superseded based upon the Talmudic principle of *kvod habriot*, our obligation to preserve the human dignity of all people.

This ruling effectively normalizes the status of gay and lesbian Jews in the Jewish community. Extending the 1992 CJLS Consensus Statement, gay and lesbian Jews are to be welcomed into our synagogues and other institutions as full members with no restrictions. Furthermore, gay or lesbian Jews who demonstrate the depth of Jewish commitment, knowledge, faith and desire to serve as rabbis, cantors and educators shall be welcomed to apply to our professional schools and associations.[8]

We are not prepared at this juncture to rule upon the halakhic status of gay and lesbian relationships. To do so would require establishing an entirely new institution in Jewish law that treats not only the ceremonies and legal instruments appropriate for creating homosexual unions but also the norms for the dissolution of such unions. This responsum does not provide *kiddushin* for same-sex couples. Nonetheless, we consider stable, committed, Jewish relationships to be as necessary and beneficial for homosexuals and their families as they are for heterosexuals. Promiscuity is not acceptable for either homosexual or heterosexual relationships.

Such relationships should be conducted in consonance with the values set out in the RA pastoral letter on intimate relationships, *"This Is My Beloved, This Is My Friend": A Rabbinic Letter on Intimate Relations.*[9] The celebration of such a union is appropriate.

Same-Sex Betrothal Blessing (2012)

Praised are You, Adonai our God, who rules the universe, creating the fruit of the vine.

Our God and God of our Patriarchs and Matriarchs, look down from Your holy abode, from heaven, and bless these loving companions, who are together creating a Covenant of Lovers. Praised are You, Adonai, who is good and does good.

Same-Sex Ceremony of Covenant (2012)

Of the following 7 blessings the officiating rabbi offers the couple, blessings 1, 2, 3, and 5 are the same as in traditional Jewish wedding rites for heterosexual couples; blessings 4, 6, and 7 are new.

The couple exchanges rings and each declares: "Be my covenanted partner, in love and friendship, in peace and companionship, in the eyes of God and humanity."

Together they say: "May it be Your will, Adonai, our God, to establish our life-long household and to bring Your presence into our lives."

1. Praised are You, Adonai our God, who rules the universe, creating the fruit of the vine.
2. Praised are You, Adonai our God, who rules the universe, whose glory is evident in all of creation.
3. Praised are You, Adonai our God, who rules the universe, Creator of humanity.
4. Praised are You, Adonai our God, who rules the universe, who created humanity in the divine image, who structured us in the image of God, and said, "It is not good for a person to live alone, I will make a fitting helper for each one" (Genesis 2:18). Praised are You, Adonai, Creator of humanity.

5. May Zion rejoice as her children return to her in joy. Praised are You, Adonai, who causes Zion to rejoice in her children.

6. Grant perfect joy to these loving companions, as You did for Your first human beings in the Garden of Eden. Praised are You, Adonai, who is good and does good.

7. Praised are You, Adonai, our God who rules the universe, who created joy and gladness, happiness and blessing, pleasure and song, delight, laughter, love, harmony, peace, and companionship. Adonai, our God, may there always be heard in the cities of Judah and the streets of Jerusalem voices of joy and gladness, voices of pleasure and song, voices of those who proclaim "Give thanks to Adonai, for God is good, God's faithfulness is eternal" (Psalms 118:1). Praised are You, Adonai, who has kept us alive and sustained us and brought us to this joyous time.

Same-Sex Marriage: Covenant of Loving Partners (2012)

On the _____ day of the week, the _____ day of the month of _____ in the year five thousand seven hundred _____, corresponding to the secular date of _____, here in _____ in the country of _____ we, _____ the daughter/son of _____, and _____ the daughter/son of _____, before the people and the congregation make this holy declaration: "Let it be known that our souls are bound one to the other with bonds of love and mutual devotion, and that it is our intention, with God's help, to be exclusively faithful to each other all the days of our lives upon this earth. As our Sages taught: 'A person should find a partner with whom to eat, drink, read, study, sleep, and share every secret, secrets of Torah and secrets of life' (*Avot D'Rabbi Natan A*, #8). We shall share from this day a complete partnership, joyfully and wholeheartedly establishing a household in common with moral and financial responsibilities for one another. We shall be loving partners for each other and will cherish, respect, sustain and assist one another in righteousness and faithfulness. With God's help may our dwelling be filled with love and harmony, peace and companionship, and may we be privileged to nurture together our Jewish heritage, our love for our fellow Jews, and the dignity of every creature."

We, the witnesses, attest that everything that is written and specified above has been done in our presence and is valid and effective.

(Signature)_____, witness

(Signature)_____, witness

Responsa on Transgender Individuals

On December 3, 2003, the CJLS accepted the new gender identity of a person who had undergone sex reassignment surgery and determined how Jewish laws applied in such cases. Rabbi Mayer Rabinowitz's responsum, "Status of Transsexuals," approved by a vote of ten in favor, two opposed, and eight abstaining (10–2–8), concluded that "only those who have undergone full SRS [sex reassignment surgery] (including phalloplasty/vaginoplasty) are to be . . . recognized [by Jewish law] as having changed their sex status."

Because in 2003 the CJLS had not yet approved same-sex marriage, the responsum included provisions to prevent Jewish recognition of such marriages as a result of a sex change: "A *get* [writ of divorce] is not necessary if one spouse undergoes SRS since the *qiddushin* [bonds of betrothal] are automatically annulled. However in the case of an MTF [male to female] person, a *get* should be given before the SRS is completed. . . . Recognition by the civil authorities of the new sex status is required in order to marry a person who has undergone SRS. This will prevent us from performing same sex marriages according to civil law." The full *teshuvah* can be found at http://www.rabbinicalassembly.org/sites/default/files/assets/public /halakhah/teshuvot/20012004/rabinowitz_transsexuals.pdf.

At the time, this responsum was on the cutting edge, for few religious authorities in any religion were seriously dealing with transgender issues. In the intervening years, however, the science behind transgender issues developed and the nomenclature changed; society increasingly came to accept that some people's gender by birth did not match the gender they felt themselves to be; and the CJLS permitted rabbis to officiate at same-sex marriages.

In light of these new developments, Rabbi Leonard Sharzer, a physician who had practiced medicine for thirty-two years before he entered rabbinical school, twenty-three of them as a plastic surgeon, wrote a responsum demonstrating that none of the usual methods used to identify a person as either male or female—anatomy, hormones, or genetics—is definitive but that gender identity in people tends to be consistent from birth, even if expressions of that identity vary over time. He therefore concludes that society generally, and Jewish law in particular, should follow what a person says about what gender that person is, whether male, female, or something else. However that person transitions from the gender assigned at birth (usually determined by anatomical characteristics)—surgery, hormonal therapy, or simply dressing as the other gender or as some combination of genders and identifying oneself as such—should be enough for Jewish law to recognize the person in the new gender. This follows the Rabbinic tradition of recognizing that some people do not fit the binary of male or female: the *androgynous* (a hermaphrodite, with bodily characteristics of both genders); the *tumtum* (a person whose genitalia are hidden or undeveloped and therefore seems to lack genitalia of either gender); the *aylonit* (a woman without a uterus or who cannot conceive for some other reason); the *saris* (a castrated man or one who is impotent for another reason).[10]

On June 7, 2017, the CJLS approved Rabbi Leonard Sharzer's responsum, "Transgender Jews and Halakhah," spelling out what this means for matters of marriage, conversion, change of name, public accommodations, burial rites, and more, by a vote of eleven in favor and eight abstaining (11–0–8). Those who abstained wanted further revision on several points before taking a vote. Here are its conclusions. To read the full responsum, visit https://www.rabbinicalassembly.org/sites/default/files/public/halakhah /teshuvot/2011-2020/transgender-halakhah.pdf.

Rulings

1. All conversion candidates require immersion in a *mikveh*. Neither circumcision nor *hatafat dam brit* [hereinafter HDB, taking a drop of blood from the head of the penis as a substitute for circumcision when

a man who is converting to Judaism has already been circumcised] is required for transgender men, whether or not they have undergone gender conforming surgery, though HDB is permissible as a spiritual act. Transgender women who have not undergone genital surgery do require either circumcision or HDB (the latter of which they may perform on themselves). Witnesses of the *tevilah* [immersion in a natural body of water or a specially constructed pool called a *mikveh*] of a transgender convert may be of any gender and the conversion candidate may immerse wearing a loose fitting garment. Values of dignity (*k'vod ha-briyot*) and modesty (*tz'niyut*) should be paramount at all times.

2. Transgender people who marry do so according to their publicly lived gender identities through the rituals established by the CJLS for same-sex and opposite-sex marriages. Specifically, Kiddushin is the appropriate ceremony for marriage between a male-identified person and female-identified person. All others marry with a Brit Ahuvim [Covenant of Lovers] ceremony. Rabbis officiating at these marriages must be familiar with the various state laws regarding gender assignment and fill out documents knowing that state law may recognize a person as belonging to a different gender than halakhah does.

3. The marriage of couples who choose to dissolve their marriage following the transition of one of them should be dissolved in the manner it was contracted, even if that means a *get* [Jewish document of divorce] being given by someone who currently presents as female or being received by someone who currently presents as male. In cases where there is refusal to give a *get*, the Beit Din of the Conservative Movement should annul those marriages according to its regular procedures.

4. The marriage of couples who choose to remain married after the transition of one partner, remains valid and no ritual is required. The couple and their rabbi may develop a ritual to signify and sanctify the ongoing nature of their relationship.

5. All medical treatments intended to alleviate the symptoms of people with gender dysphoria by more closely aligning their body with their gender identity, including pharmacological, surgical, and psychological treatments are permissible. This does not include so-called "conversion therapy" aimed at changing the gender identity of the person.

6. Decisions by transgender men to become pregnant are permissible but they should become informed about the current state of medical knowledge and possible implications for their own physical and psychological health as well as that of their offspring.

7. Healthcare professionals who treat transgender patients should do so in a respectful, caring and non-judgmental manner. They should become educated about the general and transition-related healthcare needs of transgender patients.

8. Preparation for burial (*taharah*) should be performed by members of the *ḥevra kaddisha* of the same gender identity as the deceased. However, in unusual or extenuating circumstances, *taharah* may be performed by people of any gender identity.

9. Laws of *tohorat ha-mishpahah* [family purity] apply to people of any gender who menstruate, including some transgender men and some non-binary people.

10. Obligation for Brit Milah [circumcision] applies to people of any gender who have a penis and a foreskin. This includes some transgender women and some non-binary people. This must be conveyed with care and sensitivity, and does not invalidate or contradict the gender identity of that person.

11. A transgender person is to be recognized as their publicly declared gender and to be addressed by their publicly declared name and pronouns. This change takes place when that person has gone through a process of transition, which may or may not include any medical procedures or treatments, and asserts and publicly declares their gender identity.

12. Rituals and ceremonies should be created to recognize and commemorate a person's transition, but they do not affect the transition and are not required.

Responsum and Documentation on Divorce

Although divorce is not considered a sin in Jewish tradition, as it is in some other religions, and although in some cases it is the right thing to do, it is always sad. It represents the dashing of a couple's dreams and hopes to have a lifetime relationship. It requires all those involved, including children, to make major adjustments in their lives, often with lasting negative effects. As a result, Conservative Judaism holds that divorce should be pursued only after serious consideration.

Sensitive to all the ensuing adjustments, once both members of the couple agreed to a divorce, the Jewish legal process to obtain one was always remarkably straightforward. Grounds for divorce never needed to be demonstrated to a court of rabbis; the spouses simply needed to indicate that they did not want to live together anymore. By contrast, in American law until the 1970s, almost all states required a divorcing couple to show grounds to a court, and the grounds that typically justified divorce in most states were narrow, adultery and insanity usually being the only granted reasons. (Nowadays, "irreconcilable differences" are sufficient grounds for divorce in all states.)

On the other hand, whereas in U.S. law both husbands and wives have the right to initiate divorce, in Jewish law, to this day, only the husband can start a divorce. Furthermore, even if a Jewish couple divorces by civil law, in Jewish law they are still considered married until the husband agrees to give a Jewish writ of divorce (*get*) to his wife. In the vast majority of cases, he does, and then both are free to marry in both civil and Jewish law.

In some cases, however, the man cannot be found (e.g., "lost in action" in a war or in the Holocaust with no witnesses that he died), he has become insane and therefore incapable of executing any document of Jewish law, or he refuses to grant the *get*. (He may also attempt to extort money or some other untenable concession from the woman before he will issue one.) In all these instances, the woman is considered an *agunah*, "chained" to her first husband in Jewish law and ineligible to marry someone else.

Preventing Agunot

The Conservative movement has taken multiple steps to prevent or ameliorate the hardship this law can inflict upon wives. In 1954 Conservative rabbis inserted a clause in the movement's official wedding document (the *ketubbah*) according to which the couple (really, the man) agrees to do what a rabbinical court tells them to do if they are divorced in civil law.

The court, of course, will tell the man to authorize issuing a *get*. Although in 1983 New York's highest court used that clause to force a man to issue a *get* when he wanted to remarry (*Avitzur v. Avitzur*, New York Court of Appeals, 58 N.Y.2d 108, 459 N.Y.S.2d 572), no other state has followed suit. It is questionable whether New York's decision would pass muster with the U.S. Constitution. Essentially, the court would be forcing a man to perform a religious act, which, arguably, violates the First Amendment's guaranteed separation of church and state.

The CJLS instituted a better way to avoid *agunot* in 1969, when it adopted a prenuptial agreement, "Ante-nuptial Agreement" (which follows), in which the couple (again, primarily the husband) agrees that if they divorce in civil court and the husband authorizes issuing a *get* within six months thereafter, then their marriage was valid. Otherwise, their marriage was not a marriage from the moment it was celebrated.

If the husband does not authorize the *get* within those six months, this ruling does transform the couple's sexual relations during their "marriage" from the status of sacred relations to licentiousness. However, it does not affect the woman's or man's ability to remarry or the status of their children. (In Jewish law, illegitimate children, *mamzerim*, are solely the products of adulterous or incestuous unions, not a union of two people who could be, and in this case were, married.)

The husband will still be pressed to issue a *get*, as it is the proper way to divorce in Jewish law, and if he subsequently wants to remarry, Conservative rabbis will require him to do so (*get ḥumra*, a writ of divorce out of stringency). But, again, in the meantime, the woman is free to remarry.

Ante-nuptial Agreement

On the ___ day of _____, ____, corresponding to the _____ day of _____ 57___ [in the Jewish calendar], in _____ [city and state], the groom, _____, and the bride, _____, of their own free will and accord entered into the following agreement with respect to their intended marriage.

The groom made the following declaration to the bride:

"I will betroth you and marry you according to the laws of Moses and the people Israel, subject to the following conditions:

"If our marriage should be terminated by decree of the civil courts and if by expiration of six months after such a decree I give you a divorce according to the laws of Moses and the people Israel (a *get*), then our betrothal (*kiddushin*) and marriage (*nissuin*) will have remained valid and binding.

"But if our marriage should be terminated by decree of the civil courts and if by expiration of six months after such a decree I do not give you a divorce according to the laws of Moses and the people Israel (a *get*), then our betrothal (*kiddushin*) and our marriage (*nissuin*) will have been null and void."

The bride said to the groom:

"I consent to the conditions that you have made."

Signature of the groom: _____

Signature of the bride: _____

We, the undersigned, acting as a Beth Din [court], witnessed the oral statements and signatures of the groom and bride.

_____ (rabbi)

_____ (witness)

_____ (witness)

Annulling the Marriage

Ultimately, if the couple did not complete a premarital document and the woman is an *agunah* for any of the above-mentioned reasons (usually for the third, the husband's recalcitrance), the Rabbinical Assembly's *beit din* will annul the marriage (*haf'qa'at kiddushin*). It can and does do this because the Talmud says that every Jewish marriage is valid only if the rabbis agree to it—very much like the fact that civil marriages are valid only if they fulfill the laws of the state. At the same time, because the Torah (Deuteronomy 24:1–4) and subsequent Jewish law maintain that the standard way for a couple to dissolve their marriage is for the man to give his wife a writ of divorce, the Talmud, and the Conservative rabbinate following that lead, see annulment as a measure to be used only when the man is not fulfilling his obligations in marriage and cannot or will not give his wife such a writ.

Therefore, even when a marriage is annulled, thus freeing the woman to remarry, if the man later wants to remarry, Conservative rabbis require him to give such a writ (a *get*) to his wife to reinforce the standard way to dissolve a marriage. About twenty or thirty annulments are granted in any given year, freeing the woman to marry again.

Suggestions for Further Reading

ON JUDAISM AND SEX

Martin S. Cohen, ed. *The Observant Life*. New York: Rabbinical Assembly, 2012, especially the following chapters:

> David J. Fine. "Marriage," 611–31.
> Jeremy Kalmanofsky. "Sex, Relationships, and Single Jews," 632–56.
> Elliot N. Dorff. "Same-Sex Relationships," 657–72.

Elliot N. Dorff. *Love Your Neighbor and Yourself: A Jewish Approach to Modern Personal Ethics*. Philadelphia: Jewish Publication Society, 2003. See chapter 3 for the full version of "A Rabbinic Letter on Intimate Relations," including its footnotes.

Elliot N. Dorff and Danya Ruttenberg, eds. *Jewish Choices, Jewish Voices: Sex and Intimacy*. Philadelphia: Jewish Publication Society, 2010.

Danya Ruttenberg, ed. *The Passionate Torah: Sex and Judaism*. New York: New York University Press, 2009.

ON SEXUAL AND OTHER FORMS OF FAMILY VIOLENCE

Elliot N. Dorff. *Love Your Neighbor and Yourself: A Jewish Approach to Personal Ethics*, chap. 5 Philadelphia: Jewish Publication Society, 2003.

Naomi Graetz. *Silence Is Deadly: Judaism Confronts Wifebeating*. Northvale NJ: Jason Aronson (now Lanham MD: Rowman and Littlefield), 1998.

Amy Neustein, ed. *Tempest in the Temple: Jewish Communities and Child Sex Scandals*. Waltham MA: Brandeis University Press, 2009.

PART THREE

Israel

CHAPTER TWELVE

Am Yisrael

Peoplehood

The third element of the medieval Jewish maxim that has served as the organizing principle of *Emet Ve-Emunah* and of this book—"God, Torah, and Israel are one"—is Israel. The Reform, Orthodox, and Conservative movements all affirm the importance of all three elements in Judaism, although each movement emphasizes one of the three factors over the other two—at least in practice.

The Reform movement did not acknowledge the peoplehood of Israel concept at first (this changed in later years) and has not accepted the authority of all Jewish laws (Torah). In Reform Judaism, God is the center of Judaism.

Orthodox Jews might agree that God is the center, but even more important to them is what Jews are supposed to do in obedience to God. Consequently, for Orthodox Jews, the Torah (especially its laws) is the most important of the three elements. In fact, they call their version of Judaism "Torah-true Judaism."

For the Conservative movement, although God and Torah are crucial parts of Judaism, both of these can become realities only if the People Israel make them so. The Rabbis of the Talmud and midrash said something similar: "'You are My witnesses,' declares the Lord, 'and I am God' (Isaiah 43:12). That is, *when* you are My witnesses, I am God, and when you are not My witnesses, I am, as it were, not God."[1]

Developing the Doctrine of the People Israel

Concern with the People Israel has been part of Conservative ideology from the very beginning. Rabbi Zacharias Frankel, the ideological founder of Conservative Judaism, left the Second Rabbinical Conference in Frankfurt in 1845 when it adopted Reform Rabbi Abraham Geiger's proposals to drop Hebrew from the prayer books used in affiliated synagogues and from their schools' curriculum. According to Jewish law, a Jew may pray in any language.[2] Even though Hebrew had been the Jews' first language only during the First Temple Period (and would be once again after the State of Israel's establishment in 1948), it had always been the second language a Jew learned, being the language of the Bible and the prayer book. Over the centuries, Frankel insisted, Hebrew had united Jews as a people and should continue to do so.

In the early twentieth century, Rabbi Solomon Schechter, chancellor of the Jewish Theological Seminary of America and founder of the United Synagogue of America, called the Conservative movement's attention to the importance of thinking of themselves as part of the whole People Israel, past, present, and future. He advocated a focus on "catholic Israel," his term for *k'lal yisrael*, or the entirety of the People Israel whereby "catholic" meant widespread, as in "He has catholic interests."

This perspective has shaped Conservative practice ever since. If peoplehood is primary, then current Jewish practice must reflect not only what the rabbis have written and now say but also past and contemporary Jewish customs. For example, already in Schechter's time men and women sat together in worship in Conservative synagogues, in contrast to the sexes being separated in Orthodox synagogues. Similarly, boys and girls (and later men and women) in Conservative schools studied the same curriculum in the same classes, in contrast to their Orthodox counterparts, who studied different curricula in different venues.

Moreover, inspired by the idea of "catholic Israel," Schechter and subsequent Conservative leaders initiated and realized new ventures to bring all Jews together to serve the Jewish people's needs, among them federations, synagogue councils, and many other Jewish communal organizations.

Later, in the 1930s, the early Conservative Rabbi Mordecai Kaplan avowed that Judaism was an evolving religious civilization. He called attention to the roles of the Jewish land (Israel), language (Hebrew), art, music, dance, literature, and philosophy—in addition to religion—in defining us as Jews. His understanding of Jewish rituals as "folkways" further framed Jewish identity in communal terms. And the Conservative movement widely followed his proposal to transform synagogues, which until then had been exclusively used for worship and holiday celebrations, into "synagogue centers" that encompass Jewish social, educational, cultural, social action, and even athletic activities. In short, Kaplan's emphasis on Jewish peoplehood transformed the prime institution of the Jewish people.

Today, as yet another component of his legacy, the Jewish people's creative contributions past and present are studied and encouraged. *Emet Ve-Emunah* explains: "The Conservative community fosters such creativity in Jewish scholarship, literature, and the arts through the faculties of its educational institutions, its scholarly and pedagogic publications, its conferences, its museums, its artistic and theatrical productions, and its institutes and fellowships. . . . Creative work in all of these areas enters into the corpus of Torah to be studied by present and future generations of Jews."

The Conservative emphasis on Jewish peoplehood, however, does not mean that it is interested in Jews alone. Rather, the movement's commitment to the People Israel undergirds and concretizes its commitment to help other peoples throughout the globe. To fix the brokenness of the world, Conservative Jews engage in thousands of social action activities on local, national, and international levels.

Emet Ve-Emunah on the People Israel

As the excerpts from *Emet Ve-Emunah* that follow explain, the Conservative movement affirms the Chosen People concept, interpreted as realizing, together, Isaiah's vision of the People Israel as "a light to the nations" (Isaiah 49:6, 51:4). Chosenness, however, is defined in a nontriumphalist manner. While Conservative Jews are proud of their Jewish identity and the Jewish mission to make a better world, we also have the epistemological humility to acknowledge that what God wants of all humanity is not in the exclusive hands of any one denomination or religion. Thus, Jews need to respect and to work with Jews of different beliefs and people of different faiths to repair the broken world.

God's Covenant: The Election of Israel

Few Jewish beliefs have been subject to as much misunderstanding as the "Chosen People" doctrine. Hence, the Torah and the prophets (Deuteronomy 7:7f., 9:6; Amos 3:2) found it necessary to insist that this doctrine does not imply any innate Jewish superiority. In the words of Amos: "You alone have I singled out of all the families of the earth—that is why I will call you to account for all your iniquities." Still, the teaching has been so frequently misunderstood by Jews and gentiles alike that some modern thinkers have suggested that it be abandoned.

It is undeniable that this doctrine has been distorted into an expression of moral arrogance, an attitude that the classical sources have been at great pains to deny. However, it cannot easily be given up since it has decisive importance for Jewish self-perception and is essential to an understanding of the covenant idea. The truth is that the "election of Israel" and the "covenant of Israel" are two sides of the same coin; both are central to the classical Jewish world view.

Our ancestors believed themselves chosen to be "a kingdom of priests and a holy nation" with obligations and duties that flowed from their willingness to accept this status. Far from being a license for special privilege, it entailed additional responsibilities, not only toward God but also to their fellow human beings. As expressed in the blessings at the reading of the Torah, our people always have felt it a privilege to have been selected for such a purpose. Often, however, they had to pay a bloody price for insisting on this role, enabling them to identify with Isaiah's "suffering servant" (Isaiah 53) who accepted the blows and contempt of others in order to bring the truth of God to the world.

Even those who do not accept the belief in "the Chosen People" literally can appreciate its assertion that the Jews, unlike other nations, emerged on the stage of history to be a people dedicated to the service of God. The "election of Israel," then, is the consciousness of that calling, while loyalty to the covenant suggests that its fulfillment is vital not only for Israel's continued existence, but for the well-being of all humankind.

For the modern traditional Jew, the doctrine of the election and the covenant of Israel offers a purpose for Jewish existence that transcends its narrow self-interest. It suggests that because of our special history and unique heritage we are in a position to demonstrate that a people that takes seriously the idea of being covenanted with God can not only thrive despite oppression and suffering, but be a source of blessing to its children and its neighbors. It obligates us also to build a just and compassionate society throughout the world and especially in the land of Israel, where we may teach by both personal and collective example what it means to be a "covenant people, a light of nations."

The Meaning of *K'lal Yisrael*

The Conservative Movement has always maintained the importance of safeguarding the concept of *K'lal Yisrael*, by which we mean that all Jews, irrespective of philosophical or religious persuasion, are part of one people, *Am Yisrael* [the People Israel]. We also believe that every Jew responded differently to the revelation of Torah and Sinai. As the Sages put it, each individual Jew perceived God's message according to his or her spiritual capacity or sensitivity. For us, this is the meaning of religious pluralism, and we hold this truth to be inviolate today as in the past. We do not view this as a curse or even as an unavoidable evil; rather we consider this diversity as a blessing and positive element that enriches and stimulates contemporary Jewish life and thought.

Conservative Judaism and Other Jewish Groups

We accept as fundamental in Judaism the principle that all Jews are one fellowship responsible for one another. Therefore, from the days of Solomon Schechter we have worked for the good of all Jews, setting aside our own interests at times because we believe that the welfare of *Am Yisrael* transcends all parochial interests. Furthermore, we deplore the lack of civility that mars cooperative efforts within the Jewish community and that tears asunder the fragile fabric of unity built so painstakingly over the years.

Emet Ve-Emunah on Judaism's Relations with Other Faiths

As important as the Covenant is in shaping the ideas and realities of defining Jews as Jews, the classical Rabbis long ago asserted that God, before establishing the Covenant with the People Israel at Mount Sinai, established a covenant with all descendants of Noah—that is, with all humanity. Thus Rabbinic Judaism already understands all people to have a covenant with God. At the same time, the widespread persecution of Jews over the course of history has inevitably colored what some of the classical, medieval, and early modern Jewish sources have had to say about people of other faiths.

In our own time, the world is well short of the ideal envisioned by the biblical prophets—peace among all nations. Israelis, for example, still suffer from terrorism and political and economic isolation; and even in the United States, where anti-Semitism is far below what it was in the first half of the twentieth century, the Anti-Defamation League continues to report more attacks against Jews and Jewish institutions than against any other group.

The statement in *Emet Ve-Emunah* about our relations with people of other faiths that follows is not accusatory or defensive. Quite the opposite: it affirms the Conservative movement's embrace of positive and mutually fructifying relationships with people of other faiths.

This is largely the result of the Copernican revolution in Catholic-Jewish relationships instituted in 1965 by the Vatican II document *Nostra Aetate*, in which the Catholic Church proclaimed that "not all Jews then, nor any Jews today" are responsible for the death of Jesus. Importantly, *Nostra Aetate* also rejected the long-held Christian belief in supersessionism: that the New Covenant supersedes the old one made with the Jews, who were both stubborn and immoral to cling to the Covenant of Sinai. Instead, the document affirmed that God does not retract any of the covenants God makes, and therefore both the Sinai Covenant and the New Christian

Covenant are eternally valid relationships with God.[3] Subsequently, Pope John Paul II definitively declared anti-Semitism a sin and created diplomatic relationships between the Vatican and the State of Israel.

A number of Protestant denominations have taken similar steps. In a 1994 resolution, the Evangelical Lutheran Church of America, constituting some 70 percent of America's Lutherans, officially repudiated the anti-Semitic comments of its founder, Martin Luther, and later established a commission of Lutheran theologians who met with six Jewish theologians in order to craft a new Lutheran understanding of Jews and Judaism and educational materials to foster that new view.[4]

Furthermore, despite recurring acts of anti-Semitism, Jews today no longer encounter most of the legal, political, educational, and economic barriers that previously excluded them from living in certain neighborhoods, attending the best colleges and professional schools, working in some businesses (e.g., banking), and even joining certain country clubs or staying at some hotels. Some Jews have been presidents of Ivy League universities. The percentage of Jewish senators and members of Congress has far outpaced the percentage of Jews in the United States, and three Jews currently serve on the Supreme Court.

It is only fitting, then, that, as *Emet Ve-Emunah* officially indicates, the Conservative movement has responded in kind to historic levels of Jewish inclusion (especially in the United States) by recognizing the importance of other faiths as paths to God for their adherents and by asserting that we can all learn from each other.

Some Conservative leaders were heavily involved in creating positive interfaith relations even before the 1988 writing of *Emet Ve-Emunah*. Already in the 1940s, Rabbi Mordecai Kaplan argued that instead of upholding an exclusionary Chosen People concept, the Jewish people should understand every nation and culture as having its own "vocation" that can only enrich everyone if people seek to learn from each other.[5] In the 1950s JTS chancellor Rabbi Louis Finkelstein created the Institute of Religious and Social Studies, which brought Christian and Jewish thinkers and leaders together each week to discuss and ultimately publish a series of books comprised of papers by Jews and Christians on religious and social issues. Rabbi Abraham Joshua Heschel played a major role in working with the Vatican to produce *Nostra Aetate*, and he marched with Dr. Martin Luther King Jr. in Selma to promote civil rights.

More recently, many Conservative rabbis throughout the world have engaged in interfaith activities, primarily with Christians and Muslims, but sometimes with people of Asian faiths as well. For example, Rabbi Avraham Skorka, a Conservative rabbi in Buenos Aires, became fast friends with the local cardinal who later became Pope Francis I. Rabbi Burton Visotsky, professor of midrash and interreligious studies at the Jewish Theological Seminary, has taught at pontifical colleges in Rome and has participated in interreligious engagements internationally in capitals as diverse as Washington; Warsaw; Rome; Cairo; Doha, Qatar; Madrid; Muskat, Oman; and, most recently, Marrakech, Morocco. He was the winner of the 2012 Goldziher Prize, awarded biennially by Merrimack College for work in Jewish-Muslim relations. Rabbi Elliot Dorff, the author of this volume, has participated in the Priest-Rabbi Dialogue of the Los Angeles Archdiocese (the largest in the United States) and the Board of Rabbis of Southern California since it was established in 1973 and has cochaired it since 1990. He has also taken part in interfaith conferences in Geneva, Warsaw, India, and Israel; twice taught Catholic seminary professors and seminarians in Poland; worked with the Evangelical Lutheran Church of America to create a new Lutheran theology about Jews and Judaism; taught at Fuller Theological Seminary; taught over a thousand teachers in Catholic high schools throughout the United States through the Anti-Defamation League's Bearing Witness program and its successor in Los Angeles; written articles for the World Council of Churches and Paulist Press; and chaired the Academy for Judaic, Christian, and Islamic Studies (he continues to sit on its board).

This change in attitude toward non-Jews has also had some concrete legal implications. To take a rather prosaic example, three years before the publication of *Emet Ve-Emunah*, the Conservative movement's Committee on Jewish Law and Standards approved a responsum on wine by

Rabbi Elliot Dorff in which he faced the traditional ban on wine touched by non-Jews as follows:

> In sum, then, both because of the shift in the beliefs and practices of non-Jews in the modern, Western world and because the prohibition against wine alone will not accomplish the Rabbis' goal of preventing mixed marriages in contemporary society, we should extend the approach suggested already four centuries ago by Rabbi Isserles. Specifically, while he reluctantly found reason to maintain the validity of Jewish witnesses who drink Gentile wine, we should openly assert that, unless we have specific evidence to the contrary, we can presume that the Gentiles who produce and serve wine in the Western world are not "idolaters" in the *halakhic* sense of that term . . . [and] we shall let the prohibition fall into disuse without protest.[6]

Another responsum by Rabbi Dorff resulted in the CJLS adopting procedures that encouraged Conservative synagogues to allow Christian groups to use their synagogue facilities for worship and other activities, thereby matching the welcome many churches have extended to Jewish groups trying to establish congregations of their own.[7] These warming relationships between Jews and non-Jews are reflected in the following statement from *Emet Ve-Emunah* on the relations of Conservative Jews to people of other faiths:

Relations with Other Faiths

From the time of the earliest settlement of Israelite tribes in the land of Canaan, Jews have always lived in close proximity to, and in contact with, people of other faiths and nationalities. This has been equally true in the Land of Israel and in the Diaspora. Historically, the attitude that a Jewish community has taken toward gentiles has generally depended on the nature of the relations that that community had with its immediate neighbors. . . .

As Conservative Jews, we acknowledge without apology the many debts that Jewish religion and civilization owe to the nations of the world. We eschew triumphalism with respect to other ways of serving God. Maimonides believed that other monotheistic faiths — Christianity and Islam — serve to spread knowledge of, and devotion to, the God and the Torah of Israel throughout the world. Many modern thinkers, both Jewish and gentile, have noted that God may well have seen fit to enter covenants with many nations. Either outlook, when relating to others, is perfectly compatible with a commitment to one's own faith and pattern of religious life.

If we criticize triumphalism in our own community, then real dialogue with other faith groups requires that we criticize triumphalism and other failings in those quarters as well. In the second half of the twentieth century, no relationship between Jews and Christians can be dignified or honest without facing up frankly to the centuries of prejudice, theological anathema, and persecution that have been thrust upon Jewish communities, culminating in the horrors of the *Shoah* (Holocaust). No relationship can be nurtured between Jews and Muslims unless it acknowledges explicitly and seeks to combat the terrible social and political effects of Muslim hostility, as well as the disturbing but growing reaction of Jewish anti-Arabism in the Land of Israel. But all of these relationships, properly pursued, can bring great blessing to the Jewish community and to the world. As the late Professor Abraham Joshua Heschel put it, "No religion is an island."

Theological humility requires us to recognize that although we have but one God, God has more than one nation. Our tradition explicitly recognizes that God entered into a covenant with Adam and Eve, and later with Noah and his family, as well as His special covenant with Abraham and the great revelation to Israel at Sinai. It is part of our mission to understand, respect, and live with the other nations of the world, to discern those truths in their cultures from which we can learn, and to share with them the truths that we have come to know.

Dr. Arnold Eisen on Why Our Covenant Matters

What does the Covenant at Sinai between God and the People Israel mean for Jews, especially for Conservative Jews? Dr. Arnold M. Eisen, chancellor of the Jewish Theological Seminary of America, wrote an essay (excerpted here) describing what it signifies for each of us to uphold the conviction that all Jews are part of this Covenant between God and the Jewish People.

The Covenant Continues through Us

To my mind, the question of what Conservative Judaism stands for is best answered by stating where Conservative Jews stand, and with whom. I believe that Jews alive today are the heirs to the Jewish story that began, according to Torah, with Abraham and Sarah.

We stand at Sinai with every previous generation of the Children of Israel and are called to reaffirm the promises made there to God, to one another, and to the world. I am convinced—humbly but firmly—that the Sinai Covenant continues today through us. Participation in the set of relationships entailed by the Covenant adds immeasurably to the meaning, joy, and purpose of our lives.

The fact that the Covenant at Sinai established a *people* simultaneously with *a relationship to the Holy One* stands at the heart of Conservative Judaism today and in the future. That *double covenant means, first and most importantly, that life as a Jewish human being is given ultimate meaning.* For reasons that mere mortals will never understand, but for which practicing Jews are profoundly grateful, the Creator of the universe seeks human assistance in completing the work of Creation. The world is not good enough as it is, the Torah insists, and you and I can make it better. All of us are needed for this task: Jews and non-Jews, men and women, old and young. Everything that each and every one of us bring to the task is required: the sum total of our diverse experiences and learning, our skills and our relationships, our intelligence and our passion, all the arts and all the sciences—in the Torah's words, all our hearts, all our souls, all our might. . . .

A second continuing consequence of Covenant is that Judaism has always been more than religion, even as religion has always been an integral part of Judaism. Jews are not defined as a church or sect. Rather, the Torah establishes Israel as "a kingdom," "a nation," "a people." As important as religious belief is to Judaism, it is not everything, and, arguably, is not the main thing. One cannot emphasize this point enough in a society and culture that tend to treat "religion" as a separate sphere, cut off from the major business of life, and to assume that only a high degree of separation from the beliefs and practices of the mainstream entitles one to the mantle of being "religious."

The Torah does not agree with that approach. It aims to impact the entirety of life, individual and collective, and not merely the aspect of it that other scriptures and traditions call "religion." The Torah offers a way called mitzvah that—if we walk it diligently—guides and transforms all of life: when we rise up and when we lie down, when we sit at home and when we walk upon the way.

Mordecai M. Kaplan . . . captured an important truth about Torah's insistence that Judaism is far more than "religion" when he famously defined Judaism as a "civilization" in his great book by that title (1934). Kaplan knew that Judaism had always included aspects of collective life that went beyond "religion" in the normal sense of the word: history, language, literature, folk customs, communal organizations, and intimate connection to the Land of Israel. Kaplan wanted to assure Jews whose doubts about God barred the way to faith that Judaism held an honored place for them.

This point too bears repeating today. *Individuals enter Conservative auspices from differing backgrounds and bearing differing needs.* All of our institutions should reflect this, even while offering Jews the pleasure and meaning that come from acting, worshipping, studying, celebrating, and talking together as *one caring community of Torah.*

It follows that *Conservative communities must be more than synagogues, and our synagogues must offer more than worship.* The Conservative form of Judaism is well known for the quality of ritual observances and life-cycle celebrations; the tone set for family relations in Conservative homes; the leadership roles accorded to women as well as men both on and off the *bimah* [platform where worship is led]; and for the distinctive tenor of Conservative conversation as it moves back and forth from ancient sources to contemporary politics, Hebrew to English, Shabbat *zemirot* (songs) to rock music and jazz. There is an intangible but notable warmth in our shuls and schools that comes from comfort with Judaism and one another. At our best, Conservative Jews exhibit a quiet confidence that *living fully in this century and its culture at the same time as we immerse ourselves in Jewish tradition is what Torah wants us to do.*

That confidence is crucial to our future; it is the key to successful Conservative communities and goes hand in hand with the sense that you and I—every bit as much as Jewish ancestors—are part of a reality and purpose far larger than ourselves, longer than our life span, wider than our mind can reach. Heschel said it eloquently: the Torah poses a question to which our life here and now "can be the spelling of an answer." Conservative Judaism is the most compelling interpretation of Torah that I know, a precious word in the conversation begun at Sinai, guiding covenantal work here and now that only our generation can perform.

"Covenant," in *Conservative Judaism Today and Tomorrow*, 1–3

Who Is a Jew?

Most nations occupy a piece of land and define its citizens as those who have been born within its borders or have fulfilled certain citizenship procedures. Jewish identity, however, has always been considerably more complicated than that.

Historical Precedents and Laws

From biblical times, endogamy has been the norm. That is, a Jew was directed to marry someone within the extended Jewish clan. Abraham sent his servant Eliezer back to Haran, where his family lived before they migrated to Israel, to find a wife for Isaac from among Abraham's relatives (Genesis 24). When Esau married one of the Hittite women instead of someone within the clan, his parents, Isaac and Rebekah, were so distressed that he took another wife from the family of Ishmael to please them (Genesis 26:34, 28:6–9). Later, when Dinah, Jacob's daughter, wanted to marry Schechem, one of the Canaanite men, Jacob convinced Schechem's tribesmen that they needed to be circumcised in order to marry within the Israelite clan. While they were still hurting from their wounds, two of Dinah's brothers killed Schechem, his father, and all the men of his clan—a rather nasty way of enforcing the rule of endogamy. (Jacob also protested that their actions would make it hard for his clan to live among the Canaanites [Genesis 34].)

Deuteronomy 23:4–9 later enacted the endogamy precedent into law by prohibiting Amonites and Moabites from joining the Israelites (presumably by marriage) for ten generations and barring Edomites for three. That this applied to all foreign wives and was actually carried out is attested by the fact that in the middle of the fifth century BCE, when the Persian king allowed Jews exiled to Babylonia (modern-day Iraq) to return to Israel to reestablish the Jewish community there, Ezra required all Jewish men who had married non-Jews to divorce them (Ezra 9, 10).

Some biblical figures, however, defied this ban. King Solomon, for example, married many women, among them the Queen of Sheba. King Ahab married the Canaanite woman Jezebel, who brought many Canaanite gods to the court, a graphic indication of the problems of marrying out.[8]

Rabbinic law preserved the endogamy requirement but concurrently established procedures by which non-Jews could convert to Judaism.

When a Jewish woman and a non-Jewish man did marry, the status of their progeny was unclear. The Mishnah incorporated two conflicting rulings. One said that such a child was illegitimate (a *mamzer*) and therefore could not join the Jewish people for ten generations, in accordance with Deuteronomy 23:3. The other asserted that the child of a Jewish woman and a non-Jewish man was indeed a Jew.[9] Later Jewish law followed the latter ruling, thereby deterring some men from marrying outside the Jewish people because they knew that if they did, their children would not be considered Jewish.

Intermarriage in Practice

Although it is impossible to ascertain the degree of interfaith marriage until the twentieth century, available evidence seems to indicate that it was very rare. In Muslim and Christian countries, it was often against the law for people of either faith to marry a Jew. Moreover, in many places and times, non-Jews regarded Jews with hostility, whether for religious reasons (e.g., Jews slandered as Christ-killers) or economic ones (Jews maligned when serving as tax collectors from Christian peasants on behalf of Christian landowners).

At the end of the nineteenth century and thereafter, interfaith marriage became somewhat more common (consider the stories of Hava in *Fiddler on the Roof* and *Abie's Irish Rose*), but it did not become commonplace in North America until the 1980s. When the 1990 National Jewish Population Study indicated that half of all marriages in the United States involving Jews were marriages to non-Jews, Jewish communal leaders were both surprised and deeply worried about the implications for the Jewish future. Studies done then and since have shown that the chances of children of interfaith marriages ultimately identifying as Jewish adults are slim—somewhere between 20 and 33 percent, depending on the study.[10] Furthermore, later demographic studies, such as the 2001 *National Jewish Population Survey* and the 2013 Pew study of Jewish Americans, have reported yet higher rates of interfaith marriage.[11]

Reform Rabbis Redefine Jewish Identity

To establish the Jewish status of the many children of mixed marriages in North American Reform communities, in 1983 the Central Conference of American Rabbis (CCAR), the Reform movement's rabbinical organization, adopted a resolution on "patrilineal descent." A child born to a Jewish man and a non-Jewish woman would henceforth be considered Jewish if she or he attended a Jewish school and followed a course of studies leading to confirmation. "Such procedure," the Reform rabbis wrote, "is regarded as sufficient evidence that the parents and the child himself intend that he shall live as a Jew."[12]

A year earlier, in 1982, the Conservative movement's Committee on Jewish Law and Standards had approved five diverse responsa that encouraged *keruv* (pronounced "kayruv," literally meaning "bringing close"), that is, bringing the non-Jewish spouse in an interfaith couple and their children close to the Jewish community and Judaism. The five responsa differed in approach, including the extent to which non-Jews could participate in Conservative synagogues (their worship and governance) and institutions (schools, Women's League, Men's Club, United Synagogue Youth chapters, etc.).[13]

The Reform rabbis' 1983 resolution now engendered vigorous debate in the CJLS and within the Conservative movement generally. One CJLS member, Rabbi Philip Sigal, advocated adopting the CCAR's position. Another CJLS member, Rabbi Gordon Tucker, suggested that in the name of egalitarianism and to preserve the tradition's matrilineal requirement for Jewish identity, both parents should be Jewish for any of their children to be counted as Jews by birth. Neither proposal secured more than the one vote of its author. Instead, the vast majority (15–1) at the meeting on May 1, 1985, voted for a responsum by Rabbis Joel Roth and Akiba Lubow that retains the traditional definition of Jewish identity as either being born to a Jewish woman or converting to Judaism through the traditional rites. That strong majority held when, as required for Standards of Rabbinic Practice, the entire committee was polled by mail: the final vote was twenty-one in favor of retaining the traditional definition, two against, and one abstention.

Upholding Traditional Definitions of Identity

Ultimately, the Rabbinical Assembly formally adopted this standard (printed here in its entirety) at its 1986 convention by a vote of 235 in favor and 92 opposed.

A Standard of Rabbinic Practice Regarding Determination of Jewish Identity

WHEREAS Jewishness is defined either through lineage or through conversion to Judaism; and

WHEREAS the Committee on Jewish Law and Standards has on several occasions reaffirmed its commitment to matrilineal descent, which has been authoritative in normative Judaism for many centuries as the sole determinant of Jewish lineage; and

WHEREAS rulings of the Committee on Jewish Law and Standards which govern procedures for conversions supervised by Rabbinical Assembly members, require *tevilah* [immersion in a *mikveh*, a specially constructed pool, or a natural body of water] in the case of females, and *tevilah* and *brit milah* [circumcision] in the case of males; and

WHEREAS the Committee on Jewish Law and Standards has long advocated that members of the Rabbinical Assembly welcome and assist those who wish to approach Judaism in a serious fashion and to convert to Judaism in a manner that fulfills the requirements for conversion, including those steps outlined above;

THEREFORE, BE IT RESOLVED that the Committee on Jewish Law and Standards recommends to the Convention of the Rabbinical Assembly that (a) ascription of Jewish lineage through a legal instrument or ceremonial act on the basis of anything other than matrilineal descent; or (b) supervision of a conversion that omits *tevilah* in the case of females, or *tevilah* and *brit milah* in the case of males shall continue to be regarded as violations of the halakhah of Conservative Judaism. They shall henceforth be violations of a Standard of Rabbinic Practice and be inconsistent with membership in the Rabbinical Assembly, it being understood that any member of the Rabbinical Assembly shall continue to possess the right to petition the Committee on Jewish Law and Standards for an opinion on any case of extraordinary circumstances.

> "A Standard of Rabbinic Practice Regarding Determination of Jewish Identity," http://www.rabbinicalassembly.org/sites/default/files/assets/public/halakhah/teshuvot/20012004/31.pdf

Three Decades Later

Some thirty years later, the Conservative movement still upholds this definition of Jewish identity. Given the significant increase in interfaith marriages over the last decades, however, Conservative rabbis and lay leaders continue to discuss ways to bring interfaith couples into the Jewish fold so that the Jew remains identified as a Jew, the couple raise their children as Jews, and the partner of another faith might consider converting to Judaism at a later time.

Some Conservative rabbis and lay leaders advocate changing this standard to recognize patrilineal Jews, as the Reform movement did in 1983. To date, however, the majority of Conservative rabbis and lay leaders strongly oppose such a change, and so there has been no official move in this direction.

What a non-Jewish spouse who has agreed to raise his or her children as Jews may or may not do within the synagogue and what the children of a Jewish man and a non-Jewish woman may do within the synagogue before their formal conversion to Judaism are determined by the local rabbi. Some Conservative rabbis and lay leaders would like to create movement-wide guidelines on these issues, but most rabbis want to retain the flexibility to set these policies in ways that are sensitive to the convictions and feelings of their local community. For now, then, *keruv* is the Conservative movement's primary response to interfaith marriages.

Proving Jewish Identity

In many Jewish communities, people know each other. They were raised and lived their lives as Jews in that community. When they want to marry or to be buried as a Jew, nobody in the community questions their Jewish identity.

What happens, though, when Jews move from one state or country to another and wish to marry or be buried as a Jew there? How do they demonstrate to local Jewish authorities that they are indeed Jewish?

One way to do this is to produce the Jewish wedding documents (*ketubbot*) of one's parents and maternal grandparents. Although Jewish authorities cannot be certain that the Jews whose names appear in these documents are in fact the parents and maternal grandparents of the people presenting them, it is at least probable.

The problem, though, is that few Jews have these documents. According to Jewish law, a man may not live with his wife "for even one hour" unless the woman knows where her *ketubbah* is, but couples often do not know that, let alone know where to find their parents' and grandparents' *ketubbot*.[14]

So in many Jewish communities worldwide, the local rabbi simply takes the word of the person in question that he or she is Jewish or does so after asking a few questions about his or her parents' Jewish identity, such as their Hebrew names. Some rabbis require more proof, which typically comes in either of two forms: the rabbi of the person's childhood community may be asked to write a letter attesting to the fact that he or she is Jewish, or two unrelated long-time friends may attest that they have known him or her as a Jew all their lives. Even though the chief rabbinate of Israel officially requires the parents' and grandparents' wedding documents, one or the other method of establishing a person's Jewish identity suffices in some local communities in Israel and in most other Jewish communities worldwide.

In recent decades, however, with Jews from the former Soviet Union and other formerly Communist countries in Eastern Europe immigrating en masse to North America and Israel, the problem of proving Jewish identity has grown immensely. These Jews and others, such as Ethiopian Jews, rarely have papers proving that they are Jewish, and their cases are complicated by other realities. In the former Soviet Union and Ethiopia, for example, it was often disadvantageous and sometimes dangerous to identify as a Jew, so people from these countries who now claim Jewish identity have few demonstrable ties to the Jewish communities of their youth. Furthermore, sometimes non-Jews from these nations falsely represent themselves as Jews in order to be granted permission to move to Israel or North America as refugees.

In 2011 the CJLS took up the question of what standards ought to determine Jewish identity in less than clear circumstances. Rabbi Reuven Hammer's responsum, "On Proving Jewish Identity," asked: "If an individual claims to be Jewish, either by birth or conversion, what proof, if any, is required before recognizing that individual as a Jew and permitting him or her to exercise the rights and privileges of a Jew for such matters as marriage, synagogue membership, participation in religious ceremonies, religious school, and burial?"

On May 24, 2011, the CJLS approved his responsum (excerpted here) by a vote of fifteen in favor, one opposed, and no abstentions (15–1–0). To read the full document with its accompanying notes, see https:// www.rabbinicalassembly.org/sites/default/files/assets/public/halakhah /teshuvot/2011-2020/JewishIdentity6.2011.pdf.

The Reality of Jewish Identity at This Time

Today, perhaps more than at any other time in Jewish history, we are confronted with problems concerning the status of individuals claiming to be Jews. The problem is especially acute in Israel where Jewishness is essential for *aliyah* [immigration] rights and where official marriage is controlled by the government-sponsored Chief Rabbinate. The Law of Return permits children and grandchildren of Jews (one grandparent is sufficient), as well as their spouses, to come on *aliyah*. Often those who enter Israel under that law claim to be Jewish but have difficulty proving it to the religious authorities. Furthermore, the proof of Jewishness that is sufficient for *aliyah* is not identical to that needed for halakhic purposes. The massive *aliyah* from the former Soviet Union has brought more than a million people to Israel. Reliable estimates indicate that at least a third of these are not Jews according to halakhah by their own admission.

Many immigrants who claim to be Jewish have difficulty proving their Jewishness to the satisfaction of the Chief Rabbinate because of the lack of reliable documentation. *Ketubbot* [wedding documents] have been largely non-existent among Russian Jews for over half a century. There have also been cases of forged documents. The result has been that often people who sincerely consider themselves Jews cannot prove that fact and are turned away by the official rabbinate when they wish to be married in Israel. Similar problems occur for American *olim* [immigrants to Israel] and others in Israel as well.

The well-known journalist, Gershom Gorenberg, wrote an article on such a case for the *New York Times* entitled "How Do You Prove You're a Jew?" in which he states that in previous times in Europe:

"Trust was the default position. One reason was that Jews were a per-secuted people; no one would claim to belong unless she really did. The leading ultra-orthodox rabbi in Israel in the years before and after the state was established, Avraham Yeshayahu Karlitz (known as the Ḥazon Ish, the name of his magnum opus on religious law), held the classical position. If someone arrived from another country claiming to be Jewish, he should be allowed to marry another Jew, "even if nothing is known of his family," Karlitz wrote. Several trends have combined to change that.

This situation has been further compounded by a decision of the Israeli Chief Rabbinate in 2010 to require documents proving the Jewishness of one's mother, grandmother, great-grandmother and great-great-grandmother when applying for marriage. Needless to say, this is a near impossibility for most people.

The problem of proving Jewishness is not confined to Israel, but exists in the United States and all other diaspora communities as well. As more children are born to single mothers, for example, and as there are significant numbers of couples who live together and establish families, there are numerous cases in which young people have no mother's *ketubbah* available for examination. There are also more and more people born to mothers who "converted" to Judaism. Since different groups [of Jews] have different standards for conversion, not all conversions are acceptable to the Rabbinical Assembly. A further complication has resulted from the fact that American Reform Judaism accepts those with a Jewish father and a non-Jewish mother as Jews. Therefore we often encounter young men and women with non-Jewish mothers who were brought up in Reform congregations who sincerely believe themselves to be Jews and who identify themselves as such. In an era of intermarriage, having a "Jewish name" means nothing, just as having a non-Jewish name means nothing. The question arises: when someone comes to us [rabbis] identifying him/herself as a Jew, do we adopt the "default position" of trust? If so, under what conditions, and, if not, what proof do we require? . . .

Historical Precedents

. . . Regarding marriage there was a presumption of the fitness of all families—*kol mishpaḥot b'ḥezkat kashrut hen omdot* [all Jewish families are presumed to be Jewish by the standards of Jewish law]—which became a basic principle in determining Jewish identity.

In the case of a child of unknown identity, a reasonable assumption of Jewishness can be made even where there is no actual proof, taking into account the demographic reality. The sages inclined toward declaring the child Jewish where there is nothing specific that would disprove it.

Medieval sources accept the story in the Talmud of a non-Jew who ate of the Pesaḥ [the paschal Lamb] at the Temple since no one questioned his Jewishness, as creating a principle that one who presents him/herself as a Jew is accepted with no further investigation unless there is cause to be suspicious.

In certain cases an individual's testimony about himself and his family may be accepted with no need for further evidence. . . .

. . . Even in the case of proving fitness to serve as a priest, where a thorough investigation was made, leniency was shown in that one witness [rather than the usually required two] was sufficient as long as there were none who questioned it. Thus a more thorough investigation was made only when a question was raised. Sometimes there was even a presumption of fitness—*ḥazakah*—such as when the priest has been regularly performing certain priestly duties. . . .

Concerning converts, the weight of opinion is that if someone who was thought to be a Jew reveals that he is a convert, he may be believed since he had no obligation to reveal that fact. Under certain circumstances, moreover, the Sages accept a convert's word even without witnesses to the actual conversion. The Rambam [Maimonides] would accept someone without witnesses who has been living a Jewish, mitzvah-observant life. However, in places where there was an advantage to be gained by being Jewish, proof was required, especially for purposes of marriage. . . .

Peskei Halakhah / Legal Rulings

Based upon the principle that *kol ha-mishpaḥot b'ḥezkat kashrut hen*—"all families are considered to be fit" (B. *Kiddushin* 76b), which was taken to mean that *b'torat yahadut yisrael hem*—they are all considered to be within the definition of Israelites—all who claim to be Jews are under the presumption of Jewishness (Tosafot to B. *Yevamot* 47a, Ovadia Yosef). As has been stated, *l'adam she-omer yisrael ani ain bodkin aharav*—one who says "I am a Jew" need not be investigated (Maggid Mishnah). Where one is part of a Jewish community and has been living as a Jew, there is no need to instigate an investigation into that person's Jewishness. We affirm that trust is the default position in these matters. Therefore, we do not question one's Jewishness unless there is reason to be suspicious.

However, in view of the many difficulties cited above concerning Jewish identity today and in order to avoid singling out individuals, it is appropriate to determine anyone's eligibility for synagogue membership, religious school, burial and, especially, marriage, for example, by asking for the person's Hebrew name and that of his/her father and mother. If it becomes obvious that the mother and the mother's mother were born Jewish, there should be no need for further questioning.

If, however, the person or the family is not known to us, or if there is reason to suspect that one is not Jewish, further investigation is needed. This can be done through questioning the individual, through testimony of those who know the person or knew the family, or, if available, documents that indicate a Jewish background. In many cases, especially concerning those coming from the former Soviet Union, it is understood that documentary evidence will be difficult to produce, and therefore we may rely on the evidence of friends or neighbors and on the impression made by the individual. Questioning is to be done in a sensitive way so as not to violate the honor due to human beings—*kevod ha-briyyot*—and not to shame the individual.

For matters that do not seriously affect *klal yisrael* [the Jewish community], such as a visitor to a synagogue being granted an *aliyah* to the Torah or other synagogue honors, it is not necessary to investigate individuals who state that they are Jewish unless one knows that this is not so or has very good reason to suspect it.

Where a conversion is involved, either of the individual or of that person's mother, because of variations of practice among streams of Judaism and among individual rabbis, one should investigate if the conversion included the rudimentary elements of immersion and, for a male, circumcision. If not, those should be performed in order to complete the conversion. If the mother's conversion was not valid, the individual will require a conversion, but if the individual was brought up as a Jew, it should be done as efficiently and discretely as possible within the requirements of *halakhah* [Jewish law]. As stated in previous *teshuvot* [responsa] on this matter, the rabbi must use great tact in approaching this issue, indicating that we are completing the process that was begun previously or adding the *halakhic* requirements to the individual's Jewish identity.

In places where there is a Bet Din [a local Jewish court], questions of Jewishness should be brought to the Bet Din, which is the final authority. Its decision concerning the Jewishness of a person is final and is acceptable throughout the Rabbinical Assembly. Where there is no Bet Din, the individual rabbi is the final authority. It is incumbent upon the Bet Din or the rabbi to exercise good judgment and common sense on these matters, relying on the *halakhic* principles cited above.

Suggestions for Further Reading

Louis Finkelstein, ed. *The Jews: Their History, Culture, and Religion.* New York: Harper; and Philadelphia: Jewish Publication Society, 1949; 2nd ed., 1955; 3rd ed., 1960. 2 vols.

Louis Jacobs. *God, Torah, Israel: Traditionalism without Fundamentalism*, esp. 55–80. Cincinnati: Hebrew Union College Press, 1990.

Mordecai M. Kaplan. *Judaism as a Civilization.* New York: Macmillan, 1934; latest ed., Philadelphia: Jewish Publication Society, 2010, with a new introduction by Mel Scult.

CHAPTER THIRTEEN

Tziyyonut

Zionism and the State of Israel

From the time the Romans destroyed the Second Temple and, with it, the Second Jewish Commonwealth in 70 CE, to the founding of the modern State of Israel in 1948—in other words, for nearly nineteen hundred years—Jews have lived as a people without a state. Certain historians claim that some Jews always lived in Israel, and if this is true, then the vast majority of the world's Jews have nonetheless always lived in the Diaspora (in lands outside of Israel).

Being stateless was fraught with difficulties. At best, Jews were tolerated as second-class residents. At worst, they were subjected to discrimination (harshly taxed, restricted in profession and/or residence) and persecution (maimed or murdered). For this reason and because of the Jewish people's ancient religious and historical ties to the Land of Israel, Jews over the centuries have expressed their yearning for a return to Zion (its narrow meaning referring to Jerusalem, and its broader meaning to all of Israel) three times a day in their prayers.

In 1897 Theodor Herzl, the Austro-Hungarian journalist, playwright, and political activist, called for the First Zionist Congress in Basel, Switzerland. Having witnessed blatant anti-Semitism in the Alfred Dreyfus trial in France, he concluded that Jews could not live safely in Europe, even in a country such as France that presumably operated on Enlightenment principles of individual rights and freedoms. His solution: establish a Jewish state in the ancient homeland of Israel.

Early Religious Responses to Zionism

Not all Jews endorsed Herzl's views. Some Orthodox Jews insisted that Jews needed to wait for God to bring the Messiah; to attempt to return to Israel before then would usurp God's prerogatives. To date, that remains the view of most ultra-Orthodox Jews.

On the other end of the spectrum, leading Reform thinkers such as Rabbi Abraham Geiger asserted that Jews should not isolate themselves in any one geographical area. To segregate themselves would be to deny the universalism to which Jews should aspire, in which all peoples would live together in harmony. Residing solely in the land of Israel would also inhibit Jews from fulfilling their mission to be "a light to the nations" (Isaiah 49:6), that "the remnant of Jacob be among many nations as dew from God" (Micah 5:6) and thereby influence other nations. Moreover, the Central Conference of American Rabbis' 1885 Pittsburgh Platform had proclaimed: "We consider ourselves no longer a nation, but a religious community, and therefore expect neither a return to Palestine . . . nor the restoration of any of the laws concerning the Jewish state."

In contrast, Conservative Judaism never had an anti-Zionist wing. None of Conservative Judaism's leaders were opposed to establishing a Jewish state in Israel (then called Palestine).[1]

Conservative Movement Responses to a Jewish State

Admittedly, some Conservative leaders were not heavily involved in the Zionist effort. Jewish Theological Seminary of America chancellor Louis Finkelstein (1940–72) believed it was his job to resurrect Judaism in America after the destruction of European schools of higher Jewish learning during the Holocaust. Rabbi Abraham Joshua Heschel came to feel strongly about Zionism only after the Six-Day War (1967).

Yet many Conservative leaders were active Zionists. In 1906, just nine years after the First Zionist Congress, Jewish Theological Seminary of America chancellor Solomon Schechter (1903–15) published the pamphlet *Zionism: A Statement*, asserting his support for a form of Zionism that was not only political but also religious and cultural—one that worked toward establishing a state that embodied the religious and cultural aspirations of the Jewish tradition.[2] Toward the end of his life he declared: "Zionism was, and still is, the most cherished dream I was worthy of having. It was beautiful to behold the rise of this mighty bulwark against the incessantly assailing forces of assimilation.... The Zionist Movement... again brought forth the national aspect in Jewish thought."[3]

Rabbi Mordecai Kaplan's early staunch support for Zionism flowed naturally from his conception of Judaism as a civilization encompassing a land (Israel), a language (Hebrew), Jewish music, art, architecture, dance, drama, literature, philosophy, and more. In his first book, *Judaism as a Civilization* (1934), he stated:

> Jews must clarify their position both to themselves and to the world. They cannot consider themselves emancipated unless they are granted the opportunity to foster and develop their historic civilization. This means that for the Jews no progressive corporate life anywhere is possible without the establishment of a national home in Palestine. If Judaism still possesses creative energy, it should regain the only medium through which adequate expression is possible to any civilization—a land of its own.... With the resulting enrichment of Judaism's cultural and spiritual content, Jews in the diaspora will then feel themselves members of a minority group that possesses motivation, idea, and purpose.... That steadfast hope in their ultimate return to Palestine enabled the Jews to survive as a people. It has engendered whatever spiritual and cultural potentialities they still possess.[4]

Developing his Zionist position throughout the course of his life, Kaplan came to believe that a Jewish state with moral principles at its forefront was necessary to realize the demand in the book of Exodus that Jews be "a kingdom of priests and a holy nation" (19:6). To be an ethical *nation*, for Judaism to be "a religion of ethical *nationhood*" in its fullest sense, meant that Jews had to have their own state in their own land of Israel.

This did not mean that all Jews had to reside in Israel. Already in 1934 Kaplan anticipated that even after a Jewish state in Palestine was established, most of the world's Jews would live elsewhere (given the small size of the Jewish homeland).[5] He predicted, however, in two of his books, *A New Zionism* (1955) and *The Religion of Ethical Nationhood: Judaism's Contributions to World Peace* (1970), that the Diaspora Jewish community would become more fervently Jewish because of Israel. And the very title of the latter volume indicated that for Kaplan, the State of Israel, as a Jewish state, had to be not only a center of Jewish culture but also a model of "ethical nationhood," working, among other ethical goals, toward world peace: "Peoplehood requires a homeland. . . . *The land which is a people's home should foster a humanizing way of life. The people that fails to pursue a civilized and enlightened way of life must ultimately be exiled from its homeland* [italics in the original]. The narrative parts of the Pentateuch and ancient prophecy articulate these ideas concerning the role of *Eretz Yisrael* [the Land of Israel] in the life of the Jewish people. They constitute the basic theme of ancient Israel's epic."[6]

Emet Ve-Emunah on the State of Israel and the Diaspora

Once the State of Israel came to fruition in 1948, Conservative leaders were obligated to face the ways in which it both fulfilled and failed to fulfill the early Zionist dreams. The latter included the recurring experiences and constant threats of war, which somehow none of the early Zionist thinkers had anticipated. There was also the disappointing reality that Orthodox authorities in Israel had gained control of Jewish religious life, including marriage and divorce.

In its first few decades, the new state also raised questions regarding its relationship to Conservative, Reform, and politically liberal Jews in the Diaspora. Israel's chief rabbinate did not recognize marriages or divorces conducted by Conservative or Reform rabbis. Nor did the rabbinate recognize as Jewish the Jews-by-choice who had converted to Judaism under Conservative or Reform auspices. Furthermore, the state was allocating considerable sums of money to support Orthodox synagogues and schools but almost nothing to sustain Conservative and Reform institutions. All of these realities are still true today.

In 1988 *Emet Ve-Emunah* (excerpted here) addressed many of these hopes and challenges.

Religious Freedom

The State of Israel is a unique phenomenon in history. On the one hand, it is and ought to be a democratic state that safeguards freedom of thought and action for all of its citizens. On the other hand, it is and ought to be a distinctively Jewish state, fostering Jewish religious and cultural values. Balancing the democratic and Jewish goals in Israel society presents a constant challenge.

We believe that freedom of the human spirit is a fundamental ideal of the Jewish tradition. We also believe that the essence of democracy is twofold: it expresses the will of the majority and scrupulously protects the rights of minorities. Therefore, the laws passed by the State of Israel, its cities, towns, or other political entities should not be used to support a single religious view or establishment to the exclusion of others. The State of Israel, founded for the entire Jewish people, must in its actions and laws provide for the pluralism of Jewish life. The State should permit all rabbis, regardless of affiliation, to perform religious functions, including officiating at marriages, divorces and conversions.

The Religious Factor

The Conservative movement affirms that the Jewish religion as reflected in the Jewish way of life constitutes the most significant factor that identifies, distinguishes, unites and preserves the Jewish people. Consequently, we believe that the State of Israel must encourage Jewish patterns of life in all of the agencies of the State and its political subdivisions. Without being a theocracy, Israel should reflect the highest religious and moral values of Judaism and be saturated with Jewish living to the fullest extent possible in a free society. Hence, we welcome the reality that Shabbat, *Yom Tov* [Jewish festivals], *kashrut* [the Jewish dietary laws], and other *mitzvot* are officially upheld by the civilian and military organs of the State, and that the Jewish calendar is in general use. Even in secular schools, classical Jewish sources such as Bible and rabbinic literature are taught, and Jewish observances are at least acknowledged.

While we strongly endorse the need to maintain the Jewish character and ambience of the State of Israel, we regard it as an overriding moral principle that neither the State nor its political subdivisions or agencies employ coercion in the area of religious belief and practice. In view of the wide disparity of outlook among Jews, we believe that matters of personal status should fall under secular law, which should provide civil options for marriage and divorce for those who so prefer, while empowering each religious community to handle its own ritual requirements. . . .

The Uniqueness of Israel

We hope that the State of Israel will always be a strong and secure democratic nation that will serve as a haven of refuge for Jews fleeing oppression and a welcome home for those who elect to go on *aliyah* [move to Israel]. We do not view Israel as just another state or political entity; rather, we envision it as an exemplar of religious and moral principles, of civil, political and religious rights for all citizens regardless of race, religion, ethnic origin, or sex. We believe that the litmus test of the character of a democratic Jewish state is its treatment of, and attitude toward, its religious and ethnic minorities. Having been the victims of oppression and discrimination in the lands of their dispersion, Jews should be particularly sensitive to the well-being of all the various ethnic and religious groups living in the State of Israel.

We are painfully aware of Israel's security needs and the intricacies and devious turns of international relations. We recognize that Israel must steer a hazardous course in immoral international waters. Nevertheless, we recall the prophetic injunction to our people to be "a covenant people, a light of nations." Israel reborn provides a unique opportunity for the Jewish people to be a holy people and a blessing to the nations. Consequently, it behooves Israel to set an example for other nations to build their societies on the principles of social justice, righteousness, compassion, and love for all citizens of all faiths and ethnic groups.

We hope that Israel will be true to the principles cited in its Declaration of Independence so that the State will continue to maintain the moral principles of our prophets and sages who never ceased calling for morality in government and international affairs. We look forward to the day envisioned by our prophets when "nation shall not take up sword against nation; they shall never again know war."

The Central Role of Israel

We rejoice in the existence of *Medinat Yisrael* (the State of Israel) in *Eretz Yisrael* (the Land of Israel) with its capital of Jerusalem, the Holy City, the City of Peace. We view this phenomenon not just in political or military terms; rather, we consider it to be a miracle, a reflection of Divine Providence in human affairs. We glory in that miracle; we celebrate the rebirth of Zion.

From time immemorial, *Eretz Yisrael* has played a central and vital role in the life and culture of world Jewry. The Bible indicates that God has promised the Land of Israel to our ancestors and to their descendants. The *brit* (covenant) between God and the Jewish people created an unbreakable bond between us and the geographic entity we call *Eretz Yisrael*. Throughout the ages, we have revered, honored, cherished, prayed for, dreamed of, and sought to settle in Jerusalem and the Land of Israel.

The zealous attachment to *Eretz Yisrael* has persisted throughout our long history as a transnational people in which we transcended borders and lived in virtually every land. Wherever we were permitted, we viewed ourselves as natives or citizens of the country of our residence and were loyal to our host nation. Our religion has been land-centered but never land-bound; it has been a portable religion so that despite our long exile (*Galut*) from our spiritual homeland, we have been able to survive creatively and spiritually even in the *tefutzot* (Diaspora).

Indeed, there have been Jewish communities in the Diaspora from the days of the Prophets. The relative importance of the Land of Israel and the Diaspora fluctuated through the centuries. Whether the Diaspora was more creative than Zion or Zion was more vital than the Diaspora is of little importance. What is important is that *Eretz Yisrael* enriched world Jewry even as world Jewry enriched *Eretz Yisrael*.

Conservative Judaism and Israel

We staunchly support the Zionist ideal and take pride in the achievement of the State of Israel in the gathering of our people from the lands of our dispersion and in rebuilding a nation. The State of Israel and its well-being remain a major concern of the Conservative movement, as of all loyal Jews. To be sure, the Conservative movement has not always agreed with Israel's positions on domestic or foreign affairs. We have often suffered from discriminatory policies, but we remain firm and loving supporters of the State of Israel economically, politically, and morally. The Conservative movement is a member of the World Zionist Organization. We have undertaken major efforts in Israel such as the establishment of the Masorti movement, a growing number of congregations, a rabbinical school, a *kibbutz*, a *moshav*, a youth movement, schools, and adult education programs. Increasing numbers of Conservative rabbis and laypersons have gone on *aliyah* [immigrated to Israel], and we encourage and cherish *aliyah* to Israel as a value, goal, and *mitzvah*. Each year, thousands of our teenagers visit and study in Israel to be inspired at the sources of our faith, and thousands of adults visit on pilgrimages and synagogue tours.

Conservative liturgy takes cognizance of the rebirth of Israel, and *Yom Ha-atzama'ut* (Israel Independence Day) is observed joyfully in our congregations.

Various Centers of Jewish Life

We view it as both a misinterpretation of Jewish history and a threat to Jewish survival to negate the complementary roles of *Eretz Yisrael* [the Land of Israel] and the Diaspora. Currently there are various important centers of Jewish life in the Diaspora. Diaspora Jewry furnishes vital economic, political, and moral support to Israel; Israel imbues Diaspora Jewry with a sense of pride and self-esteem. Some see the role of *Medinat Yisrael* as the cultural and religious center of world Jewry. Others insist that since the days of the Prophets, various foci or centers of Jewish life and civilization, in both Israel and the Diaspora, have sustained the creative survival of *Am Yisrael* [the Jewish people] and *Torat Yisrael* [the Jewish tradition]. *Eretz Yisrael* produced most of the Bible, the Mishnah, the Talmud of *Eretz Yisrael*, the major Midrashim, liturgy, and other great works, while the Diaspora gave us the Babylonian Talmud, Hebrew poetry, philosophical writings, commentaries, law codes, and other lasting creations. The various communities interacted in a continual symbiotic process of mutual enrichment.

We realize that Israel and the Diaspora enjoy different advantages while facing unique challenges. Only in Israel may a Jew lead an all-encompassing Jewish life. There, Shabbat, *Yom Tov*, and *kashrut* are officially observed in varied degrees by the civilian organs of state and by the military; there Hebrew is the nation's language, and the Bible is studied in every school. Paradoxically, the very ease with which Jewish identity may be expressed in the Jewish state may give the false impression that religion is not needed in Israel for Jewish survival as it is in the Diaspora. We do not believe that Jewish identity can be replaced by Israeli identity or the ability to speak Hebrew. We are convinced that Jewish religion is essential as a source of ethical and moral values. Israeli Jewry is plagued by constant pressures to survive physically in the face of implacable foes sworn to destroy the State. Israel is also challenged to maintain, preserve, and enhance Jewish moral values and ethical standards, as well as its uniquely Jewish character. For the first time in nineteen centuries, the Jewish people is master of its affairs politically, economically and militarily and must exert sovereign power in its own nation and relate to other governments.

Diaspora Jewry confronts other dilemmas. In some lands, such as the Soviet Union and Muslim nations, Jews are subjected to religious, racial, or political persecution, and the survival of Jews and Judaism is in peril. Many Jews in such communities display enormous courage and fidelity in remaining loyal to Judaism against great odds. They must be helped either to emigrate or to build a stronger cultural and religious life wherever they reside. In lands where Jews are free to practice their religion, we have yet to resolve the problem of assimilation. On the other hand, cross-fertilization with other religions and civilizations can enrich Judaism now as it has done in the past.

343

Both the State of Israel and Diaspora Jewry have roles to fill; each can and must aid and enrich the other in every possible way; each needs the other. It is our fervent hope that Zion will indeed be the center of Torah and Jerusalem a beacon lighting the way for the Jewish people and for humanity.

Conservative/Masorti Life in and for Israel

Today, many institutions fulfill the movement's Zionist convictions and advance Conservative Judaism in Israel. Within Israel, more than fifty synagogues are affiliated with the Masorti movement (the Conservative movement is called Masorti, meaning "Traditional," everywhere in the world except for the United States and Canada). Other Israel-based initiatives include a Masorti youth movement (Noam), several Ramah camps, a Conservative kibbutz (Ḥanaton), the Schechter Institute of Jewish Studies (training rabbis and educators for service in Israel and the Diaspora and publishing Jewish scholarship with academic rigor), and the Conservative Yeshiva (training rabbinical students from abroad and offering serious adult Jewish studies). Also affiliated is an extensive network of Tali schools (*tagbir limudei yahadut,* or "enriched Jewish studies"), which are officially secular, public, and government-funded but include more intensive Jewish studies (largely taught by Schechter Institute–trained teachers) than comparable Israeli public, secular schools. In addition, Mercaz, the Conservative/Masorti party within the World Zionist Congress, helps secure World Zionist Organization funds for disbursement to Masorti institutions in Israel. The Masorti movement in Israel has also created its own prayer book, *Va'ani Tefilati* (My prayer), printed entirely in Hebrew, which articulates Conservative/Masorti egalitarian, historical, and Zionist convictions in and for Israel.

In the Diaspora, the Conservative liturgy maintains the traditional Jewish liturgy's hope for a return to Zion and expands upon it. There are prayers for the State of Israel. *Hallel* is recited on Yom Ha-'atzma-ut, Israel Independence Day, and Conservative Jews include the blessings at its beginning and end that mark this as a religious holiday.

To connect North American high school students to Israel, Ramah camps and United Synagogue Youth sponsor educational trips to Israel every summer. Ramah and USY also bring educators from Israel to enhance the Israel knowledge of Ramah campers and staff and USY members and staff.

Even with all of these efforts, Israel's Masorti movement is challenged. It receives practically no government funding for its synagogues, schools, youth groups, and camps. The Israeli government funds only secular and Orthodox schools and grants allocations solely to Orthodox congregations for their buildings, maintenance, and rabbis' salaries. Furthermore, only Orthodox rabbis may officiate at a wedding of two Jews in Israel or process a divorce, and the Orthodox also control which conversions to Judaism count for eligibility to marry a Jew. These and other major problems of religious discrimination are built into the Israeli governmental system.

Why Israel Matters to Conservative Jews

Such religious discrimination, along with the Israeli government's military occupation of the West Bank (since the 1967 Six-Day War) and continued Jewish settlement building on that land, have estranged many American Jews from the State of Israel. This is especially true for young adults who never witnessed a world without a Jewish state or the wars Israel has had to fight to continue to exist. If Israel's actions do not uphold my values, many ask, why should I be concerned about Israel, see the state as part of my Jewish identity, defend it against critics, and fight politically and in other ways to preserve it?

As one example, on August 23, 2015, Dr. David Reed, a past president of the Conservative Congregation Beth El in Durham, North Carolina, wrote a letter (excerpted here) to the synagogue's board of directors questioning the conviction of the congregation and the Conservative movement generally, as articulated in Conservative prayer books, that the State of Israel has and should have religious meaning for all American Jews. In response, the author of this book asked Conservative Rabbis Benjamin Segal and Miriam Berkowitz (both raised in North America and now living in Israel); Conservative Rabbis Esther Reed, Daniel Greyber, and

Sharon Brous (all three living in the United States); and Jewish Theological Seminary chancellor Dr. Arnold Eisen to explain why they continue to be Zionists despite their disapproval of certain Israeli actions. Their replies (also adapted here) are emblematic of why Conservative Jewry as a whole may disagree strongly with particular Israeli government policies and yet remain committed to Israel's continued endurance and flourishing.

Dr. David Reed's Letter to Beth El Leaders

Chevra [Friends], I am writing to express some thoughts and anxieties that have increasingly impressed themselves on me over the past two or three years. They involve questions that seem abstract and far removed from the practical realities of synagogue leadership to which you devote yourselves, yet I think they are among the most vital issues facing American Jewish communities, and the answers that are found to these questions will have much to do with the survival of these communities.

After a good deal of reflection and discussion, I have gradually come to realize the importance of the following question, "What is (and what should be) the religious significance of the State of Israel in the Judaism of Congregation Beth El?" . . .

The clearest (but probably not the most important) example of the way in which Israel might be said to have "religious significance" for the Judaism of Congregation Beth El is what we call "The Prayer for the State of Israel." We have in *Siddur Sim Shalom*, the prayer book used by our synagogue and virtually every other Conservative synagogue, a paragraph or two labeled, "A Prayer for the State of Israel" that we regularly (although not always) recite out loud on Shabbat and Festivals. In this prayer, the words ". . . the State of Israel, the beginning of the flourishing of our redemption . . ." are included. The Hebrew word is *"geulah,"* redemption, and it is a word from the religious vocabulary of Judaism with all sorts of messianic overtones.

Just what "redemption" is meant here? How can one reasonably connect a religious notion of "redemption," which calls forth images of eternal salvation, with a specific State or country (the Hebrew phrase is *"medinat yisrael,"* "state of Israel") that has come into being at a certain time and in a certain place and that is subject to all of the changes in fortune that can happen to states or countries? Surely we all recognize that connecting a political entity with religious redemption means taking on incredible risks. Our own Jewish history is full of examples of the dangers this merging of religion and state can run into, and the histories of other religions provide many more examples. To try to detach the specific State we now have from the eternal redemption we seek to obtain, some folks have suggested replacing these words with *"may it be the beginning of our redemption," she-tehai reishit tzemiḥat ge-ulateinu.* In my view this change still places far too much weight on the human-created institution of the state to be reasonable. Following the logic of including "A Prayer for the State of Israel" in the service, it is becoming more and more common in many synagogues to include special prayers (such as "Hallel") for Israel Independence Day and Jerusalem Day, further linking our religion to specific recent historical, political, and military events.

Going outside of Beth El Synagogue you might be interested to read a short pamphlet that the Conservative Movement has produced called *Emet v'Emunah,* which is, as its subtitle says, a "Statement of Principles of Conservative Judaism" (published by the Jewish Theological Seminary, the Rabbinical Assembly, the United Synagogue of Conservative Judaism, and other related organizations). It very conveniently summarizes the Conservative Movement's view of the religious significance of the State of Israel, and the document has this to say: "We rejoice in the existence of Medinat Yisrael (the State of Israel), in Eretz Yisrael (the Land of Israel) with its capital of Jerusalem, the Holy City, the City of Peace. We view this phenomenon not just in political or military terms; rather, we consider it to be a miracle, reflecting Divine Providence in human affairs. We glory in that miracle; we celebrate the rebirth of Zion."

. . . For now, I just want to point out the clear and careful way in which the authors of the document claim that the State of Israel has a significance that goes beyond "political and military" terms, and that this significance is set out in the strongest form of religious language ("miracles," "Divine Providence"). I think it provides another good example of the type of "significance" my question is asking about.

Finally . . . there is the general understanding, spread in the world around us, that to be Jewish is to have a religious tie to the State of Israel. Most Jews seem to have this notion, the vast majority of Americans think and believe this, and most Jewish organizations, writers, and commentators encourage everyone to hold on to this idea. . . .

After pondering this topic for a number of years, I can say unequivocally that I think there cannot be and should not be any religious role for the State of Israel (or any other state) in Judaism. In that particular respect religion and state are not compatible and should not be mixed with one another. In saying this I speak for myself and no one else. It is a matter on which everyone should come to their own conclusions.

It is also a matter which, in the deepest sense, is ours to discuss as American Jews at Congregation Beth El in Durham, NC. The military and political policies of Israel or other aspects of its society and culture are rightly an Israeli matter. American Jews ultimately have little standing to enter into those discussions, and that is as it should be. How we, as American Jews, view the role of Israel in our religion is, however, something that is very much ours to discuss and determine. No one else can or should do this for us.

As you can imagine, given the many ways in which Israel takes on a religious significance at Beth El, given the official position of the Conservative Movement, and given what most people, Jews and non-Jews, have essentially accepted as "gospel" on this topic, arriving at this position has left me troubled and deeply uncertain of my place in the community. So, having started with one question, I end up with many.

* What place—if any—do I, or does anyone else who may think as I do, have in our congregation?
* How can I remain a part of Congregation Beth El without my affiliation being understood by people both inside and outside the community as support for the idea that the State of Israel has a religious significance within Judaism?
* Is there some way to make it clear to the world at large that there are Jews who are not "Religious Zionists" and who do not ascribe any religious significance to "Medinat Israel"?

*What if our Synagogue were to make it clear from the pulpit and in its By-Laws or other official documents that, in spite of what is laid out in the Conservative Movement's publications, the Congregation as a whole does not take a stand on the question of Israel's religious significance, that the matter is left to individual congregants, and that for this reason the State of Israel is not a part of Synagogue ritual and liturgy? . . . I very much appreciate your consideration of the questions I have posed.

Rabbi Benjamin Segal

We Jews have inherited a full civilization — much more than just a religion. It is a unique phenomenon among world religions and peoples. Can one legitimately ignore chapters of a book, or rooms of a house, in describing the whole?

For 2000 years we basically stayed away from Israel, even while longing for it. That is now irrelevant. Everything has come flowing back — a sense of history, the ability to act as a sovereign nation, mutual responsibility, cultural development, self-reliance, etc.

The ability to be part of all this — to contribute to creating a "Jewish" society; to have ready access to the varied treasures of our past; to confront brotherhood that transcends color, national origin and cultural chasm — is something that I can only pray you find.

Do not misunderstand me. This is not easy, and the true glory of the return to Israel is in its challenges more than in its accomplishments. We have sought power for good, but have not always so used it. When this weighs on me, I remind myself of the saying, "Ships in port are safe, but ships were not made to be in port." My greatest delight in being here, beyond the past and present, is the future. I cannot believe that I have had the good fortune to be in a position to be a small part of that, and it makes my life complete.

Our glory resides first in what we dream and work for, not always the way things happen. I sometimes recall the biblical prophets rebuking the kings of Israel and Judah and their social elites, and I recall times so bad that our kings were idolaters. If those prophets could express disgust with Jerusalem (Ezekiel says God called it a "bloody city") yet carry a different city in their hearts, a city of morality and harmony, then who am I to allow the failings of one period or another to dishearten me?

But I ramble. I know we are different. I am 75. My generation, I believe, had greater sensitivity to the often sad fate of our people over 2000 years of wandering because our parents lived during the Holocaust. Israel serving as a refuge for persecuted Jews anywhere is part of our loyalty to Israel. You may feel that less, but I would be wrong not to mention it.

One of my heroes growing up was Abraham Joshua Heschel, whose existentialism greatly influenced me. Frankly, Israel was barely on his horizon, but after he came here after the Six-Day War, he rediscovered a hidden part of himself—partially, historical association but also how much it could contribute to spiritual thought. A scion of a Hasidic dynasty, he discovered the miracle of rebirth. Coming from and returning to America, he wrote: "Nonparticipation in the drama is a source of embarrassment."

I do not suggest that you be embarrassed. I would rather say that not being part of it is a tremendous loss. Nor is this a speech for *aliyah*. There are degrees and ways of involvement. Some of those, quite honestly, are complex. If you feel public policy in any area is not reflective of the values you cherish, I would hope and pray that you would become an outspoken critic and lover, that rare combination that perhaps only we can understand. As to our accomplishments, and there are many, I hope that you can take joy in them. I, for one, delight in a nation I consider more caring for its siblings than any on earth, in the revival of Hebrew, in the integration of the most impossibly diverse populations into one society, etc. With all our failures, our achievements have been many. With all our ethical challenges, no nation struggles more or tries harder.

Next time you visit Israel, let us walk together, perhaps on a street named for the medieval scholar, to hear everyone speak Hebrew, to have the bank machine on Friday wish you a "Shabbat shalom," to read a newspaper filled with all the challenges that every living people confronts through its own culture. In one place on earth, the air bespeaks my three-thousand-year-old inheritance. It is that firm background that allows me to face the essential task of life, building for the unsure future. To end again with Heschel, "The life in the land of Israel today is a rehearsal, a test, a challenge to us all. . . . To be involved . . . is to be in labor."

Rabbi Miriam Berkowitz

My first trip to Israel was as a college student. Surprisingly for the very rational, focused person I was, Israel captured my emotions: the flowering bougainvillea and handsome soldiers awakened a sense of pride that I had not experienced growing up in Montreal, where we were double minorities as Jews and Anglophones. I found it refreshing to be in a place where Jews are the majority, where the Jewish calendar shapes the rhythm of the week and year, where the pomegranates ripen for Rosh Hashanah, and the radio plays sad songs on Yom Hazikaron [the Day of Remembrance of fallen soldiers], where the sign on the bus to stand for the elderly is taken straight from the Torah (*mipnei seiva takum* [rise before the aged]—Leviticus 19:32). I ended up moving to Israel in 1994, spending some time in the United States after getting married, and returning to Israel in 2008 for good.

I affirm the right of the Jewish people to have a country like other nations and am happy they chose this land with its historical and theological connections to the Jewish past. I am still moved that the report card of my children's school in the Old City quotes the prophet Zechariah 8:4–5: "Thus says the LORD of hosts, 'Old men and old women will again sit in the streets of Jerusalem. . . . And the streets of the city will be filled with boys and girls playing in its streets.'" I consider it a miracle and privilege to be living in these times and witnessing the rebirth of the nation in its land.

There is a sense of meaning and purpose here that I have not found in other more comfortable, peaceful, easy places to live. I love that the country is still being created, after only a few decades, that new ideas can quickly take hold, that so many young adults live near their parents, that history, nature, and archeology come to life, and that you can hear ten different languages on one city block. I love that people take their views so passionately here, vote in high percentages, demonstrate, yell, write and care so much about their view of an ideal society—even if they cannot all possibly be right.

I do fully admit all the problems and imperfections in Israel today, not least that our opportunities for self-expression have often come at the expense of other people who were and are living in this land as well. I am deeply concerned that the (untenable) limbo status of Palestinians in the West Bank and the inequalities in treatment of Arab Israelis, augmented by anti-Israel public relations by Israel's enemies, have alienated young North Americans from their Jewish identities as well as from Israel. The generation of Jews who are the most free and economically stable ever in history is self-eroding. Concern for Palestinian rights leads them to block out all the intriguing and enriching aspects of Israel; disrespect for Israel then all too often leads to shame about their Jewish identity altogether.

In Israel, young liberals have a political home and can advocate and demonstrate for liberal causes and vote for the Meretz party that represents those views but still be Zionists who serve in the army and cast their lot with the Jewish people. In North America, a young liberal Jew who does not feel the same connection to Israel might react by disconnecting from Israel and even from Jewish identity completely.

Both sides are responsible for missed opportunities, biased education, and excessively violent reactions. Religious Jews especially have an obligation to behave as ethically as possible within constraints of reality; killing Arabs randomly on supposedly religious grounds, as some ultra-orthodox Jews have done, causes *ḥillul HaShem* — a desecration of the Divine — and makes a mockery of the word "religious." On the other hand, terrorism by Arabs against Jews is beyond the pale of acceptable means of protest and is ultimately damaging to the Palestinian cause.

But even people who disagree with me and see Israel as the sole problem, oppressor, occupier, etc., can still find a way to engage with Israel instead of demonizing or distancing from it. First, this generation might see that its commitment to justice and values of fairness and respect for the Other stem directly from Biblical injunctions to protect the widow, orphan, and stranger in our midst. Second, I would encourage people on all sides of the debate over Palestinian nationhood and Israel's future to listen intently to the other narratives, gather facts, and see the situation in its historical context.

Even those who find Israel's current political policies offensive and unjust can engage with Israeli history, culture, archeology, cuisine, social life, etc. and see it as a multidimensional place with problems and achievements like all other countries. They should also recognize that there is a

vibrant liberal minority in Israel attempting to bring about transformation in Israeli society to realize its potential as a liberal democracy. Polls
show that the majority of Israelis support the two-state solution, even as
they express concerns about how a future Palestinian state would treat
its Jewish residents and its neighboring State of Israel. Israel needs the
support and participation of liberal Jews in the diaspora to argue for the
legitimacy of Israel's existence as a Jewish state to Jews and non-Jews
who would deny that and at the same time to push for social and political
change within Israel.

The words of the sage Hillel 2000 years ago still resonate as a guiding
principle: "... If I am not for myself, who will be for me? But if I am only for
myself, who am I? If not now, when?" (Ethics of the Fathers, 1:14). Alongside
these words stands the Talmudic statement, "All Jews are responsible for
one another" — *kol yisrael 'arevim zeh bazeh* (B. She'vu'ot 39a).

Soon, a majority of the world's Jews will be living in Israel, and the
majority of Jewish history, culture, literature, and philosophy will be
created in Israel. A Jew in the Diaspora is part of the Jewish people, and
we are responsible for one another, for better or for worse.

Israel is facing a double threat: an external threat of annihilation by
Iran, ISIS and others, and also erosion of liberal democracy from within.
Now is not the time to disconnect with Israel. We need you, and we need
learned, nuanced, solution-oriented voices more than ever. Hopefully this
generation of Jewish young adults can synthesize the pride in a Jewish
state restored after two thousand years of exile with the concern for the
rights, opportunities, and human dignity of our neighbors and cousins.

Rabbi Esther Reed

If I were to describe my relationship with Israel like a status on Facebook,
I would say, "It's complicated," just like my relationship with my family.
I love my mother and children deeply, but at times they drive me crazy,
and while I live my life married to a man I love and admire, boy does he
know how to push my buttons!

In Israel, everyone feels they can tell you what to do. A month after we
were married, a taxi driver asked us why we hadn't already made *aliyah*
(moved to Israel) and why I wasn't pregnant yet. A stranger will come up

to you to tell you your baby needs a warmer coat, or a hat. They ask or tell you these things, they say, because as members of my extended family, they care. As an American, I feel they are crossing a line and going too far.

But then there was the time I drove my car to Netanya for the day. At the day's end the car wouldn't start. I asked the parking attendant for help. He called his brother and father, who knew a lot about cars. They got the car to start, and explained the problem to me so that it wouldn't happen again. In America, I don't think a parking attendant and his family members would drop what they were doing to help someone who didn't know anything about cars. But in Israel, people help each other. We are family.

Whenever I'm in Israel, I join Women of the Wall to pray at the Kotel on Rosh Ḥodesh, the start of a new month. One time, we couldn't get into the Kotel area, because busloads of yeshiva girls had filled the women's section, so our group of women in Tallit and Tefillin began to pray in the plaza approaching the Kotel. People shouted, spat, whistled ferociously, and threw eggs at us. I was both sad and angry. I was sad that the Jewish community was so divided that other Jews made it hard for me to pray at the Western Wall, one of the holiest sites in Jewish history. I was angry that the government supported the Orthodox hegemony. The current leaders and the government of Israel cater to right-wing perspectives.

I think it is immoral to rule over a Palestinian population that has no opportunity to become citizens. At the same time, when I see the suffering of the Palestinians used as a weapon of propaganda on the campus where I serve as Hillel director, I cannot remain silent. People on campus who claim to care about all humanity, yet criticize only Israel, are blatantly unfair and, frankly, anti-Semitic. Couching their arguments in human rights terms draws in young people who don't understand the full picture.

One Jewish student said: "This is what was always emphasized in my Jewish upbringing: to make the world a better place, to care about people who don't have the same rights as I do, and to do everything I can to make sure they do have the same rights as I do. So standing up for Palestinians just seems like an extension of those Jewish values."

I can understand where she is coming from, and would respond this way: I have good relationships with my neighbors. We say "Hello" on the street. When the mail gets delivered to the wrong address, we bring it over to the right house. We borrow milk or sugar, or sometimes a snow shovel. If my neighbor's house were on fire, of course I would try to help. But if both our houses were on fire, I would try to save my own children first. I don't think that is racist or chauvinistic. Much as I don't want to see my neighbor suffer in any way, my family comes first.

I see the Jews in Israel as my family. Yes, there are times—such as the politics of the Israeli-Palestinian conflict and the treatment of non-orthodox rabbis and institutions—when my Israel family drives me crazy, as my own family members do. But I love my family. And when my family is under attack, I stand up to support them. It is what a family does.

Rabbi Daniel Greyber

It can be an important act of loyalty and love to yearn for Israel to be better than she is and to work towards that ideal.

Israel is the one country in the world where I am not recognized as a rabbi who can perform a Jewish marriage. Israel's movement away from a two-state solution through its continued settlement of parts of the West Bank where Palestinians hope for a future state causes me to worry for Israel's future as a democratic state that lives up to Jewish values and ideals.

And so, I do not equate criticism of Israel with hatred of Israel. The Rabbis taught, "If there is no rebuke, there can be no love."

I also accept the Zionist critique that the rabbinic Judaism that developed in the diaspora left us with enormous intellectual gifts but deprived us of wisdom that only comes with the responsibilities of self-governance. Rabbi David Hartman wrote: "Israel expands the possible range of halakhic involvement in human affairs beyond the circumscribed frameworks of the home and synagogue. Jews in Israel are given the opportunity to bring economic, social, and political issues into the center of their religious consciousness." Only because of Israel do we now have modern music, television, film, and literature in Hebrew. Only because of Israel are the Jewish people able to send help after an earthquake to Haiti or advise California on how to solve its water crisis.

In 1762, more than a century before Theodor Herzl launched political Zionism, Jean-Jacques Rousseau, writing in *Emile*, said, "I shall never believe I have heard the arguments of the Jews until they have a free state, schools and universities, where they can speak and dispute without risk. Only then will we know what they have to say."

Judaism's most audacious idea may be that, in God's eyes, we are not small. We matter. "The greatest sin of man," wrote Rabbi Abraham Joshua Heschel, "is to forget that he is a prince—that he has royal power."

It is a privilege to be a Jew. We are no better, no worse, than other peoples. We are a small, fragile fragment in a sea of human life. Our task is eternal—to bring God's light into the world. We matter. And Israel matters as a society within which the Torah can be most fully brought to life, as a culture through which our people can most fully know ourselves and the world.

She is not perfect. Nothing is. But she is ours, and she matters more than we can know.

Rabbi Sharon Brous

You've heard about many of Israel's extraordinary achievements of the past sixty-seven years, from the breathtaking advances in medicine and technology, to the against-all-odds success of the start-up nation, to the ingathering of millions of refugees and immigrants, Jews whose home countries were no longer safe or hospitable to them, Israel absorbing in its first few years hundreds of thousands of survivors from Europe, and in the next several decades nearly 1,000,000 Jews who fled or were expelled from Arab lands, 100,000 Ethiopian Jews and more than 1,000,000 from the former Soviet Union.

But Israel, for all its great achievements, has yet to live up to its own greatest aspirations—the dream of the early Zionists and Founders: a Jewish and democratic State based on freedom, justice and peace as envisioned by the prophets of Israel, one that ensures complete equality of social and political rights to all its inhabitants.

The occupation of the West Bank is now in its 48th year—older than I. I know it's at least part of the reason many American Jews are all but ready to walk away.

Here's what you need to know: Many serious, committed Zionists and serious, committed Jews, people who live in Israel and people who love Israel, believe from the core of their being—*our* being—that the treatment of the Palestinian people, the restriction of rights, the daily humiliations, the stubborn expansion of the settlements throughout the West Bank and the dual systems of justice, threaten to destroy Zionism and make a mockery of Judaism.

We need to own this. We need to acknowledge that for all the unfair and disproportionate criticism of Israel from critics around the world—some of whom, yes, are actual anti-Semites—at the end of the day Israel does not just have a PR problem; it has a policy problem.

And the American Jewish establishment has made a major miscalculation regarding this policy problem. For many years, community leadership thought it was doing the right thing by silently acquiescing when one Israeli government after another supported settlement expansion, thinking we'd eventually trade land for peace. But the peace didn't come: Arafat dodged and evaded. Rabin was murdered. And now there are nearly 400,000 Jewish settlers living in the West Bank. Initially, many were there for the view and the cheap rent. Some still are. But the script did not adjust even as the settler population began to grow more ideological, more religious, more violent, and more committed to staying forever. Instead, we built blinders and focused on growing European anti-Semitism, the Iranian nuclear threat, and the failures of the Palestinian leadership.

But in doing so, we did not calculate that we would lose you. You, frustrated by the double standard, witnessing the Jewish communal pride in its focus on the poor and vulnerable in Haiti and Katmandu and Liberia, but confounded by the communal moral blind spot when it comes to the poor and vulnerable in our own backyard—as in Arab East Jerusalem, where 79% of the population lives in poverty.

You need to know that there are many Israelis and Palestinians who are working—together—to change the script. There is strong opposition to the status quo—both here and in Israel, among activists, artists, rabbis, and even military specialists who have a different sense of how best to support Israel. Thankfully, Israel remains a place in which those voices are still heard.

Also, there are many Palestinians working every day to bring about a non-violent resolution to the conflict. They reject Palestinian terror and extremism, and risk their lives and livelihoods to make space for a different kind of conversation between Palestinians and Jews, to reach a fair and just end to the conflict.

If these Israeli Jews and Palestinians who share our Jewish and democratic values, fight tirelessly for justice and peace, and are not willing to give up, how can we walk away when they have lost so much and continue to fight?

The Jew builds a moral compass not based on the standards of criminal regimes on its borders, but based on our own values, articulated in Torah, fine-tuned over the course of thousands of years. When policies are enacted in the Jewish state that are fundamentally and dangerously incompatible with those core values, we all have an obligation to speak out.

Israel is indeed fighting for its culture, its morals, and its soul. But we shouldn't be defeatist in these battles, because they can still be won.

So please, don't walk away. We need you.

JTS Chancellor Dr. Arnold Eisen

. . . To be a Jew who cares about Israel . . . is to worry a lot about its future. To be a *Conservative* Jew, for whom intimate relationship to the State and the people of Israel stands at the very core of one's being, is to reckon with the grim possibility that peace may elude us for many years to come.

That prospect is awful to contemplate. It does not help that fewer and fewer nations are prepared to stand by Israel, or that a diminishing number of Israelis seem to share the dreams for what an Israel-at-peace should look like—dreams on which I, like most North American Jews, was raised. Even as Israel advances on many fronts and provides Jews everywhere with numerous reasons for pride, leading Israeli Orthodox rabbis declare with disturbing regularity that Conservative and Reform Judaism are heresy—and some of Israel's politicians express disdain for democracy. Jews outside of Israel seem increasingly incapable of disagreeing about Israel with civility and respect. Some (especially younger) Jews do not talk or think about Israel at all.

That is why I've been urging Jews who do care to savor the blessing of being alive at this unique moment in Jewish history and experience. Jewish life and the practice of Judaism have become infinitely richer in our generation thanks to Israel's existence and achievements. I'd like us all to affirm clearly and without equivocation—no matter what our opinions about Israeli policy—that our connection to the State of Israel and its citizens is fundamental, nonnegotiable, and unbreakable. Israel is the single greatest project the Jewish people has going right now, and the most important arena that has been available to Jews in two millennia to put our values to the test and our teachings into practice. We need it. And it needs us.

That is the heart of the matter for me. I am a religious Zionist, convinced that Jews are heirs to a unique story that we are responsible for carrying forward, and—because of history, tradition, and faith—partners in a covenant aimed at bringing more justice and compassion to the world. The sovereign, democratic State of Israel affords unprecedented scope and responsibility for the fulfillment of covenant. It presents us with the chance to do what Conservative Judaism has always urged: adapt the teachings of Jewish tradition to unprecedented circumstances and join Torah with the very best of modern thought and expertise. In Israel, Jews can and must bring the Torah to bear on every aspect of society: health care and education, foreign policy and the welfare system, treatment of non-Jewish minorities and diverse streams of Judaism, relations of war and peace, and proper stewardship of the planet's resources.

I think that Conservative/Masorti Jews are well-positioned to take the lead in undertaking three steps that will strengthen Israel and the relationship of Diaspora Jews to Israel.

First: Conservative Jews in North America can do a better job of learning about Israel and talking with Israelis. . . . Conservative Jews are well-positioned to overcome these divides. We are disproportionately represented in the lay and professional leadership of Jewish communal organizations in North America. We routinely reach across boundaries to our "left" and "right." Masorti Jews in Israel are natural allies and conversation partners. . . . Together we can make Israel a State that palpably belongs to all Jews everywhere.

Second: let's do a better job of talking with one another about Israel. Civil discourse about Israel has broken down in many synagogues, including many Conservative synagogues. I suspect the reason for our growing intolerance of each other's dissent is a combination of hopelessness about the prospects for peace and fear that any criticism of government policy gives aid and comfort to Israel's enemies. I do not minimize that danger—but we need to engage in honest discussion about the single greatest Jewish concern of our times. No Jews—particularly younger Jews—should be banished from Jewish tables, or made to feel they have no place in our community, because their views on Israel seem heretical or their criticism untempered. We need to cut ourselves a little slack where Israel is concerned. Let's trust Jewish leaders to use community agencies and forums responsibly and help individual Jews—including college students—to develop their own reasons for standing with Israel.

Third: let's make sure that the future lay and professional leaders of our Movement have every chance to know the wonderful, bewildering, changing-by-the-day reality of Israel—and so come to love it, each in his or her own way....

Israel provides opportunities for Jewish fulfillment, individual and collective, that are as yet unexplored. The State's existence and achievements carry hope to Jews and to humanity that we dare not consign to cynicism or despair. Let's embrace that hope fully—and get to work.

"Zionism"

Suggestions for Further Reading

Arnold M. Eisen. *Galut: Modern Jewish Reflection on Homelessness and Homecoming.* Bloomington: Indiana University Press, 1986.

Jeffrey K. Salkin, ed. *A Dream of Zion: American Jews Reflect on Why Israel Matters to Them.* Woodstock VT: Jewish Lights, 2007.

Benjamin J. Segal. *Returning: The Land of Israel as Focus in Jewish History.* Jerusalem: Department of Education and Culture, World Zionist Organization, 1987.

CHAPTER FOURTEEN

Teshuvot Medinat Yisrael

Masorti Responsa in and for Israel

From time to time, legal issues arise that are specific to Israel or are shared by Israel and the Diaspora but require a different treatment in Israel because of local conditions. Here are just a few examples: ceding land in a peace agreement; going on the Temple Mount in our time; milking a cow on Shabbat (on the Conservative/Masorti kibbutz, Ḥanaton); extraditing a Jewish criminal from Israel to another country; conscripting women and yeshivah students into the Israeli Defense Forces; eating legumes (*kitniyot*) on Passover (Sephardic Jews eat legumes on Passover, and at least half the Israeli Jewish population is Sephardic); riding to the synagogue on the Sabbath under work and living conditions significantly different from those in the Diaspora; donating one's body to a medical school (to advance pathology or teach anatomy in a country that depends upon first-rate medical schools and hospitals and cannot rely on non-Jewish corpses to serve these needs).

To address these and other important legal issues, in 1985 the Conservative/Masorti movement established a Va'ad Halakhah (Committee on Jewish Law) in Israel. This followed historic precedent: in some times and places, regional groups of rabbis made legal decisions for their region (see chapter 5).

The Va'ad Halakhah respected the CJLS's authority by solely treating issues specific to Israel or unique to Israel's local conditions. A Va'ad opinion became an official decision when a majority of its members voted for it. The committee began with three members and grew to eight by 1995.

The Va'ad ceased operation in 2005. Member Rabbi David Golinkin, who had edited the six volumes of Va'ad Halakhah responsa to date, could no longer carry out that task (although he continued writing his own responsa).

In 2016 the Rabbinical Assembly's Israel Region reconstituted the Va'ad, with Rabbis Shelomo Zacharov and Gil Nativ as cochairs. It now includes seven rabbis and several honorary members who served on the original committee.

In addition, under Rabbi Golinkin's direction, the Schechter Institute of Jewish Studies in Jerusalem has published many responsa and other related materials. For example, its Institute of Applied Halakhah has produced twenty-three volumes by various Conservative/Masorti rabbis encompassing scholarly works on Jewish law and thought, as well as rulings on specific legal questions. A subsection of this institute specializes in Jewish legal topics affecting women (a list of Schechter Institute of Jewish Studies schools and projects appears in the appendix). To learn more about the institute's publications on Jewish law, visit http://www.schechter.edu and click on "Books Catalog."

This chapter presents English summaries of just a few of the significant responsa on the Va'ad Halakhah's "Responsa for Today" website. To read these and other responsa in Hebrew in full, with all their legal reasoning, documentation, and sources, or to read English summaries of all of the Va'ad's responsa, visit http://www.responsafortoday.com.

Responsum on Ceding Land in a Peace Agreement

A major issue in Israel is determining Israel's borders. What are the borders that God gave the Jewish people, and may the government of Israel compromise on them for the sake of a peace agreement?

Some Torah verses (Genesis 15:18, Deuteronomy 1:7–8) state that the Promised Land extends to the Euphrates, which would mean including not only the land of modern-day Israel but also all of Jordan, Lebanon, and Syria. On the basis of these verses, some Orthodox Jews maintain that it would be a violation of God's commandments to relinquish any land within those wide borders that the Jews have been able to occupy and govern.

In the following responsum (summarized here), however, author Rabbi Tuvia Friedman points out that the actual borders of the land governed by Jews varied significantly during First Temple times (ca. 950–586 BCE) and that later, when the Jews living in Israel were governed by other regimes, the Rabbis defined the Holy Land much more narrowly. Therefore, he says, the borders of the modern State of Israel should be determined by political negotiations aimed at producing peace rather than by any considerations of Jewish law. The Va'ad Halakhah approved his responsum unanimously in 5747 (1987). The full English summary, reproduced here, can be found as the last entry in volume 2 at http://www.responsafortoday.com/eng _index.html; for the full responsum in Hebrew, with its accompanying notes, visit http://www.responsafortoday.com/vol2/9.pdf.

The Whole Land of Israel Concept

There has been much publicity in the press emanating from the Chief Rabbinate of Israel to the effect that, according to the halakhah, it is forbidden to cede even a footstep of any part of the whole Land of Israel. What is the position of our Va'ad Halakhah?

Our basic sources, Biblical and Rabbinic, do not mention the concept of "the Whole Land of Israel" as a sacred place defined by rigidly fixed borders. The reason is obvious. Throughout all periods of our history, the borders of the land expanded or narrowed for political reasons. The theoretical idealized borders were vague. Thus, major Rabbinical authorities in the Middle Ages disagreed as to the location of the "River of Egypt." Some understood this indicator of Israel's southwest border as Wadi El Arish in the Eastern Sinai, whereas others understood it to be the Nile River some 100 kilometers further west. Under King David, Israel's empire was considerably larger than the area promised to Abraham; and when Solomon ceded "twenty cities in the land of the Galilee" to Hiram of Tyre, there seems to have been no sense that any sacred territorial commitment was being violated.

After the destruction of the Second Temple, we find the Rabbis shrinking the territory to be defined as the Holy Land. There are voices arguing for the exclusion even of Acre and Beit She'an. The major factor in their reasoning may well have been economic: Those deemed to live outside of the Holy Land of Israel were exempt from observing the (seventh) Shmitah [Sabbatical] year as well as tithing and similar internal Jewish taxes. Whatever the totality of the reasons, this approach certainly demonstrates a great deal of flexibility with reference to borders.

There is also the example of two neighboring "heartland" port cities, Caesarea and Dor, roughly midway between Haifa and Jaffa. The Rabbis variously considered each as within or outside the Land of Israel, depending on the Jewish or non-Jewish nature of its population.

The status of the city of Ashkelon was complex. In some respects it was deemed to be in the Land and in some respects it was considered as outside the Land. Similarly, certain Jewish cities on the far side of the Jordan were considered as part of the Land in some respects and outside it in other halakhic respects.

Close to the year 100 CE, Rabban Gamliel of Yavneh published a list of locations considered part of the Land of Israel. About a century later, Rabbi Yehudah Hanassi issued a similar list, which differed in a number of details to reflect changes in Jewish population patterns.

By definition, the Land of Israel is Holy (holiness being defined in part by special obligations), yet the boundaries of the Holy Land were never fixed and rigid, but the opposite: flexible in accordance with the pragmatic reality of the time. To claim that the concept "the Whole Land of Israel" forbids us from conceding any part of the geographic land that happens to be under Jewish sovereignty has no support in the halakhah. The disagreement relative to the "Whole Land of Israel" concept is strictly a political dispute with no halakhic relevance whatever.

Responsum on Extraditing a Jewish Criminal from Israel to Another Country

Traditional Jewish law forbids *mesirah*, turning Jews over to non-Jewish courts for judgment.[1] This prohibition undoubtedly arose out of two concerns. First, given rampant discrimination against Jews, Jewish litigants were unlikely to receive a fair hearing. In fact, a dispute among Jews aired in a gentile court might provide the excuse for punishing both Jewish litigants and perhaps the entire Jewish community.

Moreover, rabbis over the generations wanted to make sure that Jewish law remained authoritative. Jews were using non-Jewish law as a matter of course when they engaged in business with non-Jews, and some Jews might decide it was too cumbersome and confusing to switch to Jewish law for their inter-Jewish trade. Moreover, if Jews frequently conducted business according to the norms of another legal system, they might come to assume that the same rules applied to their trade with other Jews, and it would be unfair to apply Jewish law to such transactions retroactively in a dispute.

For these political and moral reasons, Samuel, a rabbi of the early third century, announced the principle of *dina de'malkhuta dina*, "the law of the land is the law."[2] This accommodation, however, was restricted to monetary matters (and done reluctantly, for it limited the jurisdiction of Jewish law, which, in Jewish thought, is ultimately God's law). In other words, the rabbis permitted Jews to use non-Jewish law and courts solely to conduct business and to resolve disputes in commercial affairs.

How, then, could a Jew in good conscience inform non-Jewish civil authorities about another Jew who had committed a crime? And how could a Jewish state extradite a Jew accused of a crime to another country for trial and possible punishment—and thereby further diminish the authority of Jewish law?

After the Enlightenment, a number of rabbis and several sources (such as the Arukh Ha-Shulḥan, a nine-volume code of Jewish law by Rabbi Yeḥiel Epstein, 1829–1908) began issuing rulings that the *mesirah* laws no longer applied. The reasoning went as follows: Jews had been prohibited from using non-Jewish courts only when those court systems were unfair to Jews (and perhaps to others as well), and a Jewish citizen's prosecution within the system might incite persecution of the entire Jewish community. Because courts in Western democracies were no longer discriminatory toward Jews, Jews could use non-Jewish courts generally for both civil and criminal matters.[3] Indeed, in our day, legal authorities in Western democracies are unlikely to inflict penalties on the entire Jewish community because of some Jews who are criminals. Governments operating on Enlightenment principles prosecute all citizens who violate the law as individuals and not as members of a particular community.

Yet even before the Enlightenment, another strain of Jewish legal thinking maintained that government courts could be used in criminal matters where Jewish courts had no jurisdiction or power to punish. Rabbi Moses Isserles of sixteenth-century Poland cited others who lived even earlier who held that "if a person is struck by another, he may go to complain before the non-Jewish court even though he will thereby cause great harm to the assailant."[4] Today, because Jewish courts have even less power and authority to handle criminal matters than they did in pre-Enlightenment times, Ashkenazi Jews (whose ancestors came from Central and Eastern Europe) largely rely on this ruling.

Sephardic Jews, by contrast, generally follow Rabbi Joseph Karo, author of the Shulḥan Arukh, on which Rabbi Isserles commented. Rabbi Karo asserted that the prohibition of *mesirah* continues to this day, and therefore it is illegal for a Jew who is being harassed or harmed by another Jew to report the matter to civil authorities. Even Karo, though, maintained that when there is a *meitzar ha-tzibbur*, a menace to the community as a whole, *mesirah* is permissible.[5] He was likely referring to instances in which non-Jews attacked the Jewish community as a whole for the reprehensible action of one of its members; in that case, the member could be turned over to civil authorities to avoid the larger threat to the Jewish community.

How does all of this relate to extraditing criminals from Israel? Responsum author Rabbi David Golinkin explains that if the State of Israel did not extradite Jews accused of crimes to other countries where a fair trial is expected, it could not expect other countries to extradite to Israel—with deleterious consequences. In 5747 (1987) the Va'ad Halakhah unanimously approved his responsum (summarized here). To read the full responsum in Hebrew, see http://www.responsafortoday.com/vol2/5.pdf.

Why Halakhah Requires Returning a Convicted Murderer to France

Various current Rabbinic voices have been raised to the effect that it is forbidden according to the halakhah to return a convicted murderer named William Nakash to France because there is a danger to his life in a French prison. A brief halakhic investigation will prove that not only is such a transfer not forbidden, but the halakhah actually requires it.

There are five precedents in the classical literature: three in the Bible, one in the Aggadah, and one in the Talmud Yerushalmi. Even though turning over the demanded person involved mortal danger to that person's life, in four of the five instances the requested individuals were turned over. (In at least two cases, it was with the person's clear consent; in one case he was killed first.) The single instance in which there was a refusal led to a terrible civil war and the deaths of tens of thousands. However, one might argue that in the above instances there was a physical danger to the general populace if the requested individual was not turned over—something which is clearly not the case with Nakash, who therefore need not be extradited.

Our response: Granted that neither Nakash, on the one hand, nor the State of Israel, on the other, is in physical danger. Nakash is being sought for imprisonment in France, not for judicial execution, and many French rabbis have testified that the French prison system is safe. On the other hand, even though lack of extradition will not endanger Israel physically, failure to extradite would create various actual dangers for the State of Israel: *Ḥillul Hashem* [desecration of God's Name and with it besmirching the reputation of God's People], danger to the rule of the law in the state of Israel, encouragement to Jewish lawbreakers all over the world to view Israel as a haven, damage to public morality, danger to Israel's legal status among the nations with which it has signed extradition agreements, and a danger to its own populace from this particular breaker of the law if he is permitted to run free. Thus, we are required to follow the majority of precedents and surrender the particular identified individual in the interest of the general welfare. (Note: This is not to be confused with a generalized demand from a hostile power "for one of you." The latter is to be thoroughly resisted.)

Throughout Jewish history many authorities have dealt with this issue on the basis of passages found in Tosefta and Yerushalmi *Terumot*. Most rule that a Jew may be handed over to gentiles to be executed even if he is only liable according to gentile law and even if he is not liable to death like Sheva ben Bichri (II Samuel 20:14–22). If this is the halakhah in a case of extradition for execution, it is certainly the halakhah when the criminal involved is only going to be imprisoned!

Part of the concept of Ḥillul Hashem created by a refusal to extradite would be the appearance of condoning the killing of non-Jews by Jews. And so, turning William Nakash over to French judicial authorities is thoroughly in accordance with the demands of *halakhah* and raises Israel's moral stature in the world. It is an act of *Kiddush Hashem*, the sanctification of God's Name in the world.

Responsum on the Conscription of Women into the Israel Defense Forces

Some countries do not require either men or women to serve in the army during peacetime (e.g., the United States); some require men but not women to serve in the army for a period of time (e.g., Switzerland); but Israel, which has been in an actual or technical state of war with one or more of its neighbors since its founding, drafts both men and women. The required length of service for men, however, is longer than for women, and once men have completed their required army service, they alone are also subject to reserve duty until they are in their midfifties.

Ḥaredi (ultra-Orthodox) rabbis have argued that women should not be drafted at all for three reasons: (1) women should not wear the same dress (meaning uniforms and guns) as men, based on Deuteronomy 22:5; (2) women serving with men in the army will lead to sexual licentiousness; (3) the verse from Psalm 45:14, "All the honor of the daughter of the king is inside," which they interpret to mean that a woman's place is not in communal activities such as war. As a result, they call for one of three outcomes, in descending order of preference: (1) no drafting of women; (2) having women serve only in auxiliary and not combat roles and in separate units from men; (3) not drafting ultra-Orthodox women, in deference to the way ultra-Orthodox rabbis understand Jewish law. (Modern Orthodox women do serve in the Israel Defense Forces.)

In his responsum, unanimously approved in 5747 (1987) and summarized here, Rabbi Robert Harris addresses each of these contentions. To read the full responsum in Hebrew, with its accompanying references to sources, see http://www.responsafortoday.com/vol2/7.pdf.

The Service in the Army of Israel

The number of girls who identify themselves as "religious" and thus do not serve in the army is increasing. Further, the opinions of rabbis are heard that state that not only is it not proper for girls to serve, but that the *halakhah* forbids such service. What is the *halakhah* with reference to the service of girls in the Army of Israel?

The Mishnah (and Maimonides) clearly indicates that women go to war. What is not entirely clear is whether their intended service is to include the front line, or is to be restricted to behind-the-line auxiliary services. Such mandatory service is restricted to a *milḥemet mitzvah*—a "commanded war"—such as a war for the defense of the State of Israel, as opposed to *milḥemet reshut*, an "optional war"—such as a war for imperialistic aggrandizement. There remain certain specific problems having to do with aspects of the relationship between men and women.

May women carry weapons? There is the prohibition against women wearing men's clothing. It is argued that this prohibition forbids women to carry arms. The fact is that women are prohibited from wearing clothing or jewelry that are unique to men in that particular locale (the obverse is equally prohibited to men). Moreover, this prohibition holds true only in a context that could lead to forbidden sexual acts or idol worship. However, for protection against sun or storm women may wear articles of clothing that normally are associated with men. Thus, this is surely no valid objection to the carrying of arms by women. It does not mitigate against a woman's modesty and honor to carry arms and serve in the army.

It is argued that there are special dangers in men and women being thrown together in battle situations even more than in the army generally.

While it seems to us that there may be some validity to such concern, it applies equally to routine situations of modern living, at university, at work, in all kinds of situations throughout contemporary society. Various options present themselves; it is up to the individual to strive to hold appropriate moral standards within the framework of the *halakhah*. We do not find that army life presents any greater danger to morality than the modern world generally.

"The honor of the King's daughter is best maintained inside." Some understand this as favoring the isolation of women as the ideal, with special kinds of units, special kinds of service, and alternative service as minimally acceptable compromises in the interest of hoping to maintain moral standards. We can find no *halakhic* basis for this, and we most vehemently find no basis for discriminating among different categories of women ("religious" and "non-religious") for different categories of service. The basic situation is that of *milḥemet mitzvah* — a "commanded war" — for which the obligation to serve applies to women as well as men: all women and all men. That is the *halakhic* requirement as we understand it.

Responsum on the Conscription of Yeshivah Students into the Israel Defense Forces

As he prepared to declare the State of Israel's independence on May 14, 1948, David Ben-Gurion desperately wanted the entire Jewish population to participate in this momentous occasion. To induce the Orthodox to join in both the declaration and the effort to repel the Arab armies already amassing to destroy the state, Ben-Gurion granted military exemptions to students studying in Orthodox seminaries. A secular Jew, he thought that Orthodoxy would disappear in a generation or two, and, in any case, only a few hundred men had to be exempted in 1948.

This military exemption became the status quo after the War of Independence. Contrary to Ben-Gurion's prediction, however, nowadays thousands of ultra-Orthodox seminary students take advantage of it, their numbers increasing every year. Furthermore, they do not serve in the reserve duty that is required of men for some weeks each year until a man reaches his fifties.

The Modern Orthodox have created *yeshivot hesder,* in which young men have a year for Jewish study after high school and some additional study time during their mandatory three years of service. Many of the young men then enroll in officer training programs and serve as officers for some years beyond the mandatory minimum. They also participate in reserve duty.

In 2014 the Israeli government enacted legislation to remove the exemption over several years in gradual steps. Seminary students would be required to serve either in the army or in an accepted alternative form of service to the state, along with all other men their age. But as the new law took effect, riots ensued. Furthermore, the army itself was unhappy about the prospect of training these new recruits for several reasons. The ultra-Orthodox students had not been schooled in relevant secular subjects such as mathematics and technology. Moreover, most of the students were affiliated with anti-Zionist groups that believed the State of Israel was just another state (at best) or (at worst) a usurpation of God's privilege to decide when to bring the Messiah and, along with him, a restoration of the Jewish People to their homeland under Jewish rule.

In 2015 the newly elected government, whose ruling coalition had to include the ultra-Orthodox parties to secure a majority in the Knesset (Israel's Parliament), abolished the draft for ultra-Orthodox Jews. For now, it seems, resolution of this issue will completely depend on political outcomes—specifically, on whether future Israeli governments must include the ultra-Orthodox parties to form a governing coalition.

In his 1987 responsum (summarized here), Rabbi Reuven Hammer concludes that according to Jewish law, yeshivah students should not be exempted from the draft. Although the Torah specifies some exemptions from military service (Deuteronomy 20:1–9), he points out that the Rabbis interpreted the exclusions to apply only to optional wars waged to expand the borders of Israel and not to defensive wars, which all the modern state's wars have been. Furthermore, Leviticus 19:16 demands, "Do not stand idly by the blood of your brother," which the Talmud (*b. Sanhedrin* 73a) interprets to impose a duty on all Jews to rescue fellow

Jews in danger. Finally, the duty to save lives, according to the Talmud (*b. Sanhedrin* 74a), supersedes all but three other duties, and studying is not one of the exceptions. The Va'ad Halakhah unanimously approved his responsum in 5747 (1987). To read the full responsum in Hebrew, see http://www.responsafortoday.com/vol2/8.pdf.

Is IDF Service an Obligation for Every Jew in Israel?

Is service in Zahal [Israel Defense Forces] today an obligation for every Jew in Israel, or may one engaged in sacred studies request an exemption in order to devote all his time to such studies? In the State of Israel today, despite our difficult security situation, many, many thousands of young men and older men have done no military or paramilitary service whatever. The number increases from year to year. Among them are those who do not recognize the State, some who are newly religious, and others who recognize the State but feel themselves totally exempt on account of religious studies. The government permits and supports this arrangement. Our question: Does the halakhah justify this?

As a general principle, the Torah commands the responsibility of military service to every Israelite. There are temporary exceptions for those who are at a particular point in their lives and have not had the opportunity to savor specified major personal developments. And the one who is fearful—who is psychologically unfit—is exempt. The Rabbis tended to nullify the exemptions. Thus they saw the exemptions as temporarily waiving frontline duty only; there remained the obligation to perform auxiliary support services. They further restricted the exemption as applying only in the instance of an optional war. The commanded war, the necessary war, voids all exemptions. Surely *pikuaḥ nefesh*—the saving of a life—is a commandment of the highest priority. In today's world, service in Zahal, the Army of Israel, is an act of *pikuaḥ nefesh*. It is at the same time a concretization of the commandment "Do not stand idly by the blood of your neighbor."

During the Biblical period one may understand that Levites and Priests as ritual functionaries and teachers were exempt from normal military duties. But even if there were such a broad exemption, it does not appear to have extended to a period of warfare. Among the commentators, some reject this approach to blanket exemption altogether. Others would apply it only to rare outstanding individuals — not as a basis for general exemption of large numbers. There is a Talmudic approach that would exempt "rabbis" from some kinds of routine obligation. We surely do not see this as a basis for exempting large numbers of students from the commandment of saving Israel from its enemies.

Conclusion: Service in Zahal is a *halakhic* duty incumbent on every Jew living in the State of Israel. Whoever sees himself as engaged in important religious work has an even greater obligation to set an example by military service. Only in this way can he be properly prepared effectively to participate in a commanded war for the safety of the State of Israel. Not to do this involves violation of three major mitzvot: participation in a commanded war for defense of the State of Israel; "Do not stand idly by the blood of your neighbor"; and the saving of human life. To shirk this duty is to violate the *halakhah*.

Responsum on Riding to the Synagogue on Shabbat

The Va'ad Halkahah has taken a different position from that of the CJLS on the question of riding to the synagogue on the Sabbath.

In 1950 the CJLS approved a ruling by Rabbis Morris Adler, Jacob Agus, and Theodore (Tuvia) Friedman, three rabbis of large Conservative congregations in the United States who were focused on revitalizing Shabbat observance at a time when many Jews had moved to the suburbs and no longer lived within walking distance of a synagogue. Examining what happens in the combustion chamber of an automobile, the rabbis determined that the driving violations were based not on the Torah's laws but rather on Rabbinic extensions of the law, and those Rabbinic prohibitions needed to be balanced against the commandment to observe Shabbat, which has higher Torah status. Furthermore, because Shabbat observance is inherently a communal experience, if people who live beyond walking distance to a synagogue do not ride to attend services, they are unlikely to observe Shabbat while staying at home. The rabbis therefore ruled that even though it is preferable to walk to synagogue on Shabbat, if Jews could honestly say to themselves that they would not attend synagogue without having driven there, whether because of distance, weather, or handicap, they should drive to the synagogue on Shabbat.

Much has been written about this decision since its approval by the CJLS. Its detractors say that it ruined the phenomenon of a Shabbat community in which people deliberately choose to live within walking distance of one another and of their synagogue so that they can share Shabbat meals together as well as participate in services without driving. Others maintain that its legal analysis of what happens in the combustion chamber of an automobile is flawed. Its defenders maintain that it faced the reality of contemporary living conditions; any ruling that had preserved the integrity of Jewish law would simply have been unrealistic and ignored. The controversy continues today in both the Diaspora and Israel.

The Va'ad Halakhah responsum of 5750 (1990) asked a similar question to the American one but positioned it within an Israeli context: "There is no Masorti synagogue in Petach Tikvah, where we reside, and my wife will not attend an Orthodox synagogue since it makes her feel inferior. Is it permissible for us to ride to a Masorti synagogue in Hod Hasharon or Ramat Aviv in order to participate in the mitzvah of public prayer on Shabbat?"

In his ruling (summarized here), Rabbi David Golinkin criticizes the earlier CJLS ruling on legal grounds. What happens in a car engine when someone is driving, he says, violates not only Rabbinic commandments but also biblical ones, and therefore a Jew may not drive to the synagogue on Shabbat. (The appendix, however, suggests that it is permissible to hire a non-Jew to drive a Shabbat bus or taxi that will transport the elderly or the handicapped to the synagogue, providing that the bus does not leave the city limits.) To read the full ruling in Hebrew, with its notes to sources, see http://www.responsafortoday.com/vol4/3.pdf.

Practically speaking, Rabbi Golinkin's ruling may be more realistic to enact in Israel, where the vast majority of Jews live in large apartment buildings clustered close to one another and synagogues tend to be within walking distance, certainly more so than one generally finds in the Diaspora. Moreover, as Rabbi Golinkin notes, in Israel very few people work on Saturdays, and any Israeli can open a prayer book in Hebrew and pray. Notably, Rabbi Theodore (Tuvia) Friedman, who coauthored the American ruling, also endorsed this one, suggesting that, at least in his opinion, different circumstances warranted a different ruling.

Open to question is whether the Va'ad Halakhah and the CJLS may reconsider their respective rulings given the advent of new automotive technology. Fully electrically powered automobiles might avert the gasoline ignition issue, and self-driving cars presumably could be programed before Shabbat to drive to the synagogue and back at specified times.

Why Riding to the Synagogue on Shabbat Is Forbidden

. . . We have come to re-examine the lenient decision from the United States of 1950 in light of the conditions in Israel forty years later. It is clear that the reasons for that leniency do not apply. In those days most Jews in the United States worked on Shabbat, did not pray in general, did not know how to pray alone at home, and lived at great distances from the nearest synagogue. Thus, prayer at the synagogue on Shabbat was the only remnant of their Shabbat observance. This is not the case in Israel today, where almost no one works on Shabbat, where every Jew can open a siddur and pray if he so desires, and where there is a synagogue in every neighborhood. We therefore agree with the minority that it is forbidden to ride to the synagogue on Shabbat.

From a *halakhic* point of view, riding to the synagogue on Shabbat is forbidden for the following reasons:

1. Kindling a fire is a biblical prohibition (Exodus 35:3) and turning the key in the ignition creates sparks.
2. It is forbidden as a *shevut*, or rabbinic prohibition, lest the car break down and he [the driver] be forced to fix it, and then he may transgress both biblical and rabbinic prohibitions.
3. It is forbidden to go more than 2,000 cubits outside of your own city on Shabbat (*Eruvin* 49b). Therefore, in this specific case it is forbidden to travel from Petah Tikvah to Hod Hasharon or Ramat Aviv.

4. Any item that may not be used on Shabbat is considered "*muktzeh*" [forbidden to touch, lest it be used] and may therefore not be touched or carried. When one drives a car, one normally touches a wallet, money, a credit card and other forms of "*muktzeh.*" In addition, one frequently buys gas, which is also forbidden on Shabbat. It is therefore forbidden to drive on Shabbat, because it will lead to carrying and touching *muktzeh.*

5. Another type of "*shevut*" is "*uvdin d'ol*," or weekday activities. In other words, Shabbat should not look and feel like a weekday. There is nothing more weekday-like than driving a car. *Shevut* is also an activity that may lead to biblically forbidden labors. Driving may lead to biblical prohibitions, such as carrying outside of the *eruv*, commercial and agricultural transport, writing, building, fishing, and more. Thus even if driving were biblically permitted, it would be forbidden because of *shevut.*

6. Driving is also forbidden because of "*lo pelug*," which means that the rabbis do not usually decree partial prohibitions. This is because they were familiar with human nature. If we allow driving to the synagogue, many people will think it is permissible to drive everywhere on Shabbat, and, indeed, that is what happened in the United States.

7. Rabbi Moshe Sofer forbade inter-city train travel on Shabbat because of physical and mental stress. There is no question that driving a car entails physical and mental stress, which are not in keeping with the spirit of Shabbat.

8. Public prayer is not a biblical requirement. It is either a rabbinic requirement or simply a recommended form of prayer and can therefore not push aside the biblical prohibition of starting a car on Shabbat. Furthermore, many rabbis have ruled that public prayer on Shabbat does not even push aside a *shevut* or rabbinic prohibition, so even if driving is only a rabbinic prohibition, it would not be set aside for the sake of public prayer.

9. The Masorti movement wishes to create *kehillot* (communities), not just synagogues. It is impossible to create a community when every family lives a great distance from every other family, and in order to create a community that observes the Shabbat together, its members must live in close proximity to each other.

10. In light of the above, driving to the synagogue on Shabbat is a "mitzvah achieved through transgression," which is forbidden (*Berakhot* 47b, etc.).

There are, however, three possible solutions to the question that was asked:

1. Efforts should be renewed to found a Masorti synagogue in Petah Tikvah.
2. Just because a *meḥitzah* [separate seating for men and women] is not necessary does not mean that it is forbidden. We should not be as intolerant as those who refuse to pray in our synagogues. It is better to walk to an Orthodox synagogue on Shabbat than to drive to a Masorti synagogue.
3. It is also possible to move near a Masorti synagogue. This may be an expensive or inconvenient solution, but Jews have traditionally made great sacrifices in order to observe *mitzvot*. If people move to another city for the sake of a good job or a good school, why shouldn't they move for the sake of living near the *kehillah* [community] of their choice?

Suggestions for Further Reading

The responsa of the Va'ad Halakhah in Israel, available in full Hebrew text and in English summaries, are at http://www.responsafortoday.com.

Books published by the Schechter Institute of Jewish Studies on applied *halakhah* and on women in Judaism are listed at http://www.schechter.edu/book.aspx?ID=97 under the link "Books Catalogue."

Epilogue
The Ideal Conservative Jew

In the concluding section of *Emet Ve-Emunah*, the official text of Conservative Judaism, its authors defined the characteristics and acts that mark an ideal Conservative Jew, laying out what it fully means to live a comprehensive Conservative Jewish life, encompassing rituals, ethics, interpersonal relations, social action, and family and community responsibilities. (In practice, individual Conservative Jews may choose to express some meaningful components more than others.)

How does *Emet Ve-Emunah*'s description of an ideal Conservative Jew compare to what you as a reader imagine the Orthodox, Reform, and Reconstructionist movements might each consider ideal Jewish thought and practice? Does this Jewish ideal cause you to question whether Conservative Judaism is too demanding to uphold in your life—or does it challenge you to expand and deepen your Jewish commitments?

… Three characteristics mark the ideal Conservative Jew. First, he or she is a *willing* Jew, whose life echoes the dictum, "Nothing human or Jewish is alien to me." This willingness involves not only a commitment to observe the mitzvot and to advance Jewish concerns, but to refract all aspects of life through the prism of one's own Jewishness. That person's life pulsates with the rhythms of daily worship and Shabbat and Yom Tov. The moral imperatives of our tradition impel that individual to universal concern and deeds of social justice. The content of that person's professional dealing and communal involvements is shaped by the values of our faith and conditioned by the observance of kashrut and of Shabbat and the holidays. That person's home is filled with Jewish books, art, music and ritual objects. Particularly in view of the increasing instability of the modern family, the Jewish home must be sustained and guided by the ethical insights of our heritage.

The second mark of the ideal Conservative Jew is that he or she is a *learning* Jew. One who cannot read Hebrew is denied the full exaltation of our Jewish worship and literary heritage. One who is ignorant of our classics cannot be affected by their message. One who is not acquainted with contemporary Jewish thought and events will be blind to the challenges and opportunities that lie before us. Jewish learning is a lifelong quest through which we integrate Jewish and general knowledge for the sake of personal enrichment, group creativity, and world transformation.

Finally, the ideal Conservative Jew is a *striving* Jew. No matter the level at which one starts, no matter the heights of piety and knowledge one attains, no one can perform all 613 mitzvot or acquire all Jewish knowledge. What is needed is an openness to those observances one has yet to perform and the desire to grapple with those issues and texts one has yet to confront. Complacency is the mother of stagnation and the antithesis of Conservative Judaism.

Given our changing world, finality and certainty are illusory at best, destructive at worst. Rather than claiming to have found a goal at the end of the road, the ideal Conservative Jew is a traveler walking purposefully towards "God's holy mountain."

Being a committed Conservative Jew entails hard work. Conservative Judaism began and remains true to fully integrating tradition with modernity, as our ancestors did in their most creative times and places. It requires judgment to determine when to live by the tradition alone, when to live by modernity alone, and, in most cases, when and how to blend tradition with modernity. To make these judgments, one must know both the Jewish tradition and the modern world, and one must possess both the skills and experience to know when and how to combine them wisely.

As hard as this is, practicing Judaism authentically, thoughtfully, and creatively, with, as the Torah demands, "all your heart, all your soul, and all your might" (Deuteronomy 6:5), is not only the way the Jewish tradition would have us live as Jews but also the way that is most likely to enrich our lives, giving us roots, direction, communal ties, beauty, and purpose.

Appendix

Institutions of the Conservative Movement

Today's Conservative/Masorti movement is supported and coordinated by a group of academic centers, professional organizations, and national and international organizations, all of which share common goals and ideology—although they sometimes interpret and apply them differently—and cooperate in various formal and informal ways.

Academic Centers of the Conservative Movement

Jewish Theological Seminary of America

Includes an undergraduate college; professional programs for training Conservative rabbis, cantors, and teachers; and master's and doctoral programs to prepare scholars of Judaica. Auxiliary programs encompass a supplementary high school program (Prozdor); Ramah camps in Wisconsin, Pennsylvania, Massachusetts, New York, Ontario, Georgia, and Colorado; the Jewish Museum (1109 Fifth Avenue in New York); the Finkelstein Institute for Religious and Social Studies; the Melton Research Center; the Bernstein and Brand Foundation counseling centers; and *The Eternal Light* radio and television programs. 3080 Broadway, New York NY 10027. http://www.jtsa.edu.

American Jewish University (formerly University of Judaism)

Offers an undergraduate liberal arts college and professional programs to educate Conservative rabbis, educators, and managers of nonprofit institutions such as synagogues and communal and social service agencies. Auxiliary programs include two Camps Ramah in California; Brandeis-Bardin campus programs such as Camp Alonim for children and the Brandeis-Bardin Institute for college and graduate students; the Whizin Center for Continuing Education, offering adult education courses in Judaica, the arts, marriage preparation and strengthening, and personal development; and the Wagner Human Services Certificate Program, training volunteers to assist people with life challenges. 15600 Mulholland Drive, Los Angeles CA 90077. http://www.aju.edu.

Schechter Institute of Jewish Studies

Includes a rabbinical school and master's programs for training Jewish educators. Auxiliary programs encompass branch campuses in Tel Aviv and the Galilee, the Tali school system to enrich Jewish studies in Israel's secular school system, the Schocken Institute for Jewish Research, and adult education courses throughout Israel and in the Ukraine, as well as a Ramah camp in the Ukraine. 4 Avraham Granot Street, P.O. Box 16080, 91160 Neve Granot, Jerusalem, Israel. http://www.schechter.edu.

Seminario Rabínico Latinoamericano Marshall T. Meyer

Offers programs to prepare Conservative rabbis, cantors, educators, and volunteer leaders to serve Latin American synagogues. José Hernández 1750, C1426EOD Buenos Aires, Argentina. http://www.seminariorabinico.org.

Conservative Yeshiva in Jerusalem

Provides serious Jewish learning on an egalitarian, pluralistic basis for both seminary students and other adults wishing to deepen their knowledge of Jewish texts and culture and their involvement and leadership in the world Jewish community. Fuchsberg Jerusalem Center, 8 Agron Street, P.O. Box 7456, Jerusalem, Israel. http://www.conservativeyeshiva.org.

Zacharias Frankel College

In coordination with the Ziegler School of Rabbinic Studies at the American Jewish University and the University of Potsdam, the Zacharias Frankel College educates students to serve as Masorti/Conservative rabbis for European Jewish communities. P.O.B. 120852, 10598 Berlin, Germany. http://zacharias-frankel-college.de.

Professional Organizations of the Conservative Movement

Rabbinical Assembly

As an international organization of more than sixteen hundred Conservative rabbis (about three hundred of them women), the Rabbinical Assembly runs activities for the educational, social, and professional welfare of its members; determines the Conservative interpretation of Jewish law through its Committee on Jewish Law and Standards; coordinates rabbinic efforts on behalf of Israel and world Jewry; sponsors social action projects; and publishes books and other materials for use by rabbis and Conservative laypeople, including the prayer books *Mahzor Lev Shalem* and *Siddur Lev Shalem* and the Torah commentary *Etz Hayim*. 3080 Broadway, New York NY 10027. http://www.rabbinicalassembly.org.

Cantors Assembly, Jewish Educators Assembly, Jewish Youth Directors Association, and North American Association of Synagogue Executives

These professional organizations provide programs to augment their members' skills and to insure the highest standards among the professionals serving congregations. Each association cooperates with the United Synagogue of Conservative Judaism (see the description in the following section) in operating a placement service to aid congregations in obtaining qualified personnel. Cantors Assembly: http://www.cantors.org; Jewish Educators Assembly: https://jewisheducators.org; Jewish Youth Directors Association: http://www.jyda.org; NAASE: North American Association of Synagogue Executives: http://www.naase.org. (The acronym NAASE means "We will do" or, in Hebrew, "Let's do," fitting for the professionals tasked with making sure that a synagogue runs efficiently and smoothly.)

Lay Organizations of the Conservative Movement

United Synagogue of Conservative Judaism

According to its official vision statement, USCJ is "a community of kehillot—sacred communities—committed to a dynamic Judaism that is learned and passionate, authentic and pluralistic, joyful and accessible, egalitarian and traditional. . . . The United Synagogue of Conservative Judaism creates the spiritual, intellectual and managerial network that enables each of our kehillot to fulfill its sacred mission and connects all our kehillot with a common sense of community, shared mission and purpose." Its mission is "to transform and strengthen our kehillot in their effort to inspire meaningful prayer, sustain a culture of lifelong Jewish learning, nurture religious and spiritual growth, promote excellence in kehillah leadership, ensure educational excellence, . . . engage the next generation of kehillah leadership, [and] encourage and build new kehillot." 120 Broadway, Suite 1540, New York NY 10271-0016. http://www.uscj.org.

Women's League for Conservative Judaism

The parent body for more than five hundred synagogue women's groups in North America and Israel offers materials and programs designed to expand members' knowledge and involvement; is active in national, Israel, and world affairs; supports the Jewish Theological Seminary, the Ziegler School of Rabbinic Studies, and the Schechter Institute through its Torah Fund campaign; and serves as an accredited, nongovernmental observer at the United Nations. 475 Riverside Drive, Suite 820, New York NY 10115. http://www.wlcj.org.

Federation of Jewish Men's Clubs

Unifies some 250 Men's Clubs affiliated with Conservative synagogues worldwide and promotes appreciation of the Jewish heritage with involvement in Jewish communal and synagogue life: supplies mezuzot and tefillin and teaches men how to use tefillin in weekday morning services; publishes guides to holidays, alternative Shabbat experiences, and mourning rites; posts a weekly haftarah commentary; sponsors a Hebrew literacy program that has helped more than one hundred thousand people participate in Jewish worship; supports children with special needs at several Ramah camps; runs leadership training programs for both rabbis and lay leaders; translates and adapts educational materials into French, Spanish, and Hebrew to support the Masorti movement worldwide; and more. 475 Riverside Drive, Suite 832, New York NY 10115. http://www.fjmc.org.

World Council of Synagogues (Masorti Olami)

Coordinates the efforts of Conservative synagogues in twenty-six countries worldwide. 820 Second Avenue, 10th Floor, New York NY, 10017-4504, with additional offices in Jerusalem, Buenos Aires, and New York. http://www.masortiolami.org. In Israel and Latin America (especially Argentina but also Chile and Brazil), the synagogues either individually or cooperatively run seven- to fifteen-day summer camps and three- to four-day winter camps as part of Noam, an acronym for Noar Masorti (Masorti Youth). Some of those camps are called "Ramah" and some are not.

"Joint Commissions" of the Conservative Movement

These generally include representatives from several arms of the movement:

Joint Commission on Jewish Education
Joint Commission on Social Action
Joint Placement Commission
Joint Prayer Book Commission
Committee on Jewish Law and Standards, which, although a
    committee of the Rabbinical Assembly, includes members
    recommended by the president of the United Synagogue of Con-
    servative Judaism and the chancellor of the Seminary

Source Acknowledgments

1. *EMUNAH*

Bradley Shavit Artson. *God of Becoming and Relationship: The Dynamic Nature of Process Theology*, xv–xvi and 17–19 on God. Woodstock VT: Jewish Lights, 2013. By permission of Turner Publishing.

Elliot N. Dorff. *Knowing God: Jewish Journeys to the Unknowable*, 154–58. Northvale NJ: Jason Aronson, 1992. By permission of Roman and Littlefield.

Elliot N. Dorff. "In Search of God." In *Contemporary Jewish Theology: A Reader*, edited by Elliot N. Dorff and Louis E. Newman, 112–13. New York: Oxford University Press, 1999. By permission of Oxford University Press USA.

Amy Eilberg. "'Where Is God for You?': A Jewish Feminist Faith." In *Lifecycles, Volume 2: Jewish Women on Biblical Themes in Contemporary Life*, edited by Debra Orenstein and Jane Rachel Litman, 105–10. Woodstock VT: Jewish Lights, 1997. By permission of Turner Publishing.

Tamar Elad-Appelbaum. "The Radical Divinity." In *Jewish Theology in Our Time: A New Generation Explores the Foundations and Future of Jewish Belief*, edited by Elliot J. Cosgrove, 162–63. Woodstock VT: Jewish Lights, 2010. By permission of Turner Publishing.

Arthur Green. *Radical Judaism: Rethinking God and Tradition*, 1–5. New Haven CT: Yale University Press, 2010. Reprinted by permission of Yale University Press.

Excerpt(s) from *When Bad Things Happen to Good People* by Harold S. Kushner, copyright © 1981 by Harold S. Kushner. Used by permission of Schocken Books, an imprint of the Knopf Doubleday Publishing Group, a division of Penguin Random House LLC. All rights reserved. Any third-party use of this material, outside of this publication, is prohibited.

Excerpts from pages 22–25 from *For Those Who Can't Believe: Overcoming the Obstacles to Faith* by Harold M. Schulweis. Copyright © 1994 by Harold M. Schulweis. Reprinted by permission of HarperCollins Publishers. Applies only to English-language editions.

2. TEFILLAH

Bradley Shavit Artson. *God of Becoming and Relationship: The Dynamic Nature of Process Theology*, 125–29. Woodstock VT: Jewish Lights, 2013. By permission of Turner Publishing.

Mordecai M. Kaplan. *Judaism as a Civilization*, 346–48. New York: Macmillan, 1934. By permission of Reconstructionist Press.

Mordecai M. Kaplan. *Questions Jews Ask: Reconstructionist Answers*, 103–4, 105–6, 259–61. New York: Reconstructionist Press, 1956. By permission of Reconstructionist Press.

3. TALMUD TORAH

Arnold M. Eisen. *Conservative Judaism Today and Tomorrow*, 10–15. New York: Jewish Theological Seminary of America, 2015. Reprinted with the permission of The Jewish Theological Seminary of America.

4. HALAKHAH

Neil Gillman. *Doing Jewish Theology: God, Torah, and Israel in Modern Judaism*, 3–4. Woodstock VT: Jewish Lights, 2008. By permission of Turner Publishing.

Joel Roth. *The Halakhic Process: A Systematic Analysis*, 7–10, 11–12, 231–34. New York: Jewish Theological Seminary of America, 1986. Reprinted with the permission of The Jewish Theological Seminary of America.

12. AM YISRAEL

Arnold M. Eisen. *Conservative Judaism Today and Tomorrow*, 1–3. New York: Jewish Theological Seminary of America, 2015. Reprinted with the permission of The Jewish Theological Seminary of America.

13. TZIYYONUT

Arnold Eisen. "Zionism." CJ: *Kolot Magazine* 5, no. 2 (Winter 2011–12 / Chanukah 5772): 48–49. New York: Federation of Jewish Men's Clubs, United Synagogue for Conservative Judaism, and Women's League for Conservative Judaism. By permission of the United Synagogue for Conservative Judaism.

Notes

INTRODUCTION

1. Alexander Kohut, *American Hebrew* 25 (February 5, 1886), 194–95, cited in Davis, *Emergence*, 235.

2. Alexander Kohut, *The Ethics of the Fathers*, 3, 14–17, cited in Davis, *Emergence*, 222–23.

3. Alexander Kohut, "Science and Judaism," *Jewish Messenger* 59 (May 7, 1886), 4, cited in Davis, *Emergence*, 289–90.

4. *M. Sotah* 7:1; see *b. Berakhot* 13a, 15a, 40b; *b. Megillah* 17b; *b. Shevuot* 39a; Mishneh Torah, *Laws of Reciting the Shema* 2:10; *Laws of Blessings* 1:6; Shulḥan Arukh, *Oraḥ Ḥayyim* 62:2, 101:4.

5. The phrase occurs only in the Jerusalem Talmud (*j. Bava Metz'ia* 7:1 [11b] and *j. Yevamot* 12:1 [12c]), but the principle is used in the Babylonian Talmud and the later codes as well: cf. Menachem Elon, "Minhag," in *Encyclopedia Judaica*, vol. 12, cols. 5–26, esp. cols. 13–19. As Elon points out, custom could add to Jewish law in many areas and change it in monetary matters, but it could not permit that which had been forbidden in ritual areas. Only a formal *takkanah* (revision) by the rabbis could do that.

6. Gordis, "Authority in Jewish Law."

7. For example, see the papers reprinted in part 2 of Waxman, *Tradition and Change*, the earliest of which is by Louis Finkelstein, entitled "The Things That Unite Us," from the *Proceedings of the Rabbinical Assembly*, 1927. The earliest full book on Conservative ideology, *Conservative Judaism: An American Philosophy*, was written by Robert Gordis and Josiah Derby in 1945, and it has been followed by several others; see note 9 below.

8. See, for example, Levine, "Needed." See also Dorff, *Conservative Judaism*, chap. 5.

9. Some prime examples of books on the philosophy of Conservative Judaism written by individual authors include the following in chronological order: Gordis and Derby, *Conservative Judaism: An American Philosophy* (1945); Waxman, ed., *Tradition and Change: The Development of Conservative Judaism* (1958); Dorff, *Conservative Judaism: Our Ancestors to Our Descendants* (1977 ed.); Siegel and Gertel, *Conservative Judaism and Jewish Law* (1977); Gordis and Gelb, *Understanding Conservative Judaism* (1978); Siegel and Gertel, *God in the Teachings of Conservative Judaism* (1985); Gillman, *Conservative Judaism: The New Century* (1993); Schorsch, *The Sacred Cluster: The Core Values of Conservative Judaism* (1995); Dorff, *Conservative Judaism: Our Ancestors to Our Descendants*, rev. 2nd ed. (1996); and Eisen, *Conservative Judaism Today and Tomorrow* (2015).

   In addition, the following books about Conservative Judaism, again in chronological order, while dealing with Conservative Jewish beliefs and practices to some degree, are more historical or sociological in nature: Sklare, *Conservative Judaism: An American Religious Movement* (1955); Davis, *The Emergence of Conservative Judaism: The Historical School in Nineteenth Century America* (1963); Rosenblum, *Conservative Judaism: A Contemporary History* (1983); Nadell, *Conservative Judaism in America: A Biographical Dictionary and Sourcebook* (1988); Elazar and Geffen, *The Conservative Movement in Judaism: Dilemmas and Opportunities* (2000); Wertheimer, *Jews in the Center: Conservative Synagogues and Their Members* (2000); Fierstien, ed., *A Century of Commitment: One Hundred Years of the Rabbinical Assembly* (2000); and Michael R. Cohen, *The Birth of Conservative Judaism: Solomon Schechter's Disciples and the Creation of an American Religious Movement* (2012).

1. EMUNAH

1. Jacobs, *Principles*, 96–117. Rabbi Louis Jacobs (1920–2006) founded Conservative/ Masorti Judaism in England in 1964. — E.N.D.

2. For the covenant with Noah: Gen. 9. For the covenant with Abraham: Gen. 15, 17. For the covenant with Isaac: Gen. 26:2–5. For the covenant with Jacob: Gen. 28:13–15.

3. For a description of at least some of what is entailed in *tikkun olam*, see Dorff, *The Way into Tikkun Olam*.

4. *Sifra*, Kedoshim, 4:12; *Genesis Rabbah* 24:7.

5. B. *Shabbat* 31a. A. Cohen cites "Professor Kittel," who argues convincingly that even though some people today might derive different lessons from this negative formulation of the value than from the positive form in the Torah (and cited by Jesus), the people of his time would have derived the same meaning from both formulations; see A. Cohen, *Everyman's Talmud*, 214. He cites an instructive article on this by King, "The 'Negative' Golden Rule," who traces it to several pre-Christian sources, including Tobit 4:15, which Hillel may well have been quoting.

6. *Sifra*, Beḥukkotai 7:5; B. *Shavu'ot* 39a; *Numbers Rabbah* 10:5; *Tanḥuma* (Warsaw), Netzavim 2:2; *Tanḥuma* (Buber) 5.

7. M. *Avot* 2:4.

8. B. *Bava Mezi'a* 59b. Examples include Exod. 22:20, 23:9; Lev. 19:33, 25:17; and Deut. 24:14–15.

9. *Tanḥuma*, Mishpatim 1, citing Psalm 99:4.

10. *Pesikta Rabbati* xxvi, ed. Buber, p. 166b.

2. TEFILLAH

1. Kadushin, *Organic Thinking*, 237–40; and, more extensively, Kadushin, *Worship and Ethics*, 13–17, 163–98.

2. Gordis, introduction to *Sabbath and Festival Prayer Book*, viii.

3. Gordis, introduction, ix–x.

4. These include the prayer books by Rabbis Mordecai Kaplan and Eugene Kohn, *Sabbath Prayer Book* (1945), and *High Holiday Prayer Book* (1948); Ben Zion Bokser, *Ha-Siddur, The Prayer Book: Weekday, Sabbath and Festival* (1957); Sidney Greenberg and Jonathan D. Levine, *Mahzor Hadash: The New Mahzor for Rosh Hashanah and Yom Kippur* (1977), and *Siddur Hadash for Sabbaths and Festivals* (1992); and David A. Teutsch, *Kol Haneshamah for Sabbaths and Festivals* (1996), and *Kol Haneshamah Mahzor for Rosh Hashanah and Yom Kippur*. The first and last on this list were produced for Reconstructionist synagogues that were officially part of the Conservative movement until 1968, but Rabbi Teutsch is a member of the Rabbinical Assembly and thus counts as a Conservative rabbi as well.

4. HALAKHAH

1. Dorff, *For the Love*, chap. 4.—E.N.D.

2. For more on the process of creating *Emet Ve-Emunah*, see the introduction to this book.—E.N.D.

3. Elliot Dorff, the author of this volume, wrote another book, *The Unfolding Tradition: Philosophies of Jewish Law*, in which he describes and analyzes sixteen different theories of Jewish law that have been articulated by people affiliated with the Conservative/Masorti movement, together with excerpts written by the authors of each of those theories and a chapter comparing them to theories of thinkers to the right and left of the Conservative movement. Here we have room only for five Conservative theories, and then without the description and analysis in that book and with much shorter excerpts. Thus those interested in this subject may want to consult that book.—E.N.D.

4. Western philosophy beginning with Plato makes a sharp distinction between the body and the mind—so much so that the way that the two are connected is a stock issue in Western thought (the mind–body problem). Similarly, Christianity,

influenced heavily by Gnosticism, makes a sharp distinction between the body and the soul, with the ideal person (the priest, nun, or monk) denying the body as much as possible to cultivate the soul. Judaism acknowledges the distinction between our bodily functions and those of our soul; but, in sharp contrast to both Western thought and Christianity, it asserts the integration of body and soul. Here is one graphic illustration of that:

Antoninus said to Rabbi [Judah, the president, or "prince," of the Sanhedrin]: "The body and soul could exonerate themselves from judgment. How is this so? The body could say, 'The soul sinned, for from the day that it separated from me, lo, I am like a silent stone in the grave!' And the soul could say, 'The body is the sinner, for from the day that I separated from it, lo, I fly like a bird.'"

Rabbi [Judah] answered him: "I will tell you a parable. What is the matter like? It is like a king of flesh and blood who had a beautiful orchard, and in it was lovely, ripe fruit. He placed two guardians over it, one lame and the other blind. Said the lame man to the blind man: 'I see beautiful ripe fruit in the orchard. Come and carry me, and we will bring and eat them.' The lame man rode on the back of the blind man, they reached the fruit and ate it. After a while the owner of the orchard came and said to them, 'Where is my lovely fruit?' The lame man answered, 'Do I have legs to go?' The blind man answered, 'Do I have eyes to see?' What did the owner do? He placed the lame man on the back of the blind man and judged them as one. So also the Holy Blessed One brings the soul and throws it into the body and judges them as one." (B. *Sanhedrin* 91a–91b)

This interaction is not only a matter of personal responsibility: it is also at the heart of the Rabbis' recipe for a good life: "An excellent thing is the study of Torah combined with a worldly occupation, for the labor demanded by both of them causes sinful inclinations to be forgotten. All study of the Torah without work must, in the end, be futile and become the cause of sin" (M. *Avot [Ethics of the Fathers]* 2:1). For more on this, see Dorff, *Matters of Life and Death*, 20–26; and Dorff, *Love Your Neighbor and Yourself*, 20–26.

5. Psalm 145:9.
6. *Sifre Deuteronomy*, Ekev, on Deuteronomy 11:22.
7. B. *Sukkah* 14a.
8. This essay, excerpted in this book, began as a response to a challenge by Elliot Dorff in his course on theories of Jewish law in the Ziegler School of Rabbinic Studies at American Jewish University. He noted that although Jewish feminist scholars had produced theologies and new rituals, none had written a complete feminist theory of Jewish law, and he challenged anyone in the course to do so. Suskin took up that challenge through an independent study with Dorff the following year, and this essay is the product of that work. It was first published in Dorff's 2005 book, *The Unfolding Tradition*, 357–78. With the exception of Tamar

Ross' book, *Expanding the Palace of Torah: Orthodoxy and Feminism*, which was published in 2004, Suskin's essay is the very first such theory, and certainly the first written from a Conservative/Masorti viewpoint.

9. A *very* non-feminist argument in favor of complete equality of obligation might be that it is a *horaat shaah* [a decree of the hour, a temporary measure] in order to get men to fulfill their obligations!

10. Roth, "On the Ordination of Women as Rabbis."

5. P'SAK DIN

1. In an article I wrote in 1980, I noted that the English name "Conservative" invites misinterpretation, for English speakers hearing our name might well think that we are the most conservative (with a small *c*) in both religion and politics. I therefore proposed that we change our name in English to match our name in Hebrew—that is, that we call ourselves "Traditional Judaism." That name would not only have the advantage of avoiding such misinterpretations but also announce our agenda to people within the movement and outside it much more accurately and effectively. See Dorff, "Traditional Judaism."

2. See Halivni, "The Role."

3. See Finkelstein, *Jewish Self-Government*.

4. The word *teshuvah* may be familiar to readers from the High Holy Days, where it means "return [to God, or to the right path]," or, as sometimes translated, "repentance," from the Hebrew *lashuv*. Here it means "answer," from the Hebrew word *lehashiv*, meaning both "to return" an object to its owner and "to answer." The fact that *teshuvah* has all these meanings, however, should not be confusing, because the contexts in which they are used in these varying ways are quite different, and so the context will alert readers to the intended meaning.

5. The Committee on Jewish Law and Standards consists of twenty-five rabbis, fifteen of whom are chosen by the president of the Rabbinical Assembly directly, five of whom are recommended to the Rabbinical Assembly president by the chancellor of the Jewish Theological Seminary of America, and five of whom are recommended to the president of the Rabbinical Assembly by the president of the United Synagogue of Conservative Judaism (but all rabbis on the committee must be members of the Rabbinical Assembly, the professional organization of Conservative/Masorti rabbis). In addition, there are five lay members (i.e., nonrabbis) appointed by the president of the United Synagogue of Conservative Judaism who participate actively in the discussion and may even contribute to the writing of a *teshuvah* for consideration by the committee but who do not vote, and a cantor who serves in the same way. The members are each chosen for five-year terms, which are sometimes renewed, and an effort is made to insure that the committee includes both men and women and represents a variety of

different ages, geographical locations, ideological positions within the movement, and areas of expertise in Jewish law so that it can represent the movement fairly. *Teshuvot* (plural of *teshuvah*) are usually reviewed first by a subcommittee charged with the general area of Jewish law in which a particular question falls and then by the full committee. Often the *teshuvot* are revised as a result of those discussions before a vote by the full committee.

6. Gordon Tucker, "A Principled Defense of the Current Structure and Status of the CJLS," 765, https://www.rabbinicalassembly.org/sites/default/files/assets/public /halakhah/teshuvot/19912000/tucker_defense.pdf, reprinted in Dorff, *The Unfolding Tradition*, 415 in the 2005 edition, 456–57 in the 2011 edition. — E.N.D.

7. On these topics generally, including communal forums for making Jewish law, the role of custom in the law, and the Conservative movement's approach to Jewish law in contrast to that of the Orthodox and Reform movements, see Dorff and Rosett, *A Living Tree*, 337–63, 402–34, 523–45; and Dorff, *For the Love*, chap. 7.

8. See *Summary Index Supplement, 5756* of the *Summary Index: The Committee on Jewish Law and Standards* (New York: Rabbinical Assembly, 1994), 9:2. In the case of the second one of these, the one demanding a *get*, another exception to that demand that is obviously assumed, although not stated in the standard, is if the former spouse has died in the interim between the time of divorce and now, the time when the surviving spouse wants to remarry. Under those circumstances, the status of the surviving spouse changes from that of a person still married in Jewish law (despite being divorced in civil law) to that of a widowed person, and no *get* is possible or required. On the last of these standards, see *Proceedings of the Committee on Jewish Law and Standards of the Rabbinical Assembly, 1980-1985* (New York: Rabbinical Assembly, 1988), 177–78.

9. Both "A Rabbinic Letter on Intimate Relations" and "The Rabbinic Letter on the Poor" were written by Rabbi Elliot N. Dorff, the former for and with the Rabbinical Assembly's Commission on Human Sexuality and the latter for and with the Joint Social Action Committee of the Rabbinical Assembly and the United Synagogue of Conservative Judaism.

10. *Summary Index: The Committee on Jewish Law and Standards*, 9:14.

11. In an article I wrote for the journal *Conservative Judaism*, I suggested that custom may be the root of our response to the question of women serving as witnesses, especially since the legal texts seem closed to that possibility. See Dorff, "Custom Drives"; "Response to Critics"; and *For the Love*, 253–73.

12. The full paper can be read at http://www.rabbinicalassembly.org/sites/default /files/public/halakhah/teshuvot/19912000/tucker_defense.pdf. [Reprinted in Dorff, *The Unfolding Tradition*, 409–26 in the 2005 edition, 450–68 in the 2011 edition, with explanations and analysis of his article on 404–9 of the 2005 edition and 424–28 in the 2011 edition. — E.N.D.]

13. Tucker provides the following source information for this quote: Robert Cover, "The Uses of Jurisdictional Redundancy: Interest, Ideology, and Innovation," *William and Mary Law Review* 22 (1981): 640.—E.N.D.

14. The endnote for this block quote cites Cover, "The Uses of Jurisdictional Redundancy," 673–74.—E.N.D.

7. ḤAYYIM U'MAVET

1. Rabbis Kassel Abelson and Elliot Dorff, "Mitzvah Children," http://www.rabbinicalassembly.org/sites/default/files/public/halakhah/teshuvot/20052010/mitzvah_children.pdf.—E.N.D.

2. Dorff, *"This Is My Beloved, This Is My Friend": A Rabbinic Letter on Human Intimacy*, 13–15, 19–29; reprinted in Elliot N. Dorff, *Love Your Neighbor and Yourself: A Jewish Approach to Modern Personal Ethics*, Chapter 3, esp. 82–94.

3. Gen. 1:28.

4. "The Mishnah (*Ohalot* 7:6) explicitly indicates that one is to abort a fetus if the continuation of pregnancy might imperil the life of the mother.... The Rabbinical Assembly Committee on Jewish Law and Standards takes the view that an abortion is justifiable if a continuation of pregnancy might cause the mother severe physical or psychological harm, or when the fetus is judged by competent medical opinion as severely defective." Bokser and Abelson, "A Statement on the Permissibility of Abortion," *Responsa 1980–1990 of the Committee on Jewish Law and Standards of the Conservative Movement*, 817. [Also available at https://www.rabbinicalassembly.org/sites/default/files/assets/public/halakhah/teshuvot/20012004/07.pdf.—E.N.D.]

5. M. *Yevamot* 6:6 (61b). The Talmud there bases the House of Shammai's ruling on the fact that Moses had two sons. A Tosefta there asserts that the House of Shammi actually requires two boys and two girls, while Rabbi Nathan in the Talmud there says that the House of Shammi requires a male and a female and the House of Hillel either a male or a female. The Jerusalem Talmud (J. *Yevamot* 6:6 [7c]) records the opinion of Rabbi Bun, according to which the House of Shammai requires two sons and the House of Hillel, known to be more lenient than the House of Shammai, then says that *even* a boy and a girl would suffice (but two boys would definitely suffice). Although the later tradition settled on one boy and one girl, it is clear that from the very beginning there were differing traditions as to what genders one's two children had to, or could, be in order to fulfill the commandment. See Dorff, *Matters of Life and Death* 39–42 and 336, note 9.

6. M.T. *Hilkhot Ishut* 15:4.

7. S.A. *Even Haezer* 1:5.

8. ... The *Arukh Hashulhan* 1:16 mentions that some authorities hold that the *Mitzvah* of procreation can be fulfilled if there are descendants of both genders in a future generation, and it seems reasonable also to us to say that the offspring

of the broader population will balance the male-female numbers and that the important thing is to replace ourselves numerically. Ironically, in our own day, when modern technology has suddenly provided us with some control over the gender of our children but when the Jewish community simultaneously suffers from a major population deficit and values girls as much as boys, we would affirm that technologically-assisted gender selection should *not* take place, that we welcome children into our midst regardless of their gender, and that we see any two of them as fulfillment of the commandment to procreate.

9. As we write this, Rabbi Mark Popovsky is preparing a responsum on the use of preimplantation genetic diagnosis (PGD). Our stance here would agree with the one he intends to take, namely, that PGD should not be used to ensure that the child is one gender or the other except in the case of sex-linked genetic diseases.

10. M.T. *Hilkhot Ishut* 15:16.

11. Gordis, *Judaism for the Modern Age*, 254–55. Gordis dealt primarily with the question of family planning, but his analysis applies to family size as well.

12. The estimated birthrate for Jewish families is 1.8, with non-Orthodox Jews between 1.6 and 1.7. These figures are well below the 2.2 or 2.3 rate needed to replace the present Jewish population. (The rate needs to be more than 2.0 because some people will not marry or procreate, and some will have only one child or will have two children who will not themselves procreate.) See Jack Wertheimer, "Jews and the Jewish Birthrate," *Commentary*, October 2005, p. 41. He cites the *National Jewish Population Study 2000-2001*, available at www.ujc.org/NJPS. The best estimates of the Jewish population of the world and the United States can be found in the latest edition of the *American Jewish Yearbook*. See, for example, Singer and Grossman, eds., *The American Jewish Yearbook 2001*, where the estimate of the world's Jewish population is 13,254,100; see 101:540. All of these figures depend, of course, on how the demographer is defining who is a Jew, and so those like Gary Tobin who use a more expansive definition maintain that there are as many as a million more Jews in the United States. That is only temporary comfort, however, because the chances are slim that people who are only marginally Jewish will raise Jewish children. For more on the critical need for Jews to reproduce, and for strategies to increase the Jewish birth rate and make raising children Jewishly possible for people educationally and financially, see Dorff, *Love Your Neighbor and Yourself*, 98–104, 143–54.

13. Wertheimer, ["Jews and the Jewish Birthrate,"] 39–44. This article spells out in greater detail the evidence for the drop in the birthrate and points out that the Orthodox community has managed to maintain a higher birthrate and will be a larger part of the American Jewish community in the future.

14. This is also a critical part of the program for Jewish thriving suggested by Scott Shay. See Shay, *Getting Our Groove Back: How to Energize American Jewry*, chapter 2.

He also suggests there that after college women have children first and then go to graduate school and work to diminish the likelihood of infertility problems and to avoid any break between graduate school and work.

15. Dorff, *"This Is My Beloved, This Is My Friend"* (see note 2 above), 35. This theme is expanded in Dorff, *Love Your Neighbor and Yourself* (at note 2 above), 150–54.

16. This is a problem not only among Jews living in the Diaspora. In his "State of the Union talk" in May 2006 President Putin of Russia dealt with the danger a low birth rate posed to the future of Russia. He proposed subsidies to encourage families to have more children, an idea that Diaspora Jews can use as well in the form of financial support given by grandparents and the community for day care and tuition in Jewish schools, youth groups, and camps. The French and Canadian governments have expressed similar concerns. The comparatively low birthrate among Jews in Israel, in comparison to that of Israel's Arab population, poses a real dilemma for the future of Israel as both a Jewish and a democratic state.

17. B. *Kiddushin* 30a; see M.T. *Laws of Study (Talmud Torah)* 1:2; S.A. *Yoreh De'ah* 245:3.

18. See Dorff, *Love Your Neighbor and Yourself* (at note 2 above), 143–54, and Bubis, *The Costs of Jewish Living: Revisiting Jewish Involvements and Barriers*.

19. Rabbi David Feldman on abortion: http://www.rabbinicalassembly.org/sites /default/files/assets/public/halakhah/teshuvot/19861990/feldman_abortion .pdf; Rabbi Robert Gordis on abortion: http://www.rabbinicalassembly.org/sites /default/files/assets/public/halakhah/teshuvot/20012004/05.pdf; Rabbi Kassel Abelson on abortion: http://www.rabbinicalassembly.org/sites/default/files /assets/public/halakhah/teshuvot/20012004/03.pdf; and Rabbi Isaac Klein on abortion: http://www.rabbinicalassembly.org/sites/default/files/assets/public /halakhah/teshuvot/20012004/06.pdf.—E.N.D.

20. Spradling, Drumman-Barbosa, and Kai, "Stem Cells."—E.N.D.

8. *MASA U'MATTAN*

1. For the questions addressed to the Sanhedrin and their answers, see http://people.ucalgary.ca/~elsegal/363_Transp/Sanhedrin.html. For an analysis of this event, see Gil Graff, *Separation of Church and State in Thought and Practice: Application of Dina de-Malkhuta Dina in Jewish Law, 1750–1848* (University: University of Alabama Press, 1985).—E.N.D.

2. *Sifrei* on Deuteronomy 15:7; b. *Nedarim* 80b; b. *Bava Metzia* 71a; MT *Gifts to the Poor* 7:13; SA *Yoreh De'ah* 251:3.—E.N.D.

3. T. *Gittin* 3:8; b. *Gittin* 61a.—E.N.D.

4. Third Annual BSA and IDC Global Software Piracy Study, May 2006, p. 13, published online at http://www.bsa.org/globalstudy/upload/2005%20Piracy %20Study%20-%20Official%20Version.pdf.

5. Third Annual BSA and IDC Global Software Piracy Study, May 2006, p. 13, published online at http://www.bsa.org/globalstudy/upload/2005%20Piracy%20Study%20-%20Official%20Version.pdf.

6. http://www.riaa.com/issues/piracy/default.asp.

7. B. *Berakhot* 5b.

8. Ḥatam Sofer, part 5, 41.

9. Ḥatam Sofer, part 6, 57. [Translation by Schneider in his article "Jewish Law and Copyright."—E.N.D.]

10. Salamone Rossi, *Hashirim Asher Lish'lomo*, ed. by Fritz Rikko (New York: Jewish Theological Seminary of America, 1967–73), vol. 3, p. 28, quoted in "The Choral Music of Salamone Rossi," Joshua Jacobson, *American Choral Review* XXX[, no. 4] (1988).

11. Merges et al., *Intellectual Property*, 507.—E.N.D.

12. Schneider, "Jewish Law and Copyright."—E.N.D.

13. Deuteronomy 19:14.

14. B. *Bava Batra* 21b.

15. B. *Bava Batra* 21b.

16. Ḥatam Sofer, Part 5, 79. [Translation by Schneider, "Jewish Law and Copyright."—E.N.D.]

17. Tosafot, B. *Kiddushin* 59a, d.h. עני המהפך.

18. *Yabia Omer*, op. cit. [in full responsum], part 7, Ḥoshen Mishpat 9, d.h. שלום וברכה.

19. "Copying a Cassette without the Owner's Permission," Zalman Nechemia Goldberg, *Teḥumin* 6, pp. 185–207, cited in [Schneider,] "Jewish Law and Copyright," and [Kwass,] "Four Halakhic Models for Copyright Protection."

20. B. *Bava Metzia* 34a.

21. B. *Bava Metzia* 78b.

22. S.A. Ḥoshen Mishpat 359:5; see also B. *Bava Batra* 88a and Mishneh Torah, *Hilkhot Gezalah [Laws of Robbery]* 3:15.

23. Iggerot Moshe, OH, Vol. 4, 40:19.

24. The full text of the Berne Convention can be read at the World Intellectual Property Organization (WIPO) website: http://www.wipo.int/treaties/en/ip/berne/.

25. Lex2k, a website by Professor John Burke, provides a good description of some of the issues surrounding "shrink wrap" and "click wrap" licenses: http://www.lex2k.org/shrinkwrap/introduction.html. [This URL no longer exists.—E.N.D.]

26. US Code Title 17, chapter 1, paragraph 108. It can be found on the Cornell Law School website: http://www.law.cornell.edu/uscode/text/17/108.

27. See Copyright Act of 1976, Public Law No. 94-553, 90 stat 2541: Title 17; Section 110(i), available online at http://www.copyright.gov/title17/92chap1.html#110.

28. See www.cvli.com.

29. See www.mplc.com.

30. 17 U.S.C. $ 110 (3), available online at http://cyber.law.harvard.edu/is02/readings/17usc110.html.

31. "The ASCAP Concert and Recital Licenses," available online at http://www.ascap.com/licensing/pdfs/SERIOUS_CONCERT.pdf.

32. R. Yisrael Meir HaCohen Kagen, Ḥofetz Ḥayyim (Jerusalem: Mercaz Hasefer, 1952; photocopied from its original publication in Vilnius, Lithuania: A. Y. Dvorzets, 1873), Petiḥah [Introduction], pp. 21–51.

33. R. Yisrael Meir HaCohen Kagen, Ḥofetz Ḥayyim, Clal 10, p. 177.

34. R. Yisrael Meir HaCohen Kagen, Ḥofetz Ḥayyim, pp. 177–82.

35. Nachmanides commentary on Lev. 19:17.

36. B. Bava Metzia 31a.

37. B. Yevamot 65b.

38. Rambam, Mishneh Torah, Hilkhot De'ot [Laws of Ethics] 6:7.

39. B. Shabbat 54b.

40. B. Bava Kama 51a, Beit Yosef Hoshen Mishpat 410:8.

41. Maurer, Business Law Text and Cases, 131.

42. Mishneh Torah, Hilkhot De'ot [Laws of Ethics] 6:7.

43. Thank you to Rabbis Elliot Dorff, Jeremy Kalmanofsky, Levi Lauer, Daniel Nevins, and Mayer Rabinowitz for reading and commenting on earlier versions of this paper.

44. Interview conducted by Denis Johnston, SEIU 32BJ, December 2001.

45. SEIU Local 32 BJ. White Paper on "Justice for Janitors" campaign.

46. Cf. [Sh'mot Rabbah] 1:11.

47. HRW. 11.

48. For example, see Exodus 22:20 and 23:9, Leviticus 19:24 and 25:23 and Deuteronomy 10:19.

49. Cf. B. Bava Metzia 10a.

50. Jewish law differentiates between two types of workers—the po'el, who is paid by the day, and the kablan, who is paid by the task. While we are focusing on the po'el, whose situation more closely parallels that of contemporary low-wage workers, a precise delineation of the distinctions between the po'el and the kablan would be an interesting topic for further research, particularly as many companies excuse themselves from paying health benefits by classifying certain workers as contractors, rather than as permanent employees.

51. Kelley, Race Rebels, 1–13.

52. M.T. Hilkhot Matanot l'Aniyim [Laws of Gifts to the Poor] 10:7.

53. US Conference of Mayors. Hunger and Homelessness Report. December, 2001. Available: www.usmayors.org.

54. Cf. S.A. Ḥoshen Mishpat 337:20.

55. Cf. Rif on B. Bava Metzia 52b; M.T. Hilkhot Skhirut [Laws of Hiring] 13:6.

56. Cf. S.A. Ḥoshen Mishpat 337:19.

57. Bureau of Labor Statistics. *Monthly Labor Review*. 123:10 (October, 2000).

58. Stephen C. Betts. *Multiple Job Research Project*. William Paterson University.

59. The question of whether the principle of *pikku'aḥ nefesh* [the duty to save a life] can impose obligations also applies to this case, in which we might argue that the denial of benefits constitutes a threat to workers' lives.

60. [Schnall, *By the Sweat of Your Brow*, 141. —E.N.D.] Schnall's statement assumes an acceptance of the general principle "*haminhag m'vatel et hahalakhah*" [the custom abrogates the law], suggested by Rav Hoshea in J. *Bava Metzia* 7:1. The question of the general applicability of this principle is a matter of much debate. The *Or Zarua* understands this principle to apply only to an accepted *minhag*, certified by a recognized authority. (2:393) Similarly, Masekhet Sofrim permits only a "*minhag vatikin*" [a long-standing custom] to override *halakhah* [Jewish law] (14:16). The Rashba softens the necessity for earlier precedent, requiring only an "agreed-upon *minhag*." (*She'elot u'Teshuvot* 2:43.) Joseph Caro, however, seems to accept the principle, "*haminhag m'vatel et hahalakhah*" as a general rule (*Beit Yosef* and *Shulhan Arukh*. Hoshen Mishpat 232:19).

61. Schnall, *By the Sweat of Your Brow*, 130. I find extremely problematic Schnall's assumption that certain employers—notably school systems—can justify paying low wages by assuming that employees—especially teachers—will take on part-time work.

62. Schnall, *By the Sweat of Your Brow*, 127–43. As Schnall notes, the statistic that teachers are among the most likely to take supplementary jobs corresponds with the fact that most halakhic discussion around multiple employment has concerned teachers. There has been a general halakhic tendency to prohibit teachers from working after hours. 135–36.

63. Cf. M.T. *Hilkhot Skhirut [Laws of Hiring]* 9:4; S.A. *Hoshen Mishpat* 333:3.

64. M.T. *Hilkhot Mekhirah [Laws of Selling]* 14:10.

65. S.A. *Hoshen Mishpat* 231:28.

66. Oral statement, recorded in Tkhursh.

67. Qtd. in Yaron, *Mishnato shel HaRav Kook*, 164. Rabbi Shai Held called my attention to this source.

9. BEIN ADAM LAMAKOM

1. Lev. 19:28.

2. M. *Makkot* 3:6.

3. M. *Makkot* 3:6. Emphasis added.

4. Maimonides, M.T. *Hilkhot Avodat Kokhavim [Laws of Idolatry]* 12: 11.

5. Maimonides, M.T. *Hilkhot Avodat Kokhavim [Laws of Idolatry]* 12: 11.

6. *Encyclopaedia Judaica* (Jerusalem: Keter Publishing, 1972), vol. 16, p. 663ff., s.v. "Writing."

7. Isa. 44:5.

8. Isa. 49:16.

9. Job 37:7.

10. A. Cowley, *Aramaic Papyri of the Fifth Century B.C.* (1923) 28:2–6.

11. Tosafot on B. *Gittin* 20b, s.v. *b'khtovet ka'aka*.

12. S.A. *Yoreh De'ah* 180:2.

13. S.A. *Yoreh De'ah* 180:3. The *Siftei Kohen* clearly states that since the purpose is for medical purposes it is permitted.

14. And some you did not even think were capable of being pierced. In an article downloaded from the Internet, instructions were readily available on how to pierce the nostril, septum, eyebrow, Nieburh or Eric (the tissue between the eyes), the lip, cheek, tongue, navel, nipples, handweb, outer labia, inner labia, clitoral hood, clitoral triangle, clitoris, princess albertina, frenum, prince albert, ampallang, apadravya, dydoe, foreskin, and scrotum.

15. Exod. 21:6.

16. B. *Kiddushin* 21b.

17. Gen. 24:47.

18. Exod. 32:2.

19. Ezek. 16:11. See also Exod. 35:22, Num. 31:50, Judg. 8:24, and Isa. 3:21.

20. M. *Shabbat* 6:6.

21. B. *Shabbat* 11b.

22. On B. *Shabbat* 11b, Rashi explains that it was the custom of tradesmen to wear signs of their trade in the form of earrings so that when they walked in the marketplace, people would know their particular trade and could hire them.

23. Responsa on Pierced Ears, Sept. 1983, CCAR *Yearbook*.

24. M. *Shabbat* 6:6. In a discussion of what causes a permanent blemish, the Talmud, in *Bekhorot* 37a, gives piercing of the ear as an example.

25. *Noda B'yehudah* to Yoreh De'ah 10.

10. TIKKUN OLAM

1. See Dorff and Rosett (1988), 110–123, 249–257; and see Chapter Six in Dorff (2007).

2. B. *Sotah* 14a.

3. God is depicted as Israel's marital partner a number of times in the Bible, whether fondly, as in Jeremiah 2:2, or angrily, when Israel proves to be an unfaithful lover, as in Hosea, chapter 2. The phrase requiring us to go beyond the requirements of the law in our actions appears many times in the Talmud, perhaps especially B. *Bava Kamma* 100a and B. *Bava Metzi'a* 24b and 30b. God serves as a model for us in this, for in the Talmudic imagination God prays that God too will be treat people beyond the requirements of the law (B. *Berakhot* 7a) and in some cases actually does (B. *Avodah Zarah* 4b).

4. B. *Pesaḥim* 50b, and in parallel passages elsewhere.

5. Golinkin, *Proceedings of the Committee*, 3:1537–38. —E.N.D.

11. ḤAYYEI MIN U'MISHPAḤAH

1. Based on unanimous decisions of the CJLS on October 28 and December 2, 1970, and reaffirmed by the CJLS as a binding Standard on December 21, 1971. See chapter 5 for a discussion of the status of a Standard of Rabbinic Practice. —E.N.D.

2. http://www.rabbinicalassembly.org/keruv. —E.N.D.

3. http://www.rabbinicalassembly.org/story/keruv-conversion-and-jewish -peoplehood-let-s-talk-about-it. —E.N.D.

4. http://www.rabbinicalassembly.org/story/resolution-conversion-intermarriage -patrilineal-jews. —E.N.D.

5. David F. Greenberg, *The Construction of Homosexuality* (Chicago: University of Chicago Press, 1988). —E.N.D.

6. The discussion began in the mid-1980s and evolved into the Rabbinical Assembly resolution quoted here in May 1990. The United Synagogue of Conservative Judaism, the Conservative movement's synagogue arm, adopted a similar resolution subsequently in November 1991. The United Synagogue resolution uses the same language as the Rabbinical Assembly resolution that preceded it, but it leaves out the fifth "Whereas" clause and the fourth resolution of the Rabbinical Assembly version. Still, the substance and actual wording of the bulk of the United Synagogue resolution is the same as the fuller Rabbinical Assembly version reproduced here from *1990 Rabbinical Assembly Proceedings* (New York: Rabbinical Assembly, 1990), 275. —E.N.D.

7. B. *Berakhot* 19b, b. *Shabbat* 81b, 94b, b. *Eruvin* 41b, b. *Megillah* 3b, b. *Bava Kama* 79b, b. *Menaḥot* 37b, 38a, and j *Nazir* 56a. —E.N.D.

8. We expect homosexual students to observe the rulings of this responsum in the same way that we expect heterosexual students to observe the CJLS rulings on *niddah*. We also expect that interview committees, administrators, faculty and fellow students will respect the privacy and dignity of gay and lesbian students in the same way that they respect the privacy and dignity of heterosexual students.

9. Dorff, *This Is My Beloved, This Is My Friend: A Rabbinic Letter on Intimate Relations*; reprinted in Dorff, *Love Your Neighbor and Yourself: A Jewish Approach to Modern Personal Ethics*, chapter five.

10. On the *tumtum* and *androgynous*: b. *Shabbat* 136b; b. *Rosh Hashanah* 29a; b. *Haggigah* 4a, 81a, 83b; and especially b. *Haggigah* 71b–72b. On the *saris*: b. *Yevamot* 20b, 75a, and especially 79b–80a. On all three, see also M.T. *Laws of Marriage (Ishut)* 2:11–14, 24–25.

12. AM YISRAEL

1. *Midrash Psalms* on Psalm 123:1; cf. *Pesikta d'Rav Kahana*, ed. Mandelbaum, 208, and *Mekhilta, Shirata*, Beshallah, ed. Lauterbach, 2:28.

2. B. *Berakhot* 40b; MT *Laws of Shema* 2:10; *Laws of Blessings* 1:6; SA *Orah Hayyim* 62:2, 101:4, 185:1.

3. *Nostra Aetate*, http://www.vatican.va/archive/hist_councils/ii_vatican_council /documents/vat-ii_decl_19651028_nostra-aetate_en.html.
4. Evangelical Lutheran Church of America, "Declaration to the Jewish Community," April 18, 1994, http://download.elca.org/ELCA%20Resource%20Repository /Declaration_Of_The_ELCA_To_The_Jewish_Community.pdf?_ga=1.206376080 .2024737154.1486321084; Evangelical Lutheran Church of America Consultative Panel on Jewish-Christian Relations, "Lutheran Talking Points — Topics in Jewish-Christian Relations," September 1, 2002, http://www.ccjr.us/dialogika-resources /documents-and-statements/protestant-churches/na/lutheran/774-elca2002.
5. Kaplan, *The Future*, 228–30; see also Kaplan, *Questions Jews Ask*, 500–504.
6. Elliot N. Dorff, "On the Use of All Wines," http://www.rabbinicalassembly.org/sites /default/files/assets/public/halakhah/teshuvot/19861990/dorff_wines.pdf, 218.
7. Elliot N. Dorff, "Use of Synagogues by Christian Groups," http://www .rabbinicalassembly.org/sites/default/files/assets/public/halakhah/teshuvot /19861990/dorff_christiangroup.pdf.
8. Solomon married many non-Israelites: 1 Kings 3:1, 11:1–6. Ahab married a non-Israelite: 1 Kings 16:31.
9. The legal determination of Jewish identity took some time to develop. In biblical times, a person's father and his tribe determined his or her identity as part of the People Israel. The Mishnah (edited c. 200 CE) records two opinions. According to one (M. *Yevamot* 7:5; see also B. *Yevamot* 45a, 70a), the child of a Jewish woman and a non-Jewish man is illegitimate (*mamzer*) and, in accordance with Deuteronomy 23:3, may not marry a Jew for ten generations. According to the other (M. *Kiddushin* 3:12; B. *Kiddushin* 68b), such a child is a Jew, and that is the ruling that later Jewish law adopted: M.T. *Laws of Forbidden Intercourse (Issurei Bi'ah)* 15:3–4; S.A. *Even Ha-Ezer* 4:5.
10. *The National Jewish Population Survey 2000-01*, 18–19, asserts that only a third of the children in households with one non-Jewish spouse were being raised as Jews, with the interfaith parents establishing far fewer ties to the Jewish community and to Jewish life than couples who were both Jewish. The 2013 Pew study, *A Portrait of Jewish Americans*, 68, asserts that in couples in which both spouses are Jewish, 96 percent of children are being raised Jewish, while in interfaith couples "just 20% say they are raising their children Jewish by religion, and 37% say their children are not being raised Jewish."
11. The Pew study (*A Portrait of Jewish Americans*, 36) states that 17 percent of Jews who got married before 1970 had a non-Jewish spouse, but 58 percent of Jews who got married in 2005 or later have a non-Jewish spouse. By and large, the more Jewish education and social/religious ties that a person has to other Jews, the less likely it is that she or he will marry a non-Jew, but there are no guarantees.

12. "The Status of Children of Mixed Marriages," a Central Conference of American Rabbis resolution, adopted in 1983, http://www.ccarnet.org/rabbis-speak /resolutions/all/status-of-children-of-mixed-marriages-1983/.

13. The five responsa were by, respectively, Rabbis Kassel Abelson, Jacob B. Agus, Joel Roth and Daniel Gordis, Seymour Siegel, and Harry Z. Sky. They can be found at www.rabbinicalasssembly.org under the link "Jewish Law," then "Committee on Jewish Law and Standards," then "Even HaEzer," and then "Interpersonal Relations." Each of the five papers begins with the following note: "The Committee on Jewish Law and Standards unanimously adopted as 'deliberations of the Committee' the following five papers on the subject of the mitzvah of *keruv*, at a meeting on March 10, 1982. The papers were adopted without prejudice, all bearing equal value as official positions of the CJLS, in order to provide members of the Rabbinical Assembly a representative selection of views held by members of the Committee."

14. B. *Ketubbot* 57a; MT *Laws of Marriage* 10:10; SA *Even Ha-Ezer* 66:3.

13. TZIYYONUT

1. See Davis, *The Emergence*, 268–74.

2. Solomon Schechter, *Zionism: A Statement*, originally published as a pamphlet on December 28, 1906, and reprinted in Waxman, *Tradition and Change*, 457–66.

3. Solomon Schechter, preface to *Seminary Addresses of Solomon Schechter* (1915), reprinted in Waxman, *Tradition and Change*, 100.

4. Kaplan, *Judaism*, 273–74.

5. Kaplan, *Judaism*, 273–74.

6. Kaplan, *Religion of Ethical Nationhood*, 130.

14. TESHUVOT MEDINAT YISRAEL

1. B. *Gittin* 88b; M.T. *Laws of Courts (Sanhedrin)* 26:7. See Dorff and Rosett, *A Living Tree*, 320–24, 515–39.

2. B. *Nedarim* 28a; *b. Gittin* 10b; *b. Bava Kamma* 113a; *b. Bava Batra* 54b–55a. For more on how this ruling was used in Jewish legal history, see Dorff and Rosett, *A Living Tree*, 515–23.

3. *Arukh Ha-Shulḥan, Ḥoshen Mishpat* 388:7.

4. SA *Ḥoshen Mishpat* 388:7, gloss, and see comment #45 of the *Shakh* on that passage. *Shakh* there (on 338:12), in comment #60, understands Isserles to be saying categorically that "if someone is accustomed to strike others, it is permissible to hand him over [to gentile authorities] for one's protection so that he will not strike people any longer." See also glosses of Isserles to SA *Ḥoshen Mishpat* 388:9 and 26:4 and his commentary *Darkhei Moshe* to the *Tur, Ḥoshen Mishpat* 338,

comment #14. The earlier sources he cites are the *Teshuvot Maimoniot* of Maimonides (1140–1204, Spain and Egypt), *Nezikin*, Responsum #66; the Mordecai (Mordecai ben Hillel Ha-Kohen, 1240?–1298, Germany), R. Jacob ben Judah Weil (Germany, d. 1456), and Maharam of Riszburg (possibly R. Menahem of Merseburg, first half of the fourteenth century, Saxony, Germany).

5. SA *Ḥoshen Mishpat* 388:12, according to the text quoted by *Shakh* at that place, comment #59, and by the Gaon of Vilna (*Gra*), #71.

Bibliography

Abelson, Kassel, and Elliot N. Dorff. "Mitzvah Children." 2010. http://www
.rabbinicalassembly.org/sites/default/files/public/halakhah/teshuvot
/20052010/mitzvah_children.pdf.

Addison, Howard Avruhm, and Barbara Eve Breitman, eds. *Jewish Spiritual Direction: An Innovative Guide from Traditional and Contemporary Sources.* Woodstock VT: Jewish Lights, 2006.

Agus, Jacob. "Preface I." In *Abraham Isaac Kook: The Lights of Penitence, the Moral Principles, Lights of Holiness, Essays, Letters, and Poems,* translated by Ben Zion Bokser. New York: Paulist Press, 1978.

Artson, Bradley Shavit. *God of Becoming and Relationship: The Dynamic Nature of Process Theology.* Woodstock VT: Jewish Lights, 2013.

Astor, Carl N. "The Jewish Life Cycle." In Cohen, *The Observant Life,* 239–304.

Berkowitz, Miriam. "Reshaping the Laws of Family Purity for the Modern World." 2006. https://www.rabbinicalassembly.org/sites/default/files/assets/public/halakhah /teshuvot/20052010/berkowitz_niddah.pdf.

Berkowitz, Miriam, and Mark Papovsky. "Contraception." 2010. http://www
.rabbinicalassembly.org/sites/default/files/public/halakhah/teshuvot/20052010
/Contraception%20Berkowitz%20and%20popovsky.pdf.

Blumenthal, David R. *Facing the Abusing God: A Theology of Protest.* Louisville KY: Westminster / John Knox Press, 1993.

Blumenthal, Jacob. "Commerce." In Cohen, *The Observant Life,* 491–507.

Bokser, Ben Zion, and Kassel Abelson. "A Statement on the Permissibility of Abortion." 1983. http://www.rabbinicalassembly.org/sites/default/files/public /halakhah/teshuvot/20012004/07.pdf.

Bubis, Gerald. *The Costs of Jewish Living: Revisiting Jewish Involvements and Barriers.* New York: American Jewish Committee, 2002.

Cohen, Abraham. *Everyman's Talmud.* New York: E. P. Dutton and Company, 1949.

Cohen, Martin S. "Bequests and Inheritance." In Cohen, *The Observant Life*, 590–605.

———. "Intellectual Property." In Cohen, *The Observant Life*, 571–81.

———. "Israel." In Cohen, *The Observant Life*, 339–59.

———, ed. *The Observant Life: The Wisdom of Conservative Judaism for Contemporary Jews.* New York: Rabbinical Assembly, 2012.

Cohen, Michael R. *The Birth of Conservative Judaism: Solomon Schechter's Disciples and the Creation of an American Religious Movement.* New York: Columbia University Press, 2012.

Davis, Moshe. *The Emergence of Conservative Judaism: The Historical School in 19th Century America.* Philadelphia: Jewish Publication Society, 1965.

Dorff, Elliot N. *Conservative Judaism: Our Ancestors to Our Descendants.* New York: United Synagogue of America, 1977; 2nd, rev. ed., New York: United Synagogue of Conservative Judaism, 1996.

———. "Custom Drives Jewish Law on Women." *Conservative Judaism* 49, no. 3 (Spring 1997): 3–21.

———. "Family Violence." http://www.rabbinicalassembly.org/sites/default/files/public/halakhah/teshuvot/19912000/dorff_violence.pdf. Reprinted as chap. 5 of Dorff, *Love Your Neighbor and Yourself.*

———. *For the Love of God and People: A Philosophy of Jewish Law.* Philadelphia: Jewish Publication Society, 2007.

———. "In Search of God." In Dorff and Newman, *Contemporary Jewish Theology*, 112–21.

———. "A Jewish Approach to End-Stage Medical Care." 1990. http://www.rabbinicalassembly.org/sites/default/files/public/halakhah/teshuvot/19861990/dorff_care.pdf.

———. *Knowing God: Jewish Journeys to the Unknowable.* Northvale NJ: Jason Aronson (now Lanham MD: Rowman and Littlefield), 1992.

———. *Love Your Neighbor and Yourself: A Jewish Approach to Modern Personal Ethics.* Philadelphia: Jewish Publication Society, 2003.

———. *Matters of Life and Death: A Jewish Approach to Modern Medical Ethics.* Philadelphia: Jewish Publication Society, 1998.

———. "Response to Critics." *Conservative Judaism* 51, no. 1 (Fall 1998): 6–73. Reprinted in *Gender Issues in Jewish Law: Essays and Responsa*, edited by Walter Jacob and Moshe Zemer, 82–106. New York: Berghahn Books, 2001.

———. "Same-Sex Relationships." In Cohen, *The Observant Life*, 657–72.

———. "Stem Cell Research." 2002. http://www.rabbinicalassembly.org/sites/default/files/public/halakhah/teshuvot/19912000/dorff_stemcell.pdf.

———. *"This Is My Beloved, This Is My Friend" (Song of Songs 5:16): A Rabbinic Letter on Intimate Relations*. New York: Rabbinical Assembly, 1996. Reprinted as chap. 3 of Dorff, *Love Your Neighbor and Yourself*.

———. *To Do the Right and the Good: A Jewish Approach to Modern Social Ethics*. Philadelphia: Jewish Publication Society, 2002.

———. "Traditional Judaism." *Conservative Judaism* 34, no. 2 (November/December 1980): 34–38.

———. *The Unfolding Tradition: Philosophies of Jewish Law*. New York: Rabbinical Assembly [Aviv Press], 2005; 2nd, rev. ed., 2011.

———. *The Way into Tikkun Olam (Repairing the World)*. Woodstock VT: Jewish Lights, 2005.

———. *"You Shall Strengthen Them" (Leviticus 25:35): A Rabbinic Letter on the Poor*. New York: Rabbinical Assembly, 1999. Reprinted as chap. 6 of Dorff, *To Do the Right and the Good*, 126–60.

Dorff, Elliot, and Jonathan Crane, eds. *The Oxford Handbook of Jewish Ethics and Morality*. New York: Oxford University Press, 2013.

Dorff, Elliot, and Aaron Mackler. "Responsibilities for the Provision of Health Care." 1998. http://www.rabbinicalassembly.org/sites/default/files/public/halakhah/teshuvot/19912000/dorffmackler_care.pdf.

Dorff, Elliot, Daniel S. Nevins, and Avram I. Reisner. "Homosexuality, Human Dignity, and Halakhah." 2006. http://www.rabbinicalassembly.org/sites/default/files/public/halakhah/teshuvot/20052010/dorff_nevins_reisner_dignity.pdf.

———. "Rituals and Documents of Marriage and Divorce for Same-Sex Couples." 2012. https://www.rabbinicalassembly.org/sites/default/files/assets/public/halakhah/teshuvot/2011-2020/same-sex-marriage-and-divorce-appendix.pdf.

Dorff, Elliot, and Louis E. Newman, eds. *Contemporary Jewish Ethics and Morality: A Reader*. New York: Oxford University Press, 1995.

———. *Contemporary Jewish Theology: A Reader*. New York: Oxford University Press, 1999.

———. *Jewish Choices, Jewish Voices: Body*. Philadelphia: Jewish Publication Society, 2008.

Dorff, Elliot, and Arthur Rosett. *A Living Tree: The Roots and Growth of Jewish Law*. Albany: State University of New York Press, 1988.

Dorff, Elliot, and Joel Roth. "Shackling and Hoisting." 2000. http://www.rabbinicalassembly.org/sites/default/files/public/halakhah/teshuvot/19912000/dorffroth_shackling.pdf.

Dorff, Elliot, and Danya Ruttenberg, eds. *Jewish Choices, Jewish Voices: Sex and Intimacy*. Philadelphia: Jewish Publication Society, 2010.

Drazen, Paul. "The Jewish Dietary Laws." In Cohen, *The Observant Life*, 305–38.

Edwards, Tilden H. *Spiritual Friend*. New York: Paulist Press, 1980.

Eilberg, Amy. "The Siddur: A Guide to Jewish Spiritual Direction." In *Jewish Spiritual Direction: An Innovative Guide from Traditional and Contemporary Sources*, edited by

Howard Avruhm Addison and Barbara Eve Breitman, 197–208. Woodstock VT: Jewish Lights, 2006.

———. "'Where Is God for You?': A Jewish Feminist Faith." In *Lifecycles, Volume 2: Jewish Women on Biblical Themes in Contemporary Life*, edited by Debra Orenstein and Jane Rachel Litman, 104–12. Woodstock VT: Jewish Lights, 1997.

Eisen, Arnold M. *Conservative Judaism Today and Tomorrow*. New York: Jewish Theological Seminary of America, 2015.

———. *Galut: Modern Jewish Reflection on Homelessness and Homecoming*. Bloomington: Indiana University Press, 1986.

———. "Zionism." CJ: *Kolot Magazine* 5, no. 2 (Winter 2011–12 / Chanukah 5772): 48–49. New York: Federation of Jewish Men's Clubs, United Synagogue for Conservative Judaism, and Women's League for Conservative Judaism.

Elad-Appelbaum, Tamar. "The Radical Divinity." In *Jewish Theology in Our Time: A New Generation Explores the Foundations and Future of Jewish Belief*, edited by Elliot J. Cosgrove, 159–69. Woodstock VT: Jewish Lights, 2010.

Elazar, Daniel J., and Rela Mintz Geffen. *The Conservative Movement in Judaism: Dilemmas and Opportunities*. Albany: State University of New York Press, 2000.

Emet Ve-Emunah: Statement of Principles of Conservative Judaism. New York: Jewish Theological Seminary of America, Rabbinical Assembly, United Synagogue of America, Women's League for Conservative Judaism, Federation of Jewish Men's Clubs, 1988.

Feld, Edward, ed. *Mahzor Lev Shalem*. New York: Rabbinical Assembly, 2010.

Fierstien, Robert E., ed. *A Century of Commitment: One Hundred Years of the Rabbinical Assembly*. New York: Rabbinical Assembly, 2000.

Fine, David J. "Marriage." In Cohen, *The Observant Life*, 611–31.

———. "Taxation." In Cohen, *The Observant Life*, 551–55.

Finkelstein, Louis. *Jewish Self-Government in the Middle Ages*. New York: Jewish Theological Seminary of America, 1924; 2nd ed., New York: Feldheim, 1964.

———, ed. *The Jews: Their History, Culture, and Religion*. New York: Harper; Philadelphia: Jewish Publication Society, 1949; 2nd ed., 1955; 3rd ed., 1960, 2 vols.

Friedman, Theodore (Tuvia). "The Whole Land of Israel Concept." 1987. http://www.responsafortoday.com/eng_index.html, vol. 2 (English summary); http://www.responsafortoday.com/vol2/9.pdf (full responsum in Hebrew).

Gillman, Neil. *Conservative Judaism: The New Century*. New York: Behrman House, 1993.

———. *The Death of Death: Resurrection and Immortality in Jewish Thought*. Woodstock VT: Jewish Lights, 2000.

———. *Doing Jewish Theology: God, Torah, and Israel in Modern Judaism*. Woodstock VT: Jewish Lights, 2008.

———. *Sacred Fragments: Recovering Theology for the Modern Jew*. Philadelphia: Jewish Publication Society, 1990.

Golinkin, David. *Halakhah for Our Time: A Conservative Approach to Jewish Law.* New York: United Synagogue of America, 1991.

———. *An Index of Conservative Responsa and Halakhic Studies, 1917-1990.* New York: Rabbinical Assembly, 1992.

———, ed. *Proceedings of the Committee on Jewish Law and Standards, 1927-1970.* New York: Rabbinical Assembly; Jerusalem: Schechter Institute of Applied Halakhah, 1997.

———. *Responsa in a Moment: Halakhic Responses to Contemporary Issues.* Jerusalem: Schechter Institute of Applied Halakhah, vol. 1, 2000, vol. 2, 2011.

———. "Why Halakhah Requires Returning a Convicted Murderer to France." 1987. http://www.responsafortoday.com/vol2/5.pdf.

———. "Why Riding to the Synagogue on Shabbat Is Forbidden." 1990. http://www .responsafortoday.com/eng_index.html, vol. 4 (English summary); http://www .responsafortoday.com/vol4/3.pdf (Hebrew version).

Gordis, Robert. "Authority in Jewish Law." In *Proceedings of the Rabbinical Assembly, 1941-44.* New York: Rabbinical Assembly, 1944, 64-93. Reprinted in *Conservative Judaism and Jewish Law*, edited by Seymour Siegel and Elliot Gertel, 47-78. New York: Rabbinical Assembly; Hoboken NJ: Ktav, 1977; and in Dorff, *The Unfolding Tradition*, 91-121 in the 2005 edition, 87-117 in the 2011 edition.

———. *A Faith for Moderns.* New York: Bloch, 1960.

———. Introduction to *The Sabbath and Festival Prayerbook*, iv-xiii. New York: Rabbinical Assembly and United Synagogue of America, 1946.

———. *Judaism for the Modern Age.* New York: Farrar, Straus and Cudahy, 1955.

Gordis, Robert, and Josiah Derby. *Conservative Judaism: An American Philosophy.* New York: Jewish Theological Seminary of America and Behrman House, 1945.

Gordis, Robert, and Max Gelb. *Understanding Conservative Judaism.* New York: Rabbinical Assembly, 1978.

Graetz, Naomi. *Silence Is Deadly: Judaism Confronts Wifebeating.* Northvale NJ: Jason Aronson [now Lanham MD: Rowman and Littlefield], 1998.

Gratton, Carolyn. *The Art of Spiritual Guidance: A Contemporary Approach to Growing in the Spirit.* New York: Crossroad, 1998.

Green, Arthur. *Radical Judaism: Rethinking God and Tradition.* New Haven CT: Yale University Press, 2010.

Greenberg, Simon, ed. *The Ordination of Women as Rabbis.* New York: Jewish Theological Seminary of America, 1988.

Grossman, Susan, and Rivka Haut, eds. *Daughters of the King: Women and the Synagogue.* Philadelphia: Jewish Publication Society, 1992.

Halivni, David Weiss. "The Role of the Mara D'atra in Jewish Law." In *Proceedings of the Rabbinical Assembly 1976*, 38:124-29. New York: Rabbinical Assembly, 1977.

Hammer, Reuven. "Is IDF Service an Obligation for Every Jew in Israel?" 1987. http:// www.responsafortoday.com/eng_index.html, vol. 2 (English summary); http:// www.responsafortoday.com/vol2/8.pdf (full responsum in Hebrew).

———. "On Proving Jewish Identity." 2011. https://www.rabbinicalassembly.org/sites /default/files/assets/public/halakhah/teshuvot/2011-2020/JewishIdentity6 .2011.pdf.

Harris, Robert. "The Service of Girls in the Army of Israel." 1987. http://www .responsafortoday.com/eng_index.html, vol. 2 (English summary); http://www .responsafortoday.com/vol2/7.pdf (full responsum in Hebrew).

Heschel, Abraham Joshua. *Heavenly Torah as Refracted through the Generations.* Translated and edited by Gordon Tucker and Leonard Levin. New York: Continuum, 2005.

———. *The Insecurity of Freedom.* New York: Farrar, Straus & Giroux, Inc., 1972.

———. *Quest for God* (originally *Man's Quest for God*). New York: Charles Scribner's Sons, 1954.

Hoffnung, Arthur. *The University of Judaism at Forty.* Los Angeles: University of Judaism, 1991.

Jacobs, Jill. *There Shall Be No Needy: Pursuing Social Justice through Jewish Law and Tradition.* Woodstock VT: Jewish Lights, 2011.

———. *Where Justice Dwells: A Hands-On Guide to Doing Social Justice in Your Jewish Community.* Woodstock VT: Jewish Lights, 2009.

———. "Work, Workers, and the Jewish Owner." 2008. http://www .rabbinicalassembly.org/sites/default/files/public/halakhah/teshuvot/20052010 /jacobs-living-wage.pdf.

Jacobs, Louis. *God, Torah, Israel: Traditionalism without Fundamentalism.* Cincinnati: Hebrew Union College Press, 1990.

———. *A Jewish Theology.* New York: Behrman House, 1973.

———. *Principles of the Jewish Faith.* New York: Basic Books, 1964. Reprinted, Northvale NJ: Jason Aronson Press [now Lanham MD: Rowman and Littlefield], 1988.

Kadushin, Max. *Organic Thinking: A Study in Rabbinic Thought.* New York: Bloch Publishing Company, 1938.

———. *Worship and Ethics: A Study in Rabbinic Judaism.* Evanston IL: Northwestern University Press, 1964.

Kalmanofsky, Jeremy. "Participating in the American Death Penalty." 2013. https:// www.rabbinicalassembly.org/sites/default/files/assets/public/halakhah/teshuvot /2011-2020/cjls-onesh-mavet.pdf.

———. "Sex, Relationships, and Single Jews." In Cohen, *The Observant Life,* 632–56.

Kanerek, Jane. "Contracts." In Cohen, *The Observant Life,* 540–50.

Kaplan, Mordecai M. *The Future of the American Jew.* New York: Reconstructionist Foundation, 1948.

———. *Judaism as a Civilization: Toward a Reconstruction of American-Jewish Life.* New York: Macmillan, 1934. Reprinted several times by New York: Reconstructionist Press; latest edition: Philadelphia: Jewish Publication Society, 2010, with a new introduction by Mel Scult.

———. *Questions Jews Ask: Reconstructionist Answers.* New York: Reconstructionist Press, 1956.

———. *The Religion of Ethical Nationhood: Judaism's Contribution to World Peace.* New York: Macmillan, 1970.

Katz, Michael, and Gershom Schwartz. "Shabbat." In Cohen, *The Observant Life,* 98–136.

Kelley, Robin D. G. *Race Rebels: Culture, Politics, and the Black Working Class.* New York: Free Press, 1994.

King, G. B. "The 'Negative' Golden Rule." *Journal of Religion* 8, no. 2 (April 1928): 268–79.

Kushner, Harold. "Conservative Judaism in an Age of Democracy." *Conservative Judaism* 59, no. 4 (Summer 2007): 3–13. Reprinted in Dorff, *The Unfolding Tradition* (2011 edition), 397–405.

———. *When Bad Things Happen to Good People.* New York: Avon Books, 1981.

Kwass, Eliezer. "Four Halakhic Models for Copyright Protection." http://www .darchenoam.org/ethics/copyright/4mod.htm.

Leff, Barry. "Among Co-workers." In Cohen, *The Observant Life,* 529–39.

———. "Intellectual Property: Can You Steal It If You Can't Touch It?" 2007. http:// www.rabbinicalassembly.org/sites/default/files/public/halakhah/teshuvot /20052010/leff_IP.pdf.

———. "Jewish Business Ethics." In Dorff and Crane, *The Oxford Handbook,* 367–82.

———. "Whistleblowing: The Requirement to Report Employer Wrongdoing." 2007. http://www.rabbinicalassembly.org/sites/default/files/public/halakhah/teshuvot /20052010/leff_whistleblowing.pdf.

Levenson, Laurie. "Judaism and Criminal Justice." In Dorff and Crane, *The Oxford Handbook,* 472–86.

Levine, Arthur J. "Needed—a Definition." *Judaism* 26, no. 3 (Summer 1977): 292–95.

Lieber, David L., ed. *Etz Hayim: Torah and Commentary.* New York: Rabbinical Assembly, 2001.

Lubliner, Jonathan. "Recreational Sports on Shabbat." 2015. https://www .rabbinicalassembly.org/sites/default/files/assets/public/halakhah/teshuvot /2011-2020/lubliner-recreation-sports-shabbat.pdf.

Lucas, Alan. "Holy Days and Holidays." In Cohen, *The Observant Life,* 137–238.

———. "Tattooing and Body Piercing." 1997. http://www.rabbinicalassembly.org/sites /default/files/public/halakhah/teshuvot/19912000/lucas_tattooing.pdf.

Mackler, Aaron. "Jewish Medical Directives for Health Care." 1993. http://www .rabbinicalassembly.org/sites/default/files/public/halakhah/teshuvot/19861990 /mackler_care.pdf.

————, ed. *Life and Death Responsibilities in Jewish Biomedical Ethics*. New York: Finklestein Institute of the Jewish Theological Seminary of America, 2000.

————. "Surrogate Parenting." 1997. http://www.rabbinicalassembly.org/sites/default /files/public/halakhah/teshuvot/19912000/mackler_surrogate.pdf.

Mackler, Aaron, and Elie Kaplan Spitz. "On the Use of Birth Surrogates." 1997. http:// www.rabbinicalassembly.org/sites/default/files/public/halakhah/teshuvot /19912000/macklerspitz_surrogates.pdf.

Maurer, Virginia G. *Business Law Text and Cases*. New York: Harcourt Brace Jovanovich, 1987.

Medwed, Karen G. Reiss. "Prayer." In Cohen, *The Observant Life*, 5–60.

Merges, Robert, et al. *Intellectual Property in the New Technological Age*. New York: Aspen Law and Business Publishers, 2006.

Nadell, Pamela S. *Conservative Judaism in America: A Biographical Dictionary and Sourcebook*. New York: Greenwood Press, 1988.

The National Jewish Population Survey 2000–01. New York: United Jewish Communities, 2003.

Neustein, Amy, ed. *Tempest in the Temple: Jewish Communities and Child Sex Scandals*. Waltham MA: Brandeis University Press, 2009.

Peretz, Cheryl. "Between Employers and Employees." In Cohen, *The Observant Life*, 508–28.

Pew Research Center. *A Portrait of Jewish Americans*. Washington DC: Pew Research Center, 2013. http://www.pewforum.org/2013/10/01/jewish-american-beliefs -attitudes-culture-survey/.

Plaut, W. Gunther. *The Rise of Reform Judaism*. New York: World Union for Progressive Judaism, Ltd., 1963.

Popovsky, Mark. "Choosing Our Children's Genes: The Use of Preimplantation Genetic Diagnosis." 2008. http://www.rabbinicalassembly.org/sites/default/files /public/halakhah/teshuvot/20052010/Popovsky_FINAL_preimplantation.pdf.

Ratner, Joshua. "A Summary of Magen Tzedek's New Standards and Religious Underpinnings." 2011. http://www.rabbinicalassembly.org/sites/default/files/public /social_action/magen_tzedek/magen-tzedek-sources.pdf.

Reisner, Avram Israel. *Al Pi Din* (According to law). http://magentzedek.org/wp -content/uploads/2009/05/hekhsher_tzedek_al_pi_din_july_2009.pdf.

————. "Curiouser and Curiouser: The Kashrut of Genetically Engineered Foodstuffs." 1997. http://www.rabbinicalassembly.org/sites/default/files/public /halakhah/teshuvot/19912000/reisner_curiouser.pdf.

————. "A Halakhic Ethic of Care for the Terminally Ill." 1990. http://www .rabbinicalassembly.org/sites/default/files/public/halakhah/teshuvot/19861990 /reisner_care.pdf.

————. "Mai Beinaihu? [What Is the Practical Difference between Them?]." 1990. http://www.rabbinicalassembly.org/sites/default/files/public/halakhah/teshuvot /19861990/maibeinaihu.pdf.

———. "Medical Ethics." In Cohen, *The Observant Life*, 751–805.

———. "Wired to the Kadosh Barukh Hu: Minyan via Internet." 2001. http://www
.rabbinicalassembly.org/sites/default/files/public/halakhah/teshuvot/19912000
/reisner_internetminyan.pdf.

Rosen, Tracee L. "Loans and Lending." In Cohen, *The Observant Life*, 556–70.

Rosenblum, Herbert. *Conservative Judaism: A Contemporary History.* New York: United
Synagogue of America, 1983.

Roth, Joel. *The Halakhic Process: A Systematic Analysis.* New York: Jewish Theological
Seminary of America, 1986.

———. "On the Ordination of Women as Rabbis." In *The Ordination of Women as Rabbis,* edited by Simon Greenberg, 127–85. New York: Jewish Theological Seminary
of America, 1988.

Roth, Joel, and Akiba Lubow. "A Standard of Rabbinic Practice Regarding Determination of Jewish Identity." 1985. http://www.rabbinicalassembly.org/sites/default
/files/public/halakhah/teshuvot/20012004/31.pdf.

Rubenstein, Richard L. *After Auschwitz: Radical Theology and Contemporary Judaism.*
Indianapolis IN: Bobbs-Merrill, 1966; 2nd ed., *After Auschwitz: History, Theology,
and Contemporary Judaism.* Baltimore MD: Johns Hopkins, 1992.

Ruttenberg, Danya, ed. *The Passionate Torah: Sex and Judaism.* New York: New York
University Press, 2009.

———. *Surprised by God: How I Learned to Stop Worrying and Love Religion.* Boston:
Beacon Press, 2008.

Salkin, Jeffrey K., ed. *A Dream of Zion: American Jews Reflect on Why Israel Matters to
Them.* Woodstock VT: Jewish Lights, 2007.

Schechter, Solomon. *Seminary Addresses and Other Papers.* New York: Burning Bush
Press, 1959.

Schechter Institute of Jewish Studies. Books on applied *halakhah* and on women in
Judaism, listed at http://www.schechter.edu/bookscatalog/.

Schnall, David. *By the Sweat of Your Brow: Reflections on Work and the Workplace in Classical Jewish Thought.* Hoboken NJ: Ktav, 2001.

Schneider, Israel. "Jewish Law and Copyright." *Journal of Halakhah and Contemporary
Society* 21 (Spring 1991 / Pesach 5751).

Schorsch, Ismar. *The Sacred Cluster: The Core Values of Conservative Judaism.* New York:
Jewish Theological Seminary of America, 1995.

Schulweis, Harold. *Evil and the Morality of God.* Cincinnati OH: Hebrew Union College
Press, 1984.

———. *For Those Who Can't Believe: Overcoming the Obstacles to Faith.* New York:
HarperCollins, 1994.

Segal, Benjamin J. *A New Psalm: The Psalms as Literature*. Springfield NJ: Gefen Books; Philadelphia: Schechter Institute of Jewish Studies, 2013.

———. *Returning: The Land of Israel as Focus in Jewish History*. Jerusalem: Department of Education and Culture, World Zionist Organization, 1987.

Shay, Scott. *Getting Our Groove Back: How to Energize American Jewry*. Jerusalem: Devora Publishing Company, 2007.

Sheff, Craig. "Synagogue Life." In Cohen, *The Observant Life*, 61–80.

Siegel, Seymour. "A Jewish View of Economic Justice." In Dorff and Newman, *Contemporary Jewish Ethics*, 336–43.

Siegel, Seymour, and Elliot Gertel, eds. *Conservative Judaism and Jewish Law*. New York: Rabbinical Assembly; Hoboken NJ: Ktav, 1977.

———. *God in the Teachings of Conservative Judaism*. New York: Rabbinical Assembly; Hoboken NJ: Ktav, 1978.

Silverman, Morris, ed. *Sabbath and Festival Prayerbook*. New York: Rabbinical Assembly of America and United Synagogue of America, 1946.

Sklare, Marshall. *Conservative Judaism: An American Religious Movement*. Glencoe IL: Free Press, 1955.

Sosland, Abagail N. "Crime and Punishment." In Cohen, *The Observant Life*, 458–75.

Spitz, Elie Kaplan. *Does the Soul Survive? A Jewish Journey to Belief in Afterlife, Past Lives, and Living with Purpose*. Woodstock VT: Jewish Lights, 2015.

———. "The Jewish Tradition and Capital Punishment." In Dorff and Newman, *Contemporary Jewish Ethics*, 344–49.

———. "On the Use of Birth Surrogates." 1997. http://www.rabbinicalassembly.org /sites/default/files/public/halakhah/teshuvot/19912000/spitz_surrogate.pdf.

Spradling, Allan, Daniela Drumman-Barbosa, and Toshie Kai. "Stem Cells Find Their Niche." *Nature* 414 (2001): 98.

Suskin, Alana. "A Feminist Theory of Halakhah." In Dorff, *The Unfolding Tradition*, 363–89 in the 2005 edition, 352–78 in the 2011 edition.

Teutsch, David A. *Organizational Ethics and Economic Justice*. Wyncote PA: Reconstructionist Rabbinical College Press, 2007. Reprinted as part of his *Guide to Jewish Practice*, vol. 1, *Everyday Living*, 315–402. Wyncote PA: Reconstructionist Rabbinical College Press, 2011.

Tucker, Gordon. "Can a People of the Book Also Be a People of God?" *Conservative Judaism* 60, nos. 1–2 (Fall/Winter 2007–8). Reprinted in Dorff, *The Unfolding Tradition*, 422–47 in the 2011 edition.

———. " 'D'rosh vKabbel Sachar' [Study and Receive Reward]: Halakhic and Metahalakhic Arguments Concerning Judaism and Homosexuality." http://www .rabbinicalassembly.org/sites/default/files/public/halakhah/teshuvot/20052010 /tucker_homosexuality.pdf.

———. "A Principled Defense of the Current Structure and Status of the Committee on Jewish Law and Standards." http://www.rabbinicalassembly.org/sites/default/files /public/halakhah/teshuvot/19912000/tucker_defense.pdf. Also reprinted in Dorff, *The Unfolding Tradition*, 404–26 in the 2005 edition, 450–68 in the 2011 edition.

Tucker, Gordon, trans. and ed., with Leonard Levin. *Heavenly Torah as Refracted through the Generations*. A translation with critical commentary and notes of Abraham Joshua Heschel, *Torah Min Hashamayim B'aspakloria shel Hadorot* (Hebrew). New York: Continuum, 2005.

Vaad Halakhah in Israel. Responsa. http://www.responsafortoday.com (full Hebrew text and English summaries).

Waxman, Mordecai, ed. *Tradition and Change: The Development of Conservative Judaism*. New York: Burning Bush Press of the Rabbinical Assembly, 1958.

Wertheimer, Jack. *The American Synagogue: A Sanctuary Transformed*. New York: Cambridge University Press, 1987.

———. "Jews and the Jewish Birthrate." *Commentary*, October 2005, 39–44.

———. *Jews in the Center: Conservative Synagogues and Their Members*. New Brunswick NJ: Rutgers University Press, 2000.

Wolfson, Ron. *The Spirituality of Welcoming: How to Transform Your Congregation into a Sacred Community*. Woodstock VT: Jewish Lights, 2006.

Yaron, Tzvi. *Mishnato shel HaRav Kook*. Jerusalem: Moreshet Press, 1986.

Authors of Excerpted Texts

Kassel Abelson (rabbi, Jewish Theological Seminary of America [JTS], 1948) served as senior rabbi at Beth El Synagogue in Minneapolis, Minnesota, from 1957 to his retirement in 1992 and previously as a U.S. Air Corps chaplain and rabbi of Sheirith Israel Congregation in Columbus, Georgia. He was also president of the Rabbinical Assembly from 1986 to 1988. In addition, he served as chair of the Rabbinical Assembly's Committee on Jewish Law and Standards (CJLS) from 1992 to 2007; was coeditor of the volume containing CJLS-approved responsa from 1980 to 1990; and authored a number of CJLS-approved responsa. He also served on the Commission on the Philosophy of the Conservative Movement (1985–88), which produced *Emet Ve-Emunah: Statement of Principles of Conservative Judaism*, the only official statement of the ideology of the Conservative movement. It is quoted in multiple chapters in this book.

Tamar Elad-Appelbaum (rabbi, JTS, 2005) is the founder of ZION: An Eretz Israeli Congregation in Jerusalem and vice president of the Masorti Rabbinical Assembly. She served as rabbi of Congregation Magen Avraham in the Negev and as assistant dean of the Schechter Rabbinical Seminary in Jerusalem. In 2010 the *Forward* named her as one of the five most influential female religious leaders in Israel for her work promoting pluralism and Jewish religious freedom.

Bradley Shavit Artson (rabbi, JTS, 1988; DHL, HUC-JIR, 2010) is dean of the Ziegler School of Rabbinic Studies, a vice president at American Jewish University, and dean of the Zacharias Frankel College at the University of Potsdam, Germany, which ordains Conservative/Masorti rabbis for Europe. Previously he served as rabbi of Congregation Eilat in Mission Viejo, California. He has written eight books, most recently, *Renewing the Process of Creation: A Jewish Integration of Science and Spirit* (2016), and he coedited the Ziegler School's Walking with . . . book series.

Miriam Berkowitz (rabbi, Schechter Institute of Jewish Studies, Jerusalem, 1998) is a rabbi, educator, and writer who teaches in Jerusalem. The author of *Taking the Plunge: A Practical and Spiritual Guide to the Mikveh*, she also wrote two CJLS-approved responsa: one on contraception (cowritten with Rabbi Mark Popovsky and excerpted in chapter 7) and another entitled "Reshaping the Laws of Family Purity for the Modern World" (https://www.rabbinicalassembly.org/sites/default/files/assets/public/halakhah/teshuvot /20052010/berkowitz_niddah.pdf). Formerly she served as assistant rabbi at Park Avenue Synagogue in New York City.

Elliot N. Dorff (rabbi, JTS, 1970; PhD, philosophy, Columbia University, 1971) is rector and Sol and Anne Dorff Distinguished Service Professor of Philosophy at American Jewish University, a long-time visiting professor at UCLA School of Law, and founding dean of the rabbinical program at the University of Judaism (now the American Jewish University), a position he held from 1971 to 1994. He holds four honorary doctoral degrees and was awarded the *Journal of Law and Religion*'s Lifetime Achievement Award. A member of the Commission on the Philosophy of Conservative Judaism, he was an editor of its product, *Emet Ve-Emunah*. He is coeditor of the law-in-practice commentary (*Halakhah L'Ma'aseh*) of the new Conservative commentary *Etz Hayim*. A past chair of the Society of Jewish Ethics, the Academy of Jewish Philosophy, the Academy of Judaic, Christian, and Islamic Studies, and the Jewish Law Association and honorary president of the Jewish Law Association from 2012 to 2016, he has also served on three federal commissions—on health care, on reducing the spread of sexually transmitted diseases, and on research on human subjects—and currently serves on the state of California's commission on ethical guidelines for stem cell research. In addition, he is the author of more than two hundred articles and twelve books, among them *Conservative Judaism: Our Ancestors to Our Descendants* (1977; second revised edition, 1996), widely used as an introduction to Conservative Judaism; and *To Do the Right and the Good: A Jewish Approach to Modern Social Ethics* (2002), which won the National Jewish Book Award; as well as three other books that were finalists for that award. He has also served as editor or coeditor of fourteen additional books, including six volumes of the Jewish Publication Society's Jewish Choices, Jewish Voices series (three coedited with Louis Newman and another three with Danya Ruttenberg).

Amy Eilberg (MSW, Smith College School for Social Work, 1984; rabbi, JTS, 1985; DMin, United Theological Seminary of the Twin Cities, 2016) was the first woman to be ordained by the Jewish Theological Seminary. In 1986 she also became the first woman to serve on the Conservative Movement's Committee on Jewish Law and Standards. She now teaches at the Jay Philips Center for Interfaith Learning, working on peace studies, the subject of her first book, *From Enemy to Friend: Jewish Wisdom and the Pursuit of Peace* (2014). In addition, she previously served as a hospital chaplain in Philadelphia and San Francisco, where she helped found the Bay Area Jewish Healing Center.

Arnold Eisen (PhD, history of Jewish thought, Hebrew University; BPhil, sociology of religion, Oxford University) has been chancellor of the Jewish Theological Seminary in New York since 2007. He is also the author of six books, including *Rethinking Modern Judaism: Ritual, Commandment, Community* (1998); and *The Jew Within: Self, Family, and Community in America* (with Steven M. Cohen, 2000). Previously he served as the Koshland Professor of Jewish Culture and Religion and chair of the Department of Religious Studies at Stanford University, and he taught in the Tel Aviv University Department of Philosophy and the Columbia University Department of Religion.

Theodore (Tuvia) Friedman (1908–92) (rabbi, JTS, 1931; PhD, Columbia University, 1952) was the long-term rabbi of Congregation Beth El of the Oranges and Maplewood, New Jersey. He served as president of the international Rabbinical Assembly, the association of Conservative rabbis worldwide, from 1962 to 1964. In 1963 the assembly adopted his resolution to send a delegation to join protests against police brutality in Birmingham, Alabama. He also served as chair of the Conservative Movement's Committee on Jewish Law and Standards and authored significant decisions in Jewish ritual law, among them the responsum on the Sabbath (cowritten with Rabbis Morris Adler and Jacob Agus in 1950) that permitted driving to the synagogue on the Sabbath if one could not walk there. In 1970 he retired to Israel and became the founding chair of the Va'ad Halakhah from 1986 to 1988, for which he wrote the responsum on the borders of the land of Israel, summarized in this volume.

Neil Gillman (1933–2017) (rabbi, JTS, 1960; PhD, philosophy, Columbia University, 1975) was a professor of philosophy at the Jewish Theological Seminary of America for more than forty years and served as dean of its rabbinical school. He was a member of the commission that produced *Emet Ve-Emunah*. He wrote eight books on Jewish theology, including, most recently, *Doing Jewish Theology: God, Torah and Israel in Modern Judaism* (2008).

David Golinkin (rabbi, JTS, 1980; PhD in Talmud, JTS, 1988) is president of the Schechter Institutes, Inc., and president emeritus of the Schechter Institute of Jewish Studies in Jerusalem, where he also serves as a professor of Jewish law. For twenty years he was chair of the Va'ad Halakhah (Law Committee) of the Israel Region of the Rabbinical Assembly. He also serves as founder and director of the Institute of Applied Halakhah at the Schechter Institute, which seeks to publish a library of halakhic literature for the Conservative and Masorti movements; and director of the Schechter Institute's Center for Women in Jewish Law. In addition, he is the author or editor of forty-nine books, including *Halakhah for Our Time: An Index of Conservative Responsa and Halakhic Studies, 1917–1990* and *Proceedings of the Committee on Jewish Law and Standards of the Conservative Movement 1927–1970* (three volumes), and he has published more than two hundred articles, responsa, and sermons.

Arthur Green (rabbi, JTS, 1967; PhD, Brandeis University, 1975) is the founding dean of the Hebrew College rabbinical school, which he now serves as rector. He was president of the Reconstructionist Rabbinical College from 1987 to 1993; Philip W. Lown Professor of Near Eastern and Judaic Studies at Brandeis University; a cofounder of Ḥavurat Shalom, one of the first egalitarian Jewish communities; and a major figure in the Jewish Renewal movement. In addition, a widely published scholar of Jewish mysticism and Hasidism, as well as articulations of his own theology, he is editor of four books and the author of twelve more, including, most recently, *The Heart of the Matter: Studies in Jewish Mysticism and Theology* (2015).

Reuven Hammer (rabbi, JTS, 1958; DHL, JTS, 1968; PhD, Northwestern University, 1974), a past president of the Rabbinical Assembly, helped to found the Masorti movement in Israel and has served in a variety of leadership roles in it. Two of his eight books, *Sifre: A Taanaitic Commentary on the Book of Deuteronomy* (1986) and *Entering the High Holy Days: A Guide to Origins, Themes, and Prayers* (2005), received the National Jewish Book Award for scholarship. He also wrote *Or Hadash*, the official commentary on the Conservative movement's *Siddur Sim Shalom* prayer book. The Ziegler School of Rabbinic Studies awarded him the Simon Greenberg Award for Lifetime Achievement in the Rabbinate.

Robert Harris (rabbi, JTS, 1983; PhD, JTS, 1997) is associate professor of Bible and ancient Semitic languages at the Jewish Theological Seminary of America. Formerly he served as a rabbi at the Pelham Jewish Center in Westchester County, New York, and Moriah Synagogue in Haifa. He was also a visiting scholar and visiting associate professor at Hebrew University of Jerusalem, a JTS Project Judaica teacher at the Russian State University for the Humanities in Moscow, and a visiting professor at the Pontifical Gregorian University in Rome. An expert in the history of medieval biblical exegesis, he is a past president of the Society for the Study of the Bible in the Middle Ages and author of *Discerning Parallelism: A Study in Northern French Medieval Jewish Biblical Exegesis* (2004), as well as many articles and reviews in both American and Israeli journals.

Jill Jacobs (rabbi, JTS, 2003) is the executive director of T'ruah: The Rabbinic Call for Human Rights, formerly Rabbis for Human Rights—North America. She is also author of two books, *Where Justice Dwells: A Hands-On Guide to Doing Social Justice in Your Jewish Community* and *There Shall Be No Needy: Pursuing Social Justice through Jewish Law and Tradition*, as well as a *Forward* columnist. Previously she served as the rabbi in residence of Jewish Funds for Justice and as director of outreach and education for the Jewish Council on Urban Affairs.

Jeremy Kalmanofsky (rabbi, JTS, 1997) is the rabbi at Anshe Chesed synagogue in Manhattan and a member of the Rabbinical Assembly's Committee on Jewish Law and Standards.

Mordecai M. Kaplan (1881–1983) (rabbi, JTS, 1902; MA, philosophy, Columbia University), a Jewish Theological Seminary of America faculty member from the time of his ordination in 1902 to his retirement in 1963, influenced more than two generations of rabbis with his Reconstructionist approach to Judaism. He founded two synagogues in New York City, the Jewish Center and the Society for the Advancement of Judaism, both of which he also served as rabbi. Believing that Judaism encompasses not only religion but also commitment to a specific land (Israel), a specific language (Hebrew), and distinctive philosophy, art, music, dance, and literature, he proposed a school of higher learning that would both teach and create in all these areas of Jewish life, and it was realized in 1947 with the founding of American Jewish University (then called the University of Judaism) in Los Angeles. His oldest daughter celebrated what was the very first bat mitzvah ceremony in 1922, and he supported egalitarianism from then on. He was actively involved in establishing the first Jewish summer camp, Camp Cejwin in Port Jervis, New York. His idea that synagogues should serve as gathering places for social, social action, and sports activities changed North American congregational life. He and his followers were part of the Conservative movement from the early 1900s until they broke off and founded the Reconstructionist Rabbinical College in 1968. His eleven books begin with *Judaism as a Civilization* (1934).

Harold Kushner (rabbi, JTS, 1960; PhD, JTS, 1972) served as rabbi of Temple Israel of Natick, Massachusetts, for several decades. He is probably best known for *When Bad Things Happen to Good People* (1978), but he has authored many other books of note, including *To Life! A Celebration of Jewish Being and Thinking* (1994), which is widely used to introduce Jews and non-Jews to Judaism. He also edited the Midrash section of *Etz Hayim*, the Conservative movement's new Torah commentary.

Barry (Baruch) Leff (PhD, business administration, Golden Gate University, 1990; rabbi, Ziegler School of Rabbinic Studies, American Jewish University, 2002) teaches, speaks, writes, serves on the board of directors of Rabbis for Human Rights, engages in ecumenical work, and volunteers with the Masorti movement in Israel while overseeing his management and marketing business in Israel. Previously he served congregations in Tucson, Vancouver, and Toledo, and in 2016–17 he served as interim rabbi in Birmingham, Alabama. He also founded and nurtured a high technology firm in Silicon Valley into a ninety-employee business.

Jonathan Lubliner (rabbi, JTS) served congregations in Connecticut and New Jersey before becoming senior rabbi of the Jacksonville Jewish Center in 2004. He also serves on the JTS Chancellor's Rabbinic Leadership Council, the Conservative movement's Committee on Jewish Law and Standards, and the Rabbinical Assembly's Commission on Keruv, Conversion and Peoplehood. In addition, he is the author of *Petah Ha-Ohel—At the Entrance of the Tent: A Rabbinic Guide to Conversion*.

Akiba Lubow (rabbi, JTS, 1984) worked for the Rabbinical Assembly before becoming a congregational rabbi and serving congregations in St. Louis, Missouri; Rochester, New York; Winnipeg, Manitoba; Buffalo, New York; and Cranford, New Jersey.

Alan B. Lucas (rabbi, JTS, 1978) is senior rabbi of Temple Beth Sholom in Roslyn, New York, and a board member of MERCAZ, the Zionist arm of the Conservative movement. He previously served on the movement's Committee on Jewish Law and Standards, as president of the South Jersey Board of Rabbis and the Interfaith Area Clergy, and as a board member of the United Jewish Communities' Rabbinic Cabinet and the JTS Chancellor's Rabbinic Cabinet.

Aaron Mackler (rabbi, JTS, 1985; PhD, philosophy, Georgetown University, 1992) is a professor of philosophy with a specialization in bioethics at Duquesne University in Pittsburgh. Formerly a twenty-year member of the Committee on Jewish Law and Standards, he also chaired its Subcommittee on Bioethics. In addition, he authored *Introduction to Jewish and Catholic Bioethics: A Comparative Analysis* (2003) and edited *Life and Death Responsibilities in Jewish Biomedical Ethics* (2000).

Daniel Nevins (rabbi, JTS, 1994) is dean of the Jewish Theological Seminary's Rabbinical School, a member of the Rabbinical Assembly's Committee on Jewish Law and Standards, and author of numerous CJLS-approved responsa, including one (cowritten with Elliot Dorff and Avram Reisner) on same-sex relations and marriages, an excerpt of which is included in this book. He formerly served as rabbi of Adat Shalom Synagogue in Farmington Hills, Michigan.

Mark Popovsky (rabbi, JTS, 2005; JD, Columbia Law School, 2011) served as the coordinator of Jewish chaplaincy at New York Presbyterian Hospital before joining the law firm of Sullivan & Cromwell, LLP. He has written two responsa for the Committee on Jewish Law and Standards, one on preimplantation genetic diagnosis and another (with Miriam Berkowitz) on contraception, the latter excerpted in this book.

Mayer Rabinowitz (rabbi, JTS, 1967; PhD, JTS, 1974) is associate professor emeritus of Talmud and Rabbinics at JTS and chairman of the Conservative movement's Joint Bet Din, which addresses matters of marriage, divorce, arbitration, and mediation. Formerly he served as a CJLS member for twenty-five years, director of the Saul Lieberman Institute of Talmudic Research, dean of the JTS Graduate School, and the JTS librarian.

Joshua Ratner (JD, Columbia Law School, 2002; rabbi, JTS, 2012) is associate rabbi and Jewish educator at the Joseph Slifka Center for Jewish Life at Yale University. He also directs the Jewish Communal Relations Council of New Haven, Connecticut.

David Reed (MBA and JD, University of Pennsylvania; DPhil, mathematics, Oxford University) is a technology-oriented serial entrepreneur who is currently CEO of a bio-computation company, Mimetics, in North Carolina. He is also chairman of Sicha, an organization dedicated to building conversations between contemporary Jewish life and traditional Jewish texts. He formerly served as president of Congregation Beth El in Durham, North Carolina; a board member of the local Jewish Community Foundation; and vice president of the Chapel Hill Kehillah.

Avram Reisner (rabbi, JTS, 1977; PhD, Talmud and Rabbinics, JTS, 1996; MA, bioethics, University of Pennsylvania, 2002) is the rabbi of Chevrei Tzedek Synagogue in Baltimore and chair of the state of Maryland's Stem Cell Research Commission. A member of the Committee on Jewish Law and Standards for nearly twenty years, he wrote responsa on, among other things, genetically engineered foods, the status of same-sex relations (with Elliot Dorff and Daniel Nevins), and joining a minyan through the Internet, excerpts from all of which appear in this book.

Joel Roth (rabbi, JTS, 1968; PhD, JTS, 1973) is professor of Talmud at the Jewish Theological Seminary and *Rosh Yeshiva* of the Conservative Yeshiva in Jerusalem. He has served as dean of the Seminary's Rabbinical School and as chair of the Committee on Jewish Law and Standards. He is also the author of *The Halakhic Process: A Systematic Analysis* and a number of CJLS-approved responsa. His analysis of Jewish law played a major role in enabling women to become Conservative rabbis.

Harold Schulweis (1925–2014) (rabbi, JTS, 1950; ThD, Pacific School of Religion, 1972) served as the senior rabbi of Valley Beth Shalom in Encino, California, for more than four decades, becoming among the first to establish ḥavurot within and as part of a synagogue. He also instituted a para-rabbinic program, training lay people to serve as advisors to bar/bat mitzvah families and engaged couples, and a para-counseling program to help people address their life issues. He founded the Jewish Foundation for the Righteous, to collect and distribute money to non-Jews who saved Jews during the Holocaust, and Jewish World Watch, a human rights organization. One of his seven books, *Conscience: The Duty to Obey and the Duty to Disobey* (2008), won the National Jewish Book Award.

Benjamin Segal (rabbi, JTS, 1969) served as president of the Schechter Institute of Jewish Studies and later director of the Melitz program, designed to bring secular and religious Israelis together. For several decades he ran the North American Ramah camps' trips to Israel. He is also the author of *Returning: The Land of Israel as Focus in Jewish History* (1987); *A New Psalm: The Psalms as Literature* (2013); and *Kohelet's Pursuit of Truth: A New Reading of Ecclesiastes* (2016).

Leonard Sharzer (MD, Boston University School of Medicine, 1967; MS, surgery, University of Iowa, 1972; rabbi, JTS, 2003) is senior fellow in bioethics of the Finkelstein Institute of Religious and Social Studies at JTS and former clinical professor at the Albert Einstein College of Medicine. He has organized conferences entitled "Face Transplantation," "The Use of Preimplantation Genetic Diagnosis for the Purpose of Pre-natal Sex Selection," and "Medical Error and Medical Liability Reform," and he is currently working on a book on Jewish ethical issues in plastic surgery.

Alana Suskin (rabbi, Ziegler School of Rabbinic Studies, American Jewish University, 2003) is an educator, activist, and prolific writer. She is a senior managing editor of Jewschool.com, secretary of T'ruah (formerly Rabbis for Human Rights—North America), director of strategic communications for Americans for Peace Now, and a board member of American Rights at Work.

Gordon Tucker (rabbi, JTS, 1975; PhD, philosophy, Princeton University, 1979) is senior rabbi of Temple Israel Center in White Plains, New York and adjunct assistant professor of Jewish philosophy at the Jewish Theological Seminary. Formerly he served as dean of the JTS Rabbinical School and chairman of the board of the Masorti Foundation for Conservative Judaism in Israel. In addition, he served for twenty-five years as a member of the Committee on Jewish Law and Standards, writing a number of responsa, as well as the justification for the CJLS's pluralistic structure (excerpted in this book). Among his publications is *Heavenly Torah as Refracted through the Generations*, an English translation with extensive comments, essays, and notes of Abraham Joshua Heschel's study in Hebrew of the varying traditions of Rabbi Akiba and Rabbi Ishmael on God and revelation.

Index of Classical Sources

General Index

Edomites, 324
education: bar/bat mitzvah, minimum
standards of Jewish education for,
13; of children, 161, 163, 262, 277;
CJL (Conservative Jewish learning),
principles of, 90–92; Conservative
academic centers, 383–85; girls' access
to, 11, 129, 131, 139; Jewish Educators
Assembly, 385; Joint Commission on
Jewish Education, 387; procreation
affected by, 161, 164, 398–99n14
egalitarian principle in Conservative
Judaism, 14, 17–18, 61, 113, 129–30,
146–49, 151–52, 158, 326, 344, 384, 386
egg donation, 145
Eilberg, Amy, 47–51, 144, 422–23
Eisen, Arnold M., 87–92, 320–21, 346,
358–60, 423; *The Jew Within* (with
Steven M. Cohen; 2000), 15
Elad-Appelbaum, Tamar, 40–41, 421
Elazar ben Azariah, 268
Eleazar ben Rabbi Simeon/Shimon,
204, 272
election doctrine, 313–15
Eliezer (servant of Abraham), 323
Elon, Menachem, 146, 391n5
Emancipation (1760–1800), 2–3, 110, 186
embryonic stem cell research and
cloning, 171–76
Emet Ve-Emunah (1988): on Diaspora,
341–44; on Halakhah, 94–98; on the
ideal Conservative Jew, 379–80; on
interfaith relationships, 316–20; on
Israel (as people), 311, 313–16; on
prayer, 53–58; on *p'sak din* (practice),
determining, 126–27; on State of
Israel, 338–44, 347; on study of Torah,
85–87; on theology, xviii, 22–29; on
tikkun olam, 255–58; on women, 130–32
empiricism, 35, 39, 44

employers and employees, 207–22;
dignified working environment,
obligation to create, 209–11; Halakhah
and, 208, 215, 217, 218, 221, 222;
health care obligations, 216–18;
hourly workers, financial obligations
regarding, 211–16; in Jewish tradition,
208–9; labor unions, 219–22; Magen
Tzedek (Shield of Justice) program,
243, 244–46; minimum wage workers,
207–8, 212, 218, 244, 259; *po'el* and
kablan workers, in Jewish law, 401n50;
real-life experience, need to consider,
208, 218–19; responsa literature,
207–8; second jobs, employees taking,
216, 217; strikes, 220; value of work,
208–9, 264, 278; wages, determining,
218–19; whistle-blowing, 202–7; work,
employees' duty of, 215–16
end-of-life care, 176–80
endogamy, historical practice of, 323–24
environmental protections, 249–51
Epstein, Yehiel, Arukh Ha-Shulhan, 365,
397–98n8, 406n3
Eretz Yisrael (land of Israel), concept of,
338, 341–43. See also Israel (state)
eruv, 238, 239, 240, 376
Esau, 323
eschatology, 22, 23, 52n2, 52n6
ethics and morality. See morality and ethics
Ethics Committee, American Fertility
Society, 167
Ethiopian Jews, 258, 329, 356
Europe, Conservative Judaism in, 1–8,
151–52
Eve, 320
evil, problem of, 27–29, 37–38, 52n5
exercising or playing sports on Shabbat,
236–41
Exodus from Egypt, 32, 125, 209–10, 253, 258

modesty, 225, 230, 231, 276, 280, 303, 369

Modim prayer, 51

moneylending, loans, interest charges, and usury, 187, 188, 248–49, 260, 263

Montesquieu, Claude, 1, 186

Morais, Sabato, 9, 257

morality and ethics: Halakhah and, 109–10, 255; prayer and, 254; in stories, 253; study and, 254–55; theology and, 254; in Torah and Jewish literature, 252–53; traditional means of inculcating, 252–55. *See also* bioethics; business ethics; marriage and family life; sex and sexuality; *tikkun olam*

Mordecai ben Hillel Ha-Kohen, 407n4

Moses (prophet), 4–5, 23, 33, 51, 258, 397n5

Motion Picture Licensing Corporation, 199–200

Mount Sinai, 4, 5, 26, 32, 88, 253, 316, 320, 321

Musaf, 72

Musar movement, 257

music and prayer, 55, 58–59, 77, 79

Muslims. *See* Islam

mysticism: normal, 53, 112; as theology, 44–47

myths and mythmaking, 30, 34–35, 104–7

Naḥmanides (Moses ben Nahman), 204, 214–15; *Iggeret Ha-Kodesh*, 275

Nakash, William, 367–68

Napoleon, 186

nashim. See specific entries at women

Nathan (Rabbi), 397n5

National Jewish Population Survey, 325, 405n10

Nativ, Gil, 362

naturalism, religious, 35–39

Nevins, Daniel S., 158, 291, 293–97, 426

niddah (menstrual separation), 145, 149, 304, 404n8

Noah (biblical figure), 32, 41, 316, 320, 392n2

non-Jews: as birth surrogates, 169; children of marriages between Jews and, 161; French Sanhedrin on, 186, 187, 188; interfaith relationships with, 316–20; Israel's covenant with God and, 33–34; with Jewish father and non-Jewish mother, 286, 325; Jews generally living in close proximity to, 319; poverty assistance for, 262; universalism and, 256–57, 336; wine touched by, 319. *See also* interfaith marriage

normal mysticism, 53, 112

North American Association of Synagogue Executives, 385

nose piercing, 229

Nostra Aetate (Vatican II), 316, 318

nuclear weapons, 27

Obama, Barack, 181

observance. *See p'sak din* (practice), determining

olam ha-ba (afterlife), 28

The Ordination of Women as Rabbis (1988), 132. *See also* women as rabbis

Orthodox Judaism: on bioethics, 153; birthrate and demographics, 398n13; on ceding land in peace agreement, in Israel, 362–63; chief rabbinates, 119; Conservative Judaism's relationship to, xv, 14–15, 83, 84, 111, 311; gender-specific study in, 129; Israel (as people), different Jewish groups as all part of, 315–16; Israel (state), hegemony in, 119, 338–39, 345, 354; modern emergence of, 3; on sciences, 84; texts, method of approaching, 4, 83–84;

rabbis *(continued)*
  determining, role of local rabbi in, 118,
  120, 122, 126, 128; same-sex unions,
  officiating at, xv, 288–94, 296–301;
  Standards of Rabbinic Practice,
  122–24, 137, 285, 326–27, 404n1. *See
  also* women as rabbis
Rabin, Yitzhak, 357
Rabinowitz, Mayer, 287, 288, 426
Rachel (biblical figure), 165
radical feminism, 47
Ramah summer camps, 13, 77, 78, 109,
  120, 136, 139, 344–45, 383–84, 387
Rambam. *See* Maimonides
Rashba, 219, 402n60
Rashi, 4, 229, 403n22
rationalism, 29–35, 44, 66
Ratner, Joshua, 243, 427
Rav (Rabbi), 233
Rebekah (biblical figure), 323
rebuking, as responsibility, 204–6
Reconstructionist Judaism, 14, 17, 60, 71
Reconstructionist Rabbinical College, 14
Redlich, Norman, 142
Reed, David, 345, 346–49, 427
Reed, Esther, 345, 353–55
Reform Judaism: on bioethics, 153; on
  children of Jewish father and non-
  Jewish mother, 325, 331; Conservative
  Judaism's relationship to, xv, 7–9,
  15, 111, 311; emergence of, 3; God as
  center of Judaism in, 311; interfaith
  couples in, 285, 325–26, 328; Israel (as
  people), different Jewish groups as
  all part of, 315–16; Israel (as people)
  in, 311; Israel's chief rabbinate not
  recognizing Conservative or Reform
  marriages, divorces, and conversions,
  338–39, 345; Pittsburgh Platform, 8,
  336; platforms, 17; Zionism and, 336

Reisner, Avram Israel, 153, 157, 176–80,
  231, 241, 243, 291, 293–97, 427; *Al Pi
  Din* (2009), 243, 246, 250
relativism, Conservative rejection of, 26
religious freedom in Israel, 338–39, 345
religious naturalism, 35–39
Rema, Hoshen Mishpat, 210
remarriage of divorced person, 123, 131,
  305–8
remez, 44
responsa literature *(teshuvot)*: on
  bioethics, 145, 153; on business
  ethics, 189–90, 196, 207–8; on capital
  punishment, 266–72; CJLS reviewing,
  396n5; on domestic violence, 281–85;
  eradication of a responsum, 295; on
  homosexuality, 286–87, 291–95, 297–
  99; on interfaith marriage, 285–87,
  325–26, 406n13; multiple meanings
  of *teshuvah*, 395n4; on proving Jewish
  identity, 329–34; *p'sak din* (practice),
  determining, 118, 120–21; on ritual
  observance, 225, 231, 236, 241; on
  tattooing and body piercing, 225;
  on transgender individuals, 301–4;
  on women's issues, 144–51. *See also*
  business ethics; ritual observance; *and
  specific issues under* bioethics
responsa literature *(teshuvot)* in and for
  Israel, 361–77; borders and ceding
  land in peace agreement, 362–64;
  extradition of Jewish criminals from
  Israel, 364–68; Shabbat, riding to
  synagogue on, 373–77; women conscripted into Israeli Defense Forces,
  368–70; yeshiva students conscripted
  into Israeli Defense Forces, 370–73
revelation, 26–27
RIAA, 191, 195
Ricoeur, Paul, 105

CPSIA information can be obtained
at www.ICGtesting.com
Printed in the USA
LVOW11s0713230418
574401LV00005B/42/P